T5-CVF-952

ADVERTISING MEDIA

A MANAGERIAL APPROACH

ANTHONY F. McGANN
University of Wyoming

J. THOMAS RUSSELL
University of Georgia

ADVERTISING MEDIA

A MANAGERIAL APPROACH

1981

RICHARD D. IRWIN, INC. Homewood, Illinois 60430
Irwin Dorsey Limited Georgetown, Ontario L7G 4B3

ISBN 0-256-02548-7

Library of Congress Catalog Card No. 80–84716

Printed in the United States of America

1 2 3 4 5 6 7 8 9 0 M 8 7 6 5 4 3 2 1

PREFACE

ADVERTISING MEDIA is an integral part of marketing and advertising strategy. In recent years increases in media time and space costs have led to sophisticated planning, analysis, and evaluation of media purchases. This book has been designed to offer an introduction for future media planners and salespersons and an overview of advertising media for those responsible for managing the total advertising program.

Advertising Media: A Managerial Approach seeks to view the media process from three perspectives. First, the advertiser's marketing strategy, budgeting acumen, and corporate goals are considered. Second, we examine the media themselves. The unique character of the various media as business and social institutions shapes the advertising messages they carry. Finally, we discuss the role of the advertising agency, which is responsible for the planning and carrying out of the basic function between media and client.

In the past, advertisers have sometimes regarded the media-planning decisions as complementary, but secondary, to the creative aspects of advertising. Journalism advertising programs, with historical roots in news editorial training, have understandably tended to emphasize writing, production, and art in advertising curricula. Media planning was often taught as a portion of some other course and little attention was given to developing real expertise among students or to directing graduating students to jobs in the area. Business schools did not teach courses in media decisions and, until the early 70s, largely ignored any serious consideration of advertising media. Advertisers and advertising agencies tended to evaluate prospective employees on the basis of their portfolios rather than on media and marketing expertise.

In recent years this view of advertising media has changed dramatically. As the investment in advertising time and space has passed the $50 billion mark, advertisers have increasingly sought to manage these expenditures more efficiently. Journalism schools have found that they simply cannot place their students without a solid foundation in media planning and have changed their curricula accordingly. As of 1978, 21 of the 24 advertising programs accredited by the Association for Education in Journalism (AEJ) required a media course.

In business schools, marketing departments see advertising as an increasingly attractive career for their students. This has produced expansion of course offerings in the expected areas of faculty expertise: advertising management, media, and strategy. It is unrealistic to think that marketing departments will offer substantial numbers of "creative" courses in the foreseeable future. Perhaps the best evidence of the growing importance of advertising in business schools can be seen in the current membership of the American Academy of Advertising (AAA). The AAA was founded in 1958 as an organization devoted to the study and advancement of advertising education. Through the 1960s, the 120 members came largely from journalism faculties. Today 60 percent of the Academy's 400 members come from business school faculties.

This book seeks to fill the need for a text devoted to helping students learn the important managerial decisions involved in planning, buying, and evaluating advertising media. We believe that this has been accomplished in a way which also assists instructors assigned this course responsibility, and which reflects the importance now given the subject in journalism programs and business schools and by practitioners.

In contrast to others in the area, this book reflects our conviction that the study of advertising media should emphasize three areas:

1. The marketing management foundations of the media function.
2. The new technology of advertising media.
3. The quantitative nature of management problems related to the media function.

It is divided into three parts which generally correspond to each of the three emphasized areas.

Chapters 1 to 4 relate basic marketing principles to the advertising media function. Our research indicates that every accredited journalism advertising program either requires or strongly suggests a marketing minor for their advertising majors. Consequently, this first section assumes a rudimentary knowledge of basic marketing. Not to do so would eliminate the book from consideration by marketing departments and most leading journalism advertising programs.

Chapters 5 to 10 discuss the characteristics of each of the mass media as advertising vehicles. The emphasis is on the use of the various media as components in the overall marketing and promotional program. The descriptive material is kept to a minimum to avoid duplicating similar material provided in most introductory advertising texts. These chapters also emphasize the new and future technologies as they relate to marketing and advertising. Satellite communication, the vertical blanking interval potential, two-way communication, and the disappearance of distinctions between print and broadcasting are among the topics covered.

The last four chapters emphasize the management of the media function. Chapter 11 is devoted to a discussion of media selection and allocation methods which are not only available but increasingly necessary for the successful media planner. Chapter 12 furnishes an example media platform, while Chapter 13 shows how to develop and measure the effectiveness of media schedules. Finally, Chapter 14 summarizes the future of the media, including employment opportunities.

A special word of thanks goes to Ernest Larkin, University of Oklahoma, and Joseph Pisani, University of Florida. They furnished the benefit of their experience in the traditional areas of coverage and insight, and examples and encouragement in the less traditional topics. We also extend our gratitude to Robert G. Marbut, president and chief executive, Harte-Hanks Communications. His unique expression of the coming revolution in technology, management, and marketing of media enterprises provided the initial prompting about the need for this book.

The book could not have been completed without the secretarial expertise of Susan Gabriel, Amy King, and Ann Clark.

Finally, a word of thanks to patient families whose understanding and encouragement was vital to the completion of the book. Our wives, Kitty and Judy, and children, Christopher, Kevin, Angelica, Kelly, and Kenneth, were especially unselfish and deserve special thanks.

A.F.M.
J.T.R.

ACKNOWLEDGMENTS

THROUGHOUT the writing of this book the authors have benefited from the help and advice of numerous advertising professionals and academicians. We wish to acknowledge the contribution of these people and firms who have been so helpful.

Constance C. Anthes Manager communications, Arbitron.

Marcus Bartlett School of Journalism and Mass Communication, University of Georgia.

Edward I. Barz Senior vice president, Simmons Marketing Research Bureau, Inc.

Neil Bernstein Point-of-Purchase Advertising Institute.

Leo Bogart Executive vice president, Newspaper Advertising Bureau.

Hugh L. Brooks President, Traffic Audit Bureau.

Karen Burns Manager information central, Direct Mail Marketing Association.

F. R. Cawl, Jr. President, FC&A, Inc., *The Outdoor Buyer's Guide to Advertising.*

Robert J. Coen Senior vice president, McCann-Erickson, Inc.

Lawrence R. Cole Senior vice president, Ogilvy & Mather.

T. J. Donnelly Assistant communications manager, Audit Bureau of Circulations.

Richard G. Ebel Vice president, Specialty Advertising Association International.

Teresa Gannon Vice president, Media Mark Research, Inc.

Norman Glenn Editor, *Marketing & Media Decisions.*

Norman Gollin Norman Gollin Design.

Bernard Guggenheim Senior vice president, Campbell-Ewald Company.

Stan Henderson Georgia Outdoor Advertising, Inc.

John D. Leckenby Department of Advertising, University of Illinois.

Stefan Meyer Vice president, Institute of Outdoor Advertising.

Laura S. Myers Public relations department, The Advertising Council, Inc.

W. L. Weltin President, Liller Neal Weltin.

CONTENTS

ADVERTISING MEDIA

A MANAGERIAL APPROACH

1

ADVERTISING MEDIA AND THE MARKETING PROCESS

THE MANAGEMENT PROCESS AND ADVERTISING MEDIA

AS THE TITLE IMPLIES, this textbook will discuss advertising media from a managerial perspective. Management has been defined as the process by which the objectives of an organization are achieved. This process includes the functions of planning, organizing, staffing, directing, and controlling.

This book will emphasize the management functions as they are applied to advertising media. Planning, in its most basic form, is the process for determining what is to be achieved. Our discussion of planning will be directed toward the determination of advertising media objectives. Organizing includes both allocating resources and establishing procedures for accomplishing objectives. Here, the allocation of funds to the advertising budget and the distribution of these funds among the available advertising media are paramount. The organizing function depends on a thorough understanding of each advertising medium. Staffing is the process of matching human resources to necessary tasks. Staffing the advertising media tasks is discussed from the standpoint of work assignments and from the perspective of the human skills most relevant to success in those tasks. Directing is the process in which a plan is put into action. Media plans are implemented by the purchase of advertising space and time. Finally, the control function is performed to ensure that the advertiser's objectives are realized.

Students often visualize advertising as a set of activities unrelated to the other activities of business. This separation is unfortunate in that it is artificial. Virtually all advertising takes place within a business or nonprofit organization. To give you a more accurate understanding of this real-world integration between advertising media and other organizational activities, this text will introduce you to the ways in which the functional business areas such as accounting, finance, and marketing play out their assigned roles in the management of the advertising process. And, because of the very strong tie between marketing and advertising media, this chapter will be directly focused on this relationship.

This text assumes that you have had an introduction to the advertising and marketing courses, at a "principles" level. This chapter, then, will review rapidly the key concepts in advertising management which assist in the general tasks assigned to marketing management. To oversimplify, these tasks can be described as attempts to stimulate demand. In addition, this chapter will begin to suggest the ways in which other business disciplines function to give the advertising campaign, and the media employed in that campaign, direction, boundaries, and integration with the other decisions taken by the advertiser's organization.

THE MARKETING CONCEPT

Philip Kotler has defined the essence of the marketing concept as "a customer needs and wants orientation backed by integrated marketing effort aimed at generating customer satisfaction as the key to satisfying organizational goals."[1] In addition, he has specified the need for the practice of this concept in a way which is consistent with long-run consumer welfare. You can see that this widely accepted definition of the marketing concept contains four major components. Not only is each of these components important to the marketing effort, but each has particular application to the processes of media management.

Consumer orientation

While businesses can look at their activities in any number of ways, all of these approaches might be divided into two groups: those which emphasize business needs and those which emphasize customer needs. The marketing concept was revolutionary in that it focused on customer needs and customer satisfaction. Before its acceptance by businesses, most of the activities of the typical firm emphasized the satisfaction of the business needs. Thus, profits, sales, production efficiencies, and other criteria were dominant. Under the marketing concept, these criteria remain important but they are secondary to the establishment of customer satisfaction.

---

[1] Philip Kotler, *Marketing Management: Analysis, Planning, and Control,* 4th ed. (Englewood Cliffs, N.J.: Prentice-Hall, 1980), pp. 31–32.

In the management of the advertising media function, consumer preferences for media represent the single, most important "given." It is highly unlikely that advertising decisions and advertising itself will, in the short run, change consumer preferences for a particular newspaper, magazine, or television show. Rather, the advertising community accepts consumer preferences for media as they exist, assuming that those preferences can be discovered. Then, the advertising decision maker attempts to purchase media in a way which is consistent both with client needs and with consumer reading, listening, viewing, and traveling patterns.

Integration of effort

Of course the management of advertising media does not occur in a vacuum. For that matter the management of advertising is itself highly interrelated with other marketing and business activities. Sound management theory requires that the marketing activities of an organization be thoroughly integrated. But it also requires that the decisions in other areas be consonant with customer satisfaction. It is useful to recall that virtually any decision reached by a firm has implications for the marketing function and for customer satisfaction. For example, a decision to reduce the cost of a quality control program may raise the cost of the warranty service and lower the level of customer satisfaction. Also, decisions about customer credit extensions, new product development, channels of distribution, and especially advertising can materially alter levels of customer satisfaction. Throughout all areas of business, we require that marketing be integrated with other activities such as finance, production, personnel, and accounting. We also work toward integrating decisions taken in these areas with the marketing concept.

Just as marketing needs to be interrelated with other business areas, the components of marketing need to be integrated within this discipline. You will recall that almost every introductory marketing textbook examines the four major areas of marketing: product, price, physical distribution, and promotion. Within promotion, most of us include not only personal selling but also the impersonal kinds of demand-stimulating activities which are generally thought of as advertising. Integration of effort requires that advertising activities be consistent with other marketing activities.

Within advertising, the media function itself must be integrated to be effective. Media buyers must not only recognize the media consumption decisions which consumers make, but must also recognize the need to integrate these consumption preferences with all the other marketing aspects of the client's product. For example a specialty good that is produced in relatively small quantities, carries a high retail price, and is distributed through exclusive distribution channels requires advertising media support different from that needed for grocery products, commodities, and other shopping- and convenience-type products.

Satisfaction of organizational objectives

You recall that the marketing concept insists on the satisfaction of organizational objectives. Oftentimes students (and others) give enthusiastic recognition to the real benefits which flow from a focus on consumer satisfaction. Unfortunately this enthusiasm overwhelms the remainder of the marketing concept. It is unfortunate that the enthusiasm does not continue through the other major elements of the marketing concept, for a failure to recognize the importance of organizational objectives leaves the decision maker highly vulnerable to organizational disappointments—even failures and disappearance. Thus a company may define itself as being in the business of satisfying consumer beverage preferences. If it does this, however, without satisfying the need for organizational profit, then it will not be in the business of selling beverages for very long. The logic of a business enterprise is to earn a profit. This profit will permit the enterprise to remain in business and to accomplish the objectives for which it was established. In the case of not-for-profit enterprises, some other objective (for example the election of a political candidate or the solution to some social problem such as roadside litter) has been substituted for the profit motive of the corporation.

Regardless of the nature of the organization, organizational needs must be met or else the group forfeits its reason for existence. If a corporation cannot earn profits or if a nonprofit organization cannot accomplish its alternative objectives, there is no reason for the enterprise to continue to exist.

Again the media function must be brought into consonance with the need for satisfying organizational objectives. In the nonprofit enterprise, promotional activities must be performed and media for these activities managed in a way which optimizes the satisfaction of the organization's objectives. This is not to say that only traditional media can be purchased in some particular product or service class. For example a religious order reports having achieved remarkable success in its recruiting efforts by placing advertisements in the hedonistic, somewhat irreligious *Playboy* magazine. In the case of the for-profit corporation, media management must be an efficient component of advertising activities. In addition to reflecting consumer preferences for media and to being integrated thoroughly with the other aspects of the marketing effort, media management must contribute to corporate profitability and to organizational success.

Long-range social responsibility

Advertising activities are one very important way in which corporations and other organizations attempt to satisfy their long-range social responsibility. Some major advertisers, such as Sears, have withdrawn their advertising support from television programs which they considered in poor taste or socially irresponsible. On the other

Figure 1–1
An advertising industry advertisement promoting social service activity

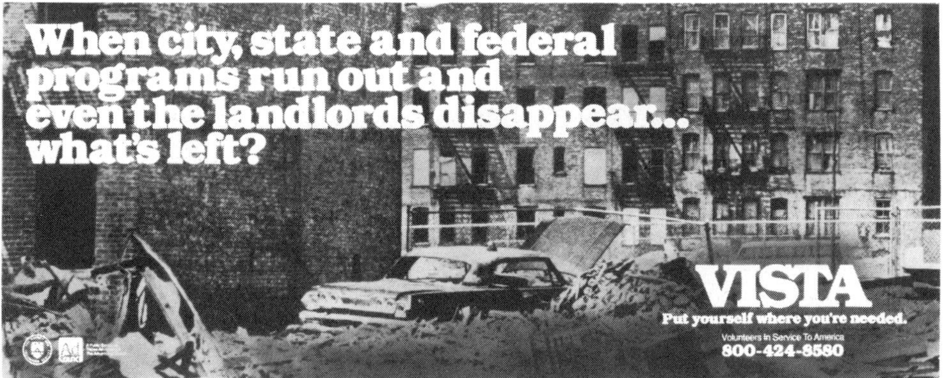

The Advertising Council, Inc.

hand, many other corporations, including Exxon, Mobil, Xerox, and IBM, have chosen particular advertising media to practice what they regard as corporate social responsibility. Examples here include the sponsorship of cultural events, entertainment, and programming.

The advertising industry itself has been in the forefront of efforts to solve social problems via advertising (see Figures 1–1 and 1–2). Advertising industry associations have been pioneers in attempts to resolve problems of discrimination, pollution, and disease.

Managing the media function is also an opportunity for public service. Just as in product advertising where media cost efficiencies must be matched with consumer media consumption patterns, so too in public interest advertising consumer markets and consumer

Figure 1–2
An advertising industry advertisement dealing with a social problem

The Advertising Council, Inc.

patterns must be matched with organizational objectives in a cost-efficient manner.

THE MARKETING CONCEPT AND EXTERNAL FORCES

Of course if management could operate in a vacuum, the marketing concept would be relatively easy to apply. In the real world, however, such a vacuum does not exist and forces beyond the control of the organization make the practice of the marketing concept more difficult. A discussion of some of the more important external forces and of their influence on marketing management follows.

Economic and technological forces

During economic boom periods, even the less than optimally managed companies have a very good prospect of making some profit. General levels of economic activity are high, and sellers enjoy economic benefits in the marketplace. From the individual consumer's standpoint, jobs are plentiful, wages are good, and economic well-being characterizes the majority. Perhaps it is not surprising that advertising (at least in the United States) tends to flourish during boom times. It is, unfortunately, also true that there is variability in macroeconomic activity levels. This implies that economic downturns regularly follow periods of economic expansion. During these downturns (depressions are the most serious type, and economic recessions are a more frequent and less devastating type), only a carefully managed enterprise survives.

It is also unfortunate that in periods of economic contraction, advertising budgets also tend to contract Dunkle and Kwan, in a 40-year study, showed that advertising and gross national product are very highly and positively correlated with each other.[2] Thus, in periods of economic downturn, advertising expenditures in general and the activities associated with media purchasing tend to be reduced.

In addition to the general economic influences imposed by expansion or recession, two specific forces—inflation and technology—have a significant impact on advertising decisions.

Inflation works its pernicious influence in many ways. Certainly during periods of continued secular price inflation, consumer confidence and purchase levels are eroded. The ability of companies to satisfy consumer expectations is impaired because increases in costs often require retail price increases. And when companies purchase

[2] As reported in F. M. Nicosia, *Advertising, Management, and Society* (New York: McGraw-Hill, 1974), p. 186.

media advertising, inflation in media space and time prices imposes a damper on the efficiency with which the advertising function can be executed.

Product innovation (particularly the development of new products which are based on a new technology) has a positive effect on the general level of economic activity. New products not only satisfy consumer needs in ways which were hitherto unavailable but also satisfy to some extent the human desire for variety.

In addition, recently developed technology offers some dramatic prospects for improving advertising efficiency. While a full discussion of this technology will be reserved for later chapters, it is safe to say that new methods of designing, producing, and distributing messages may very well revolutionize the ways in which consumers acquire information. For example the traditional distinctions between print and broadcast media may disappear in the next decade. Consumers may be able to view on their home television receivers information now carried in newspapers, and subsequently print those portions of this "electronic newspaper" that they wish to retain for future reference. This sort of technological innovation would not only revolutionize production and channels of distribution; it would also require major changes in the ways in which newspaper advertising efficiencies are computed.

Competitive pressures

With the possible exception of regulated monopolies, companies in the real world conduct their marketing activities in a competitive setting. Consumers can substitute one product for another; they can view one television show or another; they can spend their leisure time reading special-interest magazines rather than viewing television. In fact, one of the most abiding characteristics of marketplace activity is the presence of competition. When competitive pressures have diminished in our society, governmental agencies, acting on their understanding of the public interest, have taken steps to heighten competition. In this way they have sought to improve both industrial efficiency and consumer welfare.

From the standpoint of managing media activities, competition among media is highly important. In one sense the manager of advertising media activities functions as a "consumer" of advertising space and time. This person (even though acting on behalf of an advertising client) attempts to purchase certain advertising coverage at minimum cost. In this endeavor competition among enterprises in a single medium, for example among several radio stations, can improve the efficiency of the media purchase. In a similar way competition between major media classes, for example between magazines and television, can also be the basis for improved efficiency in the media function.

Political and legal influences

Virtually all business activity takes place within a framework of politics and law. In this society businesses operate within this framework. Certainly the activities we think of as marketing are quite extensively constrained by our system of law. In particular the Uniform Commercial Code and the so-called antitrust statutes very carefully specify permissible marketing activities.

Advertising is an especially regulated activity within marketing. Here standards of truthfulness and candor are carefully spelled out by both federal and state law. In addition to making literally truthful statements, advertisers must display great care to avoid claims which would tend to deceive audiences even when these claims are literally or technically "true." Further, advertisers are prohibited from making claims which have not been substantiated before their use in advertising. Since in this society the lawmaking process takes place within the political arena, advertisers must be energetic in pointing out the advantages which advertising creates for consumers. One good example is the possibility that advertising reduces retail prices.[3] And, of course, one of the most fascinating areas of marketing in the nonprofit sector is the advertising associated with political campaigns themselves. At present this area has less regulation and more lenient standards for "claim substantiation" then most other areas of advertising.

We are tempted to think that the advertising media function is separated from questions of politics and law. However, this is not the case. In the area of corrective advertising, regulators such as those at the Federal Trade Commission have gone so far as to specify the particular media which must carry a corrective message. And, for better or worse, certain media have been barred from carrying advertising for certain types of products. For example it is no longer legal to advertise cigarettes on television. In addition, self-regulation by advertisers prevents the advertising of distilled spirits in that medium. Publishers, of course, have long exercised their rights under the First Amendment to reject the advertisements of certain companies and advertisements for certain products.

We can see that these constraints complicate the already complex

[3] Robert L. Steiner, "Marketing Productivity in Consumer Goods Industries—A Vertical Perspective," *Journal of Marketing,* vol. 42, no. 1 (January 1978), pp. 60–70.

process of choosing advertising media efficiently. Nevertheless, those of us who will be responsible for the advertising media function must be sensitive to the legal and political ramifications of our activities.

INTEGRATED ESTIMATION OF DEMAND

It has been said that the function of advertising is to shift demand schedules upward and to the right. This is a technical way of saying that the function of advertising is to stimulate demand (see Figure 1–3). By and large, the claim is accurate. However, in important instances advertising is designed to destimulate, or decrease, demand for some product or service. Examples of such "demarketing" occur every day in advertising which is designed to encourage people to stop smoking, or littering, or ignoring the tragedies caused by child abuse. Nonetheless, whether used for traditional marketing purposes or for the somewhat newer demarketing objectives, advertising's role is primarily one of influencing demand for products and services.

If advertising's role in altering demand is to be successful, decision

Figure 1–3
Stimulation of demand by promotion

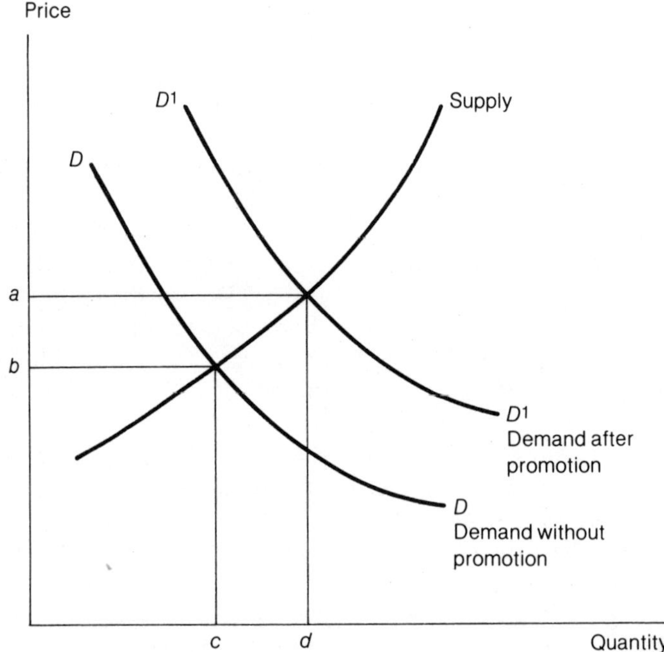

makers must understand that demand is the product of the many forces which we have just outlined. In very simple terms, the demand for some product or service is a function of consumers and their wants or needs, advertisers and their wants or needs, the competitive environment and the more general economic, political, and legal milieu. The focus of this textbook is not on altering political or legal processes directly or, for that matter, on altering consumer wants or needs in fundamental ways. At least in the short run, it accepts the premise that these are beyond the direct control of the advertiser. Its focus is, however, directed toward a careful measurement of these forces and toward a combination of these aspects of demand with efficient production of advertising messages. Inherent in advertising efficiency is the notion of efficiently selected and used advertising media.

Advertising and product demand

The ultimate goal of most advertising is to stimulate demand for a particular brand. In formulating his advertising campaign, however, it is important for the advertiser to understand fully the types of demand he is dealing with. This section deals with the various types of demand and with campaigns which might be used to stimulate them.

1. Generic demand. Before brand promotion can be effective, there must be some generic demand from consumers. An advertising campaign for Chevrolet must consider both the demand for Chevrolets and the demand for automobiles in general. Any brand advertising has elements of generic promotion within it. However, there are circumstances which require an advertiser to undertake a campaign to sell the product in general rather than only his brand. Among these circumstances would be domination of the market by a single firm. Assume that brand Y has an 85 percent share of market; brand X, 5 percent; brand Z, 5 percent; and that the remaining 5 percent is spread among several smaller firms. Firm Y can compete on a brand basis and attempt to gain a small share of market from each of these other firms (and risk antitrust problems). Or it can promote the product to nonusers or light users, recognizing that it can expect approximately its same 85 percent share of any new sales.

Another circumstance which might indicate the need for a generic campaign would be a declining industry sales trend. If sales are declining for all brands, cooperative efforts are sometimes used to stimulate generic demand. This approach recognizes that brand competition is pointless if the generic demand is soft. Of course generic campaigns are also used in industries other than those whose sales are declining. Both the Florida and California Fruit Growers

(Sunkist) cooperatives use generic themes in addition to promoting their individual brands.

2. Brand demand. Most consumer advertising is directed toward increasing the demand (sales) for a particular brand. Much of the criticism directed against advertising is that it creates temporary changes in brand preferences without causing permanent growth in the market. In fact, advertising does both. In certain industries, particularly those where usage is almost universal, brand switching is a dominant objective of advertising. On the other hand, most industries show growth in some brands *and* an increase in sales for all brands. At least a portion of this generic growth would normally be attributed to brand advertising.

3. Direct and indirect demand. Most consumer products are used and promoted for the utility they provide directly to the consumer. The advertising function is very different for products whose demand is dependent on the utility they can offer other products. Industrial goods usually fall into the indirect demand category. For instance textile sales depend on consumer demand for finished apparel; consequently, Du Pont does a great deal of consumer advertising for its synthetic fabrics although it does not manufacture wearing apparel.

The demand for a product with an indirect demand will usually demonstrate a positive correlation with the demand for the end product with which it is associated. However, sometimes the opposite is true. For instance, manufacturers of automotive parts (exclusive of those selling to new-car makers) find that as the demand for new cars decreases, the demand for replacement parts increases.

4. Advertising elasticity of demand. Like other marketing decisions, most notably, decisions regarding price, advertising may be addressed to audiences whose demand is elastic or inelastic. When demand elasticity is expressed and measured as a function of advertising, we speak of advertising elasticity. In symbolic form, the coefficient of advertising elasticity, *Ea,* can be calculated using the equation

$$Ea = \frac{Q_1 - Q_0}{Q_1 + Q_0} \div \frac{A_1 - A_0}{A_1 + A_0}$$

Where

Q_0 = Sales before the advertising change
Q_1 = Sales after the advertising change
A_0 = Advertising before the change
A_1 = Advertising after the change

When

$Ea > 1$, demand is advertising—elastic, and when
$Ea < 1$, demand is advertising—inelastic.

To review, then, recall that advertising is practiced within the general confines of the marketing concept and those orientations which the marketing concept implies. Also, recognize that the marketing concept operates within an external environment. Although marketing attempts to alter demand, demand is a function of forces beyond the direct control of the marketing manager. We now turn to the relationship between the marketing concept and the marketing plan.

THE MARKETING CONCEPT AND THE MARKETING PLAN

In simplest form, the marketing plan is the statement of how the marketing manager intends to implement the marketing concept. To be more precise, it is the plan by which the marketing manager attempts to coordinate issues of product or service, price, the physical distribution system for bringing the product or service to the marketplace, and efforts to promote the product or service. Marketing plans, then, are relatively detailed statements about how the manager will attempt to achieve integration of effort in satisfying customers and meeting organizational objectives.

PRODUCT MANAGEMENT

The management of products has long been a focus of organizational activity. Brand managers have historically attempted to bring products with certain characteristics to the marketplace—"good" or "satisfactory" products or "inexpensive" products or "durable" products. Such product characteristics have long been part of the marketing manager's emphasis. Product management has also been an area in which the marketing concept has been imperfectly applied. From the consumer's viewpoint a product is an expected bundle of benefits, and managerial emphasis on a product's technical aspects may miss the mark.

As consumers, we make purchases in the marketplace because we expect these purchases to help us solve problems. Therefore it would probably be useful for the brand or product manager to abandon some of the earlier ways of looking at products and services. Products have been traditionally categorized as either commodities or "differentiated" goods. Here theory suggested that differentiated goods (usually branded goods) were amenable to advertising's support, whereas commodities were not. Yet recent business history tells us that commodities can sometimes be successfully advertised. Chickens of a particular producer, wines from a particular country, coffee beans from a particular region, and even so ordinary a product as table salt have responded well to advertising efforts.

The notion of a product life cycle is also useful in suggesting different ways in which advertising can accomplish its assigned tasks. For example, in the introduction of new products to the marketplace, it is frequently found that initial advertising expense (per unit of goods sold) is very high. A simpleminded cost/benefit analysis of advertising for products recently brought to the marketplace would indicate that too much is being spent on advertising. However, a competent marketing manager will recognize that these initial investments in the promotion of new products pay handsome returns if and when the products reach the growth stage. Then, during product maturity, advertising has a powerful but sustaining role to play in product sales and competitive success. Finally, advertising can be efficiently employed even in the final stages of the product life cycle. At these stages advertising to clear inventory of outdated or discontinued merchandise can materially increase the profitability of products.

PRICE STRATEGY

The price of a good is itself exceptionally important information to both sellers and consumers. For most branded products, prices seem to be set by managers in one of three ways: in relation to competition, in relation to costs, or in relation to demand. While a full discussion of price theory is beyond the scope of this book, we should recognize that advertising campaigns ought to be cognizant of the pricing mechanism used by the product manager. Often an understanding of the price-setting mechanism permits the construction of effective advertising copy and illustrations. For example the advertising copy for J. C. Penney's blue jeans and other sports clothing makes direct use of the company's competition-oriented pricing mechanism. In addition, account executives should recognize that the pricing structure used for goods and services may play a material role in setting advertising budgets and that these budgets directly influence media purchases.

PHYSICAL DISTRIBUTION SYSTEMS

Like pricing, the physical distribution of goods and services is an important aspect of marketing. It is also a topic that this book cannot treat fully. Advertisers and other decision makers should recognize, however, that the ultimate success of products can be dependent on carefully managed physical distribution systems and on the channels of distribution used to bring goods to the marketplace. One recurrent pattern in the thinking of students (and some real-world executives) is that the overwhelming bulk of advertising must be directed to audiences of prospective consumers. Such an emphasis creates the serious risk that members of a channel of distribution, who are themselves intermediate markets for goods and services, will be neglected by the organization's advertising efforts. This can be a serious mistake. Case histories in the packaged goods industries are replete with instances of relatively ordinary products which were highly successful because of the support created by advertising directed to the channel of distribution. Failures in the absence of such advertising support are, unfortunately, also numerous.

Promotional plans

The promotional plans for organizations are most often divided into two major types of plans: the sales force plan and the advertising campaign. A small minority of organizations use only one or the other type of activity. That is, some organizations rely exclusively on a personal selling force, and others concentrate their entire promotional effort on advertising. Most commonly, however, advertising and personal selling enhance each other's effectiveness. Therefore it is important for sales force managers to be aware of the advertising campaign at an early stage in its development. This awareness will facilitate the development of effective presentations by those salespersons actually making calls. On the other hand information developed by a field sales force can be an invaluable contribution to the advertising strategy. Most obviously, this strategy would include contributions made to the development of effective ad copy. Less obviously, a canny sales force can provide advertisers (and those responsible for producing advertising media schedules) with current, accurate information about the media consumption habits of sales prospects. To do this, salespersons simply add to their sales call reports any information which they can detect about journal subscriptions, comments by the prospect or observations by the salesperson about broadcast media programs being consumed during the sales call, and conversational indications by the prospect about his or her sources of product information. When constructed with the benefit of information like this, advertising can provide a powerful supplement to the salesperson's ability to avoid the truly "cold" call. In addition, it can materially augment the salesperson's ability to handle prospects' objections and can thereby contribute to the overall effectiveness of the sales force. A recent version of a classic statement about the relationship between advertising and sales force effectiveness is contained in Figure 1–4.

ADVERTISING CAMPAIGNS AND ADVERTISING MEDIA

Advertising campaigns, then, are not only the units into which major advertising efforts are divided. They also suggest the plan by which these efforts are developed, coordinated, executed, and evaluated.

Advertising campaigns really have four important elements. These are the allocation, the copy plan, the media plan, and the plan for the evaluation of effectiveness. The allocation is the statement of the overall funds available for the advertising effort. You will recall that there are several major ways in which real-world advertisers solve the problem of determining how much money to devote to advertising. These ways include the use of a percentage of sales, a percentage of forecast sales, or competitive equivalencies, the "all-you-can-afford" method, the so-called objective and task methods, and several other more difficult but more theoretically correct marginal and mathematical models.

Recent evidence confirms what some have suspected all along, namely, that even the large corporations set advertising budgets in a slapdash fashion. One study of a group of the largest U.S. advertisers found that almost half of the surveyed firms never used either computer models or quantitative models for their ad budgeting activities.[4]

While budget allocation is neither the primary focus of this text nor the primary responsibility of those who plan for and coordinate media buys, it should be noted that most companies underutilize their information and their analytical talents when it comes to setting the ad budget figure. As a result it is likely that suboptimal budgeting practices are frequently used. In many organizations great benefit would be derived from the use of mathematical approaches to setting the ad allocation. As a practical matter, it would seem that persons with quantitative training (and in advertising jobs they tend to be persons who have worked in the media function) have an obligation to point out to senior decision makers (for example, brand managers, marketing executives, chief executive officers, and members of boards of directors) that optimal advertising effort depends on correctly allocating funds to the advertising function. Thus, while this is not a direct part of their day-to-day jobs, quantitatively competent media

[4] A. J. San Augustine and W. F. Foley, "How Large Advertisers Set Budgets," *Journal of Advertising Research* vol. 15, no. 5 (October 1975), pp. 11–16.

Figure 1–4
How advertising prepares the way for the salesperson

"I don't know who you are.
I don't know your company.
I don't know your company's product.
I don't know what your company stands for.
I don't know your company's customers.
I don't know your company's record.
I don't know your company's reputation.
Now—what was it you wanted to sell me?"
MORAL: Sales start before your salesman calls—with business publication advertising.
McGRAW-HILL MAGAZINES
BUSINESS • PROFESSIONAL • TECHNICAL

Reprinted with permission of McGraw-Hill Publications Company

people have genuine opportunities to improve the efficiency with which organizations make investments in advertising. The budgeting process will be discussed in detail in Chapter 3.

Selecting themes and messages—the copy plan

The copy plan in an advertising campaign is really a schedule of what things need to be said, to which persons, at what times, in what ways, through which media. The emphasis in a copy plan, though, is on designing effective messages—messages which will accomplish the advertising objectives set out in the marketing plan. To accomplish this task the "creative" people in advertising have traditionally borne the burden of developing, designing and testing copy, illustrations, scripts, music, and other audio and visual aspects of advertisements. And the development of messages has generally moved from an area of subjective whim to one where research inputs and precampaign evaluation of copy have become regular aspects of advertising life.

It is tempting to think that the creative aspects of campaigns can be divorced from the media functions for campaigns. However, it is dangerous to succumb to this temptation. The creative aspect of virtually all advertising messages is of necessity influenced by the medium which carries those messages. Thus it is not traditional to use color illustrations in newspaper advertising. Of course, this tradition has been subject to recent changes, and sophisticated newspaper publishers are now able to offer newspaper advertising and newspaper advertisers the opportunity for efficient one- and four-color illustrations. Obviously, illustrations which are appropriate in certain up-scale consumer magazines would be inappropriate in advertising to children. Radio, which relies exclusively on audible messages, plays a role different in the creative design of a campaign than from that of television, with its ability to present images of a pictorial nature. It is difficult to imagine a well-designed and -executed advertising campaign which does not thoroughly integrate the so-called creative aspects (the copy plan) with the so-called quantitative aspects (the media plan). The copy plan frequently includes three types of objectives. These are:

1. Audience identification. A major step in the development of a copy strategy is obviously to determine whom you are trying to reach. Various means of identification might be used, including demographics, psychographics and lifestyle studies. These are discussed in detail in Chapter 4.

2. Copy themes. The product analysis previously discussed is used to determine how product benefits can be used in specific advertising themes. It is crucial that the advertising campaign be built around a central persuasive idea which can give continuity to the various advertisements which will be used throughout the campaign. Often the theme becomes a slogan which continues from one campaign to another ("At GE Progress is Our Most Important Product"). At other times the theme is a background idea which is promoted but not specifically stated.

3. Specific selling ideas. A final step in the copy objectives is to determine how specific advertisements will be handled. What types of illustrations will be used? To what degree will color be used? How will advertisements adapt the central theme in the various media? All of these questions must be addressed before the actual production of advertising is undertaken.

Let us, then, turn to the media plan, which will constitute the major emphasis of the rest of this book. When one speaks of management, it is implied that managers will engage in the major activities of planning, organizing, directing, controlling, and staffing. The management of the media function is no exception. The media plan represents the way in which the carriers for advertising messages can be selected, compared, priced, evaluated and generally brought into conformity with the advertising goal. The objectives of media plans are often separated into three major parts:

1. Target audience(s). The media planner must first identify his audience. Normally audience identification in media planning lacks some of the flexibility open to the creative department. Audience identification for media purposes must conform to the information available about the media. Often this limits the media planner to demographic-oriented information.

2. Media characteristics. The media planner must coordinate his efforts with the creative objectives. Media must be selected not only on the basis of their cost efficiency in reaching the target market but also according to their ability to deliver the creative message. It should be emphasized that compromise is a two-way street and that creative approaches must often be adapted to particular media vehicles. A discussion of the individual media can be found in Chapters 5–10.

3. Other promotion. Regardless of whether the advertising agency or department is directly involved in the production of collateral promotional material, close coordination must exist among the various promotional and advertising elements.

a. Public relations. If a formal public relations program is to be conducted, it is important that it convey the same basic message as the advertising. Obviously the format must be different and news values must be emphasized, but the same marketing and/or advertising goals applicable to the advertising certainly should apply in the public relations area.

b. Point-of-purchase. In-store point-of-purchase material is the last promotional opportunity for the product. It is also a means of creating impulse buying by the customer. In either case the point-of-purchase material should tie in with media advertising so that there can be identification between the two by the consumer.

c. Collateral material. In many cases collateral material such as brochures, specialty items, and calendars are prepared as part of the total promotional effort. These items should complement the overall sales effort by promoting the basic theme and objectives of more visible promotional endeavors.

Real-world advertising campaigns often suffer from deficiencies in the statement of their objectives. Those in advertising sometimes prefer to have imprecise objectives, and one can only suspect that their desire for imprecision is generated by an apprehension about their ability to achieve more precisely stated goals.

Advertising goals can be stated at three levels: the communications level, the sales or marketplace level, and the owner or profit level. At the communications level we find that the objectives of advertising campaigns can be stated in terms of brand awareness, brand recall, inclusion of the advertised brand in an evoked set of brands for the product class, and certain other measures of favorable attitude toward the advertised good or inclination or intentions to purchase it. In addition, advertising objectives at the communications level can include changes in these measures, although the statement of an objective as a change implies a "before-after campaign" measure of that variable.

At the sales or marketplace level, advertising objectives can be stated in absolute values, for example, sales of X million units or Y million dollars. They can also be expressed as desired changes in those values, for example, a sales increase of so many thousand dollars per month during the period of the campaign. Finally, they can be expressed in competitive terms such as brand share, market penetration, ranking among the competitors of an industry or a product class, and in the case of mature products, surviving the onslaughts of recently arrived product substitutes.

The statement of advertising objectives in sales or marketplace terms is desirable from a theoretical standpoint. Advertising expenditures which are supposed to stimulate demand ought to stimulate demand, and this stimulation ought to be measurable. However, the statement of advertising objectives in these terms has been resisted by many in the advertising industry for at least two reasons. The first reason, that influences other than advertising affect sales levels, is a valid concern of advertisers. There are four marketing "P's," not one. Thus a poorly designed product, a poorly distributed product, or an incorrectly priced product can fail in the marketplace even though the advertising campaign is superb. However, it is also (and unfortunately) true that some persons in the advertising industry have resisted the statement of objectives in sales terms for a less defensible reason—a general unwillingness to have clients evaluate whether they are doing what they say they do. Thus, while an advertising account executive may tell a client that a successful ad campaign will do "wonders" for sales, that account executive may be reluctant to have the client evaluate whether the campaign has achieved those wonders.

At the owner level, advertising has consequences for the profitability of the enterprise. Here the notion of profitability is used rather generally, and it can be expanded to include the realization of objectives for groups which are not organized for profit. In the overwhelming number of cases, though, the acid test of business effectiveness is the generation of long-term profits for owners. Therefore it is theoretically correct to describe profits as a function of business effectiveness. This effectiveness would certainly include, for most organizations, the effectiveness of advertising activities. While some work has been done in the area of linkages between advertising investments and profitability,[5] it is unrealistic to assume that effective advertising is always associated with relatively high profits, or in the case of publicly held firms, with the prices for common stock shares. The effectiveness of business functions other than advertising, such as production, finance, and other aspects of marketing, all play a role in determining organizational profitability or success. Thus, while there are indications that effective advertising is associated with relatively high profitability, advertisers properly resist the notion that the entire burden for organizational success should be borne by the advertising function.

BUDGET CONSTRAINTS

The advertising allocation decision produces the upper limit on the funds which can be expended in the purchase of advertising media during an advertising campaign. The advertising allocation is one of the obvious constraints imposed on the media function in a campaign, but other budget constraints are also relevant to the manage-

[5] F. K. Reilly, A. F. McGann, and R. A. Marquardt, "Advertising Decisions and Stockholders' Wealth," *Journal of Advertising Research,* vol. 17, no. 4 (August 1977), pp. 49–56.

ment of the media function. First, the client (or other decision maker) may have specified communication objectives which call for devoting specific proportions of the total budget to several of the major media. While managers of the media function might want to question this from time to time, and to provide information about alternative weightings, a decision to accomplish certain types of communication objectives can imply the maximum which can be allocated to each of the utilized media. Also, it has been found that mathematical models sometimes allow very efficient media to "run away" with the media selection process in a way which runs counter to all reason or judgment.[6] Second, the differences which occur in the relative efficiency enjoyed by advertisements in the different media may dictate that a given proportion of the total advertising budget be spent in a particularly efficient medium. This too would impose constraints on the media function. Finally, it can be noted that budget constraints can be more flexible than they may originally appear to be if the advertiser–advertising agency combination is financially able to take advantages of cash discounts and other incentives for prompt payment. The net effect of such incentives can be to increase the effective advertising budget allocation.

SUITABILITY OF MEDIUM

One of the most fascinating and demanding tasks faced by those responsible for the advertising media function is the matching of advertiser needs with media characteristics. In this task, not only must the obvious characteristics of particular media be matched with the advertising to be carried (for example, the obvious ability of television to combine sight and sound), but more important, the audiences of the various media must be matched with the target segments which the advertiser wishes to reach. The problem here is not one of lacking data. Rather the media planner is faced with what at first seems to be a virtual flood of information. However, after that information has been sifted and graded with regard to quality and applicability, it seems that the exact information needed is often not available. Publishers and (to a lesser extent) broadcasters are quick to furnish those who buy media with the characteristics of their audiences. In particular, the print media furnish voluminous information about the demographics of their readers. In the marketplace, however, demographics are often only moderate correlates of the purchasing behavior of particular interest to an advertiser. For example, it may come as no surprise that the most frequent purchasers of a

[6] F. M. Bass and R. T. Lonsdale, "An Exploration of Linear Programming in Media Selection," *Journal of Marketing Research,* vol. 3 (May 1966), pp. 179–88.

certain over-the-counter pharmaceutical may be persons aged 55 and over. However, this correlation between a demographic variable such as age and the purchase of a particular product is only part of the story. Other factors having to do with other demographics, as well as other attitudinal and financial data, can play a *determining* role in the decision to buy or not to buy a particular pharmaceutical product. The methods by which media planners combine demographic and other information about audiences with the needs of the advertiser for precise market segments will be discussed in greater detail later. However, it is appropriate to say at this point that simpleminded attempts to match media characteristics, audience demographics, and advertiser objectives for market segmentation are virtually predestined to produce less than optimal media purchases.

Coordinating media for best effect

The next aspect of the media plan is the intermedia coordination which is designed to produce an optimum total advertising effect. Here the notion of *synergism* is relevant. Synergism says that the whole is sometimes different from (either greater or less than) the sum of the relevant parts because of the interaction of these parts. Nowhere is this truer than in advertising campaigns which use more than one medium. For several reasons synergistic effects are possible in the purchase and use of multiple media. In the first place, the audiences for one medium may very well overlap with those for another. For example automobile passengers who pass an outdoor billboard might very well be members of the audience for a television show later that evening. Thus, simply counting up the audiences for each medium may tend to overstate the size of a particular audience.

On the other hand, it has long been suspected that the effect of the second and subsequent exposures to a particular advertising message is not the same effect as that of the first exposure. The evidence from the research literature suggests that three or more exposures to an ad may be required before a consumer can reliably recall salient information from it. The evidence also suggests that, beyond this threshold, additional exposures (particularly those coming from different sources) can produce a geometrically increasing effect on consumer awareness and intentions to purchase.

In summary, one can see that management of advertising media activities occurs within the framework of an organization's advertising and marketing efforts. These, in turn, occur in a particular competitive, economic, and political setting. The marketing concept, which has contributed greatly to a new and profitable focus on the consumer, can also be used to enhance the efficiency of advertising and its major components: creative plan and media strategy.

QUESTIONS

1. What are the five major management functions?

2. Describe the marketing concept.

3. Two specific economic forces, inflation and technology, have had a significant impact on advertising decisions. Give an example of the effect of each force on advertising decisions.

4. How is efficiency influenced by competition among media?

5. Given an example of the use of advertising to "demarket" a product.

6. State the difference between advertising to direct demand and to indirect demand.

7. What is a target audience?

8. In a particular year, the Mahatma Yogurt Company spent $100,000 on advertising, and enjoyed sales of $1 million that same year. The following year, the company increased its advertising budget by 10 percent, and sales increased by $104,000. Assuming that advertising effects did not carry over from year to year, what is the apparent advertising elasticity of demand? (Hint: compute the elasticity of demand coefficient.)

2

THE ADVERTISING MEDIA-RESEARCH PROCESS

IN THIS CHAPTER you will see how the research process relates to making good advertising media decisions. Most of those who work with advertising media are consumers or users of research, as much as they are producers of research. This chapter will suggest how to use research results and will describe aspects of the process by which research is produced. In this way we hope to increase your understanding of media research as well as improve your ability to use research results effectively.

As in many other business decision areas, making decisions about advertising media requires certain intellectual disciplines. These can be summarized under the heading or name of the scientific method. To review briefly, the scientific method requires four basic steps:

1. Defining the problem.
2. Collecting pertinent facts.
3. Analyzing these facts.
4. Deriving and implementing a solution to the problem.

The scientific method requires that decision makers understand the use of models. This chapter is organized around the outline suggested by the scientific method, and includes a discussion of the nature of models and the uses to be made from them in the course of managing the advertising media process.

STATEMENT OF RESEARCH PURPOSE

When performed as part of decision making, research is *purposive.* That is, it is undertaken not to reveal basic facts about humans or their environment, as is the case for "pure" research, but to solve some practical problem in a more efficient way. In Chapter 1 you were reminded of the importance of knowing the customer in the process of implementing the marketing concept. In fact, it is virtually impossible to apply the marketing concept unless the manager knows the consumer. Marketing research is the most important means by which one comes to know the customer.

In managing the advertising media function, the problem is to maximize advertising's impact within a budget constraint. This statement of the problem is more clearly evident in the media function than in other business areas. There, one bedeviling problem the manager faces is the correct specification of the problem. Business case histories are replete with examples of instances where managers incorrectly stated the problem. In these cases any research was, at best, a costly irrelevance. Resources were expended in the research process that did not contribute to the optimal solution of the primary problem.

Of course the basic advertising media problem needs to be expressed in the particular terms of the media problem at hand. It would certainly be misleading to imply that the statement of the problem in media decisions is always simple. It is, nevertheless, a basic axiom that the research process cannot be correctly applied to problem solving in advertising media situations without a clear statement of the problem to be solved. Most often, this statement is composed of two factors:

1. A specific statement of the advertising objective to be accomplished.
2. The complete specification of the constraints to be imposed on the solution.

In managing advertising media, the statement of the problem typically requires managers to understand three concepts: the cost of information, the value of information, and the role of a research hypothesis.

The cost of information

In applying the scientific method to the research processes which solve business problems, one frequently overlooked issue is the cost of information. It is obvious that information will be required for analysis of available alternatives. Less obviously, information will often be required to formulate a statement of the problem. For either of these purposes, hypothesis formation or analysis of alternatives, the collection of relevant information is a cost-incurring activity. That is, resources are expended in the collection of information. By looking at the major kinds of information, the nature of the costs associated with their collection can be better understood.

In business decision making, information is traditionally divided into two categories: primary and secondary data. *Primary data* are those facts which are collected by the decision-making organization for its particular needs. An example of primary data might be the information which an advertising agency collects by itself to construct a demographic profile of the customers for a client's product. Primary data can be subdivided into two categories. One category comprises the data which the organization collects for the purpose of making a particular decision or set of decisions. We might call this category *decision-specific* or *problem-specific* primary data. The second category includes those facts which are collected by the organization (or possibly by the organization's client, in the case of an advertising agency) in the course of normal business activities. This kind of primary information, which we might call *general primary information,* comes from such sources as billing records, advertising budgets, client sales records, and corporate income tax returns.

In the case of general primary data, the costs of information as this relates to a particular research problem are the marginal costs of retrieving, analyzing, and interpreting these data in light of the problem at hand. For example it is likely that the client firm will have already prepared corporate income tax returns. If, for some reason, these returns are useful in solving an advertising problem, then it would not be correct to assign the entire cost of preparing the income tax returns to that problem. Rather, only the human and other economic resources required to reanalyze certain aspects of the tax returns would be relevant costs for this kind of information.

The analysis of problem- or decision-specific primary information requires the expenditure of relatively greater amounts of manpower and capital. Here, not only the analysis but the prior tasks needed to design the data collection effort, to collect the information in useful form, and to analyze it are all part of the actual cost of information. Later in this chapter some of the costs associated with the collection of primary information will be identified in greater detail. At present it is only necessary to recognize that the costs of problem- or decision-specific primary information are higher than the costs of general primary information.

The other major kind of data, *secondary data,* represents those facts which are collected by others. Secondary data include the information published by trade associations and governmental agencies such as the Bureau of the Census. Secondary data also include information collected by commercial research firms for subsequent sale to subscribers. From the standpoint of the "user" organization, data collected by Simmons Market Research Bureau and the A. C. Nielsen Company are secondary data.

The value of information

Like virtually every business process, advertising media research is an activity which requires the comparison of relevant costs with relevant benefits. In advertising media research (and, for that matter, in many other business research applications) the benefit flowing from the research process is called the value of information. This benefit, or value, is expressed on two levels: the value of perfect information and the value of imperfect information. The latter is often called the value of information under conditions of uncertainty. In the following example we will use the concepts of value of perfect information and value of information under uncertainty to illustrate the process by which a maximum value can be set on the information produced by research.

Assume that the Smith-Moore advertising agency is preparing the ad campaign for a client who wishes to market an antishark chemical, SCRAM, to skin divers and others who swim in tropical waters. SCRAM is packed in a cylindrical container about the size of a ball-point pen, and is worn clipped to the swimsuit.

Those working on the SCRAM account are trying to decide whether to augment their campaign with a direct mail appeal to proprietors and managers of retail sporting goods stores located along the southeastern coast of the United States. This direct mail augmentation would cost $15,000 to do properly.

The account people at Smith-Moore are uncertain about the response of sporting goods dealers to their direct mail appeal for SCRAM. These managers receive a large volume of such mail and may not respond to the SCRAM piece. Although it is an oversimplification, we will assume that these managers will either respond favorably to the direct mail appeal or else they will ignore it.

SCRAM company executives have guessed that a favorable response to the direct mail appeal would produce a contribution of $100,000 to net profit. However, they are pessimistic about the chances of a favorable response, and set these at a probability of only .35.

For analysis purposes, the two choices available for the campaign can be called "strategies," and the reactions of sporting goods dealers, "states of nature." Then, the four possible results, the product of each strategy and each state of nature, can be listed as follows:

1. Don't use direct mail; dealers would respond poorly. This produces a result of $0.
2. Don't use direct mail; dealers would respond well. This produces an opportunity loss of $100,000 in net profits.
3. Use direct mail; dealers would respond poorly. This produces a loss of $15,000, the marginal cost of the direct mail campaign.
4. Use direct mail; dealers would respond well. This produces a gain of $100,000 in net profits.

Figure 2–1
Two-stage decision tree

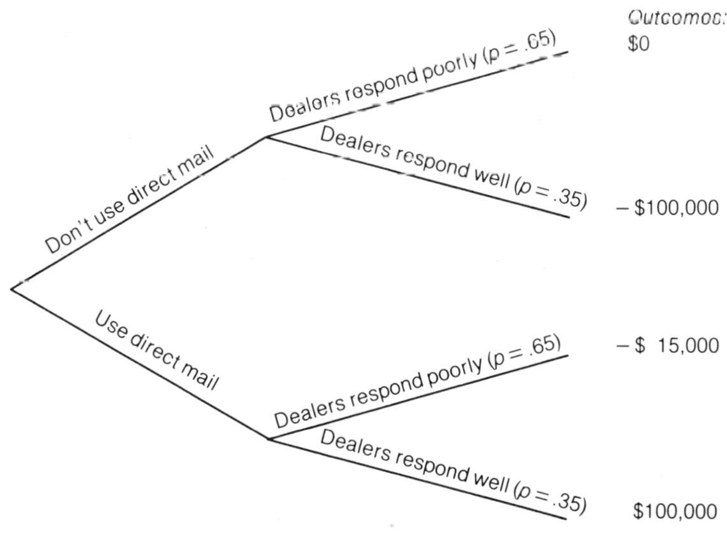

This problem, along with associated probabilities of occurrence, can be displayed in a diagram called a two-stage decision tree, shown in Figure 2–1.

The expected value of each strategy is found by multiplying the two outcomes of that strategy by the probability that each will occur. The expected value of the strategy of *not* using direct mail is:

$$EV_0 = (.65)\ (0) + (.35)\ (-\$100{,}000) = -\$35{,}000$$

Similarly the expected value of using direct mail is:

$$EV_1 = (.65)\ (-\$15{,}000) + (.35)\ (\$100{,}000) = -\$9{,}750 + \$35{,}000 = \$25{,}250$$

Thus, the decision to use a direct mail appeal, which results in an expected net profit contribution of $25,250, should be made, even though company executives think there is only about a one-in-three chance of favorable response among dealers. The other decision, not to use the campaign, has an expected loss of $35,000.

Keep in mind, though, that the probability of occurrence for each state of nature was produced by SCRAM executives' guesses, also called subjective probabilities. However, if the Smith-Moore agency could perform research which would tell, *with certainty,* whether the dealer response to direct mail would be favorable, then this *"perfect"* information could be used to choose the best strategy. You should note that the concept of the *value of perfect information* assumes no change in probabilities and outcomes; it simply computes the gain from always choosing the correct strategy.

To compute the *expected value of perfect information* (or EVPI), it is necessary to reverse the decision tree in Figure 2–1, as has been done in Figure 2–2. Then the outcomes for the best strategy are multiplied by their probability of occurrence.

If the Smith-Moore people had performed research which yielded perfect information about dealer response to the direct mail appeal, then company and agency people would simply choose the best strategy. If dealers would not respond to this appeal, it should be abandoned. If dealers would respond well, it should be used. The expected value of perfect information (EVPI) in this problem is the sum of the relevant payoffs times their probabilities. From Figure 2–2:

$$EVPI = (.65)\ (\$0) + (.35)\ (\$100{,}000) = \$35{,}000$$

How much should SCRAM executives be willing to pay for research which will produce "perfect information"? The value of such "perfect" research (or VPR) is the difference between the expected value of perfect information and the expected value under uncertainty of the best strategy. In this problem:

$$\begin{aligned} VPR &= EVPI - EV_1 \\ &= \$35{,}000 - \$25{,}250 = \$9{,}750 \end{aligned}$$

Figure 2–2
Reversed decision tree

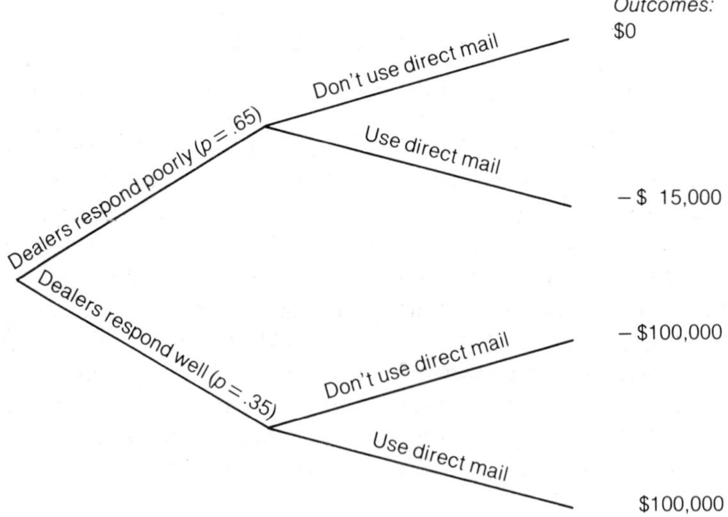

It should be stressed that the value for VPR ($9,750 in the SCRAM problem) is the *maximum* amount decision makers should be willing to pay for research-produced information. And since research is virtually never perfect in the real world, it does not produce perfect information. Thus, real-world executives should be willing to pay only a portion of VPR, since some uncertainty will still be present.

Operational hypotheses

Assuming that the decision maker has calculated (or estimated) the expected value of perfect information, and has set this figure as the upper limit of what might properly be spent on research, the first step in the research process is to state the problem in "research" form. In this form, the statement of the problem is called a *hypothesis.*

Hypotheses are assumptions, or tentative statements, about states of nature. In the preceding SCRAM problem, one hypothesis would be: "Dealers will respond well to a direct mail appeal for SCRAM." Often, hypotheses for advertising decisions involve tentative statements of a numerical nature; here the true numerical value of the state of nature is called a *parameter.*

Of course the scientific method requires more than assumptions (or hypotheses) for proper decision making. Hypotheses must be tested carefully and found to be true (more precisely, found to have an acceptably high probability of correctly describing the relevant state of nature) before the prudent decision maker incorporates them into decision making.

Hypotheses may be tested in a number of ways, but under conditions of uncertainty the most appropriate tests in advertising research are statistical tests. The usual method is to state the advertising problem in the form of a *null hypothesis.* In this form, the tentative assumption about the state of nature is that any statistical relationship is due to the unrestricted operation of the laws of chance. Our subsequent research efforts are then combined with *sampling statistics.* These are "calculated values which represent the probable deviations of sample characteristics from [parameters]."[1] Sampling stastistics, then, provide the decision maker with an objective, rigorous test of the null hypothesis, and technically speaking, the procedure is to test the null hypothesis. If it can be rejected on the basis of analysis which uses sampling statistics, we infer that the *research* (or alternative) *hypothesis* is correct. The research hypothesis is the logical opposite of the null hypothesis. An example of a pair of hypotheses (null and research) is:

[1] Frederick Williams, *Reasoning with Statistics* (New York: Holt, Rinehart & Winston, 1968), p. 7.

Null H_0: There is no significant difference between the sales response generated by an advertisement placed in *National Geographic* and the sales response generated by the same ad placed in *Cosmopolitan.*

Research H_r: There is a significant difference between the sales response to identical ads placed in *National Geographic* and *Cosmopolitan.*

To be of practical use in advertising decisions, problems must be stated in the form of *operational hypotheses.* Such hypotheses must possess two characteristics:

1. They must be "falsifiable."
2. The variables named in them must permit operational measurement.

The first characteristic, falsifiability, is necessary for any scientific hypothesis testing. Thus the statement "Ad A will eventually produce acceptable sales" is not falsifiable. If the ad does not produce acceptable sales this week, it might do so next week, or next month, or next year, or . . . If a statement cannot be disproved using agreed-upon methods, it cannot serve as a hypothesis in advertising research.

The second condition, measurable variables, simply means that we must state the hypothesis precisely enough so that subsequent measurements will lend themselves to the application of sampling statistics. "Repeat purchase rate" is a variable amenable to quantification, and we can measure this variable among a sample of customers to several decimal places. "Positive feelings about the Exxon Corporation" may or may not be a measurable variable, depending on our ability to measure them with accuracy.

Construction of models

In advertising research, particularly for problems involving advertising media, models are often used to assist the manager. A model is a simplified abstraction of selected properties of a real-world phenomenon. A manager constructs and uses this simplified representation of reality because it permits attention to be focused on the most important aspects of the problem at hand.

In other industries, physical models are sometimes used. A wavetank, which replicates the action of real ocean waves, may be used in the design of beach structures or supertankers. In advertising the most frequently employed models are symbolic, and may be either verbal or mathematical, depending on the type of symbols used to construct them. An example of a verbal model would be:

> Purchase some advertising space in magazine A, and twice as much advertising space in magazine B, in a way that maximizes the total advertising weight of both vehicles, provided that the cost of both does not exceed $3,000.

The same representation, expressed in the form of a mathematical model, would be:

$$\text{Maximize } Z = A + 2B$$

Subject to:

$A > 0$
$A + 2B \leq \$3{,}000$

Here Z is the symbolic notation given to the variable, advertising weight.[2]

In this example, the correct application of either the verbal or the mathematical model will produce the same "answer." However, mathematical models possess certain characteristics which make them particularly useful in the solution of advertising problems. These characteristics include precision, internal logic, and amenability to adjustment. By *precision,* we mean that a mathematical model can be constructed with less ambiguity than would probably be the case for a similar verbal model. By *internal logic,* we mean that the decision maker using a mathematical model is imposing the helpful discipline of logic on the process. The fallacy of $2+2=5$ is quickly recognized by all. Mathematical models also simplify the common process of *adjustment;* in the above example, an adjustment might take the form of changing $2B$ to $1.5B$. Both the nature of the change and the consequences flowing from it are highlighted through the use of mathematical models. In this book the predominant emphasis will be on mathematical models.

Types of media models

For problems in advertising media, it is useful to distinguish four classes of mathematical models, based on their linearity and cer-

[2] In algebraic notation, the statement $A > x$ means "A is greater than x," while the statement $A < x$ means "A is less than x." The symbol $\geq$ means "greater than or equal to," while the symbol $\leq$ means "less than or equal to." A beginning algebra text or one of the better dictionaries contains a more complete listing of algebraic inequality notations.

tainty. Models which employ constant proportions between variables are called *linear,* and those using varying relationships are termed *nonlinear.* Because of computational and measurement difficulties, advertising decision makers emphasize linear models, and these will also be the focus in this book. Figure 2–3 illustrates linear and nonlinear models.

Models based on certainty are called *deterministic* models. An example of a deterministic model is the media-buying model ($Z = A + 2B$) used previously. Alternatively models based on conditions of uncertainty are termed probabilistic models. For example a model which uses the concept of expected value under uncertainty (the "EVs" of the SCRAM example) is a probabilistic model, as are virtually all of the models which utilize sampling statistics.

In actual practice, advertising media models used to allocate funds among the media purchases in a campaign, and those used to choose media, are most commonly *linear* and *deterministic.* One such model type is a form of linear programming. Two examples of the use of linear programming in advertising problems are included as an appendix to this chapter.

Figure 2–3
Examples of linear and nonlinear models

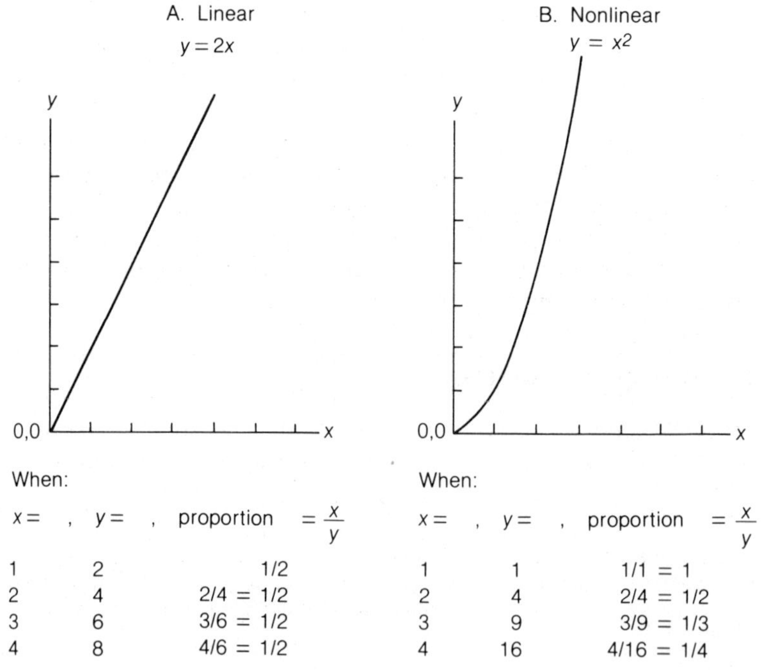

A. Linear — When:

$x =$	$y =$	proportion $= \frac{x}{y}$
1	2	1/2
2	4	2/4 = 1/2
3	6	3/6 = 1/2
4	8	4/6 = 1/2

B. Nonlinear — When:

$x =$	$y =$	proportion $= \frac{x}{y}$
1	1	1/1 = 1
2	4	2/4 = 1/2
3	9	3/9 = 1/3
4	16	4/16 = 1/4

In contrast, research to solve problems regarding the response produced by advertising most commonly uses *probabilistic* models. Among this class of models, linear forms are more frequently used than nonlinear, though the use of the more complex nonlinear variety is (and should be) growing. Extensive discussion of the application of probabilistic models to problems in advertising media will be presented in Chapter 11, Media Selection and Allocation Methods.

Choosing an optimum model

When faced with an advertising media problem, some managers (and some students) are a bit bewildered about how to proceed. This bewilderment can produce unfortunate choices and results. Sometimes the decision maker simply avoids choosing among models by making a snap judgment. We might call this the "Custer's 7th Cavalry approach." It produces sudden, dramatic, and often regrettable results. Another method is to simply take a mathematical model "off the shelf," preferably a very complex model, and force the problem into it. We might call this the "Procrustean solution," after the giant of Greek mythology who seized travelers and tied them to an iron bed. When the traveler was too short for the bed, he was stretched until he fit; when the traveler was too tall, Procrustes cut off his legs to get a fit. The travelers thus detained might well have objected to the cost of this "solution," based on a model (bed) which was not appropriate to their needs. Similarly, the Procrustean method of model selection in advertising research is often associated with suboptimal results.

An optimum model in advertising or other business decisions is one that highlights the crucial elements in the "reality" of the problem. Its elements recognize the presence or absence of certainty and linearity in this reality. The costs associated with its use are justified by the economic benefits of the information it produces. By recognizing these aspects of an optimal model and applying a modicum of logic, the advertising decision maker can select an optimal model for the problem to be solved with a high degree of confidence. This process is diagramed in Figure 2–4. You should recognize that the example models listed are just that, examples, and that a presentation of them is reserved for Chapters 4 and 11. You should also understand that it is virtually impossible for research to produce "perfect" information, though it is properly used to produce better information than was previously available. In actuality, the cost comparisons for probabilistic models should really compare ($EVPI - EV$) with *VAR*, the value of the information produced by *actual* research.

Figure 2–4
The process for selecting an optimum advertising research model

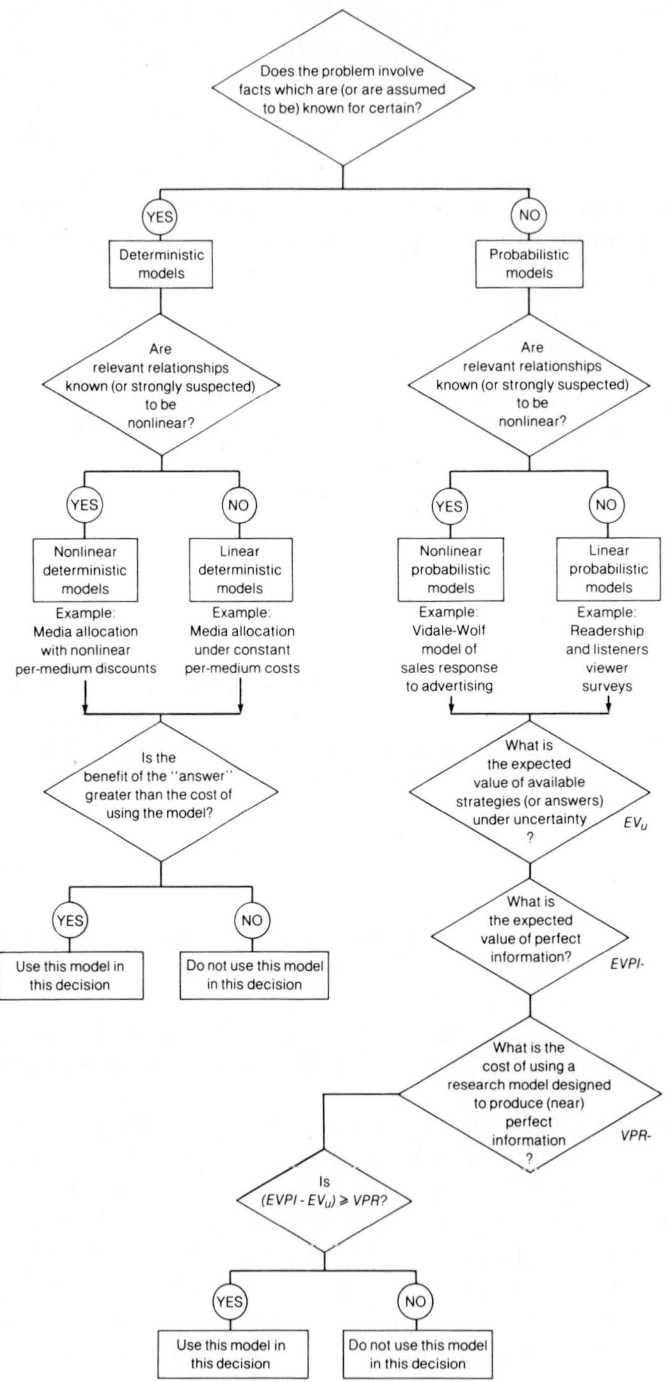

Examples and limitations of computer-assisted media model

In advertising agencies, the selection of media and the allocation of advertising weights among media is a relatively complicated process. To amplify the decision maker's ability to consider effectively many numerically expressed alternatives, computers are frequently used. Many agencies and other advertising-related organizations have constructed proprietary models which electronically process relevant information. One example is the Telmar media selection model (see Figure 2–5).

It is also important to stress at this point that all mathematical models are prey to certain limitations. In respect to linear programming models, Kotler notes four important restrictions:

1. Linear programming assumes that repeat exposures have a constant marginal effect.
2. It assumes constant media costs (no discounts).
3. It cannot handle the problem of audience duplication.
4. It fails to say anything about when the advertisement should be scheduled.[3]

More generally, Day says that linear programming is not a panacea, but an invitation to hard work and rigorous thinking, and "should never be thought of as a way of turning a problem over to a mystical black box which gives instant solutions to thorny problems."[4] And any model, to the extent that it abstracts irrelevant or tangential aspects of the real problem, has the capacity to distract the decision maker rather than enhance decision making. On balance, the advantages flowing from the use of models, especially precision, internal logic, and adjustability, are substantial. When combined with the power of computers to process and display the many alternatives available to the decision maker, the advantages outweigh the dangers. Nevertheless, as future advertising decision makers, you must recognize the care with which models must be used to enhance your decision-making ability.

COLLECTING INFORMATION

We are now at the point in the research process where the problem has been correctly stated in the form of an operational hypothesis. Analysis of the costs and value of research information has been

[3] Philip Kotler, *Marketing Management,* 2d ed. (Englewood Cliffs, N.J.: Prentice-Hall, 1972, p. 688.

[4] Ralph L. Day, "Linear Programming in Media Selection," *Journal of Advertising Research,* vol. 2 (1962), pp. 40–44.

Figure 2–5
Telmar Benchmark System II

BRAND Z - BUDGET SETTING: GOAL 70% REACH

MEDIA OBJECTIVES

BUDGET GOAL: $ 500000

RF GOAL(S):
REACH 70.0%

OPTIMIZATION
BASED ON: REACH

SELECTION PROCESS VIA MEDIAC MODEL

	MEDIA	COST	%REACH	AVG. FREQ	GRP
		CUME			
1	BBB	48000	29.33	1.00	29
1	BBB	96000	37.71	1.55	58
1	AAA	150000	53.26	1.62	86
1	GGG	180000	57.16	1.72	98
1	AAA	234000	62.50	2.02	126
1	DDD	266000	64.58	2.12	136
1	BBB	314000	67.29	2.47	165
1	AAA	368000	69.92	2.77	193
1	FFF	391000	70.91	2.77	196

*** RF GOAL(S) REACHED

BENCHMARK II SUMMARY AND ANALYSIS

USES	MEDIA	COST
3	AAA	162000
3	BBB	144000
1	DDD	32000
1	FFF	23000
1	GGG	30000
9		391000

Source: Telmar Communications Corporation, 90 Park Avenue, New York, N.Y. 10016.

made, and this analysis justifies the need for more information. An appropriate model or set of models has been tentatively selected. It is now time to collect the relevant facts which will provide grist for the research mill.

Primary data collection

The first step in primary data collection ought to be a search to discover whether the information has already been gathered by the firm (or its agents). If general primary data are appropriate and on hand, the data collection process is reduced to obtaining an intraorganization transfer of the information.

If decision-specific primary data are required, the two basic methods for gathering information are *sampling* and a *census*. In sampling, we will collect information from a portion of the total relevant group. In statistical language this group is termed a "population," even when the group is composed of objects other than persons. For example, costs of 30-second primetime television spots or magazines which offer split-run advertising can be thought of as statistical populations. By collecting values from a portion of a population and subsequently applying sampling statistics, the decision maker is able to make probabilistic inferences about population parameters.

The other method of collecting decision-specific primary data is the census. A census requires the collection of data from every member (person or object) in the entire statistical population. Any time the size of the population is large, a census is almost always *less efficient* (that is, more costly) than a correctly drawn sample. The U.S. Census of Population (and the companion Census of Agriculture, Census of Manufacturing, etc.) is an imperfect census in that not every person and household is counted. Census takers attempt to enumerate all persons, though, and the percentage of persons "missed" is relatively small.

If data are to be collected by sampling, then the researcher needs a strategy for selecting that portion of the population to be measured. If a probability distribution is employed to select subjects for measurement, then the sample obtained is a *probability sample*. The basic random sample is a probability sample in which every member of the population has an equally likely chance of being measured. Other probability samples include stratified random samples and some cluster samples.

If a probability distribution is not used to select sample units, then the sample obtained is a nonprobability or *convenience* sample. Collecting information from the first 100 persons who write for a free catalog would be an example of a convenience sample. So-called judgment and quota samples are most often nonprobability samples.

Probability samples are more difficult and more expensive to collect than convenience samples. True probability samples presume that a listing of the population can be produced, that a sampling plan based on a known probability distribution will be used to choose sampling units, and that the sampling plan is completed successfully. This last requirement precludes the real-world problems of refusals, not-at-homes, unlisted phone numbers, failures to return questionnaires or diaries, and panel mortality. However, true probability samples permit the correct application of powerful tools of statistical inference.

Convenience samples are cheaper and easier to produce. However, the absence of a probability based sampling plan impairs the power of the inferences which can be statistically derived. In practice virtually all sampling attempts to conform to the requirements for a probability sample and virtually all real-world sampling depart to some degree from a true probability sample. Actual primary data collection is conducted so as to permit as close an approximation to true probability sampling as time, research funds, and the value of information will permit. Sampling statistics are then applied as if a probability sample has been drawn. The decision maker recognizes that the "answers" developed are less certain than they would be if a true probability sample had been used.

Assuming that a probability sample of some type is desired, the next question might be, "How large a sample is required?" While a full discussion of sample size can be found in many statistics and market research texts,[5] an indication of required sample sizes for a simple random sample is given in Figure 2–6.

Secondary data sources

Secondary data, you will remember, are data collected by another organization. Such data are purchased by the user organization. Commonly used sources of secondary information which relate to advertising media decisions are presented in Figure 2–7.

Data quality

Three important issues relate to the quality of the data used in advertising decisions. These are *metricity, validity* and *reliability.*

[5] Cf. Gilbert A. Churchill, Jr., *Marketing Research* (Hinsdale, Ill.: Dryden Press, 1976), pp. 302–16.

Figure 2–6
Sample size: Simple random sample

Permitted error	*Confidence limits*	
	95 samples in 100	*99 samples in 100*
1%	9,604	16,587
2	2,401	4,147
3	1,067	1,843
4	600	1,037
5	384	663
6	267	461
7	196	339

For a simple random sample, drawn from a very large population with replacement, the formula for sample size is:

$$n = \frac{Z^2 \sigma^2}{h^2}$$

Where

σ = Standard deviation
Z = Number of standard deviations for the specified confidence internal
h = Allowable tolerance for variation

Source: C. H. Backstrom and G. D. Hursh, *Survey Research* (Evanston, Ill.: Northwestern University Press, 1963), p. 33.

By metricity, we mean the extent to which the numerical research data meet the following conditions:

$$d\overline{xx} = 0$$
$$d\overline{xy} = d\overline{yx}$$
$$d\overline{xy} \leqslant d\overline{xzy}$$

In other words, the distance from any point, *x*, to itself must be zero. The distance between two points, *x* and *y*, must be the same regardless of the direction of measurement. The distance between two points, *x* and *y*, must be less than or equal to the distance from *x*, through any third point, *z*, to *y*. (This last is known as the triangular inequalities rule.)

As a practical matter, research data are usually divided into four categories. These categories, their descriptions, and relevant classes of statistical tools are shown in Figure 2–8. These distinctions between metric and nonmetric data have important implications for media decisions. For example, one of the largest syndicated print research firms, Starch INRA Hooper, regularly furnishes information about how well a particular ad *ranked* in an issue of a magazine. Clearly such numbers represent ordinal quality data, and only nonparametric statistics are entirely appropriate for analysis of these ranks. Also, many of the behavioral measures of advertising performance, such as attitude or opinion change, are most likely to be

Figure 2–7
Sources of secondary data for advertising research: Top 23 researchers*

Rank	*Organization*	*1979 research revenues (millions)*	*% gain over 1978*
1	A. C. Nielsen Co.	$302.1	22
2	IMS International	88.8	18
3	SAMI	54.4	13
4	The Arbitron Co.	44.1	25
5	Burke International Research	42.6	15
6	Market Facts	19.3	− 7
7	Westat Inc.	14.4	50
8	Audits & Surveys	14.0	8
9	Marketing & Research Counselors	13.1	13
10	ASI Market Research	12.3	− 6
11	Chilton Research	12.0	93
12	Yankelovich, Skelly & White	11.8	26
13	Ehrhart-Babic Associates	10.4	13
14	National Family Opinion Center	10.0	
15	NPD Research	9.7	16
16	Data Development Corp.	9.6	13
17	Louis Harris & Associates	9.3	3
18	National Analysts	8.7	9
19	Opinion Research Corp.	8.2	7
20	Elrick & Lavidge	7.1	5
21	Walker Research	7.0	1
22	Starch INRA Hooper	5.5	24
23	Decisions Center	5.1	9
	Total	$719.5	+ 18 (average)

*Based on 1978 marketing/advertising research volume only.

Source: Jack Honomichl, "Top 23 Companies Post 21% Growth in Revenues," *Advertising Age,* May 19, 1980, p. 3. See also Martha Fainsworth Riche, "Non-Profit Data Sources," *American Demographics,* March 1979, pp. 36–41.

measured in a way that produces nonmetric data. This theme will be developed in Chapter 13 in the discussion of postscheduling techniques.

By *validity,* we mean how well our information actually measures what it claims to measure. Suppose we ask survey respondents how much total income is earned by members of their household. Some respondents may provide actual income figures, but others may furnish erroneous data because they don't know the actual figure or because they inflate the actual figure to appear wealthier or because they deflate the actual figure on the suspicion that the IRS might see the answer. To the extent that the measurement of any variable (e.g., household income) is contaminated by measurements or other variables (e.g., desire to impress interviewer or desire to thwart the IRS), it is an invalid measurement.

Figure 2–8
Categories of research data quality

Category of data quality	*Properties*	*Examples*	*Appropriate statistical tools*
Nominal	Numbers assigned only to classify; no arithmetic properties	0 = Present customer, past customer also 1 = Past customer, no longer customer 2 = First-time customer	Nonparametric or distribution-free statistics
Ordinal	Numbers specify ordered relations of some characteristics, without specifying the interval; rankings	1 = Most preferred brand 2 = Second-choice brand 3 = Third-choice brand	
Interval	Numbers specify ordered relationships with arbitrary but equal intervals	Centigrade temperature, household income, miles traveled	Metric statistics
Ratio	Same as interval, but scale has a "natural" or absolute zero point	Kelvin temperature, eye-pupil diameter	

Finally, *reliability* means the "repeatability" of a measurement. If it is repeatable with the same results, the measurement is reliable. Tests of data reliability, all based on correlation, include test-retest (where subjects' answers from two different measurements are compared) and alternative forms (where subjects are asked about the same thing in two or more different ways).

Instrumentation

The final issue in collecting information is instrumentation—the questionnaire, interview form, or other document on which respondent answers are recorded. Obviously instrumentation is largely the concern in primary data collection efforts.

An acceptable data collection instrument should have four properties. These are:

1. *Standardization* of questions. All respondents should be asked the same questions in the same way (provided the research design does not call for certain types of variability).
2. *Assistance* to interviewers and respondents. Areas of the instrument where questions can be expected to occur should contain clear instructions for resolving these questions.
3. *Absence* of demand characteristics. Questions and instructions should be carefully constructed so as to avoid *leading* the respondent to a particular answer.
4. *Suitability* for subsequent analysis. Instruments should be designed so that the subject's answers can be easily and accurately processed. Often this means the preparation of computer-compatible data records directly from responses. An example of a questionnaire designed for direct computer card punching is shown in Figure 2–9. Small numbers on the right of the page indicate the positions in an 80-column computer card where each answer should be key-punched.

DATA ANALYSIS AND INTERPRETATION

If our advertising research has conformed to the process outlined in the foregoing portion of this chapter, we are now at the stage where the hypotheses will be tested and the test results reported to the person responsible for reaching a decision. Major steps in the testing process are presented below.

Preparing raw data for analysis

With the data collection process completed, the next step is to prepare this information for analysis. To do this, we must first develop a procedure for handling missing data and wild codes.

By missing data, we mean those portions of responses which are not complete and those responses which are completely absent from our data set. For incomplete responses, a decision must be reached about whether to exclude missing values from the analysis or to substitute a value, such as the average of the responses at hand. Completely absent responses are a part of the nonresponse problem; while these usually impair the statistical inferences of the hypothesis tests, they do not require immediate adjustments by the analyst.

Wild codes represent impossible or highly implausible values for a variable. Suppose we were measuring "years of formal education" and this variable ranged from 0 (never attended school) to 17 (our

Figure 2 0
Questionnaire designed for computer card punching

DUPE 1-7

Statement	Definitely Disagree					Definitely Agree	
v. Once I find a brand I like, I stick with it	1	2	3	4	5	6	8
w. Eye make up is as important as lipstick	1	2	3	4	5	6	9
x. Normally, I don't try new brands until they are well accepted by others	1	2	3	4	5	6	10
y. I rarely go out of my way to shop for groceries at the store with the lowest prices	1	2	3	4	5	6	11
z. I see no particular reason to avoid preservatives	1	2	3	4	5	6	12
aa. Health foods are not worth the extra costs	1	2	3	4	5	6	13
bb. I know a great deal about nutrition	1	2	3	4	5	6	14
cc. Breakfast is the one meal a person can most often skip without any bad side effects	1	2	3	4	5	6	15
dd. There are many prepared foods that are just as good as home-made or fresh foods	1	2	3	4	5	6	16
ee. Disinfectants should be used to get your house really clean	1	2	3	4	5	6	17
ff. I have to be careful what I serve members of my family because of health problems	1	2	3	4	5	6	18
gg. I prepare each meal to be nutritionally balanced	1	2	3	4	5	6	19
hh. So called health foods are not any better for you than the well-known brands	1	2	3	4	5	6	20
ii. I buy more low calorie foods than most housewives	1	2	3	4	5	6	21

4. Are you or anyone in your household now answering questionnaires or reporting purchases regularly for any other organization or company?

Yes ( )[1] No ( )[2] 22

4a. (IF "YES") What is the name of the company? ______________________ 23-25

5. This questionnaire has been completed by: "X" one:

Female head of household ( )[1] Male head of household ( )[2] 26

Other household member (specify) ______________________ ( )[3]

Now, please check over this questionnaire to be sure that you haven't overlooked anything. It is important that we have your answer to every question. Then, return it to us in the next three or four days in the enclosed, self-addressed and postage-paid envelope.

(END OF QUESTIONNAIRE)

Courtesy Arbitron Consumer Research

code for college graduate with some advanced graduate schooling). A value of 61, for some respondent, would represent a wild code item. Perhaps the keypunch operator transposed the code 16. In such an instance, comparing the wild code with the data collection instrument can produce the appropriate correction. All variables being analyzed should be subjected to wild code checks. Wild code values which cannot be corrected should be excluded from further analysis since they can (and often do) seriously distort the hypothesis tests.

Selecting analytical procedures

In addition to using a model which correctly reflects the presence or absence of certainty as well as the property of linearity, our analytical procedure should reflect the quality of our research data. As indicated in Figure 2–5, nonparametric statistical tools should probably be used when our data are of only nominal or ordinal quality. Many analysts rely on a standard nonparametric reference, such as Siegel, for the details and limitations of these procedures.[6] The problems associated with using metric statistics on nonmetric data are illustrated below.

Assume that three magazine readers are asked to rank the following four magazines on the basis of their preference. This produces the following matrix of ranks:

	Reader 1	*Reader 2*	*Reader 3*
Cosmopolitan	1	3	4
Reader's Digest	2	2	2
Argosy	3	4	1
Literary Review	4	1	3

Now, if a decision maker wished to select the favorite magazine of the group represented by these three readers, he might be tempted to compute the average rank of each magazine, on the theory that the publication with the lowest average rank would be the overall favorite. In this case, *Reader's Digest* has the lowest mean rank (average = 2) and the other three publications are tied (at average = 2.67).

It is incorrect to compute average ranks, since ranks are ordinal data, while arithmetic averages are only appropriate for metric data. But to illustrate how dangerous it can be to apply an inappropriate

[6] Sidney Siegel, *Nonparametric Statistics for the Behavioral Sciences* (New York: McGraw-Hill, 1956).

technique, consider how many of the group represented by these three readers ever read *Reader's Digest*, if each only reads his/her favorite magazine!

Recognizing limitations

No actual research produces perfect results, but reports of hypothesis testing sometimes conceal (or at least overlook) the imperfections. Analysts have a duty to provide decision makers, and decision makers have an obligation to insist on, a careful statement of limitations on the test. The major limitations, which should always be available to decision makers as part of the hypothesis test report, are:

1. Departures from metric data quality.
2. Departures from a probability sampling plan.
3. Departures from validity or reliability to the extent that these are known.
4. Departures from certainty implied by the use of a particular probabilistic model.

You should recognize that the explicit statement of these limitations is much more than "weasel-wording." Rather these are a part of one's professional obligations in the process of using research to enhance the quality of advertising decisions.

Writing useful research reports

Research reports, which are the descriptions of hypothesis tests, are often not used (or only partly used) by decision makers. There are two basic reasons for this incomplete use. The decision maker may not have the required background to use the report, or the report may be flawed. Regarding the first cause, our efforts will be devoted to ensuring that you have the required skills to use good research.

You can also eliminate (or reduce) the second cause of incomplete research utilization by making the research reports you produce *useful*. To do this, recognize that useful reports have the following characteristics:

1. They conform to the scientific method. They marshal information in the same sequence as the research process they report.
2. They express matters clearly. Jargon is avoided. Numerical information is presented in clear tabular or graphic form. Simple declarative sentences predominate in the narrative. References and footnotes are fully presented.

3. They acknowledge costs, justify these with expected benefits, and clearly set forth limitations.

SOLVING PROBLEMS

To reiterate and summarize, purposive research can be extremely helpful in reaching good decisions. Good decisions are workable solutions to real problems. It is possible to make a good decision without benefit of research, but the odds are against it; the decision maker who makes decisions without research is in effect making the quality of the decision a hostage to chance. In the process of solving advertising media problems where the alternatives and the constraints are numerous and the dollar value of the choices is very large, careful scientific research offers the prospect of greatly improving the percentage of good decisions.

APPENDIX: EXAMPLES OF LINEAR PROGRAMMING IN ADVERTISING DECISIONS

Example 1: Benefit-maximizing mix for two media vehicles

Sunset Farms, a producer of retail pork products for a regional market, has decided to allocate the print media budget of $200,000 between two magazines: *Southern Living* (*SL*) and *Southern Outdoors* (*SO*). *SL* has a paid circulation of 1,200,000 and a single-page, four-color ad cost of $30,000. *SO* has a paid circulation of 750,000 and a four-color, full-page space cost of $20,000. Company executives wish to maximize the exposure of their ads during a 12-month campaign. They assume that audience duplication is not a problem. Both magazines will publish 12 issues during the campaign, and company executives insist that each magazine carry a minimum of one, four-color, full-page ad in 2 of the 12 issues. They further believe that an ad in either magazine will be equally effective in producing sales for Sunset.

This problem of media allocation can be stated as a linear programming problem of the form:

$$\text{Maximize readers per dollar, } Z = \frac{1{,}200{,}000(SL)}{30{,}000} + \frac{750{,}000(SO)}{20{,}000}$$
$$= 40(SL) + 37.5(SO)$$

Subject to the following constraints:

$SL \geqslant 2$
$SO \geqslant 2$
$\$30{,}000(SL) + \$20{,}000(SO) \leqslant \$200{,}000$

The linear model for Z, a *linear functional,* is called the *objective function.* You will recognize that the coefficients are simply expressions for "readers per dollar" for each magazine. The first two constraints reflect management's requirements for at least two, four-color, full-page ads in each vehicle, while the third constraint requires that the total budget not be exceeded.

In this rather simple problem, it is possible to develop an optimum solution graphically. The first step is to show the effect of the first two constaints (see Figure 2A–1).

Figure 2A–1
Graphic solution to media allocation problem (1)

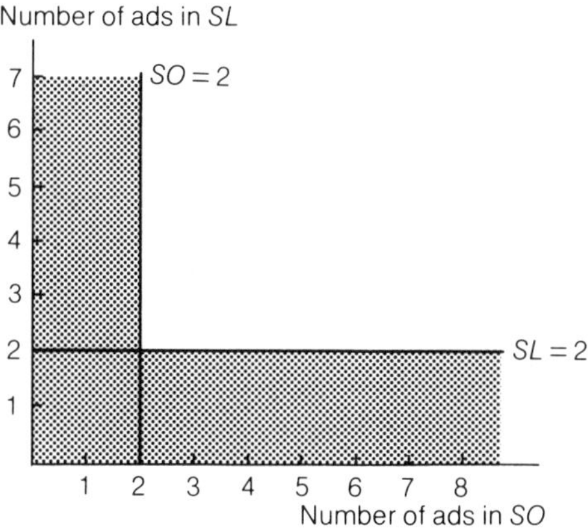

In the shaded area to the left of the vertical line $SO = 2$, and below the horizontal line $SL = 2$, one or both of the first two constraints would be violated. Therefore, no solution to the functional $Z = 40(SL) + 37.5(SO)$ can be accepted if it lies in the shaded area.

The next step is to find the values for SL and SO imposed by the budget constraint $\$30{,}000(SL) + \$20{,}000(SO) \leq \$200{,}000$. To fix this line we need to know where it intersects each axis (or we need to find the SL and SO intercepts). To find the SL intercept, we set $SO = 0$. This is equivalent to placing the entire budget (for the moment) in SL. Then:

$$\$30{,}000(SL) + \$20{,}000(0) = \$200{,}000$$

$$SL = \frac{\$200{,}000}{\$30{,}000} = 6.67$$

By the same method:

$$\$30{,}000(0) + \$20{,}000(SO) = \$200{,}000$$

$$SO = \frac{\$200{,}000}{\$20{,}000} = 10$$

Adding these intercept values and the line they determine to the graph in Figure 2A–1 produces the results shown in Figure 2A–2.

You should recognize that the only permissible solutions lie within the triangle ABC, since the areas below and to the left of this triangle violate one or both of the first two constraints. Also, the permissible solutions must be found below the line AB, since above this line the third constraint would be violated. The triangle ABC is called a *feasibility space,* which is a bounded region that must contain any permissible solution.

If a problem is such that the feasibility space is not bounded by constraints, then it is inappropriate to continue the use of linear programming. However, if a combination of all constraints produces a bounded feasibility space, then the last step is to find the value for Z_{max}. To do this, we employ a fact developed by mathematicians that the maximum permissible value for a linear functional lies at one of the cornerpoints of the feasibility space. Therefore, we substitute the *SL* and *SO* coordinates for each cornerpoint in the objective function, as follows:

	Cornerpoint coordinates *SL*	*SO*	*Objective function Z =40(SL)+37.5(SO)*
A	5.33*	2	$Z_A = 213.2 + 75 = 288.2$
B	2	7*	$Z_B = 80 + 262.5 = 342.5$
C	2	2	$Z_C = 80 + 75 = 155.0$

* Found by substituting in the equation for the budget constraint.

By inspecting values for the objective function *Z,* we can see that it has a maximum value of 342.5 readers per dollar, and this is achieved by placing the four-color, full-page ad in two issues of *Southern Living* and seven issues of *Southern Outdoors.*

Example 2: Cost-minimizing problem for an advertising agency

Melissa and Hillary are two recent hires in the media department of Oblivion Advertising, Inc., where you are vice president, media. Melissa, employed seven months ago, has completed the six-month training program and is now a qualified junior media planner. Hillary is in the second month of training and has the title of junior media

Figure 2A-2
Graphic solution to media allocation problems (2)

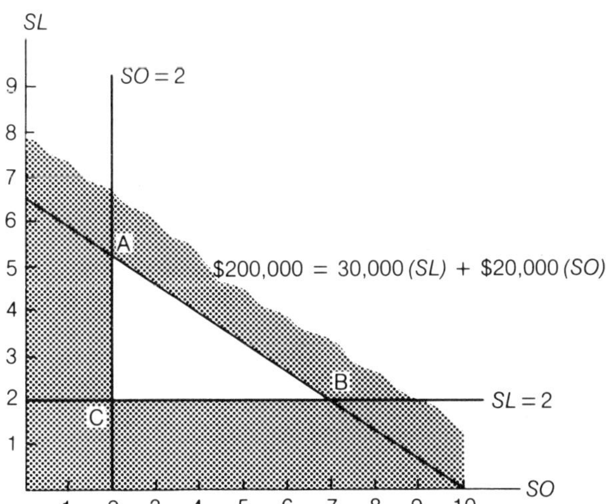

planner (trainee). Both women show great promise of developing into effective senior members of the media department. However, each woman has her own style of working. Melissa, nicknamed "Flash" by her co-workers, works rapidly, but 15 percent of her work needs to be redone by the senior media planner. Hillary, nicknamed "Pokey" by her friends at the agency, works more slowly but more accurately, and only 7 percent of her work requires corrections by the senior media planner.

At Oblivion, one task performed by the media department is the development of media schedules. This task is divided into work units, and several standards have been developed for the production of work units. These are:

a. The *minimum* expectation for trainees is 30 work units per month.
b. The *minimum* expectation for fully trained junior employees is 120 correctly produced work units per month.
c. The maximum media planning load for any employee is 200 correctly produced work units per month.
d. The expected demand for the junior group of the media department (the group composed of Melissa and Hillary) is 300 work units per month.

The cost accountant at Oblivion has just completed a meeting with you which he opened with the statement, "Holy GRPs! The cost of having the senior media planner redo incorrect work units is eating us alive!'' You and he then carefully analyze the relevant data and agree that the actual cost of each rework is \$500. Something must be done to reduce this cost.

You decide to use linear programming to assist you in minimizing rework costs, by assigning optimum numbers of work units to Melissa and Hillary. You recognize that if either or both Melissa and Hillary are not fully occupied with this task, there are a sufficient number of other duties (such as contact work with media organizations and related research work) so that both employees will be fully and productively employed by devoting any excess time to these alernatives.

In the language of linear programming, your problem is to find:

$$Z_{\text{min.}} = \$500(.15)M + \$500(.07)H$$

where M and H are the number of media planning work units assigned to Melissa and Hillary respectively. $Z_{min.}$, which is the rework cost function, can be expressed:

$$Z_{min.} = \$75(M) + \$35(H)$$

The relevant constraints, expressed as inequalities, are:

a.	$H \geqslant 30$	Production minimum for trainee (Hillary)
b.	$M + H \geqslant 300$	Estimate of work needed from junior media group
c.	$.85M \leqslant 200$ or $M \leqslant 235$	Production maximum from Melissa, after accounting for her reject rate
d.	$.93H \leqslant 200$ or $H \leqslant 215$	Production maximum from Hillary, after accounting for her reject rate
e.	$.85M \geqslant 120$ or $M \geqslant 141.2$	Production minimum for fully trained junior employees (Melissa)

You graphically place these constraints, as shown below, and determine that the feasibility space in which the objective function must be minimized is the polygon (or region) bounded by the corners *ABCD.* You also notice that the first constraint, $H \geqslant 30$, is not material in bounding the feasibility space, since Hillary's work production is already far better than this minimum. Thus, the constraint $H \geqslant 30$ is *superfluous;* no portion of the feasibility space is bounded by this constraint.

As in the preceding problem, we know that the optimum values for Z will be found at one of the cornerpoints of the feasibility space. By substituting the coordinates of the cornerpoints in the objective function, you obtain the results shown in Figure 2A–3.

Figure 2A–3
Graphic solution of work distribution problem

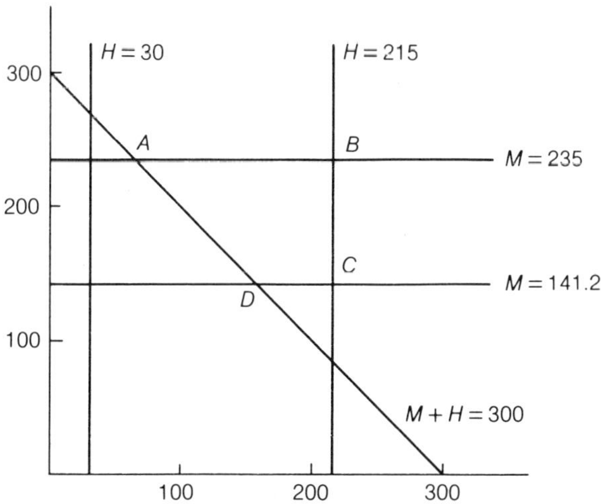

Corner point	Coordinates		Z =				
	M	H		75M	+ 35H	=	
A	235	65	Z_A =	$17,625	+ $2,275	=	$19,900
B	235	215	Z_B =	$17,625	+ $7,525	=	$25,150
C	141.2	215	Z_C =	$10,590	+ $7,525	=	$18,115
D	141.2	158.8	Z_D =	$10,590	+ $5,558	=	$16,148

Thus, the rework cost function is minimized when Melissa is assigned 141.2 work units of media scheduling, and Hillary, 158.8. At this level, 300 work units will be produced by the pair per month, and the rework cost will be $16,148.

In the short run (say, for the next month), rework costs will be minimized by this assignment. However, with a longer time horizon, an employee would be unlikely to stay with a work assignment which sets her production at the agency's minimum standard for correct monthly production. Good management practice suggests that, as her supervisor, you take steps to help Melissa reduce her rework rate or assign her other tasks in the department.

QUESTIONS

1. What are the four basic steps in the scientific method?

2. Distinguish between primary and secondary data, and give an example of each type.

3. What is the name of the upper limit on the amount you would be willing to pay for research information?

4. You wonder whether magazine advertising is effective for a particular advertising client. Translate this problem into null hypothesis form.

5. A particular newspaper offers a 2 percent discount for prompt payment of advertising space bills. Is this a linear or a nonlinear discount?

6. What is the *average* research revenue of the 23 largest U.S.-owned research firms?

7. What is the quality of the data implied by the claim "We're number one"? What is the metricity?

8. In some research done among high school students, one of the respondents has a value of 91 in the age variable. Is this a "wild code"? What should be done about this value?

3
ADVERTISING BUDGETS

AT THE FINANCIAL heart of advertising activities is the advertising budget. The advertising budget greatly influences every other aspect of advertising, but its influence on the decisions and processes involved in advertising media is especially keen. Throughout this chapter, our discussion of budgets will be segregated into two major parts: how budgets are developed and used and how they should be developed and used. To accomplish this, the nature of budgets will be explored. Then benefits accruing from the use of budgets will be outlined. Practical budgeting philosophies will be discussed, and these will be contrasted with theoretical standards. Major advertising uses of budgeted funds will be summarized. Finally, budgetary controls and their managerial applications will be described.

WHAT IS A BUDGET?

Advertising is one of the many business activities which require funds. Thus, an oversimplified statement of the financial management of advertising is that it is the process of controlling the sources and uses of advertising funds. In this chapter, you will see that advertising budgets have much in common with budgets for virtually any other business activity, such as manufacturing. You will also see that advertising budgets are different in some important respects from budgets for other business areas. And advertising budgets are a fundamental tool for managing the large sums of money involved in advertising.

In its simplest form, a budget is a plan. It describes management's intentions for future sources of funds and for future uses of these funds. Unlike all the other financial documents used by business today, which describe what has already happened, budgets state what will occur in the future. You know that the future is uncertain and cannot be forecast exactly. Since budgets plan for actions to be taken in this uncertain future, they are subject to modifications over time. In fact, the farther the budget period extends into the future, the less fixed the budget is likely to be.

While it is important to recognize the uncertainties of future periods, it is equally important to recognize the value of planning the financial aspects of the future via budgeting. In general, the budgeting process yields several kinds of benefit to managers:

1. Budgets encourage (and even require) thinking ahead. The budgeting process not only reduces managers' concentration on reacting to events, but also stimulates the processes by which management can achieve better control over those events.
2. Budgets require coordination of managerial effort. In many enterprises, preparation of a budget is the process which most effectively draws together diverse interests and problems. Budgeting is often the process by which these are resolved in light of what is best for the entire organization.
3. Budgets furnish performance standards. During and after the budget period, the budget can be used to evaluate, in relatively unambiguous quantitative terms, how effectively resources were expended and benefits realized.
4. Budgets are control devices. When properly used, budgets prevent small disturbances from becoming major problems or worse. In this sense, budgets are financial regulators which prevent unanticipated problems from creating unchecked deterioration in financial matters.

TYPES OF BUDGETS

In business several kinds of financial plans or budgets are used. The first important distinction is between *flexible* and *appropriations* budgets. As its name suggests, a flexible budget usually permits variations in revenues, in expenditures, or in both. In contrast, appropriations budgets set a ceiling on the funds available for expenditure during the budget period. Many business activities are planned by flexible budgets, while appropriations budgets are common in government agencies, and in the private sector for research activities and for advertising.

An important distinction in business budgets is the length of the planning period. Financial management theory draws a fundamental distinction between budgets for a year or less and those for more than a year. Budgets for a year or less are properly focused on plans for short-lived assets, chiefly cash. The most commonly used short-term budget is the *cash budget.* In contrast, budgets which plan for the management of assets having economic lives greater than one year are called *capital budgets.* In capital budgeting, two important concepts are incorporated into the planning. First, the concept of the "time value of money" is used. This means that a dollar received in the near future is more certain, more useful, and therefore more valuable than is a dollar received in the distant future. Second, the notion of the "rate of return" that each capital asset is projected to furnish over time is also used. Capital budgeting, then, is a process in which time-discounted rates of return are compared for competing capital projects within the constraint of the firm's cost of capital.

Advertising media budgets are almost always cash budgets of the appropriations type. In some respects this practice is unfortunate, and suggestions for modifying the nature of advertising media budgets will be presented later in the chapter. For now, let us turn to an examination of how advertising budgeting is conducted.

HOW CLIENT ORGANIZATIONS SET ADVERTISING APPROPRIATIONS

The first step in cash budgeting is to plan for the sources and volume of the funds needed. In advertising budgets, the source of funds is the client organization. The volume decision, also called the advertising allocation, is usually done in one of five ways.

1. *Percent of sales.* This method is the most popular way of determining the advertising allocation, and it is especially prevalent among small and medium-sized clients. Allocations to advertising are calculated by selecting a percentage of sales revenue, e.g., 4 percent.

Percent-of-sales allocations are roundly criticized by theoreticians who point out that this is a clear case of placing the cart in front of the horse. Advertising is supposed to stimulate demand for (and sales of) product. But here past sales are used to set the level of advertising support for the future. Critics of this method argue that when times are good and sales are high, the method may allocate "too much" to advertising. While overallocation may be associated with advertising inefficiencies, the underallocation produced by this method in hard times and from low sales is almost certain to produce less than sufficient levels of advertising.

2. *Percent of future sales.* One significant variant on the percent-of-sales allocation is the substitution of "future" or forecast sales for past sales. This substitution neatly blunts the earlier, theoretical criticism. Unfortunately, this method solves one problem by creating another, namely the uncertainty associated with the forecast figure for sales. In addition, since future sales are a function not only of advertising but also of other decisions and external forces, the method incorporates some inevitable irrelevance. Logically, allocating advertising by some percent of carefully forecast future sales would represent an improvement over the use of past sales. In prac-

tice this method is less frequently used, and its lack of popularity is probably attributable to clients' suspicions about sales forecasts.

3. Parity. By competitive parity, we mean that the client allocates funds to advertising in the same way and at the same level as the competition. As such, this method suffers from serious flaws of its own, and depending on the method of imitation used, it may also inherit other weaknesses. First, it is often difficult to discover what competitors are allocating to advertising, and so attempts to follow competitors' decisions produce imperfect imitation. In other words, even if the method were prudent, it would be difficult to apply. Second, the method fails to recognize that companies in the same industry or product group have different advertising opportunities and efficiencies. Thus, to imitate others implies a passive, defensive managerial outlook which is not consistent with either effective advertising decisions or business success. Finally, if competitors are using suboptimal advertising allocation methods, such as "percent of sales," then imitation incurs the inherent and inherited weaknesses.

4. Objective and task. In this method, advertising objectives are precisely stated. Then (its proponents claim), the tasks necessary to achieve these objectives are described carefully. Next, the funds required for these tasks are specified. Finally, the task-required costs are added and their sum is described as the advertising allocation.

Students first introduced to this method are inclined to be impressed by its logic, and the method is deductively logical. It is impractical because of two facts: it is almost impossible to know beforehand exactly what tasks (or activities) will be required to accomplish the chosen advertising objectives, and it is equally difficult to precisely determine costs for the task specified. To put the problem more philosophically, if an advertiser knew everything required to furnish the required inputs for the objective-and-task method, such as the selection of optimum objectives, there would be no need to follow the chronological steps of the method.

5. All you can afford. This method is the darling of advertising novices who are understandably struck by its implied enthusiasm for their craft. It is our sad duty to dash some cold fact on that enthusiasm. First, what the client can "afford" is not necessarily correlated with the advertising opportunities available. Wealthy advertisers could overspend and poor advertisers underspend. Second, it should be recalled that advertising is an important part of the marketing effort, but not the whole. Great differences exist among advertisers regarding the effectiveness of the advertising effort relative to that of other marketing efforts, such as product development or physical distribution. It is both simpleminded and dangerous for advertisers to assume that the benefits from added advertising weight always exceed the benefits from additional effort in the other marketing areas. Finally, and most fundamentally harmful, is the implied notion that advertising funds must come from surpluses within the advertiser organization. This notion produces an almost puritanical, invariably foolish conclusion that it is not prudent to use external funds (say, debt) to finance advertising. The discussion of a capital budgeting approach to advertising allocation, found later in this chapter, will suggest a fundamentally different alternative.

The five foregoing allocation strategies are a relatively complete listing of how a large majority of advertisers actually make the advertising allocation decision in the real world. You will recognize that none of these strategies is free from serious defect; none is free from arbitrariness. We now turn to a theoretically correct method for allocating funds to advertising.

ALLOCATION THEORY AND ADVERTISING

The economic theory of allocating funds to business activities is perversely and deceptively simple. The decision maker simply sets the marginal cost of the activity equal to the marginal revenue or return earned by that activity. Under the assumption that the activity for which the allocation is being determined does not interact with other activities and decisions, the allocation level which produces the above equality (i.e., $MC_i = MR_i$) is the *level which maximizes profit* and is therefore the optimal allocation.[1] To apply this allocation theory to actual advertising effort, the decision maker must, in effect, establish the conditions under which it is possible to measure marginal cost and marginal revenue. If you reflect on the requirements for this measurement, you will see that the necessary conditions, while they are not impossible to create, are extraordinarily restrictive. In all likelihood, a new product (not carrying an established product line, family, or company brand) will have to be both advertised and sold only through direct mail. Under these restrictive conditions, and within a range of marginal ad preparation costs (say, printing lot size) and marginal distribution costs (say, mailing lot size), an advertiser can match the marginal cost of advertising with the marginal returns (sales) from that advertising. Here the advertiser simply increases advertising allocation until the theoretical optimum is reached, or until $MC = MR$.

At this juncture, it is not uncommon to find that advertising readers are discouraged over the whole business of advertising budget allo-

[1] Joel Dean, *Managerial Economics* (Englewood Cliffs, N.J.: Prentice-Hall, 1951), pp. 363 ff.

cation. Clearly, the methods in actual use are sloppy. In contrast, the precision of the theoretically correct method is gained at the expense of restrictions and wide-ranging unsuitability. What is the prudent advertiser to do?

HOW ADVERTISERS MIGHT IMPROVE ADVERTISING ALLOCATION DECISIONS

Several possibilities exist for improving actual allocation practices by combining some aspects of advertising allocation theory with decision theory used in other business areas and with quantitative methods which estimate or isolate advertising's costs and contributions over time.

These improvements are earned at a cost. Most noticeable is the increase in the resources devoted to decision making. It is our judgment that the extra time, difficulty, and expense required to improve advertising appropriation methods are likely to improve the efficiency of advertising for most advertisers.

Empirical approaches. One way to avoid both arbitrariness and unrealistic restrictions is to try a variety of advertising allocation levels and then attempt to isolate and compare the benefits which each level produces. There are several ways to do this. You might keep in mind that most empirical approaches produce data which are mathematically evaluated. Our discussion here is largely limited to the "results" of these methods; the methods themselves are more fully presented in Chapter. 11.

Experiments. One way to let the facts speak for themselves is to conduct an experiment to find out whether one level of allocation produces significantly better results than does another. Figure 3–1 summarizes such an experiment where two per-city levels of advertising, $100,000 versus $120,000, are compared on the basis of the sales-to-advertising ratio for two groups of cities of roughly equivalent population. By simply inspecting the sales-to-advertising ratios, an advertiser could conclude that the larger appropriation produced a higher mean ratio (6.35 compared with 5.41). Use of one-way analysis of variance (ANOVA) permits the inference that the difference in these mean ratios is significant at a relatively high level of confidence. Thus, the higher per-city expenditure seems to be warranted by benefits which are larger than proportional to the increased expenditure.

Correlation methods. Often it is possible to examine historical data and, by correlating two or more such measures, reach conclusions about the presence of trends. This analysis often takes a form called regression. In one famous regression, Palda found that in com-

Figure 3–1
Advertising allocation experiment

Allocation level A: $100,000 per city	*Percent of national population*		*Test sales during month ($000)*		*Sales advertising ratio*
Wichita, Kansas	.5%		$509		5.09
San Antonio, Texas	.6		660		6.60
Richmond, Virginia	.5		494		4.94
Des Moines, Iowa	.5		501		5.01
Total:	2.1%	Average:	$541	Average:	5.41
Allocation level B: $120,000 per city					
Louisville, Kentucky	.6%		$804		6.70
Tulsa, Oklahoma	.5		828		6.90
Norfolk, Virginia	.6		707		5.87
Jacksonville, Florida	.5		710		5.92
Total:	2.2%	Average:	$762	Average:	6.35

ANOVA summary

	Sum of squares	*df*	*Mean square*	*F ratio*
Between groups	1.757	1	1.757	3.85*
Within groups	2.740	6	.457	

* $p < .10$

bination with other measures, the historical relationships between advertising allocations and sales for a patent medicine were positive but nonlinear.[2]

That is, larger advertising allocations were associated with greater sales, but at a diminishing rate of efficiency. In this situation, whether advertising allocations earn their keep by generating sales depends on the level of advertising. Using actual data (from 1950) for this regression, advertising expenditures were 974 units,[3] and these expenditures were associated with a sales figure "due to advertising" about 3½ times as large.

Koyck functions. This is the name of a family of analysis which reflects the fact that sales for any future period are a function of advertising in that period as well as a "carry-over" effect of past product success. Past success obviously includes the benefit of past advertising.

In simple form, a Koyck function might state that sales for next

[2] K. Palda, *The Measurement of Cumulative Advertising Effects* (Englewood Cliffs, N.J.: Prentice-Hall, 1964), pp. 67 ff.

[3] As reported in J. Simon, *The Management of Advertising* (Englewood Cliffs, N.J.: Prentice-Hall, 1971), p. 107.

year are a function of advertising next year and sales this year (the term reflecting past product success). Symbolically, $Sales_{t+1} = f(Advertising)_{t+1} + Sales_t)$. Relevant historical data are analyzed in one of many available correlation/regression procedures to develop the relevant coefficients or weights to be assigned to future advertising and to past success. While the mechanical aspects of this analysis are often identical to those used in any regression analysis, what differentiates the Koyck approach is the time distribution of the variables studied. The benefit from Koyck procedures is the acknowledgment of the still present benefits of past advertising effort. Thus, allocation to advertising can be made from a less artificial assumption than the assumption that all past advertising benefits have been exhausted prior to the budgeted period. The simple Koyck functions can be expanded to include terms for past success in more than one year. You should recognize that such an expansion will impose burdens of extra data analysis and extra cost on the budget decision maker, and should probably be used only when there are strong a priori hypotheses about the benefit of disaggregating "past success" into more than one component time period.

Response-decay functions. While Koyck functions attempt to account for past performance of the product in the marketplace, and thereby lump together not only advertising success but also all other aspects of marketing success, another group of procedures attempts to isolate advertising success. These procedures, called response-decay functions, focus on advertising effects, and are therefore of great potential use in advertising budgets. The procedures also combine mathematically the sales response to present advertising expenditures with the "decaying" or diminishing (but still present) effects of past advertising expenditures. In models of this genre the Vidale-Wolfe model (V-W) is probably most prominent. In it:

$$\frac{dS}{dt} = \frac{rA(M-S)}{M} - \lambda S$$

Where:

S = Rate of sales at time t.

$\frac{dS}{dt}$ = Change in rate of sales or growth rate for sales at time t.

A = Rate of advertising expenditure at time t.

r = Sales response constant, or sales generated per advertising dollar when $S = 0$.

M = Market saturation, or the ceiling level of sales which can be realistically achieved by the advertising campaign.

λ = Sales decay constant, or the proportional deterioration in sales per time period when $A = 0$.

Figure 3–2
Vidale-Wolfe version of response-decay functions in single campaign of duration *T*

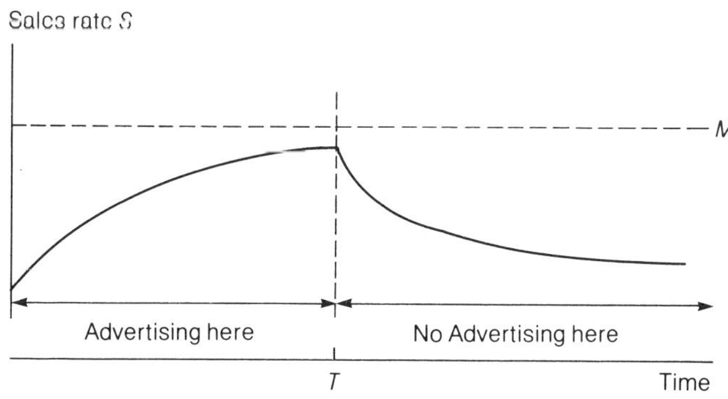

If you look at the effect of a single advertising campaign of duration *T* through the eyes of the V-W function, you will see response and decay similar to that shown in Figure 3–2. The effect of multiple campaigns across time can be visualized as the geometric sum of current advertising and all nonzero residuals in the decaying benefits of past advertising.

In V-W, *A* is the managerial decision about advertising allocation. Empirical evidence suggests that *r, M,* and λ are constants which each advertiser should estimate for each product class. If the advertiser can specify a desired growth rate for sales, it is possible to solve for the required advertising budget allocation. Symbolically:

First, let the desired growth rate, $\frac{dS}{dt}$, equal a constant, *k.*

Then, substitute *k* in the V-W function and solve for *A,* or:

$$A = \frac{k + S}{r \frac{M - S}{M}}$$

When studying the V-W application to advertising budgeting, most students are filled both with enthusiasm for this budgeting method and with disappointment because the majority of advertisers do not use it. A complete understanding of the model requires facility with differential calculus, and many decision makers simply do not have a comfortable grasp of this tool. Also, it should be emphasized that setting ad budgets by a response-decay function produces results which are no better than the estimates of *r, M,* and λ. A final point is that other response-decay models are available, chiefly those of Kuehn and Tull.[4]

Combinations of traditional methods. Most advertisers recognize that any single method for setting the advertising allocation is subject to theoretical and/or practical difficulties. So far our suggestions for empirical approaches have implied a facility with quantitative analysis, which some decision makers have not acquired (or choose not to acquire). For such decision makers, improvements in budget allocations seem to be found in combining more than one traditional method. Clearly the hope here is to offset the disadvantages of one approach with the strengths of another. Unfortunately such "improvements" often prove to be a mirage; combining frequently produces a proliferation of problems. Two such combinations are deserving of mention, if for no other reason than their frequent use.

The first of these combinations is often called the Market Share Theorem; in it, sales, which are expressed as percentage share of a market, are highly correlated with percentage expenditures on promotional activity in that market. This seems like a correlation method. In addition, empirical evidence supporting the Theorem is available, though it is highly concentrated in the performance of mature products in competitive markets. Two problems plague the Theorem approach. First, total expenditure figures for *future* periods are difficult to acquire. Second, the passive assumptions of other parity methods are present here too.

The second combination, recommended recently by Wademan, combines objective and task with break-even analysis.[5] This effort may be commended for movement in the proper direction, but break-even analysis (which fails to account for the time value of money) is inferior to the capital budgeting approach, which is discussed below.

Capital budgeting. This is the process, you will recall, which was identified as the budgeting approach relevant to the management of long-lived assets. Specifically, capital budgeting reflects the time value of money and applies this concept to assets which will produce a stream of benefits or returns for more than the current period.

A moment's reflection will indicate that advertising allocations create "assets" in the form of favorable attitudes, competitive advantages, and, most especially, decisions to purchase, which produce a stream of future benefits for the advertiser. Thus the concept of capital budgeting seems appropriate to advertising budget decisions.

---

[4] A. Kuehn, "How Advertising Performance Depends on Other Marketing Factors," *Journal of Advertising Research,* March 1962, pp. 2–10; and D. S. Tull, "The Carry-Over Effect of Advertising," *Journal of Marketing,* April 1965, pp. 46–53.

[5] V. Wademan, "How to Set Your Advertising Budget," *Public Relations Quarterly,* Winter 1975, pp. 21–24.

How might capital budgeting be applied to advertising allocation? Its advertising applications are quite similar to those for other capital budgeting problems and processes. Regardless of application, the first step in capital budgeting is to measure the cost of capital for a project. To do this, the decision maker must not only discover the *cost* of a particular source of funds but must also know the *availability* of funds from this source. And when more than one source of funds is used for a project, financial managers often weigh the after-tax proportion from each source in order to compute the effective overall cost of capital for the project.

Advertisers should recognize that the advertising use of funds generated internally (i.e., by past sales) is not costless, since these same dollars might have been applied elsewhere. They should also recognize that funding for capital projects can come from external sources. The two major sources of external funds are debt and equity, or borrowing and increased owner participation in the form of additional stock purchases. In the case of debt, the cost of capital is the effective interest rate charged on the borrowed funds.

The second step in capital budgeting is to calculate the time-discounted rate of return expected from the project. To do this, the dollar benefits expected in each future period, or cash flows, are discounted by a factor reflecting the time interval that elapses until they are received.

To calculate the discount factor, one uses the formula for the present value (PV) of a dollar, received n periods in the future, when the effective interest rate (or cost of capital) is r.

$$PV = \frac{1}{(1+r)^n}$$

By inserting values into the PV formula, you can see that the effect of having to wait a long time for a dollar (n = large number) is to reduce the present value of this future payment. Likewise, the present value of a future payment is reduced as the cost of capital is increased. To convert a future payment to its present value, one simply multiplies the size of the payment, in dollars, by the PV value (or discount factor).

A highly simplified example for an advertising campaign producing benefits over several years is shown in Figure 3–3. Here the calculations are based on a constant cost of capital of 10 percent, and a stream of sales over the campaign period and two additional years. For a given dollar amount of total benefits, if either the cost of capital or the time interval for receiving benefits increases, the present value declines. Conversely, reductions in the cost of capital or the time interval produce an increase in the present value. This is another way of saying that it is preferable to use low-cost capital to produce quick returns. When the net present value of a capital project is converted to an annualized percentage return on investment, this is called the discounted rate of return. An example of this calculation is presented in Figure 3–4. This method requires that the rate be selected which

Figure 3–3
Net present value of an advertising campaign lasting one year and producing sales over three years

Year	*Sales* due to campaign in t = 1*	*Cost of capital*	*Discount factor†*	*Present value*
Same as campaign ($t = 1$)	$100,000	10%	.909	$ 90,900
Next year ($t = 2$)	50,000	10	.826	41,300
Final year ($t = 3$)	10,000	10	.751	7,510
			Net Present value = Total =	$139,710

* A simplifying assumption was made that sales for each year were received at year-end. Since sales are likely to occur during each year, and thus become available earlier than assumed, the present values for each year and in total are conservatively understated.

† Obtained from the present value formula, $PV = \frac{1}{(1+r)^n}$

$$\text{At } t=1,\ PV_1 = \frac{1}{(1+.10)^1} = \frac{1}{(1.10)} = .909$$

$$\text{At } t=2,\ PV_2 = \frac{1}{(1+.10)^2} = \frac{1}{(1.10)\,(1.10)} = .826$$

$$\text{At } t=3,\ PV_3 = \frac{1}{(1+.10)^3} = \frac{1}{(1.10)\,(1.10)\,(1.10)} = .751$$

Figure 3–4
Rate of return on an advertising campaign lasting one year and producing sales over three years

		Present value factor and net present value if effective interest rate is:					
Period	*Cash flow**	*30 Percent*		*40 Percent*		*41 Percent*	
0	−$100,000	(0)	−$100,000	(0)	−$100,000	(0)	−$100,000
1	100,000	(.769)	76,900	(.714)	71,400	(.709)	70,900
2	50,000	(.592)	29,600	(.510)	25,500	(.503)	25,150
3	10,000	(.455)	4,550	(.364)	3,640	(.357)	3,570
			$ 11,050		$ 540		−$ 380

By interpolation, the effective rate, which lies between 40 percent and 41 percent, is about 40.6 percent.

* Assumes that the ad campaign expenses, which total $100,000, are all expended at the beginning of the first year and that the sales results flow in the same way as in Figure 3–3.

sets the sum of all time-discounted cash flows to zero. In this example the rate lies between 40 percent and 41 percent and is approximately 40.6 percent.

The third step in capital budgeting is to choose capital projects. Obviously prudent decision makers will not select projects whose cost of capital is greater than the discounted rate of return. For the remaining projects, where returns exceed costs, the decision maker usually chooses those projects which have the highest rates of return, up to the amount of available capital. Again, recall that available capital is *not* restricted to surplus funds generated internally. By available capital we mean funds from either external or internal sources which can be obtained at a cost less than the projected rate of return. In the example in Figure 3–4, and using plausible figures for cash flow, you will see that the campaign has an exceptionally high rate of return. We feel that the application of capital budgeting procedures to advertising allocations will produce high expected rates of return in many organizations; but further, we feel that financial managers will become better informed about the attractiveness of advertising campaigns relative to other, oftentimes competing, capital projects. Then if external funds are required, creditors are likely to be more willing to extend funds for a project which has been scrutinized in the capital budgeting process than for one whose costs have been arbitrarily set and whose returns are only generally surmised.

A garden variety of capital budgeting, called *payback,* is sometimes used for advertising budgeting and is deserving of passing mention. Here, one computes the time required to "pay back" the investment. If competing investments are being considered, the project with the shortest payback period is thought to have the least risk and, other things equal, is selected. Actually, other things are not often equal, and reliance on payback analysis fails to provide the decision maker with information about the relevant time-discounted cash flows.

Advertisers who use this method usually call it the *payout* method, and they use it not so much to rank competing projects as to decide whether to introduce a new product. In this application, advertising investment and projected profits are combined to give an estimate of overall investment. Then the number of periods (months, quarters, or years) required to recover this investment is estimated. Finally, some rule of thumb is applied to decide whether the payout interval is short enough to warrant introducing the product. While payout is a budgeting method that uses proper notions, it is less complete than the full capital budgeting methods, and should probably be replaced by the complete capital budgeting process.

Two final comments should conclude our discussion of capital budgeting. First, some empirical approaches to budgeting can be productively combined with capital budgeting. For example it is possible to use Vidale-Wolfe modeling to produce estimates of future cash flows. These flows, of course, are an important ingredient in calculating rate of return. Second, while capital budgeting has been discussed only within the context of decisions on total advertising allocation, it can be correctly applied to subsequent budgeting decisions for allocation to specific media. Traditionally, decisions on how to allocate total advertising funds to vehicles and to media have been made on the basis of costs per "exposure." If applied to this problem, capital budgeting offers the prospect of highlighting differences in the time that benefits are realized; but it also requires that defensible measures of return be developed.

TASKS PERFORMED BY ADVERTISING FUNDS

After the total advertising allocation has been determined, the allocation is broken down into specific expenditures of the advertising campaign. A first step in this process is to determine the legitimate charges against the advertising allocation. One of the most quoted lists of such charges appeared in *Printers' Ink* and is reprinted in Figure 3–5. This list gives some indication of the items which the industry considers reasonable charges against the advertising budget (white area); those which are doubtful (light gray); and those which the majority of firms would not classify as advertising expenses (darkest area). The gray areas are not illegal, however; they are simply not advertising.

After the advertiser decides what general areas will be funded from the advertising budget, the next step is to budget against specific tasks in the current advertising campaign. While each campaign has some unique features, there are common areas which most campaigns budgets must consider.

Space and time. At least half of most campaign budgets is expended for media space and time costs. Television is often the most costly medium for a national campaign, although most of the major media are competitive on a cost per thousand (cpm) basis. The advertiser must exercise care in space and time purchases since any unnecessary purchase of media can be a tremendous waste of money, especially at the national level. Chapter 4 discusses in detail the considerations to be incorporated into media buying.

An important development in budgeting any advertising activity is the concept of inflation accounting. At its core, inflation accounting

Figure 3–5
Ad department charges in descending order

Space and time costs in regular media
Advertising consultants
Ad-pretesting services
Institutional advertising
Industry directory listings
Readership or audience research
Media costs for consumer contests, premium, and sampling promotions
Ad department travel and entertainment expenses
Ad department salaries
Advertising association dues
Local cooperative advertising
Direct mail to consumers
Subscriptions to periodicals and services for ad department
Storage of advertising materials

Catalogs for consumers
Classified telephone directories
Space in irregular publications
Advertising aids for salesmen
Financial advertising
Dealer-help literature
Contributions to industry ad funds
Direct mail to dealers and jobbers
Office supplies

Point-of-sale materials
Window display installation costs
Charges for services performed by other departments
Catalogs for dealers
Test-marketing programs
Sample requests generated by advertising
Costs of exhibits except personnel
Ad department share of overhead
House organs for customers and dealers
Cost of cash value or sampling coupons
Cost of contest entry blanks
Cross-advertising enclosures
Contest judging and handling fees
Depreciation of ad department equipment
Mobile exhibits
Employee fringe benefits
Catalogs for salespeople
Packaging consultants
Consumer contest awards

Figure 3–5 *continued*

Premium handling charges
House-to-house sample distribution
Packaging charges for premium promotions
Cost of merchandise for tie-in promotions
Product tags
Showrooms
Testing new labels and packages
Package design and artwork
Cost of non-self-liquidating premiums
Consumer education programs
Product publicity
Factory signs
House organs for salespeople
Signs on company-owned vehicles
Instruction enclosures
Press clipping services
Market research (outside produced)
Samples of middlemen
Recruitment advertising
Price sheets
Public relations consultants
Coupon redemption costs
Corporate publicity
Market research (company produced)
Exhibit personnel
Gifts of company products
Cost of deal merchandise
Share of corporate salaries
Cost of guarantee refunds
Share of legal expenses
Cost of detail or missionary men
Sponsoring recreational activities
Product research
House organs for employees
Entertaining customers and prospects
Scholarships
Plant tours
Annual reports
Outright charity donations

attempts to distinguish between increases in expenditure which are produced by the purchase of greater volume or higher quality and increases which are created by price inflation in the goods being purchased.

When purchasing space and time in advertising media, the advertiser clearly buys a commodity whose current prices are partly the result of price inflation. Figure 3–6 shows price rises in major media groups for a recent period. Obviously a 10 percent per year increase in media purchases for a medium displaying a 15 percent per year inflation rate represents, in real terms, a shrinking volume purchased from that medium.

A second accounting concept which finds growing application in the area of budgeting media purchases is that of "zero-based" budgeting. This notion, which prohibits the carry-over of past spending levels to the future being budgeted, is as much or more a management control than an accounting practice. Zero-based budgets usually require the calculation and justification of the entire amounts planned, rather than concentrating on percentage changes from historical levels of spending. Thus, an expenditure of $1 million in network television last year is not budgeted this year on the basis of a 10 percent increase in network television purchases. Rather, the entire $1.1 million must be justified.

Like almost every popular business concept, zero-based budgeting is often misunderstood and misapplied. Without doubt, it requires more analytical work than do traditional percentage increases on a historical base figure. The principal advantage of the zero-base method is that it prevents past inefficiencies from becoming honored traditions. It also encourages decision makers to rethink the relative merits of expenditures for each budgeting period.

Mechanical work and artwork. The second largest area of budget expenditures is the actual preparation of advertising. A minimum of advertising preparation is covered by the agency commission and consequently is not an additional cost to the advertiser. However, the advertiser is normally responsible for a large portion of production costs. This is especially true for television commercials.

Some advertisers deal with their agencies on a fee basis; for example the agency may be paid on a project or hourly basis for work performed. As this fee relationship becomes more prevalent, the advertisers' share of production costs and the proportion of the advertising budget allocated to the creative area will increase.

The so-called noncommissionable media are another creative area which must be paid totally out of the advertising budget. Usually this category does not involve the media at all; it comprises brochures, direct mail pieces, annual reports, and other collateral materials prepared by an agency for an advertiser. Such materials obviously must be charged against the advertising budget.

Noncommissionable materials are sometimes placed in the category of billable services. Such services are not covered by the agency commission and are charged to the client. Nonbillable services on the other hand are the services which an agency normally provides

Figure 3–6
Media unit cost indexes (1967 = 100)

								Composite		
	Magazines	*Newspapers*	*Network TV*	*Spot TV*	*Network Radio*	*Spot Radio*	*Outdoor*	*National*	*Local*	*All*
1960	73	83	74	69	100	82	64	75	82	78
1961	80	86	76	72	101	84	68	78	84	81
1962	86	88	78	74	99	86	72	81	86	83
1963	87	89	81	80	101	86	77	84	88	86
1964	90	90	85	86	101	87	81	88	89	88
1965	94	91	90	89	100	91	88	91	91	91
1966	98	99	96	94	101	96	93	97	98	97
1967	100	100	100	100	100	100	100	100	100	100
1968	103	104	105	105	98	102	107	104	104	104
1969	106	109	114	110	100	104	116	110	108	109
1970	109	115	113	105	101	107	125	110	113	111
1971	114	120	108	104	95	103	135	111	116	113
1972	110	123	125	117	105	109	145	119	121	120
1973	110	128	140	127	105	114	155	126	126	126
1974	115	140	151	135	106	119	166	135	137	136
1975	122	160	160	145	112	125	178	145	154	149
1976	127	176	189	181	128	135	192	166	171	168
1977	137	192	227	188	154	147	209	185	186	185
1978	152	207	252	209	172	160	226	204	201	203
1979	166	226	280	230	191	173	250	224	220	222

Source: Robert J. Coen, McCann–Erickson, Inc., 485 Lexington Avenue, New York, New York 10017.

to earn its commission. These nonbillable services should be specifically stated in a contractual agreement between the agency and the client to avoid problems in this area.

Research. The costs of the research necessary to gather primary and secondary data for the advertising campaign are included in the advertising budget. The extent of billable research activities and the preliminary research performed "free" by an agency as part of its nonbillable service must be considered in budgeting for the research function.

The research budget will be determined by many diverse factors. Among the major ones will be the newness of the product, anticipation of a dramatically different creative approach, or a movement into previously unused media. Patently, the cost and value of usual information, as discussed in Chapter 2, are critical here. The type of research methodology needed will also affect the budget. For instance personal interviews, in-depth or motivation tests, or research requiring sophisticated equipment (such as eye cameras) will increase the research budget.

Administrative and miscellaneous. The advertising budget may also include items such as travel, salaries, advertising department overhead, and other expenses connected with the advertising function. Normally these administrative and miscellaneous costs are not figured as part of the campaign budget.

BUDGETARY CONTROL

After the advertising allocation has been determined and the specific budgetary areas have been covered, plans must be made for controlling the expenditure of funds. Control of the advertising budget demands a knowledge of both current and future commitments, and provision for contingencies.

Current commitments. Current commitments are those invoices which are due during the current billing period. The major element of control in this area is the responsibility to make sure all the services billed were actually performed and performed properly. The major problem is determining that media bills for space and time reflect advertisements and commercials which actually ran in the media. In the print media, tear sheets (copies of the ads or the entire publication) are routinely provided to the agency. Syndicated services such as the Advertising Checking Bureau provide a similar service for advertisers. The broadcast media are much more difficult to check, and occasionally stations have been known to bill for spots which were not run or were run in cheaper positions than those billed. In any case the advertiser and the agency have a major financial responsibility for determining that payment is made only for services satisfactorily rendered.

Future commitments. At any point during a campaign financial commitments must be made well in advance. These commitments which will come due during the ensuing weeks and months must be anticipated, and budget planning must reflect them. The extent to which a budget is tied up in these future obligations is primarily determined by (1) the type of media mix used and (2) the sophistication of the creative message. Network television, in particular, demands long-range commitments in order to guarantee availabilities during premium time periods. Newspaper media schedules conversely allow a much wider flexibility in budgeting.

Contingencies. Most of the advertising budget will be committed to specific areas of the advertising campaign prior to the initiation of the campaign. However, an ongoing review of the campaign in progress is mandatory to make sure that the campaign is progressing as expected. Some budgetary reserve is normally set aside so that weak areas in the campaign can be corrected. If changes in the campaign are necessary, it is essential that the advertising planner have complete knowledge of both current and future financial commitments.

Before concluding this section on budgeting, we must emphasize that the budgeting function is related to all other phases of the campaign and is a continuing one. A prime example is the area of research as it relates to the examination of the budget while the campaign is in progress.

Two basic approaches to the measurement of an advertising campaign are sales and communication success. Budgetary review during the campaign will often center on the success of the campaign according to one of these criteria. Sales criteria are normally measured by such techniques as store audits. These techniques may also be used to determine the geographic distribution of sales and the types of retail outlets in which sales are made. Communication success is measured by various types of recall and recognition studies conducted among listeners to and readers of the media.

Finally, it should be noted that the budgetary process is not a matter of allocating funds prior to the start of the campaign and then forgetting about them. Instead, the budgetary process of planning, expenditure and control should be viewed as an integral part of the campaign and one which must continue throughout its duration.

QUESTIONS

1. What is a budget?
2. Discuss four major managerial benefits of budgets.

3. What is the difference between a cash budget and a capital budget?

4. Describe the probable personality of a decision maker who prefers to use parity methods to develop the advertising budget.

5. In economic theory, what is the optimum level of advertising expenditure?

6. Explain the concept of a Koyck function, and how it applies to advertising budgets, to a beginning advertising student.

7. Using the formula for present value,

$$PV = \frac{1}{(1+r)^n},$$

calculate the net present value for a four-period cash flow as follows:

Period	*Cash flow*
1	$50,000
2	20,000
3	15,000
4	10,000

The effective cost of capital is 13 percent.

4

THE ADVERTISING MEDIA-BUYING PROCESS

AN INHERENT danger exists in writing a separate chapter on the advertising media-buying process. Compartmentalizing media from the other marketing and advertising functions can be a dangerous course. Media selection is basically the identification and delivery of people in the most efficient manner possible. Consequently, the media-buying function must consider identifying prospects (market segmentation), appropriating allocated funds (budgeting), developing a proper communication environment (creative), and fulfilling ultimate business goals (profits).

For advertising to do its job, well-conceived messages must reach potential prospects at the proper time and place. It is important that the media planner and creative personnel regard their specific functions as complementary rather than competitive. Some advertising practitioners take the shortsighted view that they are working on either a creative or media project rather than a *marketing* problem. In accomplishing the general marketing goals, there will be times when the creative aspects of a campaign are planned first or are given priority over the media function. Other projects may demand more of a media orientation. A successful campaign invariably embodies cooperation among creative, media, and research personnel operating in the best interests of their clients. Petty, provincial interests have no place in the creation of successful advertising.

In the discussion which follows, it will be assumed that the media planner has a clear understanding of the client's marketing strategy and that the basic creative strategy and problems have been discussed with creative persons working with the product. With this "homework" completed, the media planner is now ready to assemble a media buy. The media buy must complement the overall advertising and marketing strategy (see Chapter 1). It details the specific manner in which the media process will carry its weight in achieving overall goals.

STEPS IN THE MEDIA-BUYING PROCESS

Step 1: Prospect identification

The media process must begin with an appropriate identification of the consumer. There are many ways to describe a potential prospect for a product, just as there are many ways to describe the characteristics of a person. The media planner or researcher usually has less flexibility in identifying prospects than does his creative counterpart. The media buyer must have data which are compatible with similar information about the media to be bought. For instance a media buyer who categorizes prospects as being between 20 and 30 years old will find difficulty in matching this information with most media which designate their audiences as 18–24 and 25–34. On the other hand a company which identifies its customers as "hypochondriacs" may use this information in designing creative messages, but it will have difficulty in finding media which identify the percentage of hypochondriacs in their audiences.

In advertising there are four major means of identifying, or segmenting, subgroups within the general population:

1. Geographic identification. The oldest form of segmentation is geographic. By the late 19th century merchants recognized variance in sales by territories. Today marketers are increasingly turning to local and regional rather than national advertising strategies. For instance certain types of GM trucks are primarily advertised in the Southeast and West. The media planners find that they require regional and market-by-market data as well as national information as they buy time and space in local broadcast stations, newspapers, regional magazines, and outdoor media.

Most geographic information for advertising purposes is presented in one of two ways: by broad regional breakdown or by local markets, usually in order of population.

Regional identification. The U.S. Census has four regions—North East, North Central, South, and West. For most purposes these designations are too broad and a more traditional categorization is New England, Middle Atlantic, East Central, West Central, South East, South West, Pacific.

Market identification. The Standard Metropolitan Statistical Area (SMSA) is the most common market delineation method. Basically an SMSA includes a city of 50,000 population or a city of 25,000 with a contiguous area population of 50,000. Markets are also designated by county size as defined by the A. C. Nielsen Company. These are: A—counties in the top 25 metropolitan areas; B—counties with over

150,000 population and not in Class A; C—counties with over 35,000 population not included in A or B; D—all other counties.[1]

A major problem for media buyers is that neither media distribution nor product distribution follows these artificial boundaries. Therefore the media planner has the continuing problem of attempting to be as efficient as possible when dealing with noncompatible data. Figure 4–1 presents a hypothetical situation often faced by media planners on a much larger scale.

In Figure 4–1 our fictional media planner has market information concerning the population of a specific SMSA. However, as we can see, his sales and media areas not only do not follow the SMSA boundaries, but include territory for which he has no information.

Figure 4–1
Coverage area problems of media planners

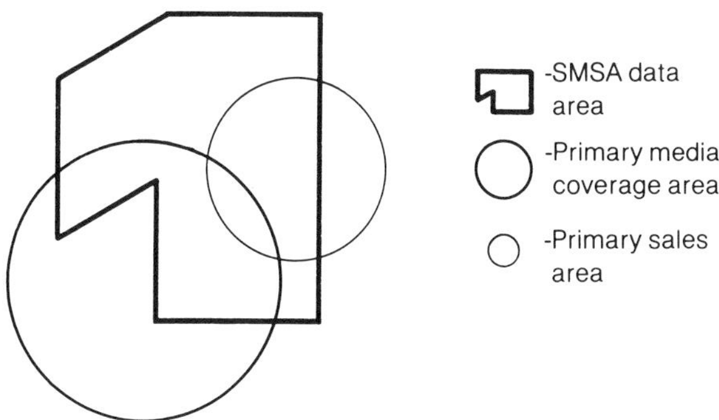

Adding to his problem is a mismatch between the sales territory and the media coverage area.

2. Demographic identification. The most common method of identifying prospects is categorization by demographic characteristics. Marketing studies usually confine these categories to such things as sex, education, age, and income. However, other media buys require information about marital status, number of children, type of living quarters, or even ethnic origin. It is a rare occurrence when one variable provides adequate information, therefore several variables are sometimes combined into a single number or index. One of the most used is the Buying Power Index (BPI) developed by *Sales & Marketing Management.* The BPI is a weighted index that converts three basic elements—population, Effective Buying Income,

[1] *Sales & Marketing Management,* July 23, 1979, p. A–43.

and retail sales—into a measurement of a market's ability to buy, and expresses it as a percentage of the U.S./Canada potential. BPI is calculated by giving a weight of 5 to the market's percentage of U.S./Canada Effective Buying Income, 3 to its percentage of U.S./Canada retail sales, and 2 to its percentage of U.S./Canada population. The total of those weighted percentages is then divided by 10 to arrive at the BPI.

Figure 4–2
Demographic matching example from MRI report

AGE (RESPONDENT) 63

BASE: MEN	TOTAL U.S. '000	18-24 A '000	18-24 B % DOWN	18-24 C % ACROSS	18-24 D INDEX	25-34 A '000	25-34 B % DOWN	25-34 C % ACROSS	25-34 D INDEX	35-44 A '000	35-44 B % DOWN	35-44 C % ACROSS	35-44 D INDEX	45-54 A '000	45-54 B % DOWN	45-54 C % ACROSS	45-54 D INDEX
ALL MEN	72485	13308	100.0	18.4	100	16434	100.0	22.7	100	11698	100.0	16.1	100	11342	100.0	15.6	100
NATIONAL ENQUIRER	6774	1850	12.4	24.4	133	1505	9.2	22.2	93	1139	9.7	16.8	104	918	8.1	13.6	87
NATIONAL GEOGRAPHIC	15319	2860	20.0	17.4	95	3749	22.8	24.5	103	2705	23.1	17.7	110	2353	20.7	15.4	99
NATIONAL LAMPOON	4112	2211	16.6	53.8	292	1344	8.2	32.7	144	253	2.2	6.2	39	*205	1.8	5.0	32
NATURAL HISTORY	1011	*157	1.2	15.5	84	309	1.9	30.6	135	*162	1.4	16.0	99	*143	1.3	14.1	90
NEWSWEEK	13291	3119	23.4	23.5	128	3593	21.9	27.0	119	2254	19.3	17.0	106	2068	18.2	15.6	100
NEW WEST	803	*132	1.0	16.4	89	221	1.3	27.5	121	*162	1.4	20.2	125	*122	1.1	15.2	97
NEW WOMAN	331	*89	.7	26.9	146	*107	.7	32.3	142	*41	.4	12.4	77	*70	.6	21.1	135
NEW YORK MAGAZINE	1107	*204	1.5	18.4	100	354	2.2	32.0	141	152	1.3	13.7	85	*162	1.4	14.6	94
NEW YORK/NEW WEST (GR)	1910	336	2.5	17.6	96	575	3.5	30.1	133	314	2.7	16.4	102	284	2.5	14.9	96
NEW YORK TIMES (DAILY)	1726	317	2.4	18.4	100	456	2.8	26.4	116	303	2.6	17.6	109	296	2.6	17.1	110
NEW YORK TIMES MAGAZINE	2120	378	2.8	17.8	97	606	3.7	28.6	126	380	3.2	17.9	111	362	3.2	17.1	110
THE NEW YORKER	1815	*285	2.1	15.7	85	538	3.3	29.6	130	246	2.1	13.6	84	274	2.4	15.1	97
OMNI	3058	1094	8.2	35.8	195	1305	7.9	42.7	188	360	3.1	11.8	73	*210	1.9	6.9	44
1,001 DECORATING IDEAS	1525	325	2.4	21.3	116	567	3.5	37.2	164	284	2.4	18.6	116	*254	2.2	16.7	107
ORGANIC GARDENING	2369	*278	2.1	11.7	64	655	4.0	27.6	122	397	3.4	16.8	104	360	3.2	15.2	97
OUI	3987	1434	10.8	36.0	196	1454	8.8	36.5	161	499	4.3	12.5	78	345	3.0	8.7	56
OUTDOOR LIFE	7521	1937	14.6	25.8	140	1929	11.7	25.6	113	1380	11.8	18.3	114	949	8.4	12.6	81
PARADE	19315	3444	25.9	17.8	97	4152	25.3	21.5	95	3385	28.9	17.5	109	3113	27.4	16.1	103
PARENTS MAGAZINE	1799	344	2.6	19.1	104	833	5.1	46.3	204	311	2.7	17.3	107	*208	1.8	11.6	74
PENTHOUSE	9778	3492	26.2	35.7	194	3478	21.2	35.6	157	1531	13.1	15.7	98	848	7.5	8.7	56
PEOPLE	10455	3001	22.6	28.7	156	3353	20.4	32.1	141	1789	15.3	17.1	106	1192	10.5	11.4	73
PETERSEN ACTION GROUP (GR)	25032	10037	75.3	40.1	218	7121	43.2	28.4	125	3859	33.0	15.4	96	2178	19.2	8.7	56
PHOTOPLAY	905	*247	1.9	27.3	148	290	1.8	32.0	141	*121	1.0	13.4	83	*106	.9	11.7	75
PICKUP VAN & 4 WD	2467	983	7.4	39.8	216	689	4.2	27.9	123	369	3.2	15.0	93	*268	2.4	10.9	70
PLAYBOY	16382	4761	35.8	29.1	158	5737	34.9	35.0	154	2947	25.2	18.0	112	1897	15.0	10.4	67
PLAYGIRL	1635	371	2.8	22.7	123	569	3.5	34.8	153	357	3.1	21.8	135	*211	1.9	12.9	83
POPULAR HOT RODDING	2599	1465	11.0	56.4	307	653	4.0	25.1	111	*292	2.5	11.2	70	*120	1.1	4.6	29
POPULAR MECHANICS	10784	2538	19.1	23.5	128	2561	15.6	23.7	104	1856	15.9	17.2	107	1731	15.3	16.1	103
POPULAR SCIENCE	7112	1473	11.1	20.7	113	1859	11.3	26.1	115	1259	10.8	17.7	110	1105	9.7	15.5	99
PREVENTION	1890	*141	1.1	7.5	41	382	2.3	20.2	89	278	2.4	14.7	91	387	3.4	20.5	131
PROGRESSIVE FARMER	1531	*247	1.9	16.1	88	*291	1.8	19.0	84	*218	1.9	14.2	88	*260	2.3	17.0	109
PSYCHOLOGY TODAY	3188	974	7.3	30.6	166	1139	6.9	35.7	157	396	3.4	12.4	77	333	2.9	10.4	67
READER'S DIGEST	25430	4153	31.2	16.3	89	5309	32.3	20.9	92	4281	36.6	16.8	104	4190	36.9	16.5	106
REDBOOK	2663	567	4.3	21.3	116	795	4.8	29.9	132	393	3.4	14.8	92	378	3.3	14.2	91
ROAD & TRACK	3612	1494	11.2	41.4	225	1213	7.4	33.6	148	471	4.0	13.0	81	282	2.5	7.8	50
ROLLING STONE	3474	2130	16.0	61.3	333	1122	6.8	32.3	142	*98	.8	2.8	17	*64	.6	1.8	12
THE ROTARIAN	339	*92	.7	27.1	147	*43	.3	12.7	56	*36	.3	10.6	66	*81	.7	23.9	153
SATURDAY EVENING POST	3402	771	5.8	22.7	123	843	5.1	24.8	109	443	3.8	13.0	81	558	4.9	16.4	105
SATURDAY REVIEW	978	*211	1.6	21.6	117	245	1.5	25.1	111	*164	1.4	16.8	104	*127	1.1	13.0	83
SCIENTIFIC AMERICAN	2313	422	3.2	18.2	99	830	5.1	35.9	158	408	3.5	17.6	109	347	3.1	15.0	96
SEA	503	*132	1.0	26.2	142	*139	.8	27.6	122	*94	.8	18.7	116	*75	.7	14.9	96
SKI	1613	735	5.5	45.6	248	486	3.0	30.1	133	165	1.4	10.2	63	*160	1.4	9.9	63
SMITHSONIAN	3271	617	4.6	18.9	103	848	5.2	25.9	114	516	4.4	15.8	98	558	4.9	17.1	110
SOUTHERN LIVING	2442	*289	2.2	12.2	66	556	3.4	22.8	100	404	3.5	16.5	102	481	4.2	19.7	126
SPORT	5622	2103	15.8	37.4	203	1344	8.2	23.9	105	876	7.5	15.6	97	624	5.5	11.1	71
THE SPORTING NEWS	2362	689	5.2	29.2	159	648	3.9	27.3	120	405	3.5	17.1	106	263	2.3	11.1	71
SPORTS AFIELD	5741	1279	9.6	22.3	121	1448	8.8	25.2	111	1187	10.1	20.7	129	814	7.2	14.2	91
SPORTS ILLUSTRATED	13111	3902	29.3	29.8	162	3852	22.2	27.9	123	2383	20.4	18.2	113	1602	14.1	12.2	78
THE STAR	3928	1070	8.0	27.2	148	912	5.5	23.2	102	625	5.3	15.9	99	502	4.4	12.8	82
SUCCESSFUL FARMING	1543	*355	2.7	23.0	125	297	1.8	19.2	85	*225	1.9	14.6	91	329	2.9	21.3	137
SUNDAY	20088	3330	25.0	16.6	90	4305	26.2	21.4	94	3662	31.3	18.2	113	3332	29.4	16.6	106
SUNSET	2170	*321	2.4	14.8	80	531	3.2	24.5	108	409	3.5	18.8	117	297	2.6	13.7	88
TENNIS	1342	589	4.4	43.9	239	345	2.1	25.7	113	211	1.8	15.7	98	*147	1.3	11.0	71
TEXAS MONTHLY	835	*295	2.2	35.3	192	229	1.4	27.4	121	*172	1.5	20.6	128	*89	.8	10.7	69
TIME	13882	2888	21.7	20.8	113	4098	24.9	29.5	130	2434	20.8	17.5	109	2046	18.0	14.7	94
TOWN & COUNTRY	606	*81	.5	10.1	55	*159	1.0	26.2	115	*134	1.1	22.1	137	*85	.7	14.0	90
TRAVEL & LEISURE	1695	*226	1.7	13.3	72	377	2.3	22.2	98	335	2.9	19.8	123	355	3.1	20.9	134
TRAVEL HOLIDAY	781	*46	.3	5.9	32	*134	.8	17.2	76	*172	1.5	22.0	137	*143	1.3	18.3	117
TRUE STORY	900	*215	1.6	23.9	130	*248	1.5	27.6	122	*162	1.4	18.0	112	*101	.9	11.2	72
TV GUIDE	23484	5690	42.8	24.2	132	6173	37.6	26.3	116	4020	34.4	17.1	106	3280	28.9	14.0	90
TWA AMBASSADOR	422	*10	.1	2.4	13	*183	1.1	43.4	191	*78	.3	18.5	115	*68	.6	16.1	103
U.S. NEWS & WORLD REPORT	6940	1273	9.6	18.3	99	1656	10.1	23.9	105	1113	9.5	16.0	99	1111	9.8	16.0	103
US	2383	888	6.7	37.3	203	841	5.1	35.3	156	319	2.7	13.4	83	265	2.3	11.1	71
VOGUE	970	*279	2.1	28.8	157	335	2.0	34.5	152	*140	1.2	14.4	89	*108	1.0	11.1	71
WALL STREET JOURNAL	2694	284	2.0	9.8	53	689	4.2	25.6	113	611	5.2	22.7	141	508	4.5	18.9	121
WEIGHT WATCHERS	928	*182	1.4	19.6	107	*191	1.2	20.6	91	*192	1.6	20.7	129	*137	1.2	14.8	95
WOMAN'S DAY	3482	522	3.9	15.0	82	932	5.7	26.8	118	610	5.2	17.5	109	593	5.2	17.0	109
WORKING WOMAN	236	*54	.4	22.9	124	*114	.7	48.3	213	*20	.2	8.5	53	*37	.3	15.7	101
WORLD TENNIS	998	421	3.2	42.2	229	245	1.5	24.5	108	*178	1.5	17.8	111	*101	.9	10.1	65
ZIFF-DAVIS NETWORK (GR)	17687	6808	51.0	38.5	209	5417	32.9	30.6	135	2323	19.8	13.1	81	1748	15.4	9.9	63

Media selection and demographic matching. The process of prospect identification by demographics involves two complementary steps. The first is to determine the prime prospects from the mass audience. The second is to gather demographic information on the various media available to the media planner. If you find that the major users and/or potential users of your product are men between the ages of 18 and 24, then the logical media choices would come from men's magazines, male-oriented television and radio shows, and certain sections of newspapers. Although we have greatly narrowed the media choices, there is still a large number from which to choose.

The media planner will normally gather information from syndicated services and media-provided sources to determine the relative popularity of the various media among our 18–24, male prospects. Figure 4–2 from Mediamark Research Inc. illustrates the procedure of demographic matching.

To use the MRI report in Figure 4–2, let us assume we are interested in finding the most appropriate magazines to reach men 18–24. The MRI report gives us several types of information.

1. *Total U.S. population.* This column tells us there are 72,485,000 men in the United States. As we go down this column we see how many men read each of the magazines listed (e.g., *People* magazine has 10,455,000 adult male readers).
2. *Column A.* Here the total number of men in each age category who read various magazines are listed. Of the 10,455,000 male readers of *People,* 3,001,000 are between the ages of 18 and 24.
3. *Column B.* As media buyers we are interested in the audience coverage. Audience coverage is the percentage of our target market reached by a media vehicle. Again looking at *People* magazine, we find:

$$\text{Column B (audience coverage)} = \frac{\text{Men 18–24 who read } \textit{People} \text{ magazine}}{\text{All men 18–24}} = \frac{3{,}001{,}000}{13{,}308{,}000} = 22.6$$

4. *Column C.* In addition to audience coverage we are interested in the composition, or audience makeup, of the media we are considering. Composition is the percentage of readers within any particular demographic or product category. In our *People* magazine example column C is computed as follows:

$$\text{Column C (audience composition)} = \frac{\text{Men 18–24 who read } \textit{People} \text{ magazine}}{\text{All male readers of } \textit{People} \text{ magazine}} = \frac{3{,}001{,}000}{10{,}455{,}000} = 28.7$$

5. *Column D.* The index in column D is a means of comparing the composition of each magazine against the national population. For instance *People* magazine has 28.7 percent of its male readers in the 18–24 age group as compared to only 18.4 percent of the total male population in this age group.

$$\text{Index} = \frac{28.7}{18.4} \times 100 = 156$$

Demographic matching: A caution. The media planner must remember that demographic matching deals with groups rather than individuals. A demographic category, no matter how carefully selected, only indicates that on the average more prospects will be found in this group than in some other. However, within any group there will be nonbuyers, just as in unlikely demographic groups (based on purchases of our product) there will probably be buyers. Dealing with groups rather than individuals can present a danger to those media planners who rely too heavily on this technique.

Look again at Figure 4–2, and consider a hypothetical situation concerning *People* magazine. As we have indicated we can reach 22.6 percent of all men 18–24 with this medium. Now assume that 22.6 percent of all men 18–24 use our product. The question facing the media planner is, How many of the 3,001,000 men in the medium's audience are the same as the 3,001,000 men who use our product? The answer, of course, is unknown, given the information available, but there is some chance that only a small proportion of users are also "consumers" of *People* magazine. Because of the uncertainty created by using a single demographic variable, the media planner will normally use at least two or three variables to reduce the risk of making an improper media buy.

3. Product-user identification. Although demographic matching is by far the most used technique for media buying, advertisers are increasingly turning to product-user matching. Product-user techniques differ from demographic matching in that their concern is with individuals rather than groups and the variable employed is product usage rather than some personal, demographic characteristics.

In theory the product-user technique is very simple. The media planner determines the heavy, medium, and light users of his product from among the audiences of the various media. Then, considering media cost, a media schedule is built around those vehicles with the highest concentration of "heavy" users.

The problem is that most national advertisers cannot identify the media habits of ultimate consumers of their products. Moreover, even if a company could gather user information for its product, few media have comparable data for their audiences. To implement product-user techniques, the media planner must have data both on individual users of the product and on their media habits; sometimes one or both sets of information are missing. Finally, product-user information does not identify potential prospects who might become users in the future.

4. Inner-directed consumer identification. In recent years techniques from psychology and small-group sociology have been increasingly applied to marketing problems. These methods are variously called lifestyle, psychographic, and benefit segmentation. Despite differences among them, these identification methods have the common task of determining *why* some consumer behavior happened. Media planners find it difficult to get valid information of this type from the media, and its use in media planning is limited.

Step 2: Media, competition, and dollars

The competitive environment of advertising was discussed in Chapter 1. Nowhere is the analysis of competition more important than in the media function. Ideally the media planner should begin by determining those media which best reach prospects without regard for competitors and their advertising strategy. However, it would be foolhardy to construct a media plan in ignorance of what advertisers of similar products are doing. If you have built a media plan which meets your needs, but is totally unlike those of your competitors, you should consider the following possibilities:

> You have found something which has been overlooked by competitors which will give you a "noncompetitive" media schedule and should be of tremendous value to your client.
>
> You have overlooked something about your schedule which your competition is aware of and which will lead to a costly mistake for you and your client.

Under normal circumstances competing advertisers use closely related media. As you flip through a magazine or watch an evening of television, notice how many competitive products use the same general media outlets for their advertising. Since advertisers tend to make similar media buys, the smaller advertiser has great difficulty in gaining a competitive advantage over companies with larger budgets. What follows are several techniques used to extend the advertising budget and to compete effectively against larger budgets.

Technique 1: The wave theory. A technique used to some degree by almost every advertiser is the so-called wave theory (often called "flighting" or "pulsing"). Figure 4–3 demonstrates a typical campaign utilizing the wave theory.

Figure 4–3 indicates an advertiser who starts a campaign with a high level of expenditure (relative to the total budget). After this initial wave or flight of advertising, the expenditure is reduced so that by March it is at the lowest advertising level of the campaign. August marks the culmination of another flight with a smaller trough in July, followed by yet another flight in beginning September.

The rationale of the wave theory is that advertising recall occurs without continuous advertising. Depending on the degree of initial impact of the advertising message, the prospect remembers the product even without constant reminders. This consumer recall is called

Figure 4–3
The wave theory

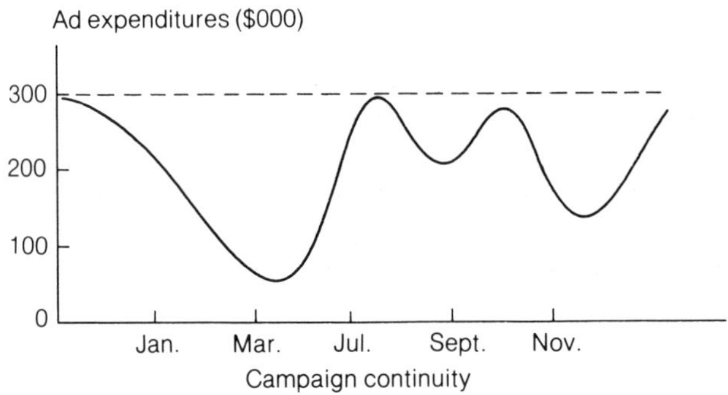

"continuity of impression" and is represented by the dashed line in Figure 4–3. Continuity of impression refers to the fact that product awareness is continuous although advertising expenditures are not.

Several precautions are in order before you develop a "flighting" campaign. The media schedule should take into account the following:

1. Quality of the advertising message. If there is to be a continuity of impression, the advertising must achieve high initial impact. This impact is also a function of the length of time you can afford to advertise at some peak level. Many advertisers make the mistake of cutting back on their advertising just when the audience is becoming aware of it.

2. Interval between flights. Perhaps the two most important considerations in determining the maximum time between flights are the level of competitive advertising and your own budget. It is important to analyze what competitive advertising activity will take place when you cut back. Obviously, the more competitive the advertising situation, the greater is the chance that the consumer will forget your advertising message. In addition you must remember that what is a wave to you might be only a "ripple" to the competition. Figure 4–4 demonstrates the importance of considering competitive activity in planning the wave theory. Product A is probably wasting its efforts on the wave theory since its maximum expenditure does not even reach the lowest levels of product B. In such a situation some alternative strategy must be found if product A wants to be competitive in the promotional area.

3. The media mix. The types of media selected for the campaign may play a major role in the advisability of using the wave theory. If television is to be the major medium in the campaign, it may be difficult to use flighting effectively. The problems are discounts and availabilities. As we will discuss later, television rates and discounts are designed with the large, continuous advertiser in mind. An advertiser who continually gets in and out of the medium will find that substantial bulk and continuity discounts are lost (see Chapter 5).

More important to the media planner considering the wave theory is the problem of availability. The broadcast media, as contrasted to the print media, deal in relatively fixed units of advertising time. We are familiar with the differences in the size of the pre-Christmas issues of popular magazines and the issues which appear shortly after Christmas. There may be a difference of 100 pages in some cases as

Figure 4–4
The wave theory and competition

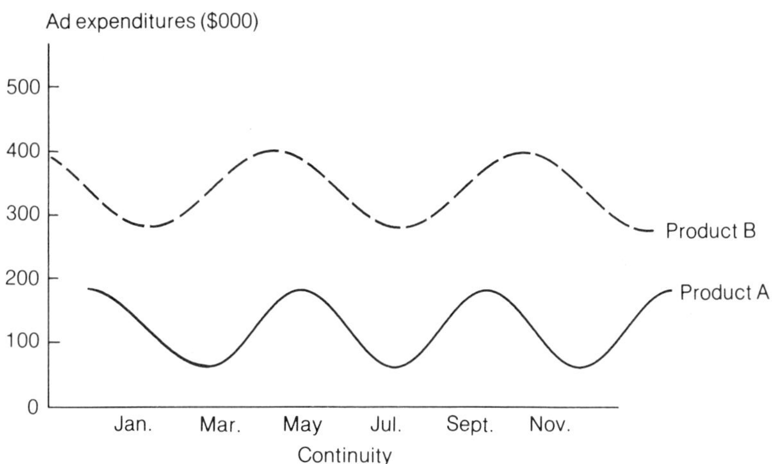

advertisers pull out after the Christmas rush. Television does not have this flexibility. Consequently, stations and networks give favorable treatment to advertisers who are willing to sign long-term contracts and agree to advertise in slack periods as well as peak seasons. The advertiser using the wave theory will find that prime availabilities are often not open to him on either the network or local station level. In effect, by losing most discounts and having a low priority for choosing advertising spots, the wave theory advertiser will pay a premium price for secondary availabilities.

Technique 2: Media dominance. Media dominance is a media-buying technique sometimes used by advertisers who find themselves in the type of relative financial disadvantage shown in Figure 4–4. Advertiser A realizes that a traditional media mix cannot achieve any particular advertising impact in the face of a much larger competitor. However, some impact might be achieved by placing all or a significant proportion of the available advertising dollars in a single medium. This avoids the mistake of spreading the advertising budget across several media and making no impression in any. On the other hand, many small advertisers have a diversified market that cannot be reached adequately by a single medium. Media dominance is essentially an attempt to achieve a compromise between these two problems.

A media dominance plan uses several media over a period of time, but it uses them sequentially. In this way the advertiser is dominant, or at least competitive, with larger competitors in a single medium. However, the product is competitive with only a narrow segment of the total audience. Figure 4–5 demonstrates how this might change the competitive situation shown in Figure 4–4.

Figure 4–5
Media dominance

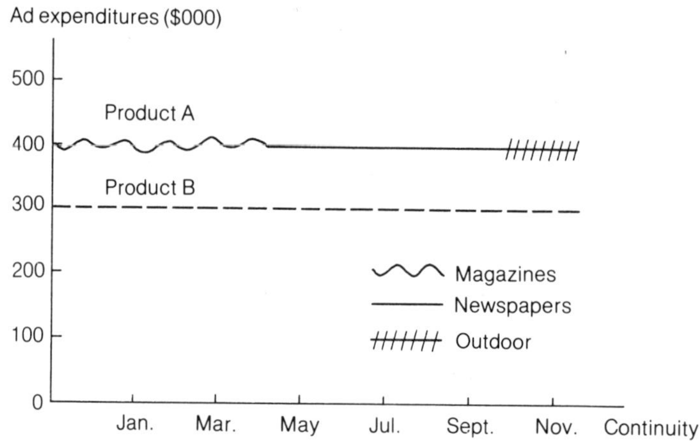

Now product A is more than competitive with product B. However, like most concepts of buying media, media dominance is far from a perfect solution to product A's problems. First, while being competitive in one medium, advertiser A is delivering no messages to prospective consumers who use other media. Second, advertiser A must take care not to use too many media and spread too thin horizontally. In determining how many media can be used, and for how long, many of the same factors considered in determining the duration of waves should be examined. Likewise, television is normally not an ideal alternative for media dominance plans for the same reasons as those discussed in connection with the wave theory.

Technique 3: Media concentration. A final media-buying technique for a small advertiser attempting to achieve parity with larger competition is media concentration. Basically media concentration is choosing the one medium which will best reach your prospects and advertising exclusively in that medium for an indefinite period of time.

An advertiser would choose media concentration over media dominance for several reasons. First, advocates of media concentration take the position that the type of coverage offered by media dominance is too risky. They feel that to be effective, advertising must be offered on a relatively continuous basis to the same audience. Another budgetary reason for using media concentration is that it allows advertisers to take advantage of media discounts and to compete for broadcast availabilities.

Figure 4–6 demonstrates a typical media concentration plan, again using products A and B from our earlier examples.

To consider media concentration, the media planner must be sat-

Figure 4–6
Media concentration (one medium)

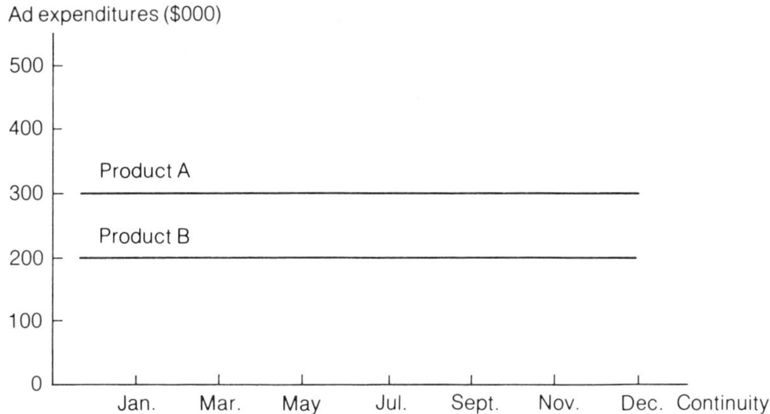

isfied that a significant number of prospects can be reached by a single medium. Media concentration often means a lower share of market for the product, and above all, in the one medium used, dominance must be achieved. It is important to remember that few advertisers (especially advertisers of consumer goods) would choose either media dominance or media concentration, given an alternative. However, the small advertiser rarely has any option other than being overwhelmed by larger advertisers if a more traditional multimedia approach is taken.

A final consideration in developing a media plan is the qualitative versus the quantitative decisions. Media is a "by-the-numbers" enterprise. However, the numbers are usually estimates, and in any case they cannot be a substitute for common sense and experienced judgment. The creative media planner must consider the quality of the media environment and its effect on the advertising message.

> Bernie Orvett, creative group head at J. Walter Thompson, states:
>
> When I look at media, I worry about environment more than audience. The same women may read *Ladies' Home Journal, Woman's Day,* and *Vogue*—but they go to *Vogue* in a different frame of mind.
>
> I used to have terrible arguments with our media department about Mink International. They kept pointing to the cpms we could get in books like *Woman's Day* and *Family Circle.* I said we couldn't sell mink in those books. I wanted *Vogue* or *Harper's.* If we had to go to a service environment, I insisted we at least go into *Ladies' Home Journal*—which has more of a fashion environment.
>
> I'm convinced that cpms can sometimes put clients into unsympathetic environments.[2]

Step 3: Basic media strategy

Once the media planner has thoroughly researched the prospective market and understands the marketing, advertising, and creative objectives, it is time to begin studying the principles which apply to the media schedule.

Reach versus frequency: The great compromise. A major dilemma of the media planner is determining what people to reach and how many times to reach them. Step 1, prospect identification, should have given the answer to the first question, but the problem of how often to reach these people is an even more difficult question.

It is obvious that few products can be sold with only a single audience exposure. Likewise, it is wasteful to continue delivering advertising messages to an audience which is not interested in your

[2] "Look Past the Numbers," *Media Decisions,* July 1977, p. 66.

product. The media planner must decide where the schedule should fall on a frequency continuum between one exposure and some point of diminishing return. He or she must also remember that each additional exposure to one group excludes reaching some other group.

The reach versus frequency problem is composed of five related factors; the media planner who finds that through study and experience he can cope with these five factors is well on the way to the "ideal" media buy.

Factor 1: Reach. The media planner must first decide what prospects (including primary and secondary prospects) he wishes to contact.

Factor 2: Frequency. Next some determination must be made concerning the number of times it will be necessary to reach each prospect. The media planner is often faced with little more than intuition when determining frequency. However, factors such as price, frequency of product purchase, level of competitive advertising, and stage in the product life cycle will offer some indication of proper frequency levels.

Another major factor in determining frequency is the theoretical conception advocated by the individual media planner. There are basically three ways of viewing the purchase of frequency in an advertising campaign; Figures 4–7, 4–8, and 4–9 demonstrate each.

The learning theory concept of frequency takes the view that each impression of an advertising message results in an additional increment of learning for the prospect. At some point (after the seventh insertion in Figure 4–7) the prospect has full knowledge of the advertiser's message, and additional repetitions will result in no further

Figure 4–7
The learning theory concept of advertising frequency

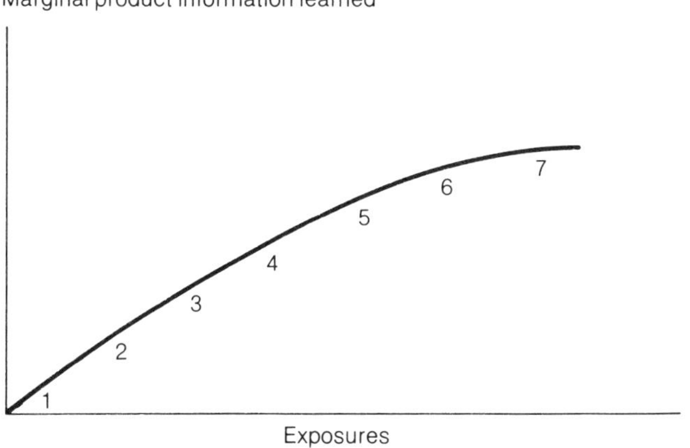

learning and consequently diminishing returns on the advertising dollar.

Figure 4–8 is a version of the learning theory concept which we might call the noise barrier concept. Here the assumption is that the first few exposures do little good since people must be made aware of the message through multiple exposure. Your advertising must break through the barrier of competing advertising. You will note in Figure 4–8 that the most effective exposures are in a middle range after the advertising has gained the attention of the prospect but before the inevitable wearing-out period begins.

Figure 4–8
The noise barrier concept of advertising frequency

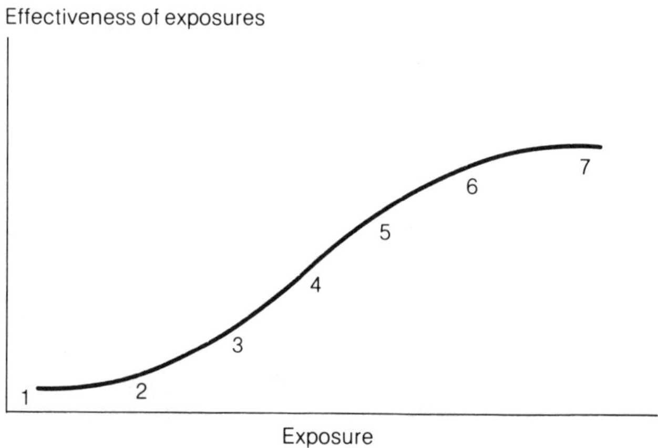

Figure 4–9, the need-perception concept of frequency, is based on advertising impact as a function of need. For instance, assume that Figure 4–9 represents a washing machine owner who is satisfied with the present washer. Although the consumer comes into contact with numerous washer ads, they make no particular impression. At some point, however, the consumer finds that a new washer is needed, and immediately the perception and the impact of the ads increase dramatically.

Figure 4–9
The need-perception concept of advertising frequency

Exposures

Shopping period

Ad impact

After a period of shopping, a new washer is purchased and the consumer's perception of washer ads drops to its former low level. The need-perception concept of frequency says that the greater the frequency of advertising, the greater is the chance that an advertising message will be available when a prospect's need for and interest in a product peaks.

Factor 3: Continuity. A third factor related to the reach versus frequency compromise is the continuity of the advertising campaign. The number of people who can be reached and the number of times they are to be exposed to your message will be determined by the length of the campaign. If the media planner is interested in a six-week introductory or special offer campaign, the opportunities to extend both reach and frequency are greater than if the same budget is to be allocated over the entire year. Regardless of the continuity, the media planner must still determine reach and frequency goals. However, flexibility in those areas will increase as the length of the campaign decreases.

Factor 4: Length and size of advertisements. The frequency of ad insertions will obviously be affected by the length of the commercial or the size of the print advertisement chosen by the media planner. Normally the most efficient ads on a cost basis are those which cost the least (i.e., the smaller ads). However, the advertisement which generates the greatest cost efficiency does not always carry out the advertising and marketing goals of the campaign.

The normal advertisement is usually 30 seconds in television; 30 or 60 seconds in radio, a full page in magazines, and a wide range of sizes in newspapers. As the ad size decreases, the number of insertion opportunities increase, along with the opportunities for added reach and frequency impact. The media planner must coordinate budgetary considerations with the considerations of his or her creative counterpart to determine the size of an advertisement. This is just one more reason why the actual purchase of time and space is usually one of the final steps in the campaign.

Factor 5: Budget. A consideration which permeates all media considerations is the size of the advertising budget devoted to the media function. In essence it is the budget which requires that compromises be made among the various elements of media strategy.

Step 4: Media evaluation

To this point the steps in the media plan have dealt with overall marketing and advertising concepts—the strategy of the plan. Now we must begin to develop the media schedule. The media schedule will designate the media (e.g., magazines, television), the specific vehicles (e.g., *Time,* "60 Minutes"), and the insertion dates of your advertising.

Chapters 5–10 will analyze each of the media in light of specific advertising requirements. Chapters 11–13 will examine techniques for intermedia research and comparisons. This section, however, will deal with some of the basic media terminology and with the calculations used in making media evaluations.

Reach. As mentioned earlier, reach is the number (often expressed as a percentage of a population) of *different* people who are exposed to your advertising or to the vehicle in which your advertising appears. The terms *coverage, unduplicated audience,* and *cume* are used as synonyms for reach. Cume, short for "accumulated audience," refers to the number of different people a medium (usually broadcast) reaches during a specified period.

Composition. In the context of the media function, composition normally refers to the percentage of some medium's total audience made up of a market segment (see Figure 4–2).

Cost per thousand. Perhaps the most used device for comparing media is the cost per thousand (CPM) calculation. The formula is:

$$CPM = \frac{\text{Cost} \times 1{,}000}{\text{Circulation}}$$

Normally CPM is calculated on a weighted basis by media planners. The simplest weighting procedure is to calculate CPM on the basis of prospects rather than total audience (see Figure 4–10). In reality much more sophisticated procedures would be used in media planning with different audience segments being given a weight equal to their importance as prospects.

Frequency. Frequency is defined as the average number of times the audience reached is exposed to a medium or an advertisement

Figure 4–10
Example of weighted CPM

CPM, *Dog & Hunter Magazine* (circulation, 5,000; one B&W page, \$100):

$$CPM = \frac{\$100 \times 1{,}000}{5{,}000} = \$20$$

18–24-year-old CPM, *Dog & Hunter Magazine* (circulation among 18–24-year-olds, 2,000; one B&W page, \$100):

$$CPM = \frac{\$100 \times 1{,}000}{2{,}000} = \$50$$

Figure 4–11
Audience frequency calculation

Week	*Total audience (000)*	*Cume (000)*
1	70	70
2	70	30
3	75	20
4	75	—
	290	120

$$\text{Frequency} = \frac{\text{Total audience}}{\text{Cume}} = \frac{290}{120} = 2.42$$

during a specified period. Figure 4–11 calculates a simple frequency problem for a local television show.

In Figure 4–11 we see that 120,000 different people accounted for 290,000 exposures (or duplicated audience). Thus, on average the members of the audience saw the show 2.42 times during the four-week period studied. Note that by the fourth week everyone in the audience had seen the show.

Audience turnover. A concept similar to frequency is audience turnover, or simply turnover. Turnover measures the number of average audiences which saw the medium during a specified period. Using the data provided in Figure 4–11, the calculations are as follows:

$$\text{Turnover} = \frac{\text{Cume}}{\text{Average audience } \left(\frac{290}{4}\right)} = \frac{120}{72.5} = 1.66$$

Note that in the case of both frequency and turnover the calculation will result in an answer between 1.0 and N (N = Total exposure opportunities, in this case 4.0). However, frequency and turnover are inversely related.

Ratings and audience share. In the broadcast media the terms *rating* and *share of audience* (or simply *share*) are the basic measures of audience. Both normally refer to television households, but the calculations can be used for individuals.

$$\text{Rating} = \frac{\text{Number of households watching a program}}{\text{Total television households in a population}}$$

A TV population will normally be either national households or households in a television market.

$$\text{Share of audience} = \frac{\text{Number of households watching a program}}{\text{Households using television (HUT)}}$$

Gross Rating Points. The broadcast media are almost always purchased in "packages," or groups of commercials, rather than on a show-by-show basis. Gross Rating Points (GRPs) are a measure of scheduling impact calculated on a weekly or monthly basis. GRP can be figured in two ways:

1. Sum the ratings of the individual shows carrying your commercial (assuming one commercial per show).

Show	*Network rating*
"Charlie's Angels"	21.1
"60 Minutes"	25.6
"Vegas"	22.1
"Fantasy Island"	21.1
	89.9, or about 90

2. Multiply reach by frequency. Here reach is expressed as a percentage of population rather than a whole number. If we assume that the four shows listed above had an average reach of 22.5 percent of TV households, then the formula would be:

$$22.5 \times 4 = 90$$

The obvious question is, Why use the second formula when it is so simple to add up the ratings? If we only want to know the GRP level for a particular schedule, we would use the addition method. However, the latter formula precisely identifies the interaction which exists between reach and frequency:

$$\frac{GRPs}{\text{Reach}} = \text{Frequency} \qquad \frac{GRPs}{\text{Frequency}} = \text{Reach}$$

The media planner must have access to the reach or frequency estimates to use these formulas. The sources of such data are numerous and will be discussed later.

It is also helpful to be able to calculate frequency estimates for combinations of media. We will provide a simple means to estimate frequency using the following data:

	Target audience		
	Reach Percent	*Frequency*	*GRPs*
Television ads	30	4.0	120
Magazine ads	20	2.0	40

In this example, reach is expressed as a percentage of the prospects in the target market exposed to television and magazine vehicles carrying your ad. Often, media people would simply sum the GRPs and let the matter drop. In fact, ads in the two media did earn 160 GRPs. But notice that by limiting this analysis to GRPs, you ignore (or assume away) the problem of audience duplication.

It is probable that some viewers of the television ads also saw the magazine ads. If this is so, the true total reach (or unduplicated audience) is less than the sum of the reach for each medium. To estimate the true reach, we use a simple adjustment process:

First, assume *no audience overlap* between media. This is done by summing the reach for each medium. This step sets the maximum value for the combined reach, and in the example above we get 30% + 20% = 50%.

Second, *subtract* from the maximum combined reach the *probable audience overlap.* A general guideline indicates that the reach for the highest reach medium (i.e., television, 30 percent) in the market is a reasonable estimate of the TV reach among magazine readers. In our example, (30%)(20%), or 6% of the total target market, saw the ads in both television and magazines. Now recall that *reach* is synonymous with *unduplicated* audience, and therefore it would be imprecise to double-count this 6 percent in the audiences for each medium. Therefore, we subtract the *duplicated* portion of the audience, 6 percent, from the value calculated in the first step, or 50% − 6% = 44%.

Since frequency is equal to GRP ÷ Reach, we can now use our estimate of combined reach to improve our estimate of the true combined frequency. In our example:

$$\text{Frequency} = \frac{160}{44} = 3.64$$

Of course, the same process of subtracting probable duplicated audience components from values for maximum reach can be applied to combinations of two or more vehicles in a single medium, and to combinations of more than two media. These problems employ exactly the same approach, though the calculations are somewhat more complex.

Cost per rating point. The media buyer often compares different broadcast buys on the basis of the cost per rating point (CPP) of various schedules, as follows:

$$CPP = \frac{\text{Schedule cost}}{GRPs}$$

Media planners often use the cost per point calculation to compare the costs of reaching certain demographic target markets. This calculation, called the cost per demographic point, adjusts for waste circulation and is used by the media buyer in much the same way as the weighted cost per thousand formula discussed earlier. Let's look at an example:

	Household rating	*Rating of women 18+*	*Rating of men 18+*	*Cost/30 second*
Daytime soap	7	5	1.2	$12,000

$$CPP = \frac{\text{Cost}}{\text{Household rating}} = \frac{\$12{,}000}{7} = \$1{,}711$$

$$\text{Cost per demographic point (women 18+)} = \frac{\text{Cost}}{\text{Rating for women 18+}} = \frac{\$12{,}000}{5} = \$2{,}400$$

$$\text{Cost per demographic point (men 18+)} = \frac{\text{Cost}}{\text{Rating for men 18+}} = \frac{\$12{,}000}{1.2} = \$10{,}000$$

The media planner can use the CPP to compare the efficiency with which different shows reach a target audience. The CPP can also be used to determine how efficiently a single show reaches different demographic groups. In the above example our soap opera does well in reaching women over 18, but as might be expected, it would be totally unacceptable as a vehicle for reaching adult males.

Use of indexes in media planning. A common comparison used in media is the index. An index compares several media on the basis of an arbitrary standard. For example, if the national rating for "Quincy," 18, is assigned an index number of 100, then the indexes based on selected local market ratings of "Quincy" would be as follows:

	Local market ratings for "Quincy"	*Index*
Atlanta	20	111
Houston	18	100
Los Angeles	22	122
New York	16	89

We arrive at these figures by dividing our base (i.e., the national rating) of 18 into each local market rating and multiplying by 100 to remove the decimal. Therefore Atlanta ($20/18 \times 100 = 111$) has an audience rating 11 percent greater than the national average, while Houston's rating duplicates the national average and New York's rating is 11 percent less than the national average.

The media planner has many other sources of information at his disposal. Among the most valuable are the general media guides published by most large advertising agencies and many media organizations. These guides are not rate cards, but they can be used to estimate audience size, demographics, and basic costs for classes of media. They can save the media planner valuable time by suggesting whether the media plan being developed is consistent with previously determined objectives. Many of the guides also offer rules for determining reach or frequency, given other media schedule data. See Figures 4–12 and 4–13 for examples of such guides.

Figure 4–12
How the media rate in terms of quantitative media factors

	TV	*Radio*	*Magazines*	*Newspapers*
Total population reach (Adults plus children)	Very strong	Good	Fair	Good
Selective upscale adult reach	Fair	Good	Very strong	Good
Upscale adult selectivity (per ad exposure)	Poor	Fair	Very strong	Good
Young adult selectivity (per ad exposure)	Fair	Very strong	Very strong	Fair
Cost per 1,000 ratios	Fair-good	Very strong	Strong	Good
National media availabilities and uniform coverage	Very strong	Poor	Good	Poor
Local market selectivity	Good	Good	Poor	Very strong
Ability to control frequency	Fair	Good	Good	Very strong
Ability to pile frequency upon reach base	Very strong	Very strong	Good	Fair
Ability to exploit time-of-day factors (in scheduling)	Fair	Very strong	Poor	Poor
Ability to exploit day-of-week factors (in scheduling)	Fair	Very strong	Poor	Very strong
Seasonal audience stability	Poor	Very strong	Good	Good
Predictability of audience levels	Fair-poor	Good	Good	Very good
Depth of demographics in audience surveys	Poor	Poor	Very strong	Fair-good
Reliability and consistency of audience surveys	Fair-good	Good	Fair-good	Good
Ability to monitor schedules	Good	Poor	Very strong	Very strong
Ability to negotiate rates	Good	Fair	Poor	Poor
Fast closing and air dates	Fair	Good	Poor	Very strong

Source: *The Media Book*, '79,

Figure 4–13
Index of HUT by household demography and daypart

Index of HUT by Household Demography and Daypart (Total HUT for each Daypart = 100)

How to read: TV households with incomes of $10,000 or less view seven percent more daytime television than does the average home viewing daytime television.

	Daytime	Early Evening	Prime Time	Late Evening	Sat./Sun. Morning
Average HUT (Total TV Homes)	25.9	48.6	63.3	26.5	19.9
Household Income					
Under $10,000	107	100	92	90	87
$10,000-$14,999	100	105	105	100	112
$15,000 +	91	97	107	112	108
$20,000 +	86	95	105	113	102
Household Size					
1-2	79	83	87	82	55
3-4	113	112	109	108	131
5 +	141	130	123	140	174
County Size					
A	94	97	101	112	97
B	103	100	98	101	96
C & D	104	103	101	84	106
Territory					
Northeast	92	103	101	94	95
East Central	122	109	108	115	120
West Central	83	83	100	128	70
South	107	99	99	97	103
Pacific	98	108	91	69	115
Selected Upper Demos					
$15,000 +, HOH POM	83	92	103	113	107
HOH 4 + Yrs. College	78	83	89	100	86

Source: A.C. Nielsen Audience Demographic Report, Nov. 1976.

Courtesy of Ogilvy & Mather

Step 5: The media schedule

The worst mistake a media planner can make is to begin media buying before completing the marketing and research steps outlined in the previous sections. The media schedule is the culmination of extensive examination of the total advertising problem, and if that examination has been done properly, the schedule based on it should fall into place naturally.

The media schedule serves two purposes: (1) It gives the client and other advertising decision makers a clear idea of the media function as part of the total marketing/advertising program; and (2) it is a working plan for carrying out the mechanics of purchasing time and space. The media schedule can take an indefinite number of different formats, but it must be unambiguous so that anyone in the media department can purchase the time and space specified in the schedule. Chapter 12 will discuss an actual media plan. After the planning and selection process for media are complete, time and space are purchased.

THE FINANCES OF MEDIA BUYING

Buying and selling advertising space and time is a $50 billion a year business. As with any other business of that size, many complex relationships exist which all parties must understand. This section will discuss the three types of firms most concerned with the advertising media process: the advertising agency, the independent media buyer, and the media representative.

The advertising agency

Most national advertising is placed by advertising agencies. Most of these agencies are independent, but some advertisers have established in-house advertising departments to carry out a portion of the advertising function. Since media expenses make up a major portion of most advertising budgets for consumer goods, the role of media in an agency-client relationship is crucial.

Normally a full-service agency's media responsibilities include the following:

1. Make basic recommendations to the client about general media strategy.
2. Enter into contracts (which set time and space prices) with the media and submit insertion orders.
3. Engage in research, usually based on syndicated data, for major media decisions.

4. Ensure that all advertising runs on schedule and that production quality meets minimum standards.

These functions are normally considered part of the basic agency function. If the agency operates on the traditional 15 percent media commission system, these functions are called nonbillable services. That is, they are included in the basic services which the commission covers. Services such as primary research, which is rarely conducted by an agency, or other specialized client services cost extra and are called billable services.

One of the major areas of the client/agency relationship is determining the method of compensation. Four systems of compensation are used:

1. Basic media commission. In the most traditional method of agency compensation, the agency bills the client at the current media rates and in turn pays the media at the same rates less 15 percent.

Figure 4–14
The 17.65 percent markup: An example

	Full page—local rate	*Full page—national rate*
Undifferentiated local/national rate	$1,000	$1,000
National rate with agency placement	$1,000 + 17.65% = $1,176.50	
Net to newspaper after agency commission is paid	$1,176.50 − 15% = $1,000	

In addition media also may offer a 2 percent discount for prompt payment. The agency generally returns this "cash discount" to the client, assuming that it has been paid in advance of the date that it must pay the media to qualify for the discount.

For noncommissionable media, such as direct mail, the agency will usually mark up its cost by 17.65 percent. This markup provides the agency with the equivalent of 15 percent of the gross bill (see Figure 4–14). The 17.65 percent markup is also used to compute billing, printing, and other production charges as well as being used in other media rate calculations. For instance some newspapers have begun to offer identical rates for national and local advertisers. However, if the national advertiser uses an agency, the newspaper will mark up the cost 17.65 percent in consideration of the agency discount.

2. Media commission method as a draw against a minimum fee. This simply means that the client agrees to pay the agency a minimum fee (usually on a monthly basis). Any media commissions or other agency fees will be deducted from this fee.

3. Retainer or fee method. Here the client contracts with an agency for specific services at a set fee. Usually this method is used where the agency-client relationship is not of long standing. For instance a brochure or a consumer research project is often paid on a per job basis. Generally, a full-service agency would not deal with clients on this basis.

4. Incentive fee method or shared profit fee method. This method guarantees the agency some minimum net profit on gross billings of the account. This can be computed either before or after taxes. A common application of the method guarantees the agency 1.5 percent profit on gross billings. If profits fall within a 1.5–2.5 percent range, there is no adjustment; and if agency profits exceed 2.5 percent, the agency returns some contracted proportion of the surplus to the client. This is to the advantage of the advertiser only when the advertising investment is heavy.

Regardless of the basic compensation method, it is crucial that a detailed letter of agreement between the client and the advertiser be completed *before* any work is done. This agreement details which charges for production, talent, and services will be included in commissions and which will not. Research charges and, occasionally, the persons or the levels of personnel that will handle the account are also specified. Finally, the agreement includes a statement of the liability of the client to the media. Some advertisers have paid their agencies only to find that the bills of third parties were not being paid. Generally the courts have held that advertisers are not liable for work contracted by an agency. A few media are requiring dual-liability contracts, and some advertisers are asking their agencies to take out insurance or a bond to protect them from having to pay twice. A simple way of handling this is for the client to ask for copies of paid invoices from the agency along with copies of any ads placed.

Agency of record. In cases where a multiline company has several advertising agencies servicing its brands, some coordination of the media function is necessary. It is important to note that corporations often qualify for media discounts higher than the total discounts for which their individual brands qualify (see Figure 4–15). Large advertisers often appoint one of their agencies as the "agency of record" to coordinate the media discounts for which the firm qualifies. The agency of record normally negotiates time and space contracts, and the firm's other agencies submit insertion orders based on these contracts.

The agency of record receives a percentage of the commissions of the other agencies. Usually this extra fee is 15 percent of the 15

Figure 4–15
Computing media discounts for companies versus brands

Acme Widget Company	Lines bought	Discount	Newspaper discount: Lines bought	Newspaper discount: Annual discount
Brand A	8,000	3%	5,000	3%
B	7,000	3	10,000	5
C	12,000	5	20,000	8
D	8,000	3	30,000	10
E	9,000	3	40,000	12
Total	44,000		50,000	15

The Acme Widget Company qualifies for a corporate discount of 12 percent. However, if each brand's discount were considered alone, the firm would receive a discount of slightly over 3 percent.

percent agency commission, or 2.25 percent. Consequently the "other" agencies of a firm utilizing an agency of record will receive only 12.75 percent instead of the normal 15 percent commission for media placement.

The independent media buyer

In contrast to the full-service agency which plans an entire campaign, independent media-buying organizations deal strictly in the purchase of media. The independent media buyer usually works either for agencies, which use them as the media department for some or all of their clients, or directly for clients who handle their own creative activities.

Most of the media purchases made by the independent media organizations are in broadcast. Fees are often set on the basis of how much the client saves compared to the prices originally quoted by the media. Since broadcast time charges are more negotiable than print charges, experienced buyers can realize major savings. Print media generally sell space on a fixed basis, with fewer opportunities for negotiated buys.

The independent media-buying services compete with the full-service agencies and are therefore often disparaged by these agencies, which contend that their media buyers are as qualified as those employed by independents. When savings are made, these agencies claim, it is because "inferior" buys are priced as if they were buys of higher quality. The independents naturally dispute this charge, claiming that since they are media specialists they can do the media-buying job better than a full-service agency, which must deal with a whole range of nonmedia functions.

Both the full-service agency and the independents are probably correct. As discussed earlier, the buying of GRPs rather than individual spots makes precise evaluation of media buys difficult. Occasionally, large clients will "test" their agencies by giving identical media assignments to the agency and one or more independent media buyers. This may keep the agency on its toes; it does little to further good agency-client relationships.

The media representative

The media representative (rep) works for media enterprises rather than advertisers. Historically the media reps functioned as media sales personnel in major markets and were paid on a commission basis for the time and space they sold. This meant that newspapers and broadcast stations could compete for national dollars without incurring the expense of having their own sales force in New York, Chicago, Los Angeles, and other major markets. The media reps still perform this basic sales function, but they have added more sophisticated services. For example the major reps, such as Blair, Eastman, McGavren-Guild, Katz, and Torbet Radio, have developed buying combines for radio, called *nonwired networks* (see Chapter 6). They now use interactive computer systems to obtain immediate information on time availabilities. Blair has recently experimented with the satellite transmission of television spots to local stations.

In addition to functioning as time and space sales organizations, the media reps have become an integral part of the total advertising media process. Media reps are excellent sources of local market information, and they increase local media revenues by bringing in national dollars to many hitherto overlooked broadcasters and publishers. Finally, the media reps provide an orderly flow of advertising from nationally oriented accounts to local media.

More and more media groups have been forming their own rep subsidiaries. These companies function similarly to the independent reps, but they restrict their clients to company-owned or otherwise related media. Gannett Newspaper Advertising Sales and NBC Spot Sales are examples of these group-oriented reps.

SUMMARY

This chapter has outlined the basic functions and terminology of media buying. At this point you should have some fundamental idea of how the buyers and sellers of advertising media function. It is important to have a clear understanding of the broad system by which advertisements and commercials progress from the initial concepts of copywriters to the mass media and ultimately to the consumers of advertisers' products.

In Chapters 5–10 we will examine and analyze various media and their specific options and limitations for the advertisers who use them. As we discuss each of the media, it is important to keep the general concepts of this chapter in mind. You must remember that advertising media buying is not done in a vacuum. Rather, every media-buying decision is also a decision not to buy various media alternatives. Only by viewing the media as an interrelated communication system can you grasp the complexities of managing the media function.

QUESTIONS

1. What are the four areas of the media-buying function?

2. Briefly describe four methods of audience segmentation. Give an example of each.

3. What is the major problem with using lifestyle or psychographic data in media planning?

4. Describe "flighting" and some considerations in using the technique.

5. Discuss the use of television in media dominance and media concentration.

6. Discuss three concepts of frequency.

7. Discuss at least two alternatives to the payment systems agency commission.

8. In a recent four-week period "Alice" had the following audience in Metropolis (6,000 TV households):

Week	*Number of households viewing*	*Unduplicated audience*
1	2,500	2,500
2	2,700	1,000
3	2,300	700
4	2,500	400

a. What was the reach during this period?
b. What was the frequency?

c. Assuming that a 30-second spot costs $150, what was the cpm/household during the first week?

d. What was the rating during the third week?

e. If the average audience in the base year 1977 was 2,100, what would the audience index be for the second week?

f. If the HUT during the fourth week was 65 percent, what was the program's share?

g. What GRP level was achieved during this period?

5 TELEVISION

AMERICA has had an uninterrupted love/hate relationship with television since 1950. Television is more than a medium of advertising and communications; it is an institution. It is criticized and praised with equal fervor by special-interest groups, legislative bodies, and organizations throughout the entire range of the political and social spectrum.

Currently the television industry is composed of more than 1,000 television stations, of which approximately 750 are commercial. Of the commercial stations, 70 percent are VHF (very high frequency) and the remainder are UHF (ultrahigh frequency). Most commercial television stations are affiliated with one of the three major networks. However, many UHF stations are independent of the networks. In 1980 television advertising revenues exceeded $8 billion, with almost half of this being spent at the network level.

The Federal Communications Commission allows a corporation or individual to own up to seven television stations; no more than five of these can be VHF. The three major networks each own five stations which are called O&Os (owned and operated). These stations are more important than their numbers would indicate. Not only are they extremely profitable, but they are the benchmark for measuring the success of certain syndicated shows, local news formats, and local market ratings. (See Figure 5–1.)

Television viewership statistics are as impressive as television rev-

Figure 5–1
Network-owned and -operated stations

American Broadcasting Company (ABC)		*National Broadcasting Company (NBC)*		*Columbia Broadcasting System (CBS)*	
WLS	Chicago	WMAQ	Chicago	WBBM	Chicago
WXYZ	Detroit	WKYC	Cleveland	KNXT	Los Angeles
KABC	Los Angeles	KNBC	Los Angeles	WCBS	New York City
WABC	New York City	WNBC	New York City	WCAU	Philadelphia
KGO	San Francisco	WKYS	Washington	KCBS	San Francisco

Figure 5–2
Concentration of television advertising ($ millions)

Product category		*Corporation*		*Percent of product category*
Food and food products	$1,200.0	General Foods	$246.7	21
		General Mills	134.9	11
Toilet goods	806.2	Johnson & Johnson	71.5	9
		Gillette	57.4	7
Automotive	653.4	General Motors	132.9	20
		Ford	110.8	17
Proprietary medicines	448.3	American Home Products	149.8	33
Confectionery and soft drinks	410.4	Pepsi Company	92.5	23
		Coca-Cola	84.5	21

Source: *Broadcasting*, April 16, 1979, p. 59.

enue data. Almost 98 percent of American households have television sets; half have two or more sets; and color-set penetration approaches 80 percent of television households. It is estimated that cable television will soon exceed 25 percent penetration of American households, and 1 percent of viewers have home video recorders.

Television is the leading advertising medium among *national* advertisers by a wide margin. In 1978 the top ten national advertisers spent $3.05 billion; of this, $1.9 billion (62.1 percent) was spent in television.[1] Television is a medium designed primarily for mass marketers, and despite a recent industry sales push to interest local advertisers in television, more than 75 percent of television advertising revenues come from network or national spot sales.

Television revenues are concentrated in a relatively few product categories, and one or two large corporations tend to dominate each category. Figure 5–2 shows the extent of this concentration by product category.

The cost of using television can be tremendous. Television CPM values compare favorably with those of other mass media. However, the real costs and message perishability which demands high frequency levels prevent most small and medium-sized advertisers from using television as their primary medium. Television is a complex medium with many quantitative and qualitative forces restricting advertising flexibility. This chapter will deal primarily with television as an advertising medium. However, we will also show the medium in the perspective of a leisure-time activity which is used over six hours per day in the average American home.

TELEVISION AS AN ADVERTISING MEDIUM

Unlike most advertising media, television is a multipurpose advertising vehicle. It appeals to different audiences and advertisers at different times. The various segments of television must be examined from a marketing perspective as if they were different media. Figure 5–3 outlines the relationships and marketing strategies of television's several faces.

Television dayparts[2]

Television is divided into several segments (or dayparts) during each broadcast day. As shown in Figure 5–1, each of these dayparts has

[1] *Advertising Age*, September 6, 1979, pp. 1 and 12.

[2] All references are to Eastern time. A network program broadcast at 8:00 P.M. in New York would be broadcast at 8:00 P.M. in the Pacific time zone and at 7:00 P.M. in the Central and Mountain time zones.

Figure 5–3
Various programming segments of television

Television segment	*Primary audience*	*Household CPM*	*Typical products*
Late fringe time	Young adults, 18–24	$3.50	Records, movies
Daytime	Women, 35+	3.00	Soaps and detergents
Primetime (8:00–11:00 P.M.)	Adults (children, and some teens until 9:00 P.M.)	5.50	Consumer goods, depends on program
Children, Saturday and afternoons	Children, 2–11	2.50	Cereals, toys
News (including "Today Show," "Good Morning America," "CBS Morning News"	Upscale adults, more women in morning and early news shows	3.00	Utilities
Sports	Men, 18–35	4.00	Automobiles, beer
Primetime access (7:00–8:00 P.M.)	Adults, 35+	3.00	Consumer goods

its own primary audience, programming, and advertising. A brief discussion of each of the major dayparts and its strengths follows.

Primetime. Primetime is the glamour segment of the medium. The stars, the major advertisers, the blockbuster shows, and, not coincidentally, 60 percent of all households are found in primetime television. The networks schedule virtually all the programming that is shown on their affiliates during this period.

During primetime the networks compete for rating points and advertising dollars with a fierceness unknown in any other medium. Costs for 30-second commercials on popular shows exceed $100,000, and program production costs are well over $500,000 per hour. With so many complaints about the quality of television programming, including an excess of sex and violence, many people wonder how television can continue to command these high primetime commercial fees.

To understand this, one must first understand the economics of television and the psychology of the television viewer. Television rates are set by market forces, that is, by supply and demand. Advertisers will buy television advertising as long as it delivers their message in a way and at a cost which cannot be equaled by other advertising media. Even at annual price increases of 15 to 20 percent for commercial time, the demand for primetime advertising remains strong because the supply of commercial time is fixed.

The demand for television commercial time is derived from, and is only as strong as, the demand by the public for television programming. Each year such groups as the National Citizens Committee for Broadcasting and Action for Children Television (ACT) publish their lists of the most violent shows. Each year these shows include some of the most popular programs. Without defending or condoning network primetime programming, a realistic appraisal of the situation would indicate that the networks and the public at least share the responsibility for current television fare. Regardless of program content or criticism, virtually every show that stays on the air is watched by millions of people.

Daytime. Daytime television is either a local or network-dominated segment, depending on the time. Networks generally provide programming from 10:00 A.M. to 4:00 P.M. The percentage of stations accepting network programs (designated as percent of clearance) varies, with many stations preempting noon programs for local news. The formula for network daytime is soap operas, 70 percent; game shows, 8–10 percent; and network reruns, 5–7 percent.

Only a few seasons ago the percentage of game shows and soap operas was almost equal. Networks would prefer to broadcast game shows since these are less expensive to produce than soap operas. However, the game shows have generally suffered when placed opposite dramas, and the networks usually program the highest rated format. In recent years only "Match Game" and "Family Feud" have held their own compared to soap operas.

The period from 9:00 A.M. to 10:00 A.M. is filled with syndicated talk shows, off-network reruns, and a few locally produced news and information programs. These shows are directed to a female-oriented audience. Early morning daytime is controlled by the networks with their news programs and CBS's "Captain Kangaroo." Independent stations counterprogram the period with inexpensive 1950s reruns of "The Three Stooges," "The Lone Ranger," and cartoons.

Fringe time. Fringe time is the period preceding and following primetime. Early fringe time starts with afternoon reruns devoted to children, and it becomes more family- and adult-oriented as primetime approaches. In recent years the 5:00–6:00 P.M. period has been hotly contested among local stations seeking strong lead-ins to their lucrative local news shows.

Late fringe is offered primarily to young adults, and it has become much more competitive than it was only a few years ago, when Johnny Carson dominated the period. Both ABC and CBS have programmed network reruns of crime/adventure shows against Carson with some success. Independent stations and a number of network affiliates choose to run movies during the period.

National and local television advertising

Although primarily a mass medium, television offers opportunities to reach different audiences. Television also provides various methods of buying time. Television advertising is divided into three categories: network, national spot, and local. National spot is the advertising purchased on individual local stations by national advertisers. That is, they "spot" their advertising instead of purchasing network time. Throughout most of the modern broadcast era, network television advertising has been the major recipient of advertising revenue, with spot advertising a distant second and local advertising representing a small percentage of total revenues (see Figure 5–4). However, in recent years local television advertising has become a significant factor, with most observers predicting that it will exceed spot revenues in the next several years.

Figure 5–4
Network, spot, and local television advertising revenues ($ millions)

	1968		*1977*	
	Amount	*Percent*	*Amount*	*Percent*
Network	$1,428.5	48.9	$3,248.1	47.4
Spot	1,000.1	34.6	1,967.3	28.8
Local	482.0	16.5	1,630.9	23.8
	$2,910.6	100.0	$6,846.3	100.0

Source: *Television/Radio Age,* June 4, 1979, p. 38.

The growing influx of local advertisers has had its effect on the medium. The demand for television time from such traditional newspaper advertisers as banks, automobile dealers, and grocery stores has further squeezed already tight inventories and has driven up both local and national spot costs. More important than these advertising cost increases, which have generally been more moderate in local television than in network costs, the local advertiser is making spot-buying strategy more difficult by decreasing available time. National advertisers find that they must commit themselves to longer schedules to guarantee desired availabilities. These long-term commitments decrease flexibility, a major reason why many national advertisers use spot television in the first place.

A large measure of the increase in local television advertising must also be credited to local stations. When independent television began to grow nationally, it appealed primarily to local advertisers. Largely ignored by national advertisers, independents had rates low enough for local retailers to experiment with television advertising. From 1973 to 1978, independent station advertising revenues grew to $650 million, an increase of almost 100 percent.[3] While spot advertisers are increasingly considering independent stations, many of the local advertisers brought to the medium have remained, and these have often expanded their television buys to local network affiliates.

National advertisers find problems in both network and spot buys. Network advertising offers lower CPMs and broad coverage with minimal administrative costs, and it often gains the prestige of network program association. On the other hand, network advertising does not allow for market-by-market variance. Many advertisers would prefer to alter copy or even substitute brands in certain markets.

One approach currently being used to offer the advertiser the convenience of network with the flexibility of spot is the cut-in. This permits the advertiser to substitute another commercial for the network commercial in certain markets. Currently all three networks offer the service primarily to very large advertisers. The cut-in can be used either to account for local market variances or to test some portion of the advertising or marketing program.

A growing problem has arisen between networks and their affiliates over cut-ins. Many affiliates see any growth in network cut-ins as a danger to national spot revenues. While networks pay a fee to stations when cut-ins are used, some stations think they should receive more from the networks, while others simply bill the advertiser directly for cut-ins. Advertisers are generally willing to pay an additional fee for a cut-in, but they want the networks and their affiliates to work out a standard fee system which satisfies all parties.

Types of sponsorship

Advertisers have a wide choice of advertising relationships with the networks and stations. This section will outline some of the basic ways in which advertisers can gain access to television.

Participating sponsorship. The most common primetime relationship between the advertiser and the networks is participating sponsorship. The networks decide on the shows they will air during the coming season. The networks then offer advertising time on these shows. Advertisers provide little or no input into the development of

[3] "Those Gutsy Indies," *Media Decisions*, January 1979, p. 1.

the shows, but rather "participate" only by buying one or more commercials. In many ways this is how advertisers buy most other media. When an advertiser purchases a page in *Time* magazine, no one considers that the advertiser has sponsored any particular section of the publication. Sometimes participating television sponsorship is known as the "magazine concept" for this reason.

Sole sponsorship. Sole sponsorship usually refers to programs which are supplied, owned, and controlled by advertisers. Since 1965 this concept has been largely confined to daytime television, where some of the mammoth advertisers such as Procter & Gamble own their own shows. In primetime most of the advertiser-controlled shows are specials and a few made-for-television movies. In the fall of 1979 Procter & Gamble brought "Shirley" to NBC, but it failed due to low ratings.

It is important to emphasize that an advertiser-owned show must meet network standards before it will be accepted. The network must consider the effect a show will have on adjacent programs and the alternative programming that could fill the same slot. The cost of program production works against an advertiser considering this type of investment. Advertisers generally refrain from spending such a large sum on one show, preferring instead to spread their budget over several shows to increase audience reach.

The appeal of sole sponsorship is the control and identification it gives the advertiser. Advertisers producing their own programming can develop projects which they think complement their marketing strategy to a greater degree than network-provided programs. In addition sole sponsorship of a successful program offers tremendous sponsor identification. The average person would be hard pressed to recall a single sponsor from a currently top-ranked show. Yet the same person might easily identify Dinah Shore with Chevrolet and Milton Berle with Texaco two decades after these shows went off the air.

Barter. Barter is defined as the exchange of goods without money. In advertising, barter takes two basic forms. In the more common form an advertiser exchanges goods for advertising time or space. Traditionally this has been done at the local market level among small advertisers, but Braniff International airlines recently announced that it would join Continental and Pan Am airlines in bartering for advertising time and space.[4]

A more formal (and expensive) form of barter is barter syndication.

[4] Josh Levine, "Braniff Betting on Better Barter," *Advertising Age,* January 14, 1980, p. 1.

The idea of barter syndication is a simple one. Advertisers supply a show to television stations. This show usually carries two minutes of commercial time for the advertiser who provided the show. In addition the station is provided three to four minutes to sell to national or local advertisers. The advertiser has a property which he controls and which fulfills his program requirements. The station has a free program plus the money it earns from nonbartered spots.

At one time bartered shows had the stigma of being those which could not be sold. However, in recent years some of television's most popular syndicated shows have been fully or partly bartered. Such shows include "Hee Haw," "Wild Kingdom," and "Carol Burnett and Friends."

Syndication

Only a few years ago television syndication was a simple process. Network shows ran their course, and when their primetime ratings started to fall, they were relegated to the minor leagues of afternoon reruns. Local stations were provided with inexpensive afternoon fillers, and networks made some extra profit in addition to what the shows had brought in during their first run.

The economics of syndicated programming changed drastically in 1971 with the passage of the FCC's primetime access rule. One of the provisions of the rule denied off-network reruns to network affiliates in the top 50 markets in the 7:00–8:00 P.M. slot formerly programmed by the networks. Independent stations in these large markets were not restricted by the rule, and they moved quickly to challenge network affiliates with syndicated shows such as the "Mary Tyler Moore Show" and "Sanford and Son." During this same period the demand by advertisers for additional commercial time was increasing, and advertisers began to buy independents. In addition the "superstation," which is an independent carried by satellite to cable systems around the country, brought network nonaffiliates or independents high advertising revenues which could then be used to buy popular programs.

In the last five years, the prices paid by stations in the largest markets for syndicated network reruns have increased dramatically. In 1970 the per-episode price for reruns of "Petticoat Junction" in these large markets was $6,500. By 1978 the price per episode of the "Mary Tyler Moore Show" was $38,000 and that of "Laverne and Shirley" was more than $60,000. These prices give stations the right to up to 14 repeats over a period of from five to seven years. It is estimated that "All in the Family" will produce gross syndication revenues of almost $80 million. This is in addition to the $40 million paid by CBS to the producer, TAT Communications, for network showings.[5]

The increase in syndication prices has not only altered the economics of reruns and their advertising rates, but has also changed the basic relationship between networks and the producers who supply the majority of television series. As the profitability of reruns increases, the networks can justify paying producers lower rates per show. According to program producers, this is happening. In recent years major producers have claimed that network fees are less than production costs. A series usually needs three to five years (75–120 shows) of network production before enough episodes are available for effective syndication. Consequently, the producer has less of a bargaining position as the length of the series run (and potential syndication profitability) increases.

Added to what is fundamentally an internal broadcast industry problem is the lack of quality (popular) series reruns. The ideal syndicated series runs one-half hour, is a comedy and appeals to a family audience. The number of network series that meet these criteria and have taped 100 or more episodes is small. Existing demand, coupled with a scarcity of shows, will continue to drive up the costs of syndication to stations and advertising rates to sponsors. This is particularly true as more stations "strip" their syndicated programs by running a single show five days a week.

FACTORS TO CONSIDER IN BUYING TELEVISION

Advertisers considering television as an advertising medium are told that it combines sight, sound, and motion with a broad potential reach. Television provides immediacy, prestige, and instant recognition to a brand. All of these features are certainly potential benefits of television and worthy of examination by a prospective advertiser. However, from a marketing and managerial perspective, other less often discussed issues should also be considered.

Inflation

In the view of many advertisers television costs got completely out-of-hand in the 1970s. While audience size showed minimal increases, overall costs and CPMs for network advertising doubled. Current predictions are for increases of 15 to 18 percent annually in the cost of network time. There appears to be no end in sight. With supplies of

[5] "Chips off Old Hit Series Transform into Big Bucks," *Advertising Age,* March 5, 1979, pp. 5–22.

commercial time virtually fixed, the quadrennial election cycle and Olympics only serve to drive prices up more sharply with new or infrequent advertisers vying for time.

The networks seem to be insulated from even macroeconomic factors such as recession and inflation. During recessionary periods in 1974 and 1979, television revenues experienced no downturn. The increases in television costs have not been accomplished without some rancor between advertisers and the networks. In 1976 advertisers were particularly incensed at what Archa Knowlton, then director of media services at General Foods, labeled "unconscionable" rate increases.[6]

Despite the complaints, most advertisers see little relief in television costs in the future. Over the past several years a few advertisers withdrew from the medium, but most returned within a few months. Some agencies and advertisers have participated in primetime syndication projects such as Mobil's "Ten Who Dared" as a "fourth network" concept to compete with the networks. However, these shows do nothing to expand the available commercial time, and, if anything, costs of advertising are exceeded only by program production costs, hardly a saving to the producer of such projects.

In addition to these problems, new categories of advertisers have come into the medium, further sharpening demand. The effects of local advertisers on national spot advertising were discussed earlier. But fast-food chains, video equipment, and national retailers have become major television advertisers in recent years. Today both Sears and McDonald's are among the top 20 network advertisers.[7]

The basic cause of the continuing inflation in television prices is that advertisers think television sells products better than alternatives. During most dayparts, television delivers audiences at a CPM significantly less than that of magazines, the major alternative for most national advertisers. As long as advertisers successfully sell their products through television, demand for time and commercial costs will remain high. *Advertising Age* estimated 30-second commercial rates at between $150,000 ("M*A*S*H") and $55,000 in the fall of 1979. Since then most rate estimates have increased substantially.

Clutter

Advertisers are concerned not only about the high cost of advertising but also about the number of television commercials. The "clutter" problem is a three-sided dispute between advertisers, station affili-

[6] Marvin H. Zim, "Inflation Isn't Over in TV Advertising Rates," *Fortune,* November 6, 1978, p. 54.

[7] *Advertising Age,* September 6, 1979, p. 62.

ates, and the networks. Stations charge that networks have expanded their commercial time and reduced the number of local primetime spots, thereby depriving local stations of millions of dollars in revenues. A study by the Station Representative Association charged that the networks carried 638 more commercial minutes in the second quarter of 1978 than were permitted under existing standards. CBS vehemently denied this charge.[8]

The problem of advertising clutter is partly one of definition. The National Association of Broadcasters (NAB) has set the maximum time for nonprogram material at 9½ minutes per hour during primetime. Nonprogram material includes commercials, program promotions, billboards, and program credits. A question has arisen as to whether some of these announcements, for instance public service announcements, should be counted against the 9½ minute limit.

Added to the confusion are recent announcements by the NAB and the Justice Department concerning clutter. Starting January 1, 1980, the NAB's TV Code Board increased the "nonprogram material" limit to ten minutes. The NAB claims that clearer definitions of nonprogram material will reduce clutter by counting material which formerly was not included in the category. However, many advertisers remain skeptical that this increase will alleviate the clutter problem.

Perhaps the most surprising entry into the clutter dispute was the U.S. Justice Department. In June 1979 the department filed a civil antitrust suit against the NAB. It sought to overturn the association's 9½-minute limit. The department contended that this limit on supply keeps television advertising rates much higher than they would be if competition were freer.[9] But adding more commercial time to an already overcrowded schedule hardly seems the solution to most advertisers.

Finally, advertisers themselves are partly responsible for the clutter problem. Their multiple product (piggyback) commercials create the illusion of excess advertising even though these commercials do not increase the number of commercial minutes. They do increase the number of exposures to product claims and brand names during any time period. The NAB Television Code specified that "a multiple product announcement shall not be scheduled in a unit of time less than 60 seconds, except where integrated so as to appear to the viewer as a single message." In fact most piggyback announcements are 30 seconds, and only the most flagrant violations (e.g., three different products) are questioned.

---

[8] "Are the TV Networks Selling Too Many Ads?" *Business Week,* September 18, 1978, p. 26.

[9] Jack Egan, "Network Advertising: The $1.6 Billion Pyramid," *New York,* July 23, 1979, p. 12.

The extent to which advertising is hurt by clutter is an empirical question. At what intensity of television advertising are consumer perception and retention of commercial messages impaired? Studies of clutter indicate that the amount, nature (advertising versus other noncommercial material), and creativity of the advertising and the advertiser's budget all play a role in how clutter affects advertising. However, there are no definitive guidelines concerning the exact point at which advertising is damaged by clutter.

The fragmented audience

In the past television advertisers had two alternatives for their advertising schedule. At the national level the three networks provided the only television coverage. In all but the largest markets advertisers could only choose among the three affiliated stations. Even in the few major markets where independent television stations existed, these alternatives were largely ignored by national advertisers.

In the late 1970s several factors combined to increase the options and complexities of buying television advertising. These changes included:

1. *New technology.* Advertisers found that a number of innovations made the system of networks and affiliates only one of a number of options. Independent stations and "superstations" are examples of such expansion. It should be noted, however, that predictions of the demise of the network/affiliate relationship are premature at best.
2. *Greater demand for commercial time.* The relatively fixed inventory of television commercial minutes and increasing demand for this time forced advertisers to look for nontelevision advertising alternatives. Some advertisers moved into other media; others looked to forms of television that they had formerly ignored or underutilized.
3. *Aggressive selling by independents and cable.* Taking advantage of the increased demand for television time, independent stations and a few cable operators began to compete aggressively for advertising dollars.
4. *Changing emphasis in marketing strategy.* National advertisers began to examine the value and desirability of audience segmentation. They found that in some cases nontraditional broadcast outlets offered specialized programming (particularly sports) more suited to their needs and often at a lower CPM than network or affiliate buys.

For the last decade marketing theory has trumpeted the advantages of developing more specialized media. The supposition was that an increasingly fragmented audience would be an advantage to all parties. Programming would be more specifically directed to individual rather than mass tastes. The fragmented audience would offer the communication industry more opportunities for entry, thereby creating an expanded information and entertainment industry. Finally, advertisers would benefit by decreasing the waste circulation found in current mass media outlets.

In recent years both advertisers and the television industry have started to realize that segmentation carries with it risks and costs that will require future adjustments. For instance the historical rule of thumb for measuring the success of a network show was that it should attain a 30 share of audience. Under normal circumstances anything less than a 27 share placed the show's existence in jeopardy.

The 30 share guideline is no longer the standard. While the network share of noncable households remains approximately 90 percent, network programming makes up only about 80 percent of viewing in cable homes. As cable penetration increases from its present 20 percent of households, networks will show a decrease in share of overall viewing.

Since each program source has to cover certain overhead expenses regardless of audience size, we will not see a drop in advertising rates proportionate to the decrease in per-channel audience. Fragmentation of what has been an audience divided "into thirds" means that CPMs will increase significantly (see Figure 5–5). Part of this increase in CPM will be offset by lower waste circulation. Thus the advertiser will have a more favorable CPM/prospect cost. However, even with this more favorable targeting of prospects, advertisers must expect higher real costs in the future.

As the hypothetical case in Figure 5–5 demonstrates, advertisers are faced with increasing CPM. In addition more astute media planning will be required to reach the fragmented audience of the 1980s. Figure 5–5 points up another problem which is potentially more ominous than higher advertising costs. As we have noted, four of the ten viewing alternatives are noncommercial. The introduction of videotape recorders (VTRs) allows viewers to record programs for viewing at their preference (time-shift viewing), and some VTRs can delete commercials from the program. Consequently, the advertiser runs the risk of having an audience different from the intended audience view the show or of having no audience at all for commercial messages.

Let's take a brief look at the best prospects for the fragmented television of the future.

Cable television. The oldest of the "new" technology, cable has changed from a means for transmitting weak signals to isolated areas to a major force in broadcasting. Currently 4,000 cable systems covering approximately 16 million households are in operation. By 1985 cable penetration should be close to 50 percent, or about 40 million households. The distribution of distant signals as well as the expansion of types of television service will offer greater diversity to the public and new problems for media planners. The expansion of satellite transmission has created opportunities for networklike systems such as the superstations. These independent stations, such as WGN in Chicago and WTBS in Atlanta, have gained national coverage through cable systems.

The full utilization of cable as an advertising vehicle rather than a carrier of other programming has yet to be achieved. Cable-originated programming is largely confined to weather displays or news spots. A few cable systems have programmed movies or local programs, but advertiser interest is almost nonexistent.

Pay television. There are two basic systems of pay television: pay cable and subscription television. Pay cable provides noncom-

Figure 5–5
Effects of audience fragmentation on TV costs in a local market

1975: Three-station market (market population = 100,000 TV households)	*Average primetime audience*	*Share of audience*	*Cost per 30 seconds*	*CPM per household*
ABC affiliate	22,000	38.6	$150	$ 6.82
NBC affiliate	15,000	26.3	90	6.00
CBS affiliate	20,000	35.1	130	6.50
Average HUT	57,000 (57%)			
1980: Four-station market with cable (market population = 120,000 TV households)				
ABC affiliate	18,000	22.7	180	10.00
ABC affiliate*	11,000	13.8	100	9.09
NBC affiliate	16,000	20.0	130	8.13
CBS affiliate	17,000	21.4	170	10.00
CBS affiliate*	10,500	13.2	120	11.43
Home Box Office—pay TV†	3,500	4.4	2	—
Cable news network	1,200	1.5	2	—
Cable system channel	1,150	1.4	40	34.78
Videodisc and other off-broadcast video equipment†	300	.3	2	—
Educational station†	800	1.0	2	—
Average HUT	79,450 (66.2%)			

* A second network affiliate brought in by cable.
† Noncommercial

mercial programming to cable subscribers at an additional cost over the basic service charge. Most programs are transmitted by satellite to local cable systems and then sent to homes equipped with a decoder to unscramble the signal. The two largest pay television companies are Home Box Office (HBO) and Showtime.

Subscription television provides pay television through over-the-air signals which are decoded by a box in subscribers' homes. The advantage of subscription television is that it is not limited to cable households. However, at present subscription television is much less popular than pay cable. While pay television systems are noncommercial, some consideration is being given to accepting limited amounts of commercial time in the future. Pay television may well be yet another advertising alternative in the near future.

Home video equipment. Another source of audience fragmentation is the videocassette recorder and the videodisc player. The videocassette recorder can play bought or rented tapes or record programs off a regular television set. Videodisc players can use only purchased discs, usually movies. Discs vary widely in price but usually sell for approximately $60. In 1979 videocassette player sales fell far below industry expectations. Whether this shortfall was a result of economic recession, indecision about which of the several incompatible systems to purchase, or a real softening of the market for such players remains unclear.

Home information technology. Systems for the transmission of words have been developed recently. There are basically two systems under the generic name videotext. The first of these systems is teletext. Teletext uses the black lines at the top of the television picture (hidden by the cabinet), called the "vertical blanking interval," to carry signals which allow words and symbols to be displayed on the screens of sets equipped to convert the signals.

The British Broadcasting Corporation (BBC) has experimented with teletext since 1972. Currently 25,000 homes in Great Britain have access to the three channels provided by the BBC or its commercial counterpart. In this country experiments with some form of videotext are being conducted by KSL-TV in Salt Lake City, by KMOX-TV in St. Louis, and by Knight-Ridder in Miami.

Broadcasters have some apprehension about home information systems. Some stations and advertisers fear that viewer control over information might drastically reduce the audience for commercials. However, others see major opportunities to increase advertising revenues by providing advertising with a more narrowly defined audience of prospects. This concept of narrowcasting as opposed to broadcasting may have particular applications to classified advertising which appeals to only a small minority of the audience on any given day. With the addition of printers, sales literature with commercial messages could be delivered to a select, interested audience.

A significantly more complex type of videotext is viewdata. Whereas teletext is broadcast, viewdata utilizes telephone or cable systems to make the home television receiver interactive with a central computer. Viewdata gives the viewer access to several data sources and a virtually limitless amount of data. Teletext is limited to about 200 "pages." Providers of information, or data banks, sign up with the computer company for a fee, and the viewer pays a small amount to the company on a per-page-viewed basis as well as an initial hookup charge. In England the data banks provide a wide range of information, including adult education materials, airline schedules, mail-order offers, and even television games.

Another version of home information technology is the individually owned computer. The home computer can be purchased for about $500, but the problem has been in obtaining software programs to give the computer broad utility to the owner, who is usually unskilled in computer programming. Telecomputing Corporation of America (TCA) is providing this utility to the home computer through a data retrieval system called The Source.

The Source offers several information data sources, including all United Press International wire services, through its New Share system. In addition the home user has access to several syndicated news services, including the *New York Times.* The Source's retrieval capability also has long-range implications for direct selling and advertising.

Assume that a person is considering the purchase of a boat. The specifications of the desired boat could be placed in the computer, and all newspaper classified advertisements could be made available to the prospective buyer. Several newspapers already sell advertising in combination with cable television systems. As we will discuss in a later chapter, many advertisers see classified advertising as the most viable short-term use of the computer-based "electronic newspaper."

Two-way cable. The era of two-way cable began in this country in December 1977, when Warner Communications introduced its QUBE system in Columbus, Ohio. Cable households could call up any of 30 available channels, including normal network and independent stations. Like the videotext systems, QUBE allows the viewer to control the information received. Unlike videotext, QUBE and other two-way cable systems are not limited to text. The QUBE subscriber can request variable-length commercials called Qubits as well as other specialized programming of an entertainment, educational, and commercial nature.

Not only do two-way cable systems provide versatility to the viewer, but they have many implications for realistic advertising research. Since these systems allow instant identification of the consumers who request certain information, it is easier and more accurate to conduct audience research by using two-way cable than by using general sampling techniques which must search for these same people in the general population. However, the full utilization of two-way cable for research must await the day when it has gained more acceptance in the general population. Current users of such systems are not representative of the general population.

BUYING TELEVISION

When the media planner has considered all the dayparts, formats, and programs offered by television, the job of buying time has only begun. The buying of television advertising time is divided into several categories, depending on the nature of the buy. There are three areas of buying television:

1. Primetime network buys.
2. National spot buys.
3. Local buys.

Primetime network buys

At the television network level you are dealing with experienced experts in buying and selling time. Corporate advertising directors, agency media executives, and network salespeople must consistently prove that their selling and negotiating skills and judgment are better than those of their competitors. The major buying period for network advertising is in the early spring. Figure 5–6 examines a hypothetical network and advertiser as the firm makes its network buys for the following season.

National spot buys

In some ways planning television spot buys in major markets requires even more skill than buying network advertising. Instead of buying three networks, the media planner is faced with more than 700 station coverage areas and audiences in approximately 200 major television markets.

These areas are usually referred to as Areas of Dominant Influence (ADIs), a term used by the Arbitron Syndicated Research Service to designate a unique group of counties served by a particular market's

Figure 5–6
Buying network

January 1981

The Smith-Moore Advertising Agency meets with its client, Xenia, Inc., to outline the marketing strategy, budget, and advertising schedule, including television, for the coming year. Since Xenia devotes a major portion of its advertising budget to network advertising, emphasis is given to the fall television season.

March 1981

The United Television System (UTS) announces its tentative fall schedule with a presentation of pilot shows to major agencies. The schedule is divided into three categories and costs as follows:

	Anticipated average audience share	*Average 30-second cost*
Returning hits, major films, specials	33	$100,000
Returning shows, new shows with promise (known talent, good lead-in, etc.)	30	80,000
Marginal shows (unknown talent, scheduled opposite highly rated show, etc.)	26	60,000

April 1981

The networks begin negotiations with major advertisers who are willing to buy early at a premium rate to have a better selection of shows (called up-front buys). Smith-Moore places $4 million (25 percent) of Xenia's $16 million network television budget in up-front UTS buys. Another $7 million is spent on other network time, leaving $5 million designated for later network advertising. Smith-Moore agrees to pay approximately 85 percent of UTS's original asking price.

June 1981

The networks begin to reduce their prices as the best spots on major properties are bought. Smith-Moore places all but $3 million in these "inexpensive" spots at an average cost of $48,000 per 30-second commercial.

August 1981

Based on the scheduling of other networks and evaluations by agency buyers and network programmers, UTS decides to cancel two upcoming shows and to shift three others to different times or days. Xenia had spots on all five shows. Network salespeople offer Smith-Moore the same time

Figure 5–6 (*continued*)

on the shows which were moved and spots are available on the substituted shows. Smith-Moore agrees to keep its spots on the three rescheduled shows and asks the network for a 10 percent reduction in price. It settles on a 6 percent price adjustment. One of the new shows is acceptable; the other is not. Smith-Moore cancels the contract on the second show and moves the spots to CBS.

October 1981

"The National Clown Hour," one of the new UTS shows purchased by Smith-Moore, achieves a rating of 11 and an audience share of 16. It is canceled after six embarrassing weeks, and Smith-Moore asks for a substantial rebate since an 18 rating/30 share had been anticipated. After some negotiation the network agrees to schedule a Xenia spot for six weeks in each of UTS's top three rated shows and to price the spots at 15 percent below the market price.

March–August 1982

Smith-Moore takes advantage of advertiser cancellations and a small number of unpurchased network spots to spend the remaining $2 million allocated to network television.

stations. An ADI includes all counties in which the central market's stations receive the major viewership. There are currently 209 ADIs, and these are reevaluated annually, with counties being added or deleted as station coverage patterns change.

ADIs are normally determined by the concentration of population, with large metro areas including as few as three or four counties in their ADIs, while the Salt Lake City ADI covers all of Utah and parts of Idaho and Wyoming. The ADI may be used not only to buy television but also to designate general market areas for local advertising buys in all media. Thus a national advertiser may plan regional magazine buys to conform as closely as possible to spot television bought on the basis of ADIs. The A. C. Nielsen Company has a similar technique to measure coverage areas known as the Designated Market Area (DMA).

The astute media planner will generally use the services of a station representative when buying spot television. The job of the television representative has expanded from simply selling time to advising local television stations on a host of topics, including rate setting, programming, and overall station sales policies. The primary task of the rep remains selling, and recent developments in computer-based research and inventory control have been directed toward this function.

Television reps are paid a commission of from 5 to 15 percent by the stations they represent. The average commission is about 10 percent. A rep in a major market may earn $50,000–75,000, and $25,000 is the average annual earnings of reps in medium-sized markets. The two largest reps both in revenues and in stations represented are Blair and Katz.

Local buys

Normally local television sales are handled by a station's own sales force. A station in a "top 20" market may have as many as 20 salespersons, while a station in a small market may have only two or three persons in the sales department.

In small markets the station sales department is responsible for local advertising. In large markets a local salesperson may approach national spot advertisers as well as local concerns. Since the station's rep may attempt to sell the same company, disagreements sometimes arise between the rep and the station over who actually sold the time.

To prevent this problem, reps may agree not to approach certain advertisers. In the future we may see a station pay the rep a lower percentage of all station billings. In rare instances the station may turn over its entire sales operation to a rep organization. When problems arise between a station's sales force and its rep, it is important not to involve the advertiser. Advertisers are not interested in internal station sales problems, and rather than become involved they may take their business elsewhere.

Television rate structure

Regardless of the level at which television time is bought, the same basic rate structure applies. Throughout television, the fixed rate is disappearing, if not gone. Rates are computed on length of continuity requested, demand from other advertisers, and volume of annual business. However, most television time is purchased by negotiation and in "packages" of several commercials rather than single spots. Normally neither an advertiser nor the station/network could (or would) quote a price for a single spot. The cost per rating point (CPP) or the average cost per spot can be computed, but not the single commercial price. As discussed in Chapter 4, the weight of a schedule is measured in Gross Rating Points (GRPs), and various estimating guides are used to give the buyer a preliminary idea of broadcast costs.

When rate cards or directory listings (such as *Spot Television SRDS*) exist, they are usually intended as a general guide. Because of the negotiated nature of television buys, price lists, called grids, are often coded so that some or all prices are not given for specific spots. There are three types of grid cards: full disclosure cards, nondisclosure cards, and partial disclosure cards, which give rates for only a portion of the schedule. Within these grids prices are also quoted for fixed (guaranteed) rates and preemptible rates (when another advertiser agrees to pay a higher rate than the fixed rate) (see Figure 5–7).

Figure 5–7
Examples of grids in television pricing

Full-disclosure grid: Primetime, 30 seconds

	Fixed	*I*	*II*
"60 Minutes"	100*	†	†
"Archie's Place"	90	80	60
"The Jeffersons"	90	75	55
"Alice"	80	60	50

Nondisclosure grid: 30 seconds

Code ‡			
1	100	6	55
2	90	7	50
3	80	8	45
4	70	9	40
5	60	10	35

* Units in dollars.
† No preemptible rate available.
‡ Average rates for estimating: Early morning (9/10); daytime (4/8); fringe time (5/7); primetime (1/4).

Because of the complex nature of television rates, the rep can be valuable to the spot advertiser. Since the rep's firm is aware of the rate structure of the client stations, the rep can save the media buyer much time which would be spent either in contacting stations or in making wrong estimates.

Television discounts and special features

Three types of television discounts are offered. (For a discussion of the broadcast discounts most applicable to radio, see Chapter 6.) These are:

1. *Bulk discount*—offered for purchasing a certain number of spots, usually within a month or year.
2. *Volume discount*—based on dollars spent during a set period.
3. *Continuity discount*—given for consecutive advertising over a set number of weeks.

In addition two other features are often associated with television prices:

1. *Product protection.* Many stations attempt to keep a ten-minute separation between competing products. However, most stations will not offer rebates unless competing commercials are back to back.
2. *News and special features.* Stations may have different rates for news and other special features. The media buyer should check the rate card carefully or contact the station when considering such purchases.

TELEVISION RATINGS

Television, more than any other medium, lives and dies by the rating numbers. As we have mentioned earlier, a shift of only one rating point can mean a difference of millions of dollars annually to a network. Ratings are no less important to the revenues of a local station. Currently television ratings are dominated by two firms: Arbitron and Nielsen. Arbitron is stronger in the local station ratings, while Nielsen dominates the national ratings. Although there are some differences in the methodology and the reports of the two services, basically the services are quite similar. In order to give an overview of the basic rating services we will briefly outline the primary Nielsen services.

Nielsen Television Index (NTI)

The NTI, based on a national sample, is one of the two major reporting systems offered by the A. C. Nielsen Company. The foundation of the NTI System is the Storage Instantaneous Audimeter (SIA, or simply Audimeter). The Audimeter is a device which is mechanically and electrically fixed to the television receiver. It automatically records the time of day and the date, whether the receiver is turned on and when, and the electronic frequency of the station being received. The Audimeter is supplemented with a viewer diary called an Audilog.

The national Nielsen service uses two samples of national household ratings. The NTI provides household ratings based on 1,200 metered households. The National Audience Composition (NAC) sample of 3,200 reports individual diary data. The major NTI and NTI/NAC reports include:

1. *NTI National Nielsen TV Ratings.* This is the most familiar report, often referred to as the "pocket piece" because of its size.

Figure 5–8
1980–81 Nielsen Station Index measurement schedule

Market	Oct.	Nov.	Jan.	Feb.	Mar.	May	July
Abilene-Sweetwater		V		V		V	V
Ada-Ardmore		V		V		V	V
Akron		V		V		V	
Albany-Schenectady-Troy		V		V		V	V
Albany, GA		V		V		V	V
Albuquerque		V		V		V	V
Alexandria, LA		V		V		V	V
Alexandria, MN		V		V		V	V
Alpena, MI		V		V		V	V
Amarillo		V		V		V	V
Anniston		V		V		V	
Atlanta	V	V	V	V		V	V
Augusta, GA		V		V		V	V
Austin		V		V		V	V
Bakersfield		V		V		V	V
Baltimore	V	V	V	V		V	V
Bangor		V		V		V	V
Baton Rouge		V		V		V	V
Beaumont-Port Arthur		V		V		V	V
Beckley-Bluefield-Oak Hill		V		V		V	V
Bend, OR		V		V		V	
Billings		V		V		V	V
Biloxi-Gulfport		V		V		V	V
Binghamton		V		V		V	V
Birmingham		V		V		V	V
Boise		V		V		V	V
·Boston	V	V	V	V	V	V	V
Bowling Green		V		V		V	
Buffalo	V	V	V	V		V	V
Burlington-Plattsburgh		V		V		V	V
Butte		V		V		V	V
Casper-Riverton		V		V		V	V
Cedar Rapids-Waterloo		V		V		V	V
Champaign & Springfield-Decatur		V		V		V	V
Charleston-Huntington		V		V		V	V
Charleston, SC		V		V		V	V
Charlotte		V		V		V	V
Charlottesville		V		V		V	
Chattanooga		V		V		V	V
Cheyenne-Scottsbluff-Sterling		V		V		V	V
Chicago	V	V	V	V	V	V	V
Chicago-M/M Weeklies	•	•	•	•	•	•	•
Chico-Redding		V		V		V	V
Cincinnati	V	V	V	V		V	V
Clarksburg-Weston		V		V		V	V
·Cleveland	V	V	V	V	V	V	V
Colorado Springs-Pueblo		V		V		V	V
Columbia-Jefferson City		V		V		V	V
Columbia, SC		V		V		V	V
Columbus-Tupelo, MS		V		V		V	V
Columbus, GA		V		V		V	V
Columbus, OH		V		V		V	V
Corpus Christi		V		V		V	V
·Dallas-Ft. Worth	V	V		V		V	V
Davenport-Rock Island-Moline		V		V		V	V
Dayton		V		V		V	V
Denver		V		V		V	V
Des Moines-Ames		V		V		V	V
·Detroit	V	V	V	V		V	V
Dothan		V		V		V	V
Dubuque		V		V		V	
Duluth-Superior		V		V		V	V
El Paso		V		V		V	V
Elmira		V		V		V	
Ensign-Garden City		V		V		V	
Erie		V		V		V	V
Eugene		V		V		V	V
Eureka		V		V		V	V
Evansville		V		V		V	V
Fargo-Valley City		V		V		V	V
Farmington, NM		V		V		V	
Flagstaff		V		V		V	
Flint-Saginaw-Bay City		V		V		V	V
Florence (Muscle Shoals), AL		V		V		V	
Florence, SC		V		V		V	V
Fresno (Visalia)		V		V		V	V
Ft. Myers-Naples		V		V		V	V
Ft. Smith		V		V		V	V
Ft. Wayne		V		V		V	V
Gainesville		V		V		V	V
Glendive		V		V		V	V
Grand Junction-Montrose		V		V		V	V
Grand Rapids-Kalamazoo-Battle Creek		V		V		V	V
Great Bend		V		V		V	
Great Falls		V		V		V	V
Green Bay		V		V		V	V
Greensboro-High Point-Winston Salem		V		V		V	V
Greenville-New Bern-Washington		V		V		V	V
Greenville-Spartanburg-Asheville		V		V		V	V
Greenwood		V		V		V	V
Hagerstown		V		V		V	V

Market	Oct.	Nov.	Jan.	Feb.	Mar.	May	July
Harlingen-Weslaco		V		V		V	V
Harrisburg-Lancaster-Lebanon-York		V		V		V	V
Harrisonburg		V		V		V	V
Hartford & New Haven		V		V		V	V
Hattiesburg-Laurel		V		V		V	V
Hays-Goodland		V		V		V	
Honolulu		V		V		V	
·Houston	V	V		V		V	V
Huntsville-Decatur		V		V		V	V
Idaho Falls-Pocatello		V		V		V	V
Indianapolis		V		V		V	V
Jackson, MS		V		V		V	V
Jackson, TN		V		V		V	V
Jacksonville		V		V		V	V
Johnstown-Altoona		V		V		V	V
Jonesboro		V		V		V	V
Joplin-Pittsburg		V		V		V	V
Kansas City	V	V	V	V		V	V
Knoxville		V		V		V	V
LaCrosse-Eau Claire		V		V		V	V
Lafayette, IN		V		V		V	
Lafayette, LA		V		V		V	V
Lake Charles		V		V		V	V
Lansing		V		V		V	V
Laredo		V		V		V	V
Las Vegas		V		V		V	V
Lexington		V		V		V	V
Lima		V		V		V	V
Lincoln & Hastings-Kearney		V		V		V	V
Little Rock-Pine Bluff		V		V		V	V
Los Angeles	V	V	V	V	V	V	V
Los Angeles-M/M Weeklies	•	•	•	•	•	•	•
Louisville		V		V		V	V
Lubbock		V		V		V	V
Macon		V		V		V	V
Madison		V		V		V	V
Manchester		V		V		V	
Mankato		V		V		V	V
Marquette		V		V		V	V
Mason City-Austin-Rochester		V		V		V	V
Medford-Klamath Falls		V		V		V	V
Memphis		V		V		V	V
Meridian		V		V		V	V
·Miami-Ft. Lauderdale	V	V		V		V	V
Milwaukee	V	V	V	V		V	V
Minneapolis-St. Paul	V	V	V	V		V	V
Minot-Bismarck-Dickinson (Williston)		V		V		V	V
Missoula		V		V		V	V
Mobile-Pensacola		V		V		V	V
Monroe-El Dorado		V		V		V	V
Monterey-Salinas		V		V		V	V
Montgomery		V		V		V	V
Nashville		V		V		V	V
New Orleans	V	V		V		V	V
New York	V	V	V	V	V	V	V
New York-M/M Weeklies	•	•	•	•	•	•	•
Norfolk-Portsmouth-Newport News		V		V		V	V
North Platte-Hayes-McCook		V		V		V	V
Odessa-Midland-Monahans		V		V		V	V
Oklahoma City		V		V		V	V
Omaha		V		V		V	V
Orlando-Daytona Beach		V		V		V	V
Ottumwa-Kirksville		V		V		V	V
Paducah-Cape Girardeau-Harrisburg		V		V		V	V
Palm Springs		V		V		V	
Panama City		V		V		V	V
Parkersburg		V		V		V	V
Peoria		V		V		V	V
·Philadelphia	V	V	V	V	V	V	V
Phoenix		V		V		V	V
·Pittsburgh	V	V	V	V		V	V
Portland-Poland Spring		V		V		V	V
Portland, OR		V		V		V	V
Presque Isle		V		V		V	V
Providence		V		V		V	V
Quincy-Hannibal-Keokuk		V		V		V	V
Raleigh-Durham		V		V		V	V

Market	Oct.	Nov.	Jan.	Feb.	Mar.	May	July
Rapid City		V		V		V	V
Reno		V		V		V	V
Rhinelander		V		V		V	V
Richmond-Petersburg		V		V		V	V
Roanoke-Lynchburg		V		V		V	V
Rochester		V		V		V	V
Rockford		V		V		V	V
Roswell		V		V		V	V
Sacramento-Stockton		V		V		V	V
Salisbury		V		V		V	V
Salt Lake City		V		V		V	V
San Angelo		V		V		V	V
San Antonio		V		V		V	V
San Diego		V		V		V	V
San Francisco-Oakland	V	V	V	V	V	V	V
San Francisco-Oakland-M/M Weeklies	•	•	•	•	•	•	•
Santa Barbara-Santa Maria-San Luis Ob.		V		V		V	V
Sarasota		V		V		V	
Savannah		V		V		V	V
Seattle-Tacoma	V	V		V		V	V
Shreveport		V		V		V	V
Sioux City		V		V		V	V
Sioux Falls (Mitchell)		V		V		V	V
South Bend-Elkhart		V		V		V	V
Spokane		V		V		V	V
Springfield-Holyoke		V		V		V	V
Springfield, MO		V		V		V	V
St. Joseph		V		V		V	V
·St. Louis	V	V	V	V		V	V
Syracuse		V		V		V	V
Tallahassee-Thomasville		V		V		V	V
Tampa-St. Petersburg		V		V		V	V
TerreHaute		V		V		V	V
Toledo		V		V		V	V
Topeka		V		V		V	V
Traverse City-Cadillac		V		V		V	V
Tri Cities, TN-VA (Bristol-Johnson City-Kingsport)		V		V		V	V
Tucson (Nogales)		V		V		V	V
Tulsa		V		V		V	V
Twin Falls		V		V		V	V
Tyler		V		V		V	V
Utica		V		V		V	V
Waco-Temple		V		V		V	V
·Washington, DC	V	V	V	V		V	V
Watertown		V		V		V	V
Wausau		V		V		V	V
West Palm Beach-Ft. Pierce		V		V		V	V
Wheeling-Steubenville		V		V		V	V
Wichita Falls & Lawton		V		V		V	V
Wichita-Hutchinson		V		V		V	V
Wilkes Barre-Scranton		V		V		V	V
Wilmington		V		V		V	V
Worcester		V		V		V	
Yakima		V		V		V	V
Youngstown		V		V		V	V
Yuma-El Centro		V		V		V	V
Zanesville		V		V		V	V

MONTH	DATE	# MARKETS
October, 1980	9/25-10/22	23
November, 1980	10/30-11/26	ALL
January, 1981	1/8-2/4	18
February, 1981	2/5-3/4	ALL
March, 1981	3/5-4/1	7
May, 1981	4/30-5/27	ALL
July, 1981	7/9-8/5	ALL DMA's

V - Viewers in Profile

·Preview's are issued for selected measurement periods.

•Weekly Reports

Issued biweekly, it reports ratings for all network programs 48 weeks during the year.

2. *NTI Multi-Network Area Ratings (Fast MNA).* The Fast MNA reports the weekly network audience for the largest 70 markets with full network service.
3. *NTI Market Section Audiences.* The MSA report, issued nine times annually, describes the households tuned to network programs on ten variables, including household income, education of head of household, and household size.
4. *NTI Brand Cumulative Audience Report.* The BCA Report measures how advertising for individual brands performs against competition. It is issued three times a year.
5. *NTI/NAC Audience Demographics (NAD).* The NAD is the basic demographic report of the Nielsen service. Issued 15 times a year, it provides estimates of individual viewing of network programs. In addition to the basic NTI/NAC service four supplementary reports are issued.

Nielsen Station Index (NSI)

Diaries and meters are combined to gather data for the NSI reports. However, Nielsen's basic local market reports utilize primarily the Audilog diary. NSI issues three principal reports:

1. NSI metered services reports are issued for New York, Los Angeles, Chicago, and San Francisco. These markets include approximately 20 percent of U.S. TV households.
2. Three times a year—November, February, and May—all television markets are measured. These are the "sweep" periods, and the *Viewer in Profile* report provides the results of these ratings. Since the ratings are conducted so infrequently, they are extremely important to local station spot sales and local advertising. A continuing controversy surrounds the artificial inflation of ratings by networks and local stations which schedule extraordinary programming during these periods.
3. Five times a year NSI issues a key markets rating to supplement the regular *Viewer in Profile* report. See Figure 5–8 for a typical schedule of measurement periods.

Local Nielsen ratings report audience levels for three different geographic areas surrounding the station: (1) the Metro Area, (2) the Designated Market Area (DMA), or Area of Dominant Influence (ADI) in Arbitron reports; and (3) the NSI Area (the Total Survey Area in Arbitron). See Figure 5–9 for a full description of these areas. These reports are recapitulated in Figure 5–10.

Figure 5–9
***Viewer in Profile* market data**

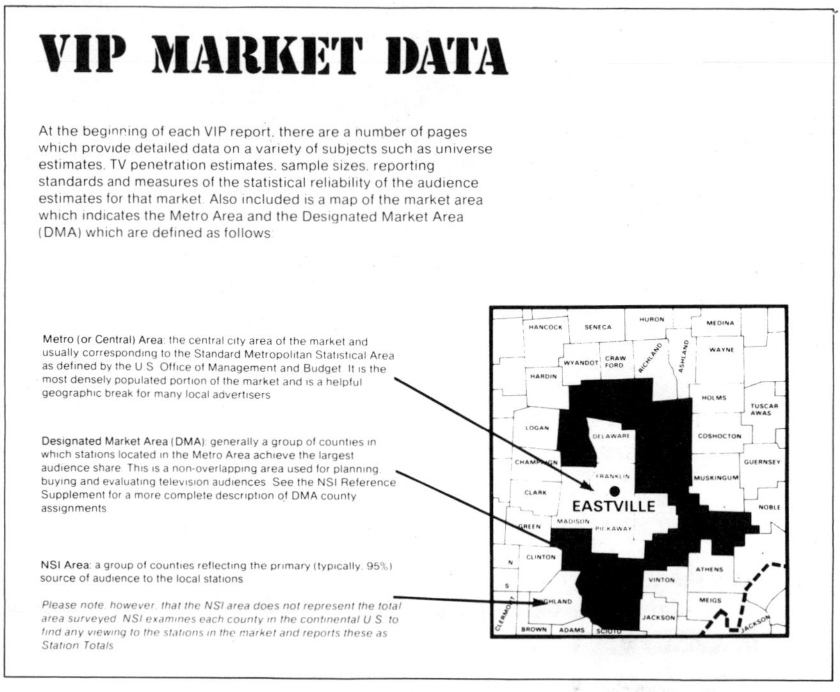

VIP MARKET DATA

At the beginning of each VIP report, there are a number of pages which provide detailed data on a variety of subjects such as universe estimates, TV penetration estimates, sample sizes, reporting standards and measures of the statistical reliability of the audience estimates for that market. Also included is a map of the market area which indicates the Metro Area and the Designated Market Area (DMA) which are defined as follows.

Metro (or Central) Area: the central city area of the market and usually corresponding to the Standard Metropolitan Statistical Area as defined by the U.S. Office of Management and Budget. It is the most densely populated portion of the market and is a helpful geographic break for many local advertisers.

Designated Market Area (DMA): generally a group of counties in which stations located in the Metro Area achieve the largest audience share. This is a non-overlapping area used for planning, buying and evaluating television audiences. See the NSI Reference Supplement for a more complete description of DMA county assignments.

NSI Area: a group of counties reflecting the primary (typically, 95%) source of audience to the local stations.

Please note, however, that the NSI area does not represent the total area surveyed. NSI examines each county in the continental U.S. to find any viewing to the stations in the market and reports these as Station Totals.

Courtesy: A. C. Nielsen

Many of the NTI and NSI services are available at extra cost on a "day-after" basis through computer terminals. In addition to the services discussed here, both Nielsen and Arbitron provide specially designed studies for individual clients. Some of these services utilize the telephone coincidental method. Here phone surveys are conducted while a program is being broadcast.

Both Nielsen and Arbitron have plans for regular cable audience measurements. Nielsen published a preliminary study of cable audiences in early 1979. In the foreseeable future both companies will have reports summarizing a whole range of new electronic viewing habits, including not only cable but also videocassette and videodisc viewing. These studies will probably be limited to the top 10 or 20 markets initially, with general measurement by the end of this decade.

Other television research

Most of the familiar television rating services measure households and/or people's viewing habits. Another category of less well known

Figure 5–10
Primary Nielsen television reports

Nielsen Television Index	*Abbreviation/ trade nickname*	*Purpose*	*Sampling frame*	*Data collection method*	*Frequency/ publication time*
National TV Ratings	NTI/Pocket Price	Reports ratings for network programming	1,200 households in national sample	Audimeter	Biweekly
Multi-network Area Ratings	Fast MNA	Reports ratings for network programming	70 largest markets	Audimeter	Weekly
Market Section Audiences	MSA	Reports values for ten demographic variables for households viewing network programming	Combination of NTI and NAC samples	Audilog/ Andimeter	9 times per year
Brand Cumulative Audience Report	BCA Report	Reports advertising performance by brand	Combination of NTI and NAC samples	Audilog/ Andimeter	3 times per year
Audience Demographics	NAD	Individual viewing of network programming	1,200 households in national sample	Audilog/ Andimeter	15 times per year; 4 supplements
Nielsen Station Index: *Viewer in Profile* (Meter Market)	"Overnights"	Next-day report of ratings in four key markets	Sample households in New York, Los Angeles, Chicago, and San Francisco	Audimeter	3 weekly
Viewer in Profile	"Sweeps"	Comparative ratings of stations in a local market	220 largest markets	Primarily Audilog	November, February, and May
NSI Plus	"Supplements"	Special information such as spot/network duplication, ethnic and children viewership	Same as local market *Viewer in Profile* samples	Primarily Audilog	5 times per year

services measures the degree of audience involvement or popularity for a brand, program, or individual performer. Two of the major firms doing this type of research are Burke International Research Corporation and Marketing Evaluations, Inc., which produces the TVQ report.

Burke offers a host of specialized client services for advertisers. However, the best known of Burke's research studies is the Day-After-Recall technique for measuring effectiveness, exposure, memorability, and content retention. This research is conducted for either pretesting or posttesting of commercials or both on a before and an after basis.

TVQ publishes two reports. The most common is the annual "Performer Popularity Poll," which measures the popularity of individual performers. In addition the television program TVQ, issued seven times a year, measures program popularity. In both cases the research does not measure the number of people watching a show, but how well liked the program (or performer) is among those people who do watch. The report gives two scores for a program or performer—the percent of familiarity (FAM score) and the percent of likability (Q score). The Q number is found by dividing the percentage of people saying the program or performer is "one of my favorites" by the percentage familiar with the program or performer.[10]

$$Q = \frac{FAV}{FAM}$$

Advertisers use the TVQ score in casting celebrities in commercials. The television networks use the studies to measure the popularity of present performers and to make decisions about shows or performers they might wish to schedule in the future. Fred Silverman, president of NBC, was quoted as saying the TVQ score of Joe Don Baker was a contributing factor in cancellation of his series "Eischied."[11]

THE OUTLOOK

Any attempt to predict the future of television is a risky enterprise where 50 percent accuracy would be a high score. While we have no crystal ball, we can point out several areas of television where change is inevitable during the next decade.

1. Inflation. The cost of television advertising during the 1980s

[10] Edwin Diamond, "The Mysterious Q: TV's Secret Casting Weapon," *New York,* May 26, 1975, p. 53.

[11] "NBC Will Be No. 1 by Next Christmas: Silverman," *Advertising Age,* December 31, 1979, p. 28.

will be discussed, criticized, and reviewed. None of the rhetoric, however, will alter the continuing upward spiral of commercial pricing. Both real costs and CPMs will increase by a minimum of 10–15 percent annually until at least 1985. The fact is that most advertisers, particularly at the national level, view television advertising as more effective than available alternatives. If this attitude and the accompanying advertiser demand continue, there is no way the television pricing structure will significantly change in the foreseeable future.

2. Government deregulation. It is unclear exactly what form future deregulation of the broadcast industry will take. However, it is clear that the government has made a decision to return broadcasting to the free market as it interprets that concept. Radio may experience the most dramatic short term effects. However, recent decision on importation of cable signals, increase in FCC licensing of earth station satellite receivers, and liberal court interpretation of potential copyright infringement by private citizens may have greater impact on broadcasting in the long run.[12]

3. Broadcast diversity and advertising. Some of the technology, such as satellite receivers and electronic newspapers, is probably still years away from extensive use at the household level. However, in the next decade we will see greater utilization of these scientific developments at the broadcaster level. Most of the work will concentrate on narrowcasting—identifying and reaching small, better-defined market segments. Of course these audiences will be reached at a premium cost to advertisers.

The 1980s will be a period of establishing which of the diverse outlets will survive. By 1990 we may well have only one or two pay cable (or subscription) television networks, one sports network, and a superstation or two. There is only so much household time and advertiser money, and ultimate decisions about where to allocate these resources will have to be made. We may well look back on the 1980s as a period in which broadcast technology developed beyond the ability of the public's time, money, and interest to utilize it fully.

QUESTIONS

1. What are O&Os, and why are they so important?

2. Describe the sources of television revenues, including dayparts, types of advertisers, and any changes in revenues during the last decade.

[12] A Los Angeles district court ruled in 1979 that noncommercial home use of recordings of broadcasts over public airwaves did not constitute copyright infringement.

3. What is barter? Barter syndication?

4. How did the primetime access rule change the economics and content of syndication?

5. Discuss the concept of the fragmented audience and some of the technologies that are bringing it about.

6. Discuss "sweep weeks" ratings and how they differ from national ratings.

7. Discuss the "package" concept of television commercial buys.

6

RADIO

FEW INDUSTRIES could have successfully made the transition required of radio in the last 30 years. From its struggling start in the 1920s, to a major national advertiser of the 1930s and 40s, to its predicted demise in the 1950s, radio has found change the normal situation. Radio has never been healthier. Its advertising revenues in 1980 should surpass the $3 billion mark (see Figure 6–1).

GENERAL CHARACTERISTICS OF RADIO

Radio's major characteristics are its individuality and its specialized formats. It is difficult to talk about *the* radio medium since many categories of radio must be treated as almost unique media rather than subcategories of radio. In this section we will discuss three of the major areas of radio: AM, FM, and network.

AM radio

Amplitude modulation (AM) radio is the oldest and most popular form of transmitting broadcast signals. Currently there are four major categories of AM radio among the approximately 4,000 commercial AM stations:[1]

1. *Class I: Clear channel stations.* These normally operate on the maximum power assigned AM stations (50,000 watts). There are currently 25 Class I stations in the country, and many of them, such as WLS-Chicago, WSB-Atlanta, WHO-Des Moines, and WJR-Detroit, can be heard for several hundred miles at night. In 1979 the FCC and the Carter administration announced plans to cut back the power of the Class I stations drastically in favor of opening up access to 120 to 700 new local stations.
2. *Class II: Secondary clear channel stations.* These stations are designed to serve a population center and a surrounding rural

[1] For a full discussion of AM and FM radio, see *Broadcasting Yearbook, 1979,* pp. A–4–5.

Figure 6–1
Trends in radio advertising revenues

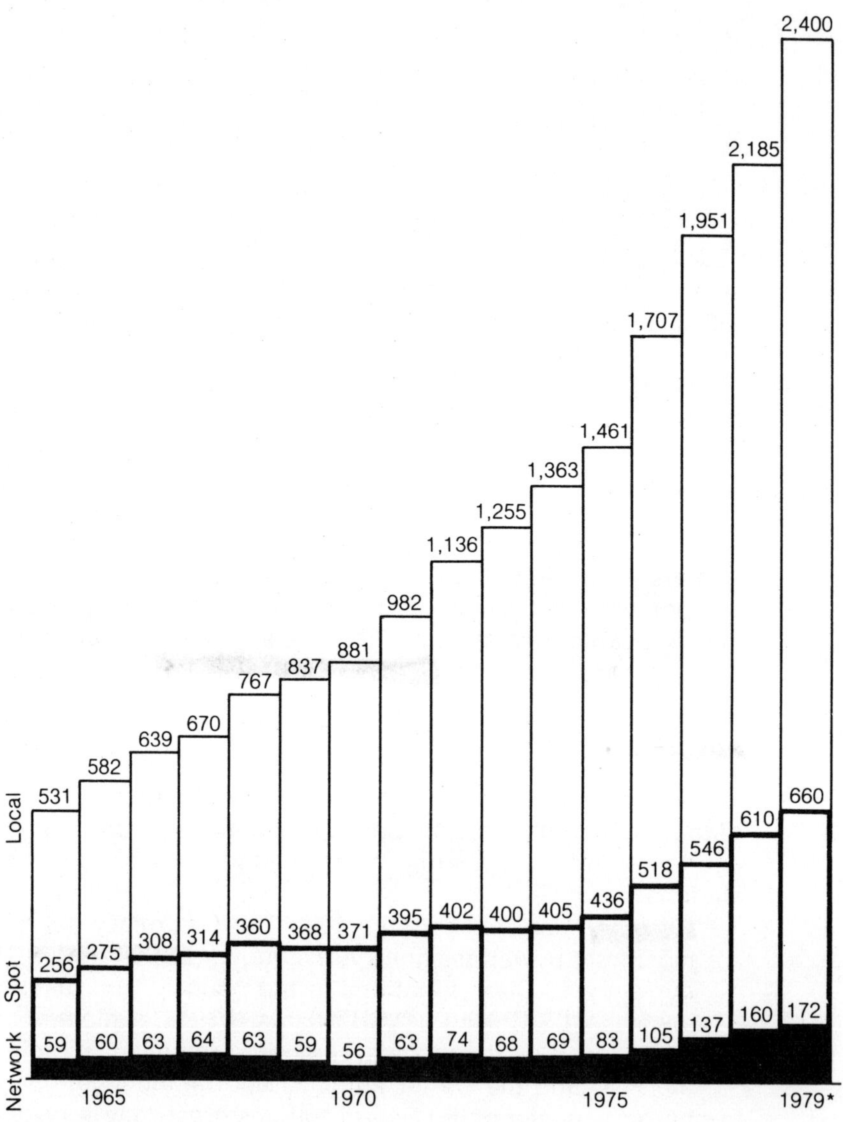

Data source: *McCann-Erickson. Estimates* (*) by Blair Research.

area. They do not interfere with the Class I clear channel stations and operate with 250–50,000 watts of power.

3. *Class III: Regional stations.* A regional station operates on a maximum of 5,000 watts and shares a channel with several other stations located far enough away to eliminate signal interference.
4. *Class IV: Local stations.* Local stations operate on a maximum of 1,000 watts and often are on the air only during daylight hours.

Revenues for AM and AM-FM outlets should pass the $2 billion level in 1980 as compared to $700 million, for FM-only stations. The gain in total radio revenues has been in the 10–12 percent range for the last several years, and this trend should continue at least for the near future.

FM radio

Frequency modulation radio was developed as a practical means of communication shortly before World War II. However, it was not until the early 1960s that the FCC took some steps to position FM as a vital part of radio. In 1963 the FCC assigned commercial FM channels to states and communities and ruled that FM programming could not duplicate more than half of AM programming among jointly owned stations in markets with more than 100,000 population. In the long term the trend is probably toward separate ownership of AM and FM stations.

Currently FM stations are allocated according to national zones and classes (assigned by power among these zones). Figure 6–2 summarizes these assignments.

Once many of the technological and administrative problems of FM were solved, it began a dramatic growth period. FM radio's image of classical music, few commercials, and a small, commercially insignificant audience is gone forever. Today FM stations are among the top stations in virtually every top 50 market. In New York WKTU-FM

Figure 6–2
Classification of FM stations

Zone I: 18 Northeastern states and Washington, D.C.	*Class A:* Low-power, maximum 3 kilowatts; located in all zones
Zone I–A: Southern California	*Class B:* Maximum 50 kilowatts; located in Zones I and I–A
Zone II: The rest of the country	*Class C:* Most powerful, up to 100 kilowatts; located in Zone II.

came out of nowhere with its disco sound to replace WABC as New York's top station. If anything, critics point to what is called *AManization* as a future drawback to FM as a distinct medium.

From 1973 to 1977 FM advertising revenues grew from less than $200 million to approximately $500 million. By 1981 FM revenues should approach $800 million. Despite these significant gains, FM revenues and profits are still trailing even greater increases in audience ratings. Many older media decision makers still regard FM in its stereotypic image of the 1950s and automatically buy only AM. FM will eventually overcome this problem, but it will remain a concern for the next few years.

NETWORKS

Wired networks

The major radio networks, once the prestige medium, almost went out of existence during the late 1960s. The only regular network programming was short newscasts. Total network revenues, which reached a high of $133 million in 1948, had fallen to $35 million by 1960.[2] However, in the years since 1975, network revenues have grown at an annual rate of 15–28 percent. Despite this growth, network radio only accounts for about 6 percent of total radio revenues.

During the last several years much of the publicity surrounding network radio has concerned the return of radio drama. The "CBS Radio Mystery Theater" is credited with providing the push for more recent programming such as the "Sears Radio Theater," begun in January 1979, and National Public Radio's "Masterpiece Radio Theater." However, for all the attention given these shows, network programs remain mostly five-minute newscasts and occasional short fillers. Special events such as major sport contests, news conferences, and miscellaneous programs make up a minute portion of network programming.

Major problems of network radio

1. Program clearance. In Chapter 5 network television clearances were discussed. It was noted that most network programs are carried by 98–99 percent of affiliates. A top ten market television affiliate failing to carry a program is regarded as a serious problem to

[2] "Radio Billings, 1935–1977," *Broadcasting Yearbook, 1979,* p. C–342.

network programmers. In radio, unlike television, stations depend on local programming for their audiences, and network is regarded by most stations as secondary to their own programming.

Consequently, radio networks have different relations with their affiliates than do television networks. Radio networks expect to have a far lower percentage of stations carrying their programs (known as percent of *clearance*).

In addition to the traditional system of paying affiliates for carrying their programs radio networks, have other ways of dealing with affiliates. For instance a local station may buy a network program and then exclude the network commercials in favor of local spots.

Radio networks may even present different formats of the same programs to different affiliates. The CBS "World News Tonight" is a 15-minute evening newscast. but many stations carry only the first 5–7 minutes. The format of the program provides a break which allows stations to do this. Moreover, stations are permitted to move network programs to other times more often in radio than in television.

2. Credibility. Network radio, like FM radio, faces the intangible problem of a lack of credibility. Many advertisers think of radio only in terms of local AM stations. Often network advertising is not even considered when a media schedule is being built. This avoidance of network overlooks the fact that network radio is usually available at a lower CPM than are the same stations individually.

3. Quality of affiliates. Unlike television, where network programming determines the strength of the affiliates, in radio the local stations decide how strong the network is. Consequently, there is diversity in audience demographics from one station to another within a network's lineup. In signing new stations, networks have begun to pay more attention to the quality of a station's audience and to its compatibility with the audiences of other network affiliates. However, advertisers continue to regard network buys as difficult because of inconsistency in audience profiles.

Structure of wired networks

Soon after commercial radio began, radio networks were created as a means of reaching national audiences and spreading program costs among several local stations. The network era began in 1926, when the National Broadcasting Company was formed by its parent company, the Radio Corporation of America (RCA).

Currently there are five major radio networks. The networks and

Figure 6–3
Wired networks and their affiliates

Network	*Approximate number of affiliates*
National Broadcasting Company (NBC)	260
Mutual Broadcasting System (MBS)	950
Columbia Broadcasting System (CBS)	276
National Black Network (NBN)	90
American Broadcasting Company (ABC)	1,565
ABC Contemporary	400
ABC Entertainment	475
ABC Information	500
ABC FM	190

the approximate number of affiliates in each are shown in Figure 6–3. The Mutual Broadcasting System (MBS) is the largest single network, while the American Broadcasting System (ABC) has the largest number of affiliates under its four-network system.

Advertising costs and ratings for network radio are very low when compared to television. A typical drivetime, one-minute network commercial averages around $4,000. The low cost and the ability to reach specific audience segments with certain types of programs (news, sports, features) make network radio attractive to many advertisers. Radio is used as a supplemental medium by some advertisers (General Motors), while others see it as a major medium in their overall advertising strategy (Blue Nun wine). Figure 6–4 lists typical network radio coverage.

Nonwired networks

In the last several years a new type of radio network had been formed. The so-called nonwired networks are in fact stations which the radio rep sells in combination as a network. (For a full discussion of the role of the media rep, see Chapter 4.) The nonwired networks do not sell programs or even simultaneous advertising, as do the wired networks. Instead the rep, through a network of clients, allows an advertiser to purchase all or a sizable number of stations with one invoice. The time is usually placed within a particular daypart (e.g., drivetime) on a run-of-schedule basis.

Currently there are five major radio reps with nonwired networks: Torbet Radio, Blair, Eastman, McGavren-Guild, and Katz. In addition there are several smaller groups. The major advantage promoted by

Figure 6–4
Network ratings: Average quarter-hour audiences by networks

			Wired networks							Nonwired networks				
Total adults in United States: 6:00 A.M.–midnight, Monday–Friday	*U.S. total*	*Total radio*	*Adult contemporary*	*ABC entertainment*	*ABC FM*	*ABC information*	*CBS*	*Mutual*	*NBC*	*Blair*	*Eastman*	*Katz*	*McGavren-Guild*	*Torbet-Lasker*
Total (000)	153,218	26,936	1,736	1,516	1,251	1,794	1,446	1,775	2,253	2,455	1,744	2,485	1,961	2,253
Rating	100.0	17.6	1.1	1.0	.8	1.2	.9	1.2	1.5	1.6	1.1	1.6	1.3	1.5
Age														
18–24	28,041	5,848	411	168	646	149	122	181	202	660	457	632	367	408
Percent of composite	18.3	21.7	23.7	11.1	51.6	8.3	8.4	10.2	9.0	26.9	26.2	25.4	18.7	18.1
Rating	100.0	20.9	1.5	.6	2.3	.5	.4	.6	.7	2.4	1.6	2.3	1.3	1.5
25–34	33,697	6,570	633	335	332	345	246	477	362	597	399	508	498	432
Percent of composite	22.0	24.4	36.5	22.1	26.5	19.2	17.0	26.9	16.1	24.3	22.9	20.4	25.4	19.2
Rating	100.0	19.5	1.9	1.0	1.0	1.0	.7	1.4	1.1	1.8	1.2	1.5	1.5	1.3
35–44	23,937	4,684	334	296	105	370	157	411	412	407	333	367	355	473
Percent of composite	15.6	17.4	19.2	19.5	8.4	20.6	10.9	23.2	18.3	16.6	19.1	14.8	18.1	21.0
Rating	100.0	19.6	1.4	1.2	.4	1.5	.7	1.7	1.7	1.7	1.4	1.5	1.5	2.0
45–54	23,984	4,158	195	219	24	395	375	382	382	310	215	432	320	288
Percent of composite	15.7	15.4	11.2	14.4	1.9	22.0	25.9	15.9	17.0	12.6	12.3	17.4	16.3	12.8
Rating	100.0	17.3	.8	.9	.1	1.6	1.6	1.2	1.6	1.3	.9	1.8	1.3	1.2
55–64	20,887	3,237	126	294	68	268	253	212	565	348	98	247	243	460
Percent of composite	13.6	12.0	7.3	19.4	5.4	14.9	17.5	11.9	25.1	14.2	5.6	9.9	12.4	20.4
Rating	100.0	15.5	.6	1.4	.3	1.3	1.2	1.0	2.7	1.7	.5	1.2	1.2	2.2
65 or over	22,672	2,439	38	204	76	267	293	211	33	133	242	299	177	192
Percent of composite	14.8	9.1	2.2	13.5	6.1	14.9	20.3	11.9	14.6	5.4	13.9	12.0	9.0	8.5
Rating	100.0	10.8	.2	.9	.3	1.2	1.3	.9	1.5	.6	1.1	1.3	.8	.8
18–49	96,582	18,789	1,466	892	1,092	998	709	1,228	1,171	1,806	1,285	1,690	1,334	1,479
Percent of composite	63.0	69.8	84.4	58.8	87.3	55.6	49.0	69.2	52.0	73.6	73.7	68.0	68.0	65.6
Rating	100.0	19.5	1.5	.9	1.1	1.0	.7	1.3	1.2	1.9	1.3	1.7	1.4	1.5
35–49	34,845	6,372	422	389	114	504	341	570	608	550	430	551	469	639
Percent of composite	22.7	23.7	24.3	25.7	9.1	28.1	23.6	32.1	27.0	22.4	24.7	22.2	23.9	28.4
Rating	100.0	18.3	1.2	1.1	.3	1.4	1.0	1.6	1.7	1.6	1.2	1.6	1.3	1.8

Source: Reprinted with permission, Simmons Market Research Bureau, copyright 1978. *Advertising Age*, May 21, 1979, p. S–22.

the nonwired networks is that they combine the flexibility of market-by-market spot advertising with the convenience of network. However, critics of the nonwired concept charge that when dealing with a rep the client really has only one station to choose from in each market. Consequently, much of the flexibility of the nonwired network is an illusion. Figure 6–5 lists the major advantages and disadvantages of wired and nonwired networks.

Figure 6–5
Claims and counterclaims of wired versus nonwired radio networks

Advantages claimed by all networks

Easy to buy; permit larger margin of profit for the agency then market-by-market spot.

One order and one invoice.

One affidavit.

Pre- and postbuy analyses at no extra cost to advertiser.

Promotion and merchandising from station at no extra charge to advertiser.

Both competitive with market-by-market spot buys.

Advantages claimed for wired networks

The CPM for a wired network is half or less than half that for a nonwired network.

The wired networks offer a wide spectrum of audience profiles collectively: ABC via its contemporary (C), entertainment (E), information (I), and FM networks; MBS via its general marketing and black networks; CBS via its news and information and drama networks.

NBC through its National News and Information Service network, due to debut in June, expects to achieve a maximum of station clearance for commercials, since the affiliated stations will get six commercial minutes to sell against each NNIS-oritented program (three in the program, and three following).

The CBS, NBC, ABC, MBS network names provide the national advertiser with familiar prestigiousness that he can capitalize on in dealing with brokers, distributors, and retailers.

Advantages claimed for nonwired networks

Greater flexibility in implementing a national marketing plan.

Better control over station clearances. Can deliver larger percentage of stations and commercial clearances than wired networks.

Stations are more inclined to cooperate with nonwired networks since stations' share of nonwired network revenue is greater.

Figure 6–5 (*continued*)

The advertiser can vary his weight of schedules and impressions per market and select the daypart and programming adjacent to his commercial and compatible with his product's local or regional requirements. Starting dates of schedule per market can also be varied.

Nonwired networks combine the best features of both wired and market-by-market spot, adding reach to the wired network's frequency.

Nonwired network stations generally cooperate better on promotion and merchandising than do wired network affiliates.

Rep network salesmen are more likely to take the advertiser's marketing objective into account. Therefore, presumably, if a market-by-market spot campaign seems more appropriate, he would recommend spot. The premise here: the rep network is not pitching against spot but rather against wired networks.

If an advertiser's target is so many gross rating points per market, he can use a wired network as a base and fill in the holes or heavy-up as needed with a nonwired network.

Duplicates of taped commercials are made and distributed to stations on nonwired network without added expense to the advertiser.

Source: *Media Decisions,* April 1975, p. 67.

RADIO AS AN ADVERTISING MEDIUM

Strengths

1. Selectivity and audience segmentation. Radio is a medium of selective tastes. Through the wide range of formats offered by radio, an advertiser can reach virtually every demographic audience with a minimum of waste circulation. The *Spot Radio SRDS* lists more than 160 radio station formats, from "Acoustic Music" to "Young & Beautiful." Many stations use as many as four format descriptions to describe various parts of their programming.

Figure 6–6 presents some of the major formats and the age groups most likely to listen to each. Since these format designations are made largely by the stations themselves, advertisers must use some judgment in selecting a specific station.

2. Out-of-home audience. One of radio's major strengths is its ability to effectively reach the out-of-home audience. However, in recent years the stereotype of drivetime (approximately 7:00–9:00 A.M. and 5:00–7:00 P.M.) as a mostly male, automobile audience has been challenged by radio audience research. One such study by

Figure 6–6
Average quarter-hour audiences by formats

Total adults in United States: 6:00 A.M.–midnight, Monday–Friday	*U.S. total*	*Total radio*	*Adult contemporary*	*All news*	*Beautiful music*	*Black*	*Classical/semi-classical*	*Country*	*Golden oldies*	*Middle of the road*	*Progressive*	*Soft contemporary*	*Standard*	*Talk*	*Top 40*
18–24															
Percent of composite	18.3	21.7	38.8	6.6	5.7	37.0	9.1	11.8	49.8	14.9	39.0	41.1	9.3	5.0	39.1
Index	100	119	212	36	31	202	50	64	272	81	213	225	51	27	214
25–34															
Percent of composite	22.0	24.4	30.7	14.6	15.2	30.8	12.4	21.2	29.8	28.5	43.9	36.8	13.8	8.0	30.7
Index	100	111	140	66	69	140	56	96	135	130	200	167	63	36	140
35–44															
Percent of composite	15.6	17.4	10.5	13.3	23.1	18.6	28.6	27.8	11.9	18.3	8.1	6.5	21.3	14.1	14.9
Index	100	112	67	85	148	119	183	178	76	117	52	42	137	90	96
45–54															
Percent of composite	15.7	15.4	8.0	24.3	22.8	10.9	33.2	15.9	3.1	19.6	2.3	6.5	23.3	26.8	8.3
Index	100	98	51	155	145	69	211	101	20	125	15	41	148	171	53
55–64															
Percent of composite	13.6	12.0	6.9	19.0	20.3	1.6	11.2	15.2	2.8	10.6	6.1	6.9	16.6	21.1	3.9
Index	100	88	51	140	149	12	82	112	21	78	45	51	122	155	29
65 or over															
Percent of composite	14.8	9.1	5.1	22.2	12.8	1.2	5.4	8.2	2.3	8.2	0.7	2.6	15.7	25.3	3.2
Index	100	61	34	150	86	8	36	55	16	55	5	18	106	171	22
18–49															
Percent of composite	63.0	69.8	83.0	46.0	54.1	92.4	57.7	69.8	93.7	70.2	91.7	87.8	53.8	36.0	87.6
Index	100	111	132	73	86	147	92	111	149	111	146	139	85	57	139
35–49															
Percent of composite	22.7	23.7	13.6	24.8	33.2	24.7	36.1	36.8	14.1	26.8	8.8	9.8	30.7	22.9	17.9
Index	100	104	60	109	146	109	159	162	62	118	39	43	135	101	79

Source: Reprinted with permissicn, Simmons Market Research Bureau, copyright 1978. *Advertising Age*, May 21, 1979.

RADAR (Radio All-Dimension Audience Reseach) showed that the in-car share of the drivetime audience was only 21.2 percent. This study also indicated that women made up a sizable portion of the drivetime audience.[3]

These data have implications for FM radio. Many advertisers eliminate FM radio from their drivetime radio buys because of the low FM set penetration in automobiles. If these figures are correct (see Figure 6–7), then most listeners are at home during all dayparts. However, this does not mean that drivetime, out-of-home listeners are not an important target segment for many advertisers. It does mean that

Figure 6–7
Drivetime radio audiences
How listening by men and women differs by time of day

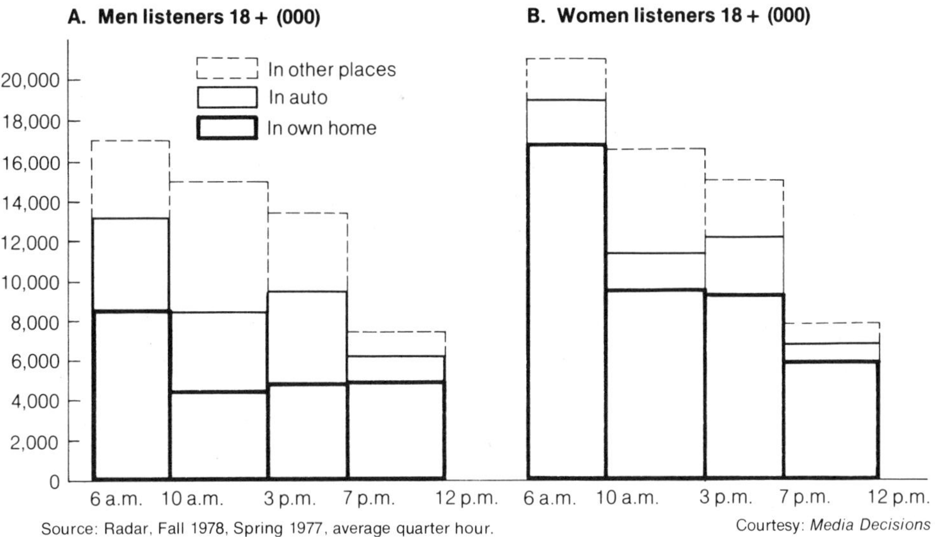

Source: Radar, Fall 1978, Spring 1977, average quarter hour.

Courtesy: *Media Decisions*

drivetime buys should be made on the basis of available research, not traditional wisdom.

3. Low unit cost. As we have noted, all media advertising rates have risen dramatically during the last decade. However, radio has had the smallest overall increase in CPM. This increase has been far below the overall rate of inflation and only about one third of comparable increases in television and newspapers (see Figure 6–8).

The relatively low cost of radio allows advertisers to utilize the

[3] "Who's Listening in Drive Time?" *Media Decisions,* November 1977, p. 126.

Figure 6–8
Radio's cost per thousand increase, 1967–1978

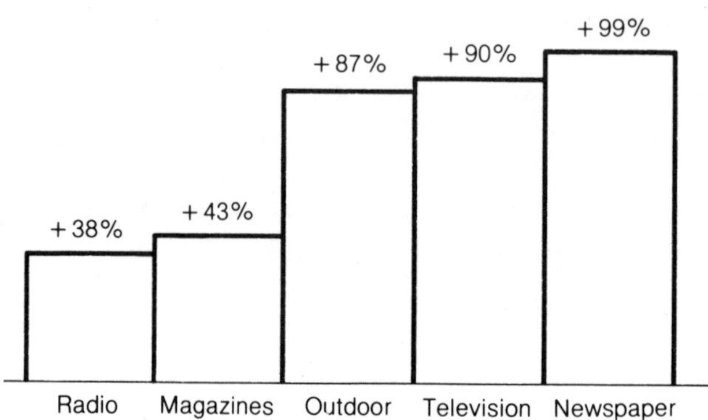

Source: *Radio Facts*, p. 14. RAB Research Department.

medium to gain supplemental reach (new audience) or to generate heavy frequency by buying multiple spots on a few stations. Heavy frequency also permits advertisers to qualify for various discounts, making the cost of radio even lower.

4. Inexpensive copy opportunities. With the costs of television and print production going up at a rate similar to that of the costs for these advertising media, inexpensive radio production costs are welcomed. Radio's low (often negligible) production costs in turn allow quick copy changes and short scheduling deadlines. Radio can take advantage of short-term changes in the marketplace without junking expensive advertisements prepared before these changes occurred.

5. Cooperative advertising. Radio has become more aggressive in going after the co-op dollar in recent years. While co-op is used predominantly in newspapers, several events have made co-op more of a multimedia enterprise:

Because of media cost inflation, advertisers have been looking for ways to save money, and co-op has become a consideration in all media.

The Radio Advertising Bureau (RAB) has led industry-wide efforts to encourage advertisers to consider radio co-op.

Greater emphasis is being placed on local market strategies. Major manufacturers realize the local retailers know the customer best and are giving them more flexibility in spending co-op dollars.

Better controls of co-op have been developed. Radio stations are routinely required to sign affidavits attesting to performance in co-op. A station signing an improper affidavit could lose its license under FCC rules.[4]

Weaknesses

1. Low attention levels. Perhaps radio's greatest drawback is that it can easily be ignored. Because radio lacks the visibility of the other media, listeners use it as background while they engage in other activities. As more and more products are "presold," the inability of radio to provide package identification is a major problem for certain classes of advertisers, such as advertisers of detergents and packaged/prepared foods.

2. Frequency expensive. Because the average quarter-hour audience of any radio station is relatively low, radio advertising schedules must have extremely high frequency to obtain broad reach. Radio audiences are smaller than television audiences, and these audiences are spread over more stations, with less attention being given to the medium.

RATE STRUCTURE IN LOCAL RADIO

The structure for radio time sales is regarded as complex by media buyers. In some cases buying radio seems complex because television buyers are often assigned to buy radio "on the side." Since they may be largely unfamiliar with the medium, they naturally find radio more difficult to buy than the medium they work with on a regular basis. In addition radio exaggerates the buying problem by providing an unstandardized system of rate cards, including fixed rates, grid rates, and a number of different combination or package discount rates. Most of the grid rates are similar to those discussed in Chapter 5 in connection with television. However, most radio grid cards offer fewer options than does the similar system in television.

Nevertheless, radio time sales are similar in many ways to those of television since prices are set largely by demand and ratings. However, radio rates are less subject to negotiation. The media buyer will need to confirm rates (largely through contracts agreed upon previously) and availabilities. Since most radio time is bought during dayparts rather than within a participating program, as in television, there is greater flexibility for the station to place commercials.

The potential radio advertiser considers several factors in buying a station:

[4] "Can You Control Co-op?" *Marketing and Media Decisions,* October 1979, p. 75.

1. Format. Most stations are bought primarily on the basis of format. Local advertisers, of course, know the general program format of stations in the community. National advertisers must depend primarily on descriptions provided by stations. Most stations provide program descriptions under their listings in the *Spot Radio SRDS*. A few stations also have a system which permits advertisers to hear recorded program segments by telephone.

2. Coverage area ratings. Stations are bought on the basis of ratings over a specific geographic area:

Metro Survey Area (MSA). The MSA conforms to a Standard Metropolitan Statistical Area (SMSA).

Total Survey Area (TSA). The TSA is the Metro Survey Area plus certain adjoining counties. The number of counties included in a TSA is determined by the number of stations which achieve minimum coverage in these counties.

Area of Dominant Influence (ADI). As discussed in Chapter 5, this is primarily a television term. However, national advertisers sometimes define markets in terms of ADIs and buy other media, including regional magazines and newspapers, to conform to these areas.

The advertiser is not interested in the coverage area of a station per se. Rather he is interested in the audience reached by the station in its coverage area. Radio advertising is normally bought in one of two ways or a combination thereof:

a. Gross rating points. This strategy of buying broadcast time has already been discussed in Chapter 5. Compared to television, any particular level of GRPs in radio usually requires a greater number of spots since the average rating per spot is lower.

b. Cume. Short for accumulated audience, this is simply radio terminology for reach. However, radio audience surveys commonly report the number of different households (or of individuals in certain age categories). The advertiser using cumes buys a specified number of different households, whereas GRPs only provide a specified level of exposure, with no indication of extent of duplication.

3. Daypart. While station format and coverage area ratings are perhaps the two most important factors in choosing a station, the advertiser must also schedule the commercial in the most advantageous daypart. Stations vary greatly in the daypart segments they make available to advertisers. Most stations offer a minimum of two dayparts, however, and a few have more than four. Dayparts are usually designated by letters, with AAA often being the highest priced period. There is no consistency to these designations, and the media

Figure 6–9
Daypart letter designations for two stations

WYOR-FM (Coral Gables, Florida)			*WWOK (Miami)*		
AAA	Monday–Saturday	10:00 A.M.–8:00 P.M.	AAA	Monday–Saturday	6:00–10:00 A.M. and 3:00–7:00 P.M.
AA	Monday–Saturday	5:30–10:00 A.M.	AA	Monday–Saturday	10:00 A.M.–3:00 P.M.;
				Sunday	6:00 A.M.–7:00 P.M.
A	Monday–Saturday	8:00 P.M.–5:30 A.M.	A	Monday–Sunday	7:00 P.M.–midnight
B	Monday–Sunday	8:00 P.M.–5:30 A.M.			
C	Monday–Sunday	Midnight–5:30 A.M.			

planner must designate times rather than letters when giving instructions to buyers. Figure 6–9 shows how two stations use different letter designations for the same times.

4. Commercial time. Next a decision must be made as to the length of the commercial messages to be purchased. Normally radio commercials are for one minute, although stations will permit 30-second spots. Most stations will also allow 10- and 20-second spots, but these are rarely used in radio. Before considering a spot of less than one minute, the advertiser should examine the cost differential. It is not uncommon for stations to charge up to 80 percent of the one-minute price for commercials of less than one minute. For most advertisers this saving is not worth the loss of commercial time.

5. Discounts. Radio stations typically offer a wide range of discounts to regular advertisers. While discounts vary from station to station, they generally fall into one of two categories.

a. Bulk discounts. The *bulk* or frequency discount is given for buying a certain number of spots during a specific time period (normally one month or one year). When the discount is based on money spent rather than commercials purchased, it is called a *volume* discount. Volume discounts are more common in television than in radio.

b. Package discounts. Radio stations offer a wide array of discounts based on the purchase of certain dayparts or on the use of some pattern in scheduling commercials. Some of the most common discounts are:

Annual discount. This discount requires an advertiser to purchase a 52-week schedule with a minimum number of spots per week. It is sometimes referred to as a continuity discount.

Consecutive week discount (CWD). This is similar to the annual discount, but it usually requires only 13 weeks to qualify.

Rotations (also called *Orbits*). Rotations are offered on either a horizontal or vertical basis. A horizontal rotation places a spot at the same time on different days. A vertical rotation moves a spot through dayparts.

Run of Station (ROS). An ROS buy allows the station to place the advertiser's spots at its discretion. It is the cheapest buy, but many advertisers think they need more control over their advertising than it affords. Stations often list ROS as Best Times Available (BTA) in their rate cards.

Total Audience Plan (TAP). The TAP discount permits the advertiser to buy several spots in each of the dayparts. The price for these spots is determined by the proportions of the spots that are scheduled for each of the dayparts. A typical listing for a TAP plan would be: ⅓ AAA, ⅓ AA, ⅓ A. In this case, one third of the spots would run in each of the three time periods.

c. *Other discounts.*

(1) *Combination rates.* Often, when more than one station is owned by the same company, an advertiser can buy the stations in combination at a reduced price. In radio, combination rates are most common where AM/FM stations are held by the same company in a specific market. In smaller markets the advertiser may have no choice if the FM station is simulcast (i.e., carries most of the same programs broadcast by its AM sister station). Other combination buys are available through regional agreements under which stations allow themselves to be sold with other stations.

(2) *Preemptible rates.* An advertiser may save money by paying less than the maximum price for a spot with the understanding that his commercial may be preempted, or bumped, by an advertiser paying a higher price for the same spot. This system is known as fixed and preemptible rates, and it is usually indicated on a rate card in this way:

	I	*II*	*III*
AAA	100	90	80
AA	70	65	60
A	50	40	30

The letters indicate the daypart (e.g., AAA might be 7:00–9:00 A.M. daily), and the Roman numerals give the prices which the station charges for this time. In the example above, I–AAA is called fixed time. An advertiser who buys this time is guaranteed the time indefinitely. On the other hand, an advertiser who buys III–AAA is taking a chance that no other advertiser will pay more than $80 and thus preempt the time. Levels II and III differ in the length of notice an advertiser will be given by the station before being preempted. For instance, II might mean two weeks' notice, while III might be only 24 hours.

Sometimes stations will not offer their most valuable time on a preemptible basis. The lack of preemptible rates for certain time periods usually indicates that demand is great enough so that the station can always sell this time at the fixed rates. A typical rate card might indicate this as follows:

	I	*II*	*III*
AAA	100	*	*
AA	70	65	60
A	50	40	30

* Preemptible rates not avaiable.

In addition to buying at these discounts, advertisers sometimes want to buy spots at certain times. When a station guarantees to run a spot at a specific time, this is called a *fixed position*. This can cost the advertiser 10–25 percent extra. Not all stations carry fixed positions.

Two final comments should be made about radio rates. In the station listings in the *Spot Radio SRDS,* under the heading "Time Rates," some stations will say, "National and local rates same." If this statement does not appear, it is assumed that the quoted rates are for national advertisers. Also radio stations usually do not give the 2 percent discount for cash (see Chapter 4 for a discussion of this discount).

SOURCES OF RATES AND AUDIENCE DATA

Buying radio is often disorganized, and many aspects of the problem are misunderstood. With so many stations, formats, and pricing structures, the radio media buyer has a difficult time making and justifying radio buys. In this section we will discuss the major information sources available to the radio media buyer.

1. Spot Radio Standard Rate and Data Service. The SRDS is the general information book for the media buyer. The SRDS listing for a station gives, in addition to rates, information concerning station policies, reps, network affiliation, and power. However, SRDS is viewed as a guide rather than the definitive word on rates. As discussed in Chapter 5 broadcast rates are usually negotiable, and the buyer will contact the station before making a final decision.

2. Estimator books. In Chapter 4 we discussed the use of media guides in estimating rates. These and more elaborate references are available from reps, broadcast industry associations, and most major agencies. These "estimating books" are not used for final advertising pricing, but they can be useful for an idea of costs. They can also be helpful in giving the media buyer a starting point for negotiation. Figure 6–10 presents a section from a typical estimating guide.

Advertisers should also consider the rep as a valuable source of information. Advertisers should evaluate rep information as coming from a salesperson. However, the rep knows that future sales depend on how accurate and candid they are with media buyers. Media reps are in an advantageous position to know local markets and special factors which will not show up in general audience information sources.

3. Syndicated audience services. For local radio audience ratings there is only one major report, *Arbitron Radio*. With the demise of The Pulse, Inc., several other organizations attempted to compete with Arbitron. Most recently Audit & Survey (TRAC-7) and Burke Broadcast Research, Inc. (BBR), attempted to challenge Arbitron without success. Arbitron reports include average quarter-hour ad cume listening estimates for men and women reported by various age groups. These data are reported by metro, total, and ADI survey areas (see Figure 6–11).

Arbitron Radio uses the diary method of gathering data. This method enables Arbitron to report not only listening levels but also the demographics of the audience. Recently Arbitron has taken steps to report more adequately ethnic audiences (primarily black and Spanish listeners). Since diaries are placed in telephone households, Arbitron has also developed a computer random dial system (called Expanded Sample Frame) to reach unlisted numbers. Arbitron reports are available from one to four times a year, depending on the size of the market. The April/May survey is conducted in every Arbitron market and is the radio equivalent of the sweep periods in television.

While the basic rating mathematics of radio are similar to those used in television, some differences should be noted. Radio ratings are almost always based on age/sex rather than on households. Tele-

Figure 6–10
Radio estimator: Market-by-market costs per minute announcements

National rank	Markets	Morning traffic 1st	2d	3d	4th	Average	Daytime 1st	2d	3d	4th	Average	Afternoon traffic 1st	2d	3d	4th	Average
44.	Akron, Ohio	$ 65	$ 45	$ 40	$ 40	$ 48	$ 47	$ 40	$ 40	$ 40	$ 42	$ 55	$ 46	$ 46	$ 41	$ 47
42.	Albany–Schenectady–Troy, N.Y.	105	65	60	45	69	75	55	45	37	53	85	60	52	50	62
69.	Albuquerque, N.Mex.	43	41	36	33	38	43	32	32	28	34	48	33	31	30	36
136.	Allentown–Bethlehem–Easton, Pa.–N.J.	37	37	37	24	34	34	34	32	22	31	37	37	37	24	34
147.	Altoona, Pa.	21	18	16	15	18	18	15	13	13	15	21	18	16	15	18
104.	Amarillo, Tex.	23	22	18	14	19	21	19	16	14	18	23	22	16	15	19
101.	Anchorage, Alaska	34	28	25	24	28	23	22	21	21	22	28	25	24	24	25
143.	Ann Arbor, Mich.	19	18	17	17	18	18	16	15	14	16	19	18	17	17	18
22.	Atlanta, Ga.	270	150	145	105	135	145	100	95	77	104	145	135	117	105	126
103.	Augusta, Ga.-S.C.	40	20	17	16	23	34	18	15	11	20	40	20	17	13	21
85.	Austin, Tex.	41	27	27	25	31	31	25	22	20	25	41	27	27	24	30
76.	Bakersfield, Calif.	25	23	21	15	21	22	21	20	13	19	25	22	21	15	21
15.	Baltimore, Md.	140	130	89	75	109	105	85	73	56	80	115	95	89	75	94
117.	Baton Rouge, La.	24	24	24	24	24	22	22	17	17	20	24	24	24	24	24
119.	Beaumont–Port Arthur–Orange, Tex.	19	19	19	18	19	18	18	16	16	17	22	22	19	19	21
43.	Birmingham, Ala.	63	63	54	50	58	46	46	38	34	41	52	52	50	44	50
6.	Boston, Mass.	350	325	225	125	256	150	120	110	110	123	190	150	140	125	151
29.	Buffalo, N.Y.	110	110	86	54	90	90	85	60	58	73	110	85	79	74	87
93.	Canton, Ohio	55	21	21	15	28	29	19	18	13	20	35	21	18	15	22
145.	Casper, Wyo.	21	18	14	12	16	20	14	13	12	15	21	18	14	12	16
78.	Cedar Rapids, Iowa	46	29	23	19	29	34	26	19	19	25	46	29	23	19	29
137.	Charleston, S.C.	31	31	28	28	30	29	29	22	22	26	31	31	28	28	30
89.	Charleston, W.Va.	42	38	37	18	34	38	33	32	26	32	38	38	37	18	33
36.	Charlotte–Gastonia, N.C.	185	100	63	45	98	130	81	58	45	79	135	81	75	50	85
109.	Chattanooga, Tenn.–Ga.	70	43	43	21	44	38	38	25	25	32	43	43	30	30	37
3.	Chicago, Ill.	303	300	280	260	286	194	180	180	175	182	280	242	233	200	239
25.	Cincinnati, Ohio-Ky.	125	95	80	73	93	95	80	70	63	77	105	95	73	70	86
19.	Cleveland, Ohio	101	95	92	88	94	95	92	79	70	84	101	95	92	80	92
126.	Colorado Springs, Colo.	21	17	16	14	17	20	16	12	12	15	21	16	14	14	16
81.	Columbia, S.C.	59	34	31	27	38	36	32	26	24	30	45	34	27	27	33

Based on 12 per week for 13 weeks for the four (when available) highest cost stations (and their average) in each daypart. Markets shown are the top 150, arranged in alphabetical order.

Source: *Katz Spot Radio Planning Guide, 1979–80.*

Figure 6–11
Cume listening estimates

CHICAGO
APRIL/MAY 1978

Cume Listening Estimates

CUME PERSONS—TOTAL SURVEY AREA, IN HUNDREDS

STATION CALL LETTERS	TOT. PERS. 12+	MEN 18-24	MEN 25-34	MEN 35-44	MEN 45-54	MEN 55-64	WOMEN 18-24	WOMEN 25-34	WOMEN 35-44	WOMEN 45-54	WOMEN 55-64	TNS. 12-17
WAIT	335			69	26			16	11		79	12
WBBM	4149	26	327	372	390	467	55	140	233	307	465	49
WBBM FM	489	55	62	24	27		132	121		4		44
WBMX	1259	93	267	122	43		199	168	112	27	13	215
WCFL	663	28	52	43	140	43	21	43	40	115	76	28
WCLR	680	108	120	48	82		93	41	76	24	35	53
WDAI	926	291	123				177	65		34		236
WEFM	462	37	69	9	26		34	24	11	25		227
WFMT	26				26							
WFMT FM	452		6	47	93	73	21	41	19	40	91	
TOTAL	477		6	47	118	73	21	41	19	40	91	
WFYR	1059	105	115	93			183	346	57			160
WGCI	374	139	24				46	31	34	16		84
WGN	6018	80	241	317	745	777	87	237	515	945	638	60
WIND	1619	59	227	163	31	148	116	209	144	76	169	90
WJEZ	478		24	112	53	43	13	23	22	54	48	27
WJJD	436	38	22	53	27	21			42	33	90	14
WJPC	263		77	20	26		51	31	11			47
WKQX	945	145	108	78	24		214	22		67		256
WLAK	1031		28	69	134	164		40	109	94	131	73
WLOO	1622		44	255	144	255	34	83	130	175	239	
WLS	4990	570	636	228	163	75	511	705	304	201	71	1483
WLUP	689	134	66			18	102	78	19			272
WRAQ	3813	130	607	397	367	171	334	393	328	321	282	134
WMET	1263	143	140	20			149	82	16	24		689
WRIB	68					22					18	
WVON	1331	125	72	137	73	35	77	94	146	48	50	430
WXFM	114				26	20				24	20	
WXRT	292	55	44			21	42	41		22	18	49
WYEN	248	28	97	26	27		42					28

CUME PERSONS—METRO SURVEY AREA IN HUNDREDS

STATION CALL LETTERS	TOT. PERS. 12+	MEN 18-24	MEN 25-34	MEN 35-44	MEN 45-54	MEN 55-64	WOMEN 18-24	WOMEN 25-34	WOMEN 35-44	WOMEN 45-54	WOMEN 55-64	TNS. 12-17
WAIT	291			69	24			16	11		73	12
WBBM	3422	21	245	248	366	378	55	119	181	278	371	49
WBBM FM	469	55	62	24	27		126	117				44
WBMX	1224	84	249	122	43		191	168	112	27	13	215
WCFL	539	28	23	43	130	43	21		38	91	65	26
WCLR	680	108	120	48	82		93	41	76	24	35	53
WDAI	813	237	94				157	65		24		236
WEFM	416		69		26		34	24	11	25		227
WFMT	26				26							
WFMT FM	405			47	93	73	21	41	19	24	87	
TOTAL	430			47	118	73	21	41	19	24	87	
WFYR	1029	105	115	93			183	339	57			137
WGCI	365	139	24				42	31	34	14		81
WGN	5182	64	185	244	628	674	80	165	445	848	580	30
WIND	1497	29	221	142	27	148	93	181	144	76	169	90
WJEZ	449		24	102	53	43	13	23	22	44	48	18
WJJD	376	23	22	51	27	21			38	33	71	
WJPC	234		48	20	26		51	31	11			47
WKQX	746	136	92	35			174	22		43		213
WLAK	941		22	69	134	126		40	109	81	98	73
WLOO	1579		44	212	144	255	34	83	130	175	239	
WLS	2771	253	392	159	84	41	195	506	213	127	63	707
WLUP	680	134	66			18	93	78	19			272
WRAQ	2064	54	244	249	246	82	46	166	207	209	238	51
WMET	1263	143	140	20			149	82	16	24		689
WRIB	68					22					18	
WVON	1331	125	72	137	73	35	77	94	146	48	50	430
WXFM	114				26	20				24	20	
WXRT	292	55	44			21	42	41		22	18	49
WYEN	232	28	91	26	27		42					18
TOTAL LISTENING IN METRO SURVEY AREA	27796	1451	2348	1939	2161	1998	1811	2470	2004	2278	2258	3298

Footnote Symbols: (*) means audience estimates adjusted for actual broadcast schedule (+) means AM-FM Combination was not simulcast for complete time period. **ARBITRON**

Source: The Arbitron Company, *Arbitron Radio Market of Chicago,* April/May 1978, p. 67.

vision uses a four-week period for analysis of reach and frequency levels, but radio commonly uses both one- and four-week periods.

Local radio ratings encounter the same "sweep weeks" hypoing problem that was discussed in Chapter 5. If anything, the problem of ratings inflation is even more serious in radio than in television. Since most radio markets are rated only once or twice a year, any ratings problem means that an advertiser will buy from the wrong numbers for up to a year. To address the problem, Arbitron carries a list of the stations which engaged in promotional activities during the rating period. It is important to remember that Arbitron is not a regulator of broadcast practices, and consequently its ability to prevent hypoing is limited.

Some agencies will not buy stations which call attention to rating diaries or engage in extraordinary promotions during a rating period. From a practical standpoint this position is effective only if a few stations which your client didn't need in the first place engage in the practice. To emphasize the seriousness of hypoing, Arbitron has begun to carry the following statement in its rating books:

> The FTC Guidelines Regarding Deceptive Claims of Broadcast Audience Coverage contain language which points out that **RADIO STATIONS . . .**
> "should not engage in activities calculated to ***DISTORT*** or ***INFLATE*** such data—for example, by conducting a ***SPECIAL CONTEST,*** or otherwise varying . . . usual programming or instituting ***UNUSUAL ADVERTISING*** or other promotional efforts, ***DESIGNED TO INCREASE AUDIENCES ONLY DURING THE SURVEY PERIOD.*** Such variation from normal practices is known as ***'HYPOING'.***"
>
> It is the opinion of Arbitron that while many radio stations that engage in promotional activities during a survey period are not attempting to hypo audiences, many other stations conduct their promotional activity for the specific purpose of increasing audiences artificially during the rating period.
>
> This activity could distort the behavior of the listening audience by making the estimates higher than they would have been if no promotional activity had been conducted during the survey period.
>
> The purpose of this notice is to call attention to the text of the FTC Guidelines and to call attention to report users where there is a possibility that some kind of hypoing might have been conducted during the survey period by one or more stations in the market.

Network radio audience ratings are measured by two primary sources: Arbitron and RADAR. Arbitron offers the more extensive network radio services. It uses the diary method to provide information on both wired and nonwired networks and gives ratings for 162 geographic areas. RADAR uses the telephone coincidental technique with a sample of approximately 6,000.

4. Intermedia approaches to buying radio. As we discussed earlier in this chapter, radio is seldom used alone or as the primary medium in a campaign. Radio is a complement to other media, and most advertisers buy radio time on the basis of how it fits into their overall schedule. For some time the RAB and other industry groups have promoted radio as part of an intermedia schedule.

One of the most widely known studies of radio and other media is

Figure 6–12
Example from ARMS II report

Product: Shampoo
Target: Females, 12–34
Weekly budget: $9,250

			Cumulative frequency distribution			
Schedule	*Net reach*	*Average fre-quency*	*One or more times/ week*	*Two or more times/ week*	*Three or more times/ week*	*Four or more times/ week*
100% spot TV	29.9%	1.4%	29.9%	8.0%	3.4%	1.4%
⅔ TV, ⅓ radio	40.2	1.8	40.2	19.0	8.5	2.7
⅓ TV, ⅔ radio	48.9	2.3	48.9	27.8	16.3	10.1
100% spot radio	51.7	3.1	51.7	34.5	23.9	17.8

Source: Radio Advertising Bureau.

the RAB's All-Radio Marketing Study (ARMS II). The details of this comprehensive study show how radio fits into schedules using different levels of television and newspaper advertising (see Figure 6–12).

THE OUTLOOK

There is little doubt that radio is undergoing a renaissance. By any standard, radio's growth since the early 1970s has been phenomenal. The weekly audience is at an all-time high of 166 million adults. In 1977, profits were $250 million on revenues of $2.3 billion, compared to 1972 figures of $97 million and $872 million, respectively.[5] Radio also demonstrated lower CPM increases during the same period than any other major medium, and this has increased its attractiveness to advertisers.

The future for radio as an advertising medium appears solid. Radio is becoming aggressive and innovative in its competition for audiences and advertising dollars. One of the most obvious areas of change in radio has been the return to programming at both the local and network levels. As discussed earlier, several network-produced programs have met with success. However, the largest number of new programs are offered by syndication.

Radio syndication includes both reruns of well-known programs of

[5] "Radio's Rennaissance: Now It's Giving TV a Run for the Money," *U.S. New & World Report*, January 16, 1978, p. 48.

the 1930s and 40s such as "The Lone Ranger" and "The Shadow" and first runs of new programs such as "Alien Worlds," released in mid-1979. However, the bulk of syndicated programs are short subjects, from 90 seconds to five minutes in length, on a host of entertainment and public affairs issues. Shows such as "Home Handyman" can charge premium advertising rates because of higher ratings and because the conventional wisdom is that listeners will pay more attention to "talk" programs than to a steady diet of music.[6]

Radio is being helped immeasurably by cost increases for television advertising. With 30-second commercials on major primetime series costing $100,000 or more, advertisers look to alternatives to stretch limited budgets. Traditionally, magazines have been the major supplement to television. However, radio has been starting to get a larger share of the advertising dollar.[7] Since neither radio's popularity nor television's costs show any signs of abatement, the future of radio as an alternative to television looks bright.

Implications of radio deregulation

Two years ago the Communication Act of 1978 was introduced into the U.S. Congress. Since that time many of the bill's original provisions have been revised or deleted. However, one of the bill's major provisions, radio deregulation, seems destined to go forward sometime soon. Radio deregulation is too complex to cover here, but some implications for the future of radio should be mentioned. The intent of the deregulation process is to create diversity through increased competition. Let's look at three of the proposed deregulation provisions and their implications for advertising.

1. *Deletion of the "public interest" section of the Communication Act of 1934.*[8] Will this lead stations to forgo news and public affairs programming? Will candidates be denied access to broadcast facilities for political advertising if the Fairness Doctrine is abolished? Will stations expand commercial minutes per hour since they will not have to answer to a public interest criterion for license renewal?

2. *Station log requirements.* Currently a station must keep an extensive log (or diary) of its broadcast day. Part of this log includes commercials broadcast, and the log is valuable to the advertiser in checking station affidavits of performance. Current FCC regulations

[6] "Syndicators Thrive on Radio Features," *Business Week*, April 16, 1979, p. 56.

[7] Edmund M. Rosenthal, "Broadcast Advertising Bullish despite Recession," *Television/Radio Age*, September 10, 1979, pp. 105–106.

[8] "Public interest" means that a station is serving the needs of the community. Licenses are required to ascertain these needs and program accordingly. The FCC does not prescribe a standard format.

also provide that stations involved in improper practices dealing with co-op advertising can lose their licenses. Some advertisers fear that without a station log a few stations would engage in improper practices, knowing that violations would rarely be caught.

3. *The question of diversity.* At the heart of the argument over deregulation is the question of whether diversity would really result. Cyril Penn, director of media, Shaller Rubin Associates, sees just the opposite effect:

> The new commission would be denied authority over all intrastate cable systems and the role in communications of the antitrust division of the Department of Justice would specifically be curtailed.
>
> In my opinion, this may not lead to diversity through competition in the free marketplace. In 1956, Bell Telephone came to an agreement with the Department of Justice, in the face of pending antitrust action, to refrain from going into other unregulated businesses which could interface with its existing services.
>
> Bell has now applied for permission to establish cable telecommunications systems. If cable transmission of radio and other origination of programming becomes unregulated, Bell's monopolistic power may not, in fact, lead to development of alternative technologies and services. Under the new act, there would be no regulation of competitive rates by common carriers.
>
> Deregulation of the communications industry will not necessarily promote the kind of desirable diversity that radio as an advertising medium can benefit by. Further market segmentation in radio would please many advertisers, but the public could soon find that its only means of obtaining quality programming, even of a mass entertainment nature, would be by direct subscription.[9]

The final decision on deregulation is yet to be made. However, it is probable that radio is soon going to gain some freedom from current regulation. Advertisers will have to be aware of and adjust to these changes over the next several years.

Research

While radio's future looks bright, audience research remains a major problem for the industry. The primary problem is the nature of the medium itself. Radio has a sizable out-of-home audience which is virtually impossible to measure accurately. In addition the number of stations in the major markets and the lack of programming lead to confusion among respondents reporting their listening behavior. Finally, a lack of money to tackle these problems puts radio research

[9] Cyril Penn, "The Future of Radio—Will It Be Diversity or Monopoly?" *Advertising Age,* June 25, 1979, p. 66.

Figure 6–13
Comparative ranks of advertising research and advertising revenue dollars

Ad research dollars	*Ad revenues*
1. Television	1. Newspapers
2. Magazines	2. Television
3. Newspapers	3. Radio
4. Radio	4. Magazines

far behind television in the development of audience measurement techniques.

One must remember that no particular relationship exists between the advertising research problem to be solved and the money available to solve it. Figure 6–3 shows the comparative ranks of advertising research dollars expended and advertising revenues among the various media.

You will note that advertising research dollars roughly follow advertising expenditures by national advertisers. Television and magazines, which rank first and second among national advertisers, are the subject of the most research. On the other hand, newspapers, the leader by a wide margin in total advertising revenue, rank a comparatively poor third in research dollars. Radio, with the smallest percentage of national advertising dollars, is last in research expenditures.

QUESTIONS

1. Describe some of the major changes in radio revenues and radio stations during the last decade.
2. How is a nonwired network organized, and what is its purpose?
3. How does radio differ from television as an advertising medium?
4. Discuss radio as an out-of-home medium.
5. Discuss MSA and TSA as they relate to radio ratings.
6. Discuss some of the implications of radio deregulation for advertising.
7. What steps have been taken to discourage hypoing in radio ratings?

7

NEWSPAPERS

GENERAL CHARACTERISTICS

Despite the advent of new media during the last several decades, newspapers continue to occupy a predominant position among advertisers. There are about 1,760 daily newspapers with a combined circulation of over 62 million readers. In addition some 7,500 weeklies cover rural and metropolitan suburban readers throughout the country. Advertisers searching for more selective newspaper readership may look to the ethnic press. Currently 1 percent of newspaper advertising dollars are being spent in the black press.

Traditionally the evening daily newspaper has accounted for the majority of total newspaper circulation. At present, it comprises more than 58 percent of daily newspaper circulation (35 million readers). The strong competition from television news has decreased the percentage of circulation held by evening newspapers. Many evening newspapers are published only five times per week. The Saturday evening newspaper is often combined with morning editions of jointly owned papers in most major markets, as has been traditionally done on Sundays.

To some extent both the Sunday and Saturday morning editions differ as advertising media from their daily counterparts. The almost 700 Sunday newspapers are often used by national advertisers as introductory vehicles and by retailers for announcements of sales during the next week. The Saturday newspaper has changed to a feature and human interest emphasis from a strict news orientation, and it is an excellent outlet for youth and young adult markets. Entertainment guides and similar features of many Saturday newspapers offer excellent opportunities for record, movie, and restaurant advertisements. Food and household product categories continue to make the Wednesday or Thursday newspaper the major weekday revenue producers.

If asked, the average person would probably name television as the dominant advertising medium in terms of advertising revenues. However, newspapers are by far the leading advertising medium (over

$15 billion in 1980), with a 30 percent share of total advertising expenditures to television's 20 percent. While television's share of advertising dollars has increased steadily over the last decade, the newspapers' share has remained constant. Despite adjustments and changing marketing conditions the trend toward localization of advertising efforts suggests continued prosperity for newspapers.

NEWSPAPERS AS AN ADVERTISING MEDIUM

Categories of newspaper advertising

1. Local. Local advertising is the economic foundation of newspapers. Virtually all local businesses use newspaper advertising to some extent. Local advertising accounts for more than $12 billion, or 85 percent, of total newspaper advertising revenues. As discussed later in this chapter, the use of cooperative advertising makes this figure somewhat misleading in terms of the sources of these funds. However, it is significant that one quarter of total U.S. advertising is placed in newspapers by local advertisers.

All local businesses, including local chain outlets, generally qualify for local rates, which run 25–50 percent less than national rates. Newspaper circulation is sometimes divided into three geographic categories: city zone, retail trading zone, and other. Normally the "other" category is inconsequential, although a newspaper such as the *New York Times* has a significant number of out-of-city readers. Local rate information is usually obtained from individual rate cards provided by the newspapers (see Figure 7–1).

2. National. The national advertising category accounts for approximately $2 billion. The national rate normally provides for the 15 percent agency commission as well as a 10–20 percent commission for the media representative (for a full discussion of the media rep's role, see Chapter 4). National rate information can be obtained from the newspaper edition of Standard Rate and Data Service. A version of this service is also available for a limited number of weekly newspapers.

National advertisers use newspapers for a variety of reasons. In order, the four largest categories of national newspaper advertisers are cigarettes, automobiles, airlines, and liquor.[1] Since liquor has never had access to the broadcast media to any extent and cigarettes have been banned since 1971, it is natural that they would use the print media on a large scale. Airlines in this era of deregulation are competing on a price basis, which must be done market by market.

---

[1] "National Newspaper Ad Dollars," *Media Decisions,* June 1977, p. 74.

Figure 7–1
Newspaper rate card

Retail:

ATHENS BANNER-HERALD
The Daily News

December 30, 1979

Rates:

Open Rate . . . . . 45¢ per line
$6.30 per column inch

Sunday Combination Rate . . . . . 45¢ per line
$6.30 per column inch

Banner-Herald (evenings) only . . . . . 38¢ per line
$5.32 per column inch

Daily News (mornings) only . . . . . 38¢ per line
$5.32 per column inch

Split Combination . . . . . 64¢ per line
$8.96 per column inch

- Ad appears in our Sunday combination papers and any single issue on Monday, Tuesday, or Friday with no copy changes.

Business Page . . . . . $10.36 per column inch

- 13-week contract required, 1.5 inch minimum

Classic Scene:

- A weekly Sunday magazine featuring television logs, stories on the arts, entertainment and features of local interest. A 5-column tabloid format.

Open Rate . . . . . $6.30 per column inch
13-week Contract . . . . . $6.02 per column inch
26-week Contract . . . . . $5.74 per column inch
52-week Contract . . . . . $5.46 per column inch
Church Pages . . . . . $6.30 per column inch

- Contracts for these pages are the same as Classic Scene above. Six-column format. 1-inch minimum.

Hi-Fi Page . . . . . $760 less earned discount
Flex Forms . . . . . $700 less earned discount

- A maximum of 90 column inches is allowed, plus one color at no extra charge.

Card Ad, minimum one inch, in multiples . . . . . $140 inch net

- Ad runs in both newspapers plus every shopper each week for 30 days.

The Northeast Georgia News and Shopping Guide:

Open Rate . . . . . 19¢ per line
$2.66 per column inch

13-week Contract . . . . . $2.52 per column inch
26-week Contract . . . . . $2.38 per column inch
52-week Contract . . . . . $2.24 per column inch

- Contract Rates require a minimum of 10 column inches weekly and are subject to no further discounts.
- Ads run in The Northeast Georgia News and Shopping Guide are to run in both the Banner-Herald and The Daily News two weeks prior to or following the weekly Shopper date desired.

Georgia News only . . . . . $4.20 per column inch
Hi-Fi Page $300
Flex-Form $285

- A maximum of 90 inches is allowed, plus one color at no extra charge.

Courtesy: *Athens Newspapers, Inc.*

The need for localized copy and the detailed nature of fares and schedules featured in most airline advertising dictate a heavy expenditure in newspapers. Finally, national automotive companies supplement their general, national appeals with hard-sell advertising at the local level. These four groups of advertisers and their varied reasons for using newspapers demonstrate the fact that the newspaper advertising of each national advertiser has its own specific objectives. The opportunity for couponing, introductory messages to a broad audience, and supplemental advertising to markets inadequately covered by national advertising schedules are other reasons why national advertisers choose newspapers.

Despite substantial increases in the use of newspapers by national advertisers, some newspaper media planners remain unsophisticated. Let's briefly examine two frequent mistakes made by media planners. First, duplicated coverage by two dailies is often ignored. Too often, media planners will total the morning and evening coverage, which may grossly inflate actual reach (see Figure 7–2). The media planner using the data from the *Morning Sun* and the *Evening Herald* will overestimate coverage by figuring on 86 percent reach versus the actual unduplicated coverage of 57 percent.

A second major error of newspaper media planners is using metro area coverage as the basis for media planning. Metro area coverage of many large markets ignores the growing, affluent suburbs. Often one or more suburban daily or weekly newspapers in combination with a daily newspaper give better coverage of the *total* market than does the traditional morning/evening metropolitan newspaper. However, the national media planner who gives adequate consideration to the suburban press is in the minority.

National advertising and the Newspaper Advertising Bureau[2]

Since the late 1970s newspapers have become aggressive in their efforts to increase national advertising. The Newspaper Advertising Bureau, a nonprofit sales and research organization, has been active in promoting newspapers to national advertisers. Among its major services are the one-order/one-bill insert placement service; Newsplan, a national advertising newspaper discount plan; and research reports.

[2] The information included in this section was provided by the Newspaper Advertising Bureau.

Figure 7–2
Newspaper coverage and duplication

	Total circulation	Metro circulation	Percent metro coverage	Unduplicated coverage
Morning Sun	25,000	20,000	40%	40%
Evening Herald	30,000	23,000	46%	17%

NAB insert service

The NAB Insert Division makes it possible for national advertisers to place inserts in most U.S. daily newspapers while dealing only with the NAB. The NAB gathers cost information on specified newspapers, reserves space, and obtains all applicable mechanical specifications. After the inserts have been placed, NAB provides the advertiser or agency with an invoice detailing all newspapers used, actual insertion dates, gross billings, net billings, and cash discounts.

NAB Newsplan

At one time a major complaint among national advertisers was a lack of competitive space discounts among daily newspapers comparable to those offered local advertisers. In addition many advertisers wished to purchase national space in modular units (full page, half page, etc.) rather than line or column inch units. The NAB has developed Newsplan, a cooperative agreement among approximately 800 daily newspapers, to offer discounts to national advertisers based on annual contracts. Currently national advertisers can earn discounts of 10–30 percent (see Figure 7–3).

NAB research services

1. **Computer Analyzed Newspaper Data On-Line (CAN DO).** The NAB provides a series of reports through the CAN DO service. These reports use individual newspaper readership reports for 160 newspapers which account for 48 percent of total daily circulation. The four basic CAN DO reports are described in Figure 7–4.

2. **National Advertised Brands Scanning Reports (NABSCAN).** In the NABSCAN program, product movement data are gathered from ten major retail chains such as A&P. These data are used in retail reports and sold to national advertisers. The NAB is

Figure 7–3
Newsplan discounts

Here's how you can earn discounts with NEWSPLAN:

1. Plan your advertising on an annual basis to make sure your cumulative space — in lines or modular units equals 6 pages, 13 pages, 26 pages, or 52 pages. Discounts at these page levels are now in effect in 823 newspapers across the country.
2. Issue a contract.

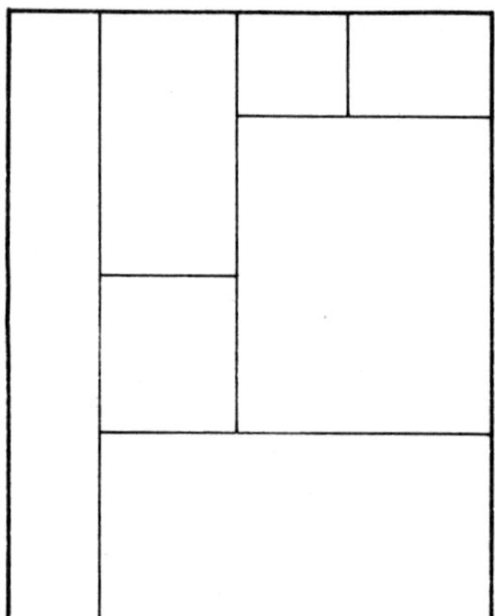

650 newspapers allow advertisements in any dimension, in any linage combination of your choice. You can cume all linage to earn discounts at the 6, 13, 26, or 52 page levels.

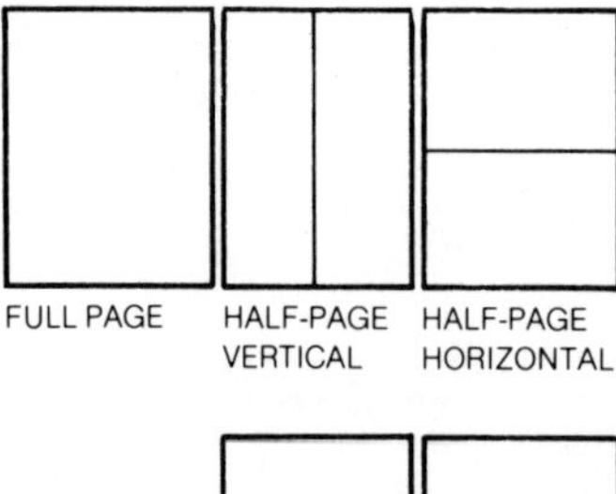

175 newspapers require advertisements in modular units—1/8, 1/4, 1/2, and full-page sizes. You can cume any combination of these modular units to reach full pages and earn discounts at the 6, 13, 26, or 52 page levels.

Source: Newspaper Advertising Bureau, *Newsplan Discounts for Continuity,* pp. 2–3.

Figure 7–4
The CAN DO reports

Report 1: Total Newspaper Report

Shows audience (total or specific demography) for a list of newspapers for one or multiple insertions. Total summarized by total estimated and grand total.

Report 2: Regional Newspaper Detail Report

Shows aggregates of circulation of newspapers and readers by market, including spill-in of outside markets and spill-out to other markets. Summarized for the schedule. Total reach and average frequency of each market and the schedule may be added.

Report 3: Regional Summary Report

Summarizes circulation, audience, and newspaper gross impressions by market and total schedule. Total reach and average frequency of each market and the schedule may be added.

Report 4: Total Schedule Frequency Distribution

Shows reach and frequency detail for the schedule, including spill-in, by the number reached 0, 1, 2, . . . *n* times and the number and percent of audience exposed. Also shows coverage, frequency of exposure, and Gross Rating Points of exposure by quintile (or other divisions of the audience).

Reports available for any newspaper schedule and for the total audience or specific demography.

Source: Newspaper Advertising Bureau, *Newspaper CAN DO,* p. 3.

the first organization to make regular use of the new sales data resulting from scanners and the Universal Product Code. With these data the retailer and manufacturer can learn within 24 hours what advertising is really moving the product.

3. Cooperative advertising. A hybrid advertising category with aspects of both local and national advertising is cooperative advertising, or simply co-op. Current estimates of co-op expenditures are more than $4 billion, most of which is spent in newspapers. Co-op dollars spent by national advertisers account for as much as 20 percent of local newspaper dollars according to some estimates.

The concept of co-op advertising is simple. National advertisers pay some percentage, typically one half or more, to support retailer-scheduled local advertising. Co-op serves several major purposes of national advertisers:

a. Financial savings. The national advertiser is able to stretch the media budget by splitting the cost of local advertising with a retailer and placing the advertising at local rates.

b. Localization of promotion. Co-op advertising allows the national advertiser to provide a local tie-in with each market. This market-by-market approach enables consumers to identify not only with the national brand but also with the local distributor. In addition it permits more price advertising and the advertising of unique services which are provided by dealers in one area but are not available throughout the country.

c. Strengthening local distribution. Done properly, a co-op program allows the national advertiser to demonstrate support to its retailers. It may also be used to develop coordinated merchandising programs for sales and special promotions between national and local advertising.

A major problem of co-op advertising is the control which national advertisers must exercise over expenditures. Naturally the national advertiser must make certain that co-op dollars are spent properly and that the advertiser is paying for space which actually ran at a rate which fairly reflects the cost to the retailer.

Double billing occurs when retailers request an advertising allowance from the national advertiser greater than the retailer actually paid for the advertising. The term *double billing* is used because such retailers send dummy (or double) bills to national advertisers which show an amount greater than the retailer actually paid. The national advertiser then reimburses the local advertiser based on this fraudulent bill. The retailer thus obtains a reduced price (or even free) advertisement plus extra cash. We wish to emphasize that double billing is an uncommon occurrence, but national advertisers should take steps to ensure that they are not the victims of this practice. The usual procedure is to have the newspaper send a copy of the advertisement (called a tear sheet) to ensure its publication plus some type of rate verification.

Large co-op advertisers often engage the services of an independent firm to control the expenditure of co-op dollars. Among the largest of such services is the Advertising Checking Bureau, Inc. (see Figure 7–5).

The national advertiser engaging in co-op must be in compliance with Federal Trade Commission regulations which require that expenditures for co-op advertising be distributed to retailers on a basis proportionate to the volume of the goods they purchase. Despite the problems that national advertisers encounter in utilizing co-op adver-

Figure 7–5
The Advertising Checking Bureau

If your Co-op program's a circle of frustration, let ACB run it—and make more money for you!

Problems with Billings? Rate verification? Paying? Conformance? Hours and hours of time spent by too many people trying to make your Co-op work better? And those hidden costs on top of it all—how much do *they* run?

Let ACB take over and change frustration into success! ACB will do *all* the nitty-gritty work for you—the planning, checking, auditing, paying and reporting.

And ACB will give you complete Co-op control for far less than doing it yourself.

You see, we're the largest, most experienced Co-op audit, payment and verification service in the country, handling more than 600 plans, processing more than one million claims every year.

So break the circle of Co-op frustration and let your Co-op make money for you. Call your nearest ACB representative. Or, if you'd like more information first, send for our comprehensive Co-op Booklet 500.

Call your nearest ACB office.

NEW YORK: 2 Park Avenue, 10016; Phone 212/685-7300
CHICAGO: 434 South Wabash Avenue, 60605; Phone 312/922-2841
COLUMBUS, OHIO: 941 North High Street, 43201; Phone 614/294-4761
MEMPHIS: 52 South Second Street, 38103; Phone 901/526-3281
SAN FRANCISCO: 1453 Mission Street, 94103; Phone 415/626-6546
ORLANDO: 1010 Executive Center Drive, 32803; Phone 305/898-7680

tising, it is an alternative worth considering when newspaper advertising is expected to be a major feature of a national campaign.

In recent years the number of co-op offers and the number of companies offering co-op arrangements have grown tremendously. To make retailers aware of co-op opportunities, several reference books have been compiled to outline the sources and types of available co-op plans. Local media space and time salesmen also find that these catalogs of co-op plans can be invaluable in gaining additional advertising from retailers. Figure 7–6 shows a typical listing from one of the standard co-op guides.

Figure 7–6
Listing from a co-op guide

—A—

A-1 KOTZIN COMPANY
1300 South Santee Street
Los Angeles, Calif. 90015
TRADEMARK-Tobias
PRODUCTS COVERED-All Tobiam (TM)
Slacks, Jeans, and Tops. Also Angels Flight
PRO RATA SHARE OF COSTS-Up to 50% depending on media.
BILLING PROCEDURES-Send invoices and tear sheets to A-1 %: Checking-Bureau, P.O. Box 3419 Rincon Annex, San Francisco, Calif. 94119 within 60 days.
MEDIA APPROVED-Radio, Newspaper. Manufacturer's Co-Op Limitations-Prior approval on radio.

ABBOTT CONSUMER PRODUCTS DIVISION
Abbott Park
North Chicago, Ill. 60064
Advertising Manager-Susan Bartaux
PRODUCTS COVERED-Abbott CPD Products
PRO RATA SHARE OF COSTS-5% of net purchases from Oct 1'77-Sept 30 '78.
BILLING PROCEDURES-Invoices must be submitted no later than 60 days after performance dates.
MEDIA APPROVED-Radio, Newspaper, Outdoor, and TV.
Manufacturer's Co-Op Limitations-Funds earned and allocated advertise another brand. Signed contract #5426 must be on file at CPD headquarters before any claims can be processed for payment.

ACCO SEED
P.O. Box 9
Div. of Anderson, Clayton & Company
515 River Avenue North
Belmond, Iowa 50421
Advertising Manager-Lynn O. Henderson
TRADEMARK-Acco Seed
PRODUCTS COVERED-Seed Sales
BILLING PROCEDURES-Copy of tear sheet and invoice.
MEDIA APPROVED-Radio, Newspaper, Television, Direct Mail.
AIDS AVAILABLE-Spots, Mats, Film Clips, Shopper, and Glossies.
Manufacturer's Co-Op Limitations-50%
Special Co-Op Instructions-Dealers pay entire invoice; 50% credit is then paid to their accounts.

ACE MANUFACTURING COMPANY
P.O. Box 114
Abington, Pa. 19001
TRADEMARK-Ace "Servespoon," "Drain 'R Cut Spoon," Slice'a Slice, "Serves' Fork"

Figure 7–6 (*continued*)

BILLING PROCEDURES-1%, 10 net-30.
MEDIA APPROVED-Newspaper and Direct Mail.
AIDS AVAILABLE-Glossies, limited number, 24 or 30 sheet posters.
Special Co-Op Limitations-Portion of Ad cost paid on approval only.

ACTIVATED CHEMICALS & PRODUCTS CO.
Chemical Research
110 West Ash Avenue
Burbank, Calif. 91502
Advertising Manager-Ben Goldman
TRADEMARK-Sea Cal and Sea Chem
PRODUCTS COVERED-Sea Cal and Sea Chem Enzyme Septic Tank and Cesspool Activator, Sea Chem Enzyme Grease Trap Cleaner.
PRO RATA SHARE OF COSTS-50% paid by manufacturer, 50% by distributor; 20% of purchases allowed for advertising.
BILLING PROCEDURES-Advertising allowance deducted from invoice upon receipt.
MEDIA APPROVED-Newspaper.

AIDS AVAILABLE-Mats.
Manufacturer's Co-Op Limitations-Time limit for claiming allowance 90 days.

ADELAAR BROTHERS, INC.
525 7th Street
New York, N.Y.
Advertising Manager-Charles Jarver
TRADEMARK-Suitable
PRODUCTS COVERED-Adelaar
PRO RATA SHARE OF COSTS-50-50 basis up to a maximum of 1½% of net purchases made in the previous year within the same seasonal range for total of 3% for advertising. (Seasons are Jan-June and July-Dec.)
BILLING PROCEDURES-Send a tear sheet of the ad, accompanied by an invoice showing the newspaper, date of ad, size of ad, rate, and total cost at 50% to Adelaar, New York, New York.
MEDIA APPROVED-Newspaper
AIDS AVAILABLE-Mats and Glossies
LIMITATIONS-Must be 1st quality.

Courtesy: *TRIPAC, Inc. Middlesboro, Kentucky*

Figures 7–7 through 7–9 show some forms suggested by the Newspaper Advertising Bureau to aid retailers in planning, requesting, and obtaining reimbursement of advertising dollars. It is important to emphasize the term *cooperative* in this type of advertising. Cooperative advertising can be beneficial to media, national advertisers, and retailers. However, to carry out its mission effectively, it must be planned with the same types of marketing objectives and advertising strategy as are applied to other forms of advertising.

4. Classified advertising. A final category is newspaper classified advertising. While all of us are familiar with the "want ad" section of our newspaper, few realize its importance. It is estimated that classified advertising accounts for double the revenue (or approximately $4 billion) obtained from national advertising in newspapers, and this revenue is generated at a lower cost than national advertising. The

Figure 7–7
Co-op advertising information request

Gather co-op program information using a form like this

Co-Op Advertising Information Request

Date *February 1, 1980*

Manufacturer's Name *Nordstrom Manufacturing Co.*

Home Office Address *1435 Sanders St.*

Bell City, Ohio 06512

Attn. National Sales Manager

I am budgeting a yearly advertising program for my store. In order to take advantage of any Co-op Advertising allowances offered by vendors supplying me, I would appreciate your filling out the following information and returning it to me by *March 15, 1980* (Date)

Thank you for your help.

Cordially, *Frank W. Wilson*

Frank's Appliance Store

Lebanon, Missouri 61202

1
Does your company offer a co-op ad allowance that I qualify for? YES ☒ NO ☐

2
If answer to question #1 is YES, and your company has a printed Co-op Program, simply send the program and answer only those questions NOT covered in your printed plan. If NO, please return the entire form to me in the enclosed envelope.

3
What is the basis of accrual of co-op funds? (Example: 3% of net purchases, 5% of net purchases, unlimited, or 50¢ per unit, etc.)

10% of your purchases

4
What is the time period that the accrual is based on? (Example: based on last calendar year's purchases)

This year's purchases

5
How much ad allowances, based on my purchases, have I available to spend?

Dollar figure: *$1,500.00*

6
Please stipulate whether your Co-op Program is on a 50/50—75/25—100% paid, or a fixed line rate basis.

100% paid

7
What are the time limits in which the Co-op ads must appear in the paper, to insure your company's participation?

March 1st thru August 31st

8
What "proof of performance" does your co-op plan require? (Example: tear sheet, newspaper invoice, store invoice, etc.)

A tear sheet and duplicate net invoice from your newspaper

9
How soon after an ad appears must we submit "proof of performance" to your company and whom do we mail it to in order to get paid?

30 Days

1435 Sanders St., Bell City, Ohio 06512

Attn. Co-op Auditing Dept.-Nordstrom Mfg. Co.

10
What requirements does your company have in order for us to comply with their co-op plan. (Example: ads must use illustrations of product, registry symbols, product logo, (your policy on competing products in same ad, etc.)

Logo and trademark - a picture

11
Are there any restrictions in your co-op plan regarding newspaper classified advertising?

No! As long as a picture of our product and our logo appear in the newspaper ad

If your company has a printed Co-Op Plan and/or retail kit, will you please enclose it with this form and mail to me today.

This form has been completed by

Name *Thomas C. Nordstrom*

Title *National Sales Mgr.*

Phone *614-222-3156*

Frank W. Wilson
Retailer authorized signature

Source: Newspaper Advertising Bureau, *Newspaper Advertising Planbook, 1980,* p. 12.

Figure 7–8
Calculating co-op money

Calculate Co-op Money

Cooperative advertising control sheet

Company *Jones Camera Co.*

Product(s) *35 mm still cameras, lenses, accessories*

Co-op terms *5% of net purchases 50/50 participation*

Accrual period *Jan. 1 – Dec. 31*

Sales representative *Jim Roberts (914) 557-1883*

Reimbursement requirements *Claim must be submitted within 45 days after insertion*

Send to *Co-op Dept. Jones Camera Co. 44 Short St., Anytown, U.S.A. 00388*

Planned $ merchandise purchases	$ available for co-op	Date & size of ad	Co-op $ spent	Date invoice & tear sheets submitted	Date re-imbursement received	Balance of co-op $ available
12,000	600	6/12 40 col. in.	120	6/30	7/28	480
		11/12 50 col. in	150	11/28	12/28	330
		12/15 110 col. in	330	12/30	1/21	0

Summary of planned allocation of co-op funds for year ending *Dec. 31, 1980*

JAN.	FEB.	MAR.	APR.	MAY	JUNE	JULY	AUG.	SEPT.	OCT.	NOV.	DEC.
					40"					50"	110"

NOTES:

June, November and December are months when camera sales are greatest.

Source: Newspaper Advertising Bureau, *Newspaper Advertising Planbook*, 1980, p. 13.

Figure 7–9
Cooperative advertising claim

Collect co-op money using a form like this

Cooperative
Advertising Claim

To:
Co-op Auditing Dept.
Nordstrom Manufacturing Co.
1435 Sanders St.
Bell City, Ohio 06512

From:
Frank's Appliance Store
185 Madison St.
Lebanon, Missouri
61202

We submit the following cooperative advertising claim in accordance with the terms of your cooperative advertising program. Proof of advertising is enclosed in the form of duplicate bills and newspaper tear sheets.

Your prompt issuance of a credit or a check covering payment of this claim is expected and will enable us to continue and extend use of your cooperative advertising program.

Newspaper	Date of Advertisement	Space Used	Net Rate	Total Cost	Vendor's Co-op Cost
Lebanon Daily Record	April 15, 1980	80 inches	$5.00 per inch	$400.00	$400.00

I certify that the above is billed at my exact LOWEST NET RATE, computed after all normally earned discounts and expected rebates—and that the amount billed does not include (1) production costs, (2) special or preferred position premiums. If any further discounts, or rebates, other than those already computed, are earned by us for space used, your share will be promptly refunded.

Date May 3, 1980

Signature Frank W. Wilson

Source: Newspaper Advertising Bureau, *Newspaper Advertising Planbook*, 1980, p. 14.

three major types of classified advertisers are help wanted, real estate, and automotive, which account for almost 90 percent of newspapers' classified revenues.[3] In most newspapers advertisers have

[3] E. S. Lorimor, "Classified Advertising: A Neglected Medium," *Journal of Advertising*, Winter 1977, p. 19.

the option of placing all-text notices or display advertisements within the classified section.

Major advertising considerations for newspapers

As has been pointed out, the newspaper is an extremely adaptable medium for advertisers. The advertising community's respect for the medium is reflected not only in the billions of dollars that advertisers spend in newspapers but also in the number and diversity of the advertisers that regularly use newspapers as a primary or secondary advertising vehicle. Nevertheless, certain major characteristics of the newspaper must be considered by an advertiser before investing in the medium. Major advantages and disadvantages of the newspaper as an advertising vehicle are discussed below.

Problems and solutions in co-op advertising

Problem	Solution
1. **Vendor rates, or the rate established by the retailer for use when billing co-op advertising to his suppliers.** Normally, vendor rates are based on the local rate paid by the store, plus a charge for ad production and other overhead expenses incurred by the retailer in developing a local ad. It's common knowledge that these rates are inflated. It's just a question of how much. One co-op expert says vendor rates can turn a retail store's ad department into a major profit center.	The solution to many of these problems rests in most cases with the manufacturer. Says one industry observer: "The manufacturer who is willing to be strong and up-front in his co-op program and is selling a quality product, will have far fewer problems in dealing with retailers." One company which is said to have good relationships with stores is Arrow Shirts. Arrow has a predetermined set policy on co-op and sticks by it. There are no variations within the plan and each store is treated equally within a given market. It is generous in its co-op allowance and for good reason: that's one way to get around the store's vendor rate. "We pay two thirds of co-op and the retailer pays one third," says Bob Clark, ad director at Arrow. "We don't pay the vendor rate. We think we're very fair paying two thirds. It makes the program very cut and dry. Our policies and terms are set down and are equal for everyone." Arrow will go along with a store in advertising in any recognized medium. It also assists the stores in utilizing co-op funds. "The media mix comes into that planning," says

Problems and solutions in co-op advertising (*continued*)

Problem	Solution
	Clark. "We would recommend certain media to the store."
2. Catalog costs. This is one area where the manufacturer has almost no control at all in what he must pay to have his merchandise appear in a catalog. Retailers reportedly charge different manufacturers different rates for equal space in a catalog.	In some cases, the bigger the company and the better its product, the more clout it has with retailers. Kodak is an example of this. The company refuses to pay what retailers charge for catalog costs and instead follows its own equal payment policy all the way. The company requires the store to submit all its bills for the catalog and Kodak pays 75 to 100 percent of its share of the cost. The cost is determined by dividing the total cost of the catalog by the number of pages. Kodak gets a per page cost and then a per square inch cost and gets a figure from there. "If the retailer refuses to submit his bills, then we use a set scale where we pay a certain amount for a one-color or two-color page and we ignore what the store asks for," says John Allen. Michael Horen, formerly of London Fog and now a manager of marketing services for Pulsare Time Inc., says he had his own way of dealing with catalogs when he worked for London Fog. "We had a fixed line for catalogs, based on circulation and size. We didn't care what the store said it cost. "We went to printers and asked how much it cost to print the catalogs. We also decided it shouldn't cost more to appear in a catalog than to run an ad in the *New York Times Sunday Magazine.* Some retailers spend one half to three quarters of a million dollars on these catalogs and then try to make up the cost by billing manufacturers. The small companies get killed on this. They don't have the volume or the markup to meet the cost. Horen was instrumental in developing the idea for Catalog Clearing House, a brand-new service offered by Pinpoint Marketing Inc., a co-op advertising auditing firm in New York. The Clearinghouse analyzes what one company

Problems and solutions in co-op advertising (*continued*)

Problem	Solution
	pays to be in a catalog compared to another company. "We analyze catalog competitors," says Irene Ferber, VP client services at Pinpoint Marketing. "Basically, we tell manufacturers how much they're being overcharged by the retailer. Everybody knows they're being overcharged, but they don't know how much. If they do know, then they can negotiate with the store on a price."
3. Double billing. While the Federal Communications Commission clamped down on this by threatening to lift a TV or radio station's license if it goes along with this practice, the problem still exists although to a lesser degree. Many manufacturers fear that double billing will increase if radio is deregulated and the FCC ruling eliminated. Said one major manufacturer, "Small radio stations can come under a lot of pressure from retailers if the FCC drops out of the picture." The commission is currently considering the question of radio deregulation as proposed by the	Some manufacturers are afraid that they themselves might be in the auditing business if the radio industry is deregulated and the station logging procedure eliminated. "How do you check on billing if there is no logging," asked Arthur Ginsberg who heads up the FCC Complaints and Compliance Division. "The FCC may throw the burden on someone else and that may be the manufacturer. The question has been raised of whether the commission should be policing this industry at all. I can't predict what will happen because the commission hasn't met yet. But the question of deregulation will be placed before the public in open hearings and everyone, including advertisers, can voice their concern." Besides the logging issue, there is also the question of whether or not the FCC will lift its policy on double billing. Erwin Krasnow, general counsel for the National Association of Broadcasters, which proposed deregulation, says deregulation doesn't automatically mean the end of the double-billing rule. He says the NAB is more concerned with the broader issue of freeing radio from unnecessary government restraints. Comparing the broadcast and print media, Krasnow said, "There's a clear consensus that broadcasters are discriminated against by the federal government." Still, manufacturers are concerned about

Problems and solutions in co-op advertising (*concluded*)

Problem	Solution
National Association of Broadcasters. Hearings on the subject were scheduled for September of this year.	radio deregulation. While many of them say they are in favor of less government regulation in broadcast, they agree it could create problems in co-op advertising on radio. "If the FCC shield is taken away, radio could be in a terrible situation," says Ed Crimmins, a consultant on co-op to many manufacturers. "The electronic tear sheet and the double-billing rule resulted in a lot of co-op money for radio. But manufacturers could withdraw it overnight if they have to."
4. Control of co-op. How much of it should be institutional in nature, and how much of it should be devoted to the retail store? This is an ongoing problem among retailers and manufacturers and is one reason why so much co-op money goes unspent.	Manufacturer-based co-op offers a company greatest control. It's one way to escape vendor rates, retail copy, and it's usually very appealing to a small retailer, but not the larger ones. The big stores prefer to call the shots on co-op. One way to get around the power struggle and still stay in control is reserve the space or time in the appropriate media and notify the retailer so he can drop in the ad. The type of ad, the cost, and frequency are all decided beforehand. Ed Crimmins, a consultant on co-op to manufacturers, said the Florida Citrus Division was one of the first to use this type of co-op. Now it's done by many packaged good companies. "The plan has an interesting twist," says Crimmins. "Somebody is doing all the buying for the retailer, but they're telling him beforehand what he will pay." The plan is similar to what Art Fay of Direct-to-Media Inc. is doing. Fay, formerly with the Advertising Checking Bureau and the U.S. Suburban Press, proposes a plan where the manufacturer buys media up-front for retailers in key markets and allocates the buys in proportion to the individual retailer's sales. Fay says his plan offers manufacturers greater continuity and frequency in local markets and ties local advertising in with the national program.

Source: *Marketing & Media Decisions*, October 1979, pp. 76–77.

Pro

1. Audience coverage. Newspaper penetration covers all strata of society with the exception of the very young and the very poor. In some major markets newspapers cover as many as 70 percent of all households. Newspapers provide an excellent vehicle of high-intensity coverage for product introductions and sales.

2. Flexibility. As advertisers increasingly develop localized market plans, the newspaper offers the ability to reach customers on a market-by-market basis with messages designed specifically for the conditions of the locality. Because of its short production closing deadline the newspaper can be used to tie in advertising messages with changing market conditions and current news and sport events.

3. Editorial association. Many opportunities exist for the advertiser to associate a product with a section of the newspaper designed for a particular audience. The financial, entertainment, sports, travel, and food sections all provide advertisers with opportunities to associate their products with the proper editorial environment and increase advertisers' chances of directing their messages to prospects.

4. Long copy. Advertisers find that newspapers allow them to provide in-depth product information and prices impossible in most other media. Broadcasting and outdoor advertising restrict copy length, while magazines are not a practical advertising alternative for many advertisers.

Con

1. Lack of audience selectivity. A few major newspapers have made some progress in audience segmentation by offering advertisers some simple circulation breakouts. Most of these attempts have involved only geographic buys rather than the demographic segmentation needed by the majority of advertisers. Many newspaper executives think that greater utilization of the computer and the natural advantage newspapers have in controlling their own distribution will lead to audience segmentation of circulation in the future. However, today the newspaper is not a totally acceptable medium for an advertiser with specific audience requirements.

2. Clutter. The term *clutter* is usually associated with television. However, while television normally schedules 15 to 25 percent of its time for nonprogram content, the average daily newspaper runs in excess of 60 percent advertising.[4] In recent years studies have indicated that the adult reader usually spends less than 40 minutes with the newspaper. It is obvious that a newspaper advertisement must compete with many other messages during a relatively short time.

3. Lack of quality color reproduction. In the years since the ad-

[4] *Facts about Newspapers,* American Newspaper Publishers Association, 1978.

vent of offset printing, newspapers have made strides in improving color reproduction. However, the quality of color advertising is still uneven from newspaper to newspaper. This lack of guaranteed color quality reduces the use of newspapers by some major national advertisers and causes others to use preprinted supplements and inserts as alternatives to advertising within the newspaper itself. Other advertisers needing both local coverage and high-quality color have used other media such as outdoor, direct mail, and regional editions of magazines.

4. Buying difficulties. National advertisers have difficulty in purchasing newspaper advertising. Not only are national rates higher than local rates for comparable space, but the national advertiser must fill out separate insertion orders and deal with each newspaper individually. Attempts in the past by advertisers and media organizations to standardize rate cards (e.g., the AAAA model rate card) and develop national buying plans have met with limited success.

NEWSPAPER RATE STRUCTURE

National rates versus local rates

Most newspapers feature a rate structure different from that used by the majority of other advertising media. Newspapers normally charge national advertisers significantly higher rates compared to local advertisers. The amount of the local-national rate difference varies from as little as 10 percent to as much as double the local rate. Regardless of the amount, the practice is prevalent, with less than 100 daily newspapers (approximately 5 percent) offering a single rate schedule for national and local advertisers.

While some national advertisers are vocal in their opposition to the national-local rate differentiation, newspapers give several reasons for the practice. Most national advertising is placed through advertising agencies which qualify for an agency discount, usually 15 percent (see Chapter 4 for a discussion of media discounts to agencies). In addition a major portion of national advertising is solicited by media reps which are normally paid a percentage of the space costs. Finally, newspapers argue that the national advertiser normally obtains full advantage of the entire circulation of a newspaper, while a local business may serve only a portion of a market. There is also the intangible factor that newspapers have long regarded local merchants as "their" customers, while they have seen national advertisers as outsiders—a perception which the national-local differentiation reinforces.

National advertisers have criticized the rate differentiation on the basis that they often receive fewer services from the newpaper than does the local retailer who pays a reduced rate. Many critics of the higher national rate claim that it is self-defeating and has kept some national advertisers out of newspapers. In addition many of the abuses of co-op advertising stem primarily from these higher costs to national advertisers.

Units of purchase

The basic units of purchase for newspapers are the agate line (usually simply called "lines") and the column inch. There are 14 lines in a column inch, and the typical newspaper page is 8 columns by approximately 21½ inches. A full page in an eight-column newspaper will be equivalent to approximately 2,400 lines. This will vary according to the page size of the newspaper, so each paper must be checked for accurate rate and mechanical information.

Figure 7–10
Comparing advertising costs of newspapers with varying column formats

	Number of columns	*Length of newspaper*	*Cost/ line*
Newspaper A	6	21 inches	10 cents
Newspaper B	8	21	8
Newspaper C	9	21	7

In the past few years many newspapers have adjusted their column widths, commonly changing to either a six- or nine-column format from the traditional eight columns. The agate line and column inch remain one column wide in these newspapers, regardless of whether a six-, eight-, or nine-column format is used. In figuring rates, the media buyer must be careful to compare newspapers of different formats on a common base. The most convenient method for doing this is to compute full-page costs and compare different newspapers on this basis (see Figure 7–10).

Assuming that the circulations of the three newspapers in Figure 7–10 are the same, the careless media buyer, ignoring the different formats of the three newspapers, would of course choose newspaper C as the least expensive. However, converting each of the line rates to a full-page price (Number of columns × 14 lines/inch × 21-inch depth × Cost), we find that newspaper A has the lowest page cost:

Newspaper A = \$176
Newspaper B = \$188
Newspaper C = \$185

Figure 7–11
SRDS listing for six-column newspaper

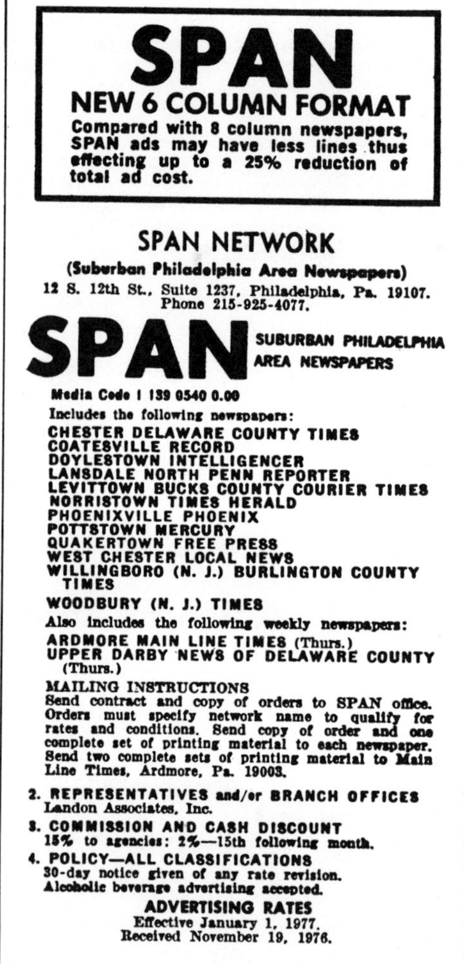

SPAN
NEW 6 COLUMN FORMAT
Compared with 8 column newspapers, SPAN ads may have less lines thus effecting up to a 25% reduction of total ad cost.

SPAN NETWORK
(Suburban Philadelphia Area Newspapers)
12 S. 12th St., Suite 1237, Philadelphia, Pa. 19107. Phone 215-925-4077.

SPAN SUBURBAN PHILADELPHIA AREA NEWSPAPERS

Media Code 1 139 0540 0.00
Includes the following newspapers:
CHESTER DELAWARE COUNTY TIMES
COATESVILLE RECORD
DOYLESTOWN INTELLIGENCER
LANSDALE NORTH PENN REPORTER
LEVITTOWN BUCKS COUNTY COURIER TIMES
NORRISTOWN TIMES HERALD
PHOENIXVILLE PHOENIX
POTTSTOWN MERCURY
QUAKERTOWN FREE PRESS
WEST CHESTER LOCAL NEWS
WILLINGBORO (N. J.) BURLINGTON COUNTY TIMES
WOODBURY (N. J.) TIMES
Also includes the following weekly newspapers:
ARDMORE MAIN LINE TIMES (Thurs.)
UPPER DARBY NEWS OF DELAWARE COUNTY (Thurs.)
MAILING INSTRUCTIONS
Send contract and copy of orders to SPAN office. Orders must specify network name to qualify for rates and conditions. Send copy of order and one complete set of printing material to each newspaper. Send two complete sets of printing material to Main Line Times, Ardmore, Pa. 19003.
2. REPRESENTATIVES and/or BRANCH OFFICES
Landon Associates, Inc.
3. COMMISSION AND CASH DISCOUNT
15% to agencies: 2%—15th following month.
4. POLICY—ALL CLASSIFICATIONS
30-day notice given of any rate revision.
Alcoholic beverage advertising accepted.
ADVERTISING RATES
Effective January 1, 1977.
Received November 19, 1976.

Courtesy: *Standard Rate and Data Service*

The problem of media buyers not taking note of the different newspaper formats is so serious that special notices are often placed on the rate cards and directory listings of six- and nine-column newspapers. Figure 7–11 shows such a listing from the *Newspaper SRDS* for a six-column newspaper.

A few newspapers offer local advertisers modular space buys. This space unit may become prevalent in the future as newspapers move toward the modular plan for national advertising discussed earlier in this chapter.

Open rate versus flat rate

Newspaper rate schedules fall into one of two categories: open rate (also called sliding scale) or flat rate. An open-rate newspaper offers bulk discounts based on the amount of space purchased or the number of continuous weeks a product is advertised. Most metropolitan dailies offer some form of discount to their advertisers. A flat-rate paper is one which charges the same price per line or column inch regardless of the amount of space bought. The flat rate is most prevalent among weeklies and smaller daily newspapers. The newspaper whose rates are shown in Figure 7–12 charges a flat rate for display advertising but offers bulk and continuity discounts to classified advertisers. Likewise, a flat-rate newspaper may use a local-national rate differentiation but give no discounts to either type of advertiser.

Recently the U.S. Justice Department brought suit against the *Los Angeles Times,* charging that its sliding scale constituted restraint of trade since it unfairly favored large advertisers. The matter is being challenged by the Times Mirror Company, the *Los Angeles Times* parent company, but any future judgment by the courts in favor of the Justice Department's charges could have major implications for the rate structure offered by many major newspapers.

Short rate versus rebate

Normally newspaper advertising contracts are price-setting devices based on the anticipated advertising of a firm in a particular newspaper. In a flat-rate newspaper this is no problem since each line of advertising is purchased at the same rate. In an open-rate newspaper, the newspaper and the advertiser agree on a rate to be paid for some period, usually a year, then make necessary adjustments at the end of the contract period. Figure 7–13 demonstrates typical short-rate and rebate situations.

In example 1, advertiser A originally agreed to pay the maximum line rate of \$1.50. However, at the end of the contract period it was found that the advertiser had qualified for the lower \$1.40 rate and the newspaper owed the advertiser a rebate of \$500. In example 2, advertiser B failed to qualify for the rate (\$1/line) agreed upon at the beginning of the contract period. At the end of the period, advertiser B had to make up the difference between what should have been paid and what was actually paid. This difference, a short rate, was \$2,000.

Figure 7–12
The advertising rates of a flat-rate newspaper

HAYWARD

Alameda County—Map Location B-6
See SRDS consumer market map and data at beginning of the State

	Households	Population
Corporate city population (1970 govt. census)		93,058
ABC city zone ('70 census)	78,903	254,017
ABC retail tr. zone ('70 census)	59,946	218,946

REVIEW

A Sparks Newspaper
116 W. Winton, Hayward, Calif. 94544.
Phones 415-783-6111, 351-6210.

Media Code 1 105 2925 2.00
EVENING AND SUNDAY.

1. PERSONNEL
Publisher—Floyd Sparks.
National Advertising Manager—John Sandoval.
Nat'l Adv. Sales Representative—Connie Conrad.

3. COMMISSION AND CASH DISCOUNT
15% to agencies; 2% 15th following month.

4. POLICY—ALL CLASSIFICATIONS
60-day notice given of any rate revision.
Alcoholic beverage advertising accepted.

5. BLACK/WHITE RATES
Flat, per agate line (daily or Sunday) .... .47

6. GROUP COMBINATION RATES—B/W & Color
U. S. Suburban Press, Inc. Newspaper Network—see listing in National Newspapers Section.
Also sold in combination with Fremont Argus, Tri-Valley Herald and Tri-Valley News (tri-weekly), extra .39 per line. Same copy, same calendar week.
Circulation:
Argus—Net Paid A.B.C. 9-30-76—Morn 15,434; Sun 15,409.
Tri-Valley Herald—Net Paid A.B.C. 3-31-76—Morn 10,766; Sun 10,713.
Tri-Valley News—3-31-76.
After three requests, publisher has failed to file circulation statement on SRDS form.
Daily Review Shopping News (Wednesday) extra, per agate line .... .32
(Ad must run in Review & Argus same calendar week.)
Circulation—Sworn 9-30-76:
Hayward edition—Total non-paid 39,825.
San Leandro Area—Total non-paid 26,000.
Washington Township Area -- Total non-paid 39,285.
Deadline: Review Shopping News—4:30 p.m. Friday.

COLOR RATES AND DATA

B/w 1 c, 2 c and 3 c available daily, Sunday thru Saturday. 2 day leeway required weekdays. Minimum 560 lines.
Use b/w line rate plus the following applicable costs:

	b/w 1 c	b/w 2 c	b/w 3 c
Extra (excl. Shopping News)	336.00	606.00	876.00

CLASSIFICATION AND OTHER RATES

Amusements, Theater, Restaurants, per agate line .86; Political (cash with order), per agate line .86.

7. COLOR RATES AND DATA
B/w 1 c, 2 c and 3 c available daily, Sunday thru Saturday. 2-day leeway required weekdays. Minimum 560 lines.
Use b/w line rate plus the following applicable costs:

	b/w 1 c	b/w 2 c	b/w 3 c
Extra	120.00	210.00	300.00

Closing dates: Reservations 1 week in advance; printing material and cancellations 3 days in advance, daily; Sunday, 4 days in advance.

8. SPECIAL ROP UNITS
FLEXFORM PAGES
Available daily or Sunday. No restrictions regarding size or shape of ads other than following: Maximum space cannot exceed 65% of page (1529 lines). Individual units of ad form must be at least 1 column wide or multiple of standard column widths. All ad borders must be parallel to the chase. No other ad appears on page; make-up and content of editorial material inserted around ad form is responsibility of newspaper.

	b/w or b/w 1 c	b/w 2 c	b/w 3 c
Flat, per page	746.89	836.89	926.89

Linage applies toward regular R.O.P. contracts for volume discount.
Closing dates reservation and printing materials: 10 days before publication date.
Mechanical measurements:
Standard column widths—See Section 15.

11. SPECIAL DAYS/PAGES/FEATURES
Best Food Day: Wednesday.
Financial page, daily except Monday; Teen Times, Saturday; Home and Garden, Friday; Automotive, Thursday and Friday; Fashion Page, daily; Night and Day Around the Bay, Friday; TV Preview, Home Section, Sunday; Outdoor Outlook and Brightside, alternate Sundays.

12. ROP DEPTH REQUIREMENTS
As many inches deep as columns wide. Ads over 266 lines deep charged full column.

13. CONTRACT AND COPY REGULATIONS
See Contents page for location of regulations—items 1, 2, 3, 7, 10, 11, 12, 13, 14, 16, 18, 24, 28, 30 31, 32, 34, 35, 42.

14. CLOSING TIME
Noon, 2 days before publication; Sunday, noon, 4 days before publication.

15. MECH. MEASUREMENTS (Offset)
For complete, detailed production information, see SRDS Print Media Production Data.
8/10-9/3—8 cols/ea 10 picas-9 pts/3 pts betw col.
Lines to col. 294; page 2352; dbl. truck 4851.

16. SPECIAL CLASSIFICATION/RATES
Restaurants, Amusements, Theatres, per agate line .50; Political (cash with order), per agate line .47.

17. CLASSIFIED RATES
Classified Advertising Dir.—Philip E. Dutton.
Available in combination only. Same ad, all papers, same issues. Ads appear Tues. Hayward Review and Livermore, Tri-Valley Herald also run Wed. Review-Argus Shopping News and Tri-Valley News (charged as add'l issue.) All ads initially appear pm; then follow am.

COMBINATION RATES

	Per Day 1-2 ti	3 ti	4-6 ti	7-9 ti	(*)
3- 27 lines....	1.68	1.52	1.31	1.15	1.07
28- 72 lines....	1.32	1.27	1.09	.96	.89
74- 146 lines....	1.03	.98	.93	.88	.83
147- 300 lines....	1.01	.96	.91	.86	.81
301- 601 lines....	.99	.94	.89	.84	.79
602- 902 lines....	.97	.92	.87	.82	.79
903-1203 lines....	.95	.90	.85	.80	.79
1204-1504 lines....	.93	.88	.83	.79	.79
1505 2407 lines....	.91	.86	.81	.79	79
2408 lines or more..	.89	.84	.79	.79	.79

(*) 10 or more times.

Box number charge 4.00; mailed 5.50. Minimum 3 lines; average 5 words per line. Classified Display minimum 2 column inches.
Deadline: Mon. thru Sat. material 54 hours before publication; Sunday 4:00 p.m. Wed.
Regulations, see Contents—C-1 thru 15, 19 thru 22, P-1 thru 6, T-3, T-4.

18. CIRCULATION
Established 1891. Per copy Daily .15, Sunday .35.
Net Paid—A.B.C. 9-30-76 (Newspaper Form)

	Total	CZ	TrZ	Other
Eve	38,085	28,711	9,230	144
Sun	38,408	29,006	9,250	243

Max-Min rate (flat): Eve 12.13; Sun 12.03.
For county-by-county and/or metropolitan area breakdowns, see SRDS Newspaper Circulation Analysis.
Submitted by John Sandoval.

Courtesy: *Standard Rate and Data Service.*

Figure 7–13
Short rate and rebate: Newspaper XYZ sliding scale

Number of lines purchased within one year	*Cost/ line*
1,000	$1.50
3,000	1.45
5,000	1.40
10,000	1.30
50,000	1.15
100,000	1.00

Example 1: rebate

Advertiser A contracts for maximum line rate and uses 5,000 lines:

5,000	Lines used
× $1.50	Estimated contract cost
$7,500	Amount paid
5,000	Lines used
× $1.40	Actual cost
$7,000	Amount owed
$7,500	
− 7,000	
$ 500	Rebate

Example 2: Short rate

Advertiser B contracts for minimum line rate and uses 5,000 lines:

5,000	Lines used
× $1.00	Estimated contract cost
$5,000	Amount paid
5,000	Lines used
× $1.40	Actual cost
$7,000	Amount owed
$7,000	
− 5,000	
$2,000	Short rate

Milline rate

Often advertisers wish to compare the relative cost efficiency of newspapers with different circulations. Normally the milline rate is computed to make such comparisons. The milline rate is the cost per line to reach 1 million readers. The formula for figuring the milline rate is:

$$\text{Milline rate} = \frac{1{,}000{,}000 \times \text{Line rate}}{\text{Circulation}}$$

Using the newspaper in Figure 7–12, the milline rate would be:

$$\text{Milline rate, } \textit{Hayward Review} = \frac{1{,}000{,}000 \times \$.47}{38{,}085} = \$12.34$$

The milline rate is simply a means for comparing rates among newspapers and is never used as a rate to purchase newspaper space.

Often rate cards or SRDS listings will give the milline rate. In other cases instead of the milline rate a "Max-Mil" listing will be shown. Max-Mil stands for maximil and minimil. The maximil rate is defined as the maximum cost per 1 million readers, which is figured on the one-time, one-line rate. The minimil rate uses the same formula, but the discounted line rate. If the advertiser qualifies for a cash discount, the cost is multiplied by .983. The following formulas are used.

With the 2 percent cash discount:

$$\text{Maximil rate} = \frac{.983 \times \text{Maximum line rate} \times 1{,}000{,}000}{\text{Circulation}}$$

$$\text{Minimil rate} = \frac{.983 \times \text{Minimum line rate} \times 1{,}000{,}000}{\text{Circulation}}$$

With no cash discount:

$$\text{Maximil rate} = \frac{\text{Maximum line rate} \times 1{,}000{,}000}{\text{Circulation}}$$

$$\text{Minimal rate} = \frac{\text{Minimum line rate} \times 1{,}000{,}000}{\text{Circulation}}$$

When using the minimal rate formula, the advertiser will use the appropriate discount for which he qualifies rather than the minimum rate.

The media buyer must be sure that all newspapers being compared have the same number of columns, or some conversion must be made to take account of the differences. Otherwise we encounter the same problem discussed above, where the newspaper which appears to have the lowest advertising space costs might actually not be the least expensive. The media buyer may consider using the full-page rate rather than the line rate in making these comparisons. By using the large page cost rather than line costs, the comparisons can be made on a cost per 1,000 (CPM) basis (see Chapter 4). Using CPM rather than milline rate comparisons overcomes the variable-column problem. It also allows comparisons with other major media, assuming that cost is the only consideration. Again using the example of the *Hayward Review,* the page comparison would be computed as follows:

Lines per page	2,352
Cost per line	$ .47
Cost per page	$1,105.44

$$CPM = \frac{1{,}000 \times \$1{,}105.44}{38{,}085} = \$29.03$$

Run-of-paper and special rates for newspaper advertising

Most newspaper space is bought on a run-of-paper (ROP) basis. ROP simply means that the newspaper may place the advertisement wherever it wishes. Advertisers often request a particular position, and when possible the newspaper will try to accommodate them. Remember that it is to the newspaper's advantage to give an advertiser the best possible position to make the advertising effective.

In addition to ROP many newspapers charge special rates for placing advertising in certain sections or on especially visible portions of a page. Advertisers may have to pay a premium to guarantee space in, say, the sports section. Or newspapers may charge extra for guaranteeing that an advertisement will be placed at the top of a column next to a news story. This is generally known as full position. The types of premium rates vary with individual newspapers, and the advertiser must check rate cards or inquire as to the availability of such special rates.

Combination rates

As the number of major cities with jointly owned morning and evening newspapers increases, advertisers find that they are often able (or required) to purchase a combination of these newspapers. Generally the space must be bought in consecutive editions and the same space and copy must be used. For the advertiser the combination rate usually offers significant savings over buying the two newspapers individually.

Auditing the newspaper audience

Since newspapers set their rates largely according to circulation, it is important for advertisers to know that newspaper circulation figures are correct. Beginning in 1914 the Audit Bureau of Circulations (ABC) has provided verified circulation figures for major newspapers and consumer magazines. The ABC report provides information not only concerning paid circulation, but also the circulation in city, trade and other zones as well as the number of subscribers who received the newspaper at a discount and the newspapers sold at the newsstand versus subscription.

ABC issues two major reports. The Publisher's Statement is issued twice a year and covers the periods ending March 31 and September 31. The ABC Audit Report is issued annually after an on-premise audit of the publisher's circulation data. In addition ABC also provides custom-order information on circulation, population, household, and demographic data for almost 2,000 magazines and newspapers through its *Circulation Data Bank Report.* The newest ABC service is the *Newspaper Audience Research Data Report,* which provides customized demographic reports on newspaper audiences.

THE OUTLOOK

Move to the suburbs. The movement to the suburbs during the last two decades has had profound effects on American culture. Education, housing, and transportation are only a few of the areas which have been changed by the transition from an urban to a suburban society. The traditional metropolitan daily newspaper has also been forced to adapt to this movement away from the inner city.

Long after the pattern of suburban living was established, the metropolitan daily continued to ignore the suburban population as a distinct audience. Local news coverage concentrated on city-wide issues, and the specific concern of the suburbs were usually covered by small weeklies or not at all. This neglect was largely a result of financial considerations. National and large local advertisers such as department stores largely ignored the suburban press, and consequently the metro newspapers saw no need to expend time and effort to cultivate or compete for a market which advertisers felt these newspapers were reaching adequately.

In the last several years, however, the suburban market and the suburban press serving it have become increasingly difficult to ignore. Suburban readers are beginning to view themselves as part of a community distinct from the metropolitan area. They have problems unique to the suburbs, and they are turning to suburban newspapers as a supplementary source of information. From an advertising viewpoint the market is simply too lucrative to overlook. As national advertisers turn their attention to local market strategies, they will treat the suburban audience as an audience separate from the larger metropolitan population.

Several large metropolitan newspapers are meeting the competition of the suburban press with zoned editions or local supplements for outlying areas. Both the *Chicago Tribune* and the *Chicago Sun-Times* provide suburban supplements up to five times a week to various metropolitan areas. A combination of 30 weekly newspapers called the Suburban Newspapers of Greater St. Louis claims 93 percent coverage of the metropolitan market. In the future the competition for the suburban audience will intensify as it becomes apparent that appealing to this group is the only way to maintain or increase newspaper circulation (and advertising revenues).

In the short term the suburban press will remain a local, retailer-oriented medium. The daily metropolitan press will continue to increase the zoned distribution approach to keep national advertisers and bring small retailers into the fold. The suburban press will entice national advertisers with incentives such as an upscale audience, greater selectivity, and easier national buys through such representative organizations as the U.S. Suburban Press, Inc., which services suburban newspapers through a nationwide network. (See Figure 7–14.)

Local market research. Despite the massive investment by advertisers in newspapers, the medium's research expenditure has been meager. In the past newspapers have often assumed that they were the only practical retail advertising vehicle and that there was therefore no reason to spend funds to prove what to them was obvious. In recent years, however, other media—regional editions of national magazines, radio, and television—have started to compete for advertising dollars once conceded to newspapers.

As a result newspapers have had to demonstrate their value as compared with that of other media. When William Simmons' Three Sigma company contracted with 26 media clients, including 8 newspapers in the New York area, for a local market comparison of the audiences of these media, many advertisers hoped that this would be the beginning of general syndicated research on a market-by-market basis.[5] In the future advertisers will expect newspapers to provide comparable audience data similar to the data which have long demanded of other media.

Unsuccessful efforts to develop a newspaper data bank indicate that the availability of broadly based newspaper audience data may be further from reality than advertisers would wish. Despite efforts by

[5] "Media Research: The Trend is to Local Multi-Media Studies," *Media Decisions*, February 1977, p. 68.

Figure 7–14
Rate card of U.S. Suburban Press, Inc.

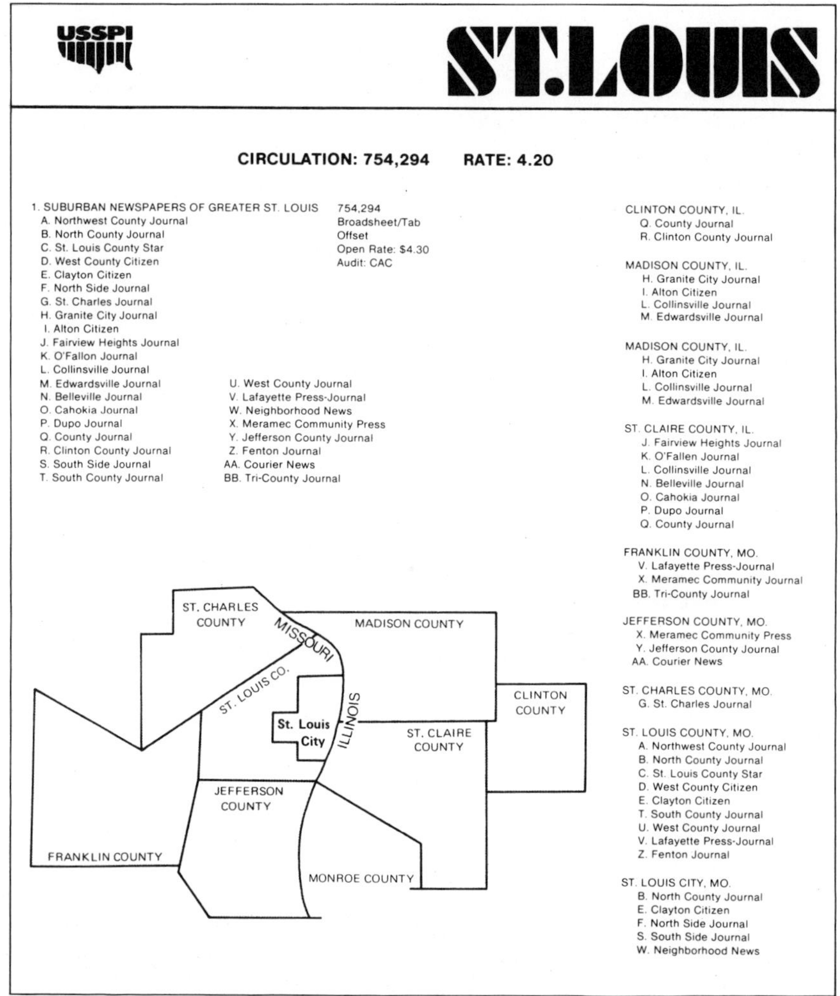

USSPI

ST. LOUIS

CIRCULATION: 754,294 RATE: 4.20

1. SUBURBAN NEWSPAPERS OF GREATER ST. LOUIS
   A. Northwest County Journal
   B. North County Journal
   C. St. Louis County Star
   D. West County Citizen
   E. Clayton Citizen
   F. North Side Journal
   G. St. Charles Journal
   H. Granite City Journal
   I. Alton Citizen
   J. Fairview Heights Journal
   K. O'Fallon Journal
   L. Collinsville Journal
   M. Edwardsville Journal
   N. Belleville Journal
   O. Cahokia Journal
   P. Dupo Journal
   Q. County Journal
   R. Clinton County Journal
   S. South Side Journal
   T. South County Journal
   U. West County Journal
   V. Lafayette Press-Journal
   W. Neighborhood News
   X. Meramec Community Press
   Y. Jefferson County Journal
   Z. Fenton Journal
   AA. Courier News
   BB. Tri-County Journal

754,294
Broadsheet/Tab
Offset
Open Rate: $4.30
Audit: CAC

CLINTON COUNTY, IL.
Q. County Journal
R. Clinton County Journal

MADISON COUNTY, IL.
H. Granite City Journal
I. Alton Citizen
L. Collinsville Journal
M. Edwardsville Journal

MADISON COUNTY, IL.
H. Granite City Journal
I. Alton Citizen
L. Collinsville Journal
M. Edwardsville Journal

ST. CLAIRE COUNTY, IL.
J. Fairview Heights Journal
K. O'Fallen Journal
L. Collinsville Journal
N. Belleville Journal
O. Cahokia Journal
P. Dupo Journal
Q. County Journal

FRANKLIN COUNTY, MO.
V. Lafayette Press-Journal
X. Meramec Community Journal
BB. Tri-County Journal

JEFFERSON COUNTY, MO.
X. Meramec Community Press
Y. Jefferson County Journal
AA. Courier News

ST. CHARLES COUNTY, MO.
G. St. Charles Journal

ST. LOUIS COUNTY, MO.
A. Northwest County Journal
B. North County Journal
C. St. Louis County Star
D. West County Citizen
E. Clayton Citizen
T. South County Journal
U. West County Journal
V. Lafayette Press-Journal
Z. Fenton Journal

ST. LOUIS CITY, MO.
B. North County Journal
E. Clayton Citizen
F. North Side Journal
S. South Side Journal
W. Neighborhood News

the Audit Bureau of Circulations and other interested parties, newspaper data remain a largely individualized enterprise, with some newspapers providing extensive audience and market data and others virtually none.

The newspaper as a delivery system. When discussing the newspaper as an advertising medium, we often overlook the fact that in addition to providing space for advertisements, the newspaper is also used as a delivery vehicle for separate material. National adver-

Figure 7–14 (*continued*)

ST. LOUIS

Metro Newspaper Circulation/Coverage Comparison

	Total Circ. (000)	Metro Circ. (000)	Metro Cov. %	City Zone* Circ. (000)	City Zone* Cov. %	Bal. Metro Circ. (000)	Bal. Metro Cov. %
HOUSEHOLDS		796.7		188.3		608.4	
GLOBE DEMOCRAT (M)	263.8	213.3	26.8	61.5	32.7	151.7	24.9
POST DISPATCH (E)	256.9	232.5	29.2	64.9	34.5	167.6	27.6
TOTAL	520.7	445.8	56.0	126.5	67.2	319.3	52.5
USSPI	754.3	739.1	92.8	146.6	77.9	592.5	97.4

Metro County Circulation Breakdown

County	HH's (000)	Globe Democrat Circ. (000)	Globe Democrat Cov. %	Post Dispatch Circ. (000)	Post Dispatch Cov. %	USSPI Circ. (000)	USSPI Cov. %
CLINTON, IL.	9.5	1.4	14.2	.5	5.8	6.2	64.9
MADISON, IL.	85.9	16.4	19.1	7.2	8.4	85.9	99.9
MONROE, IL.	6.4	1.4	22.3	.6	9.5	.4	5.5
ST. CLAIRE, IL.	94.9	15.2	16.0	5.8	6.2	79.3	83.5
FRANKLIN, MO.	21.5	2.7	12.7	2.3	10.9	20.5	95.4
JEFFERSON, MO.	38.3	6.7	17.5	5.5	14.3	38.1	99.5
ST. CHARLES, MO.	35.8	8.2	23.0	6.0	16.8	38.8	99.9
ST. LOUIS, MO.	316.1	99.7	31.5	139.6	44.2	323.3	99.9
ST. LOUIS CITY	188.3	61.5	32.7	64.9	34.5	146.6	77.9
TOTAL	796.7	213.3	26.8	232.5	29.2	739.1	92.8

Source: Circulation '78/'79: USSPI publisher records. *St. Louis City - Circulation '78/'79 does not report newspaper circulation in the core city. For purposes of analysis, USSPI shows circulation in City Zone (if available) or home county, whichever, by definition, is nearest the core city.

Market	% Population	% Households	% Total E.B.I.	Average E.B.I.	% Total Retail Sales	% Food Sales	% Auto Sales
ST. LOUIS METRO	100.0	100.0	100.0	$18,754	100.0	100.0	100.0
CITY**	21.2	23.6	18.3	14,543	20.0	19.9	15.3
SUBURBS (Balance of Metro)	78.8	76.4	81.7	20,058	80.0	80.1	84.7

Source: Sales Management's 1978 Survey of Buying Power. **Metro City: St. Louis

U.S. SUBURBAN PRESS, INC.

NEW YORK
122 E. 42nd St., Suite 818
New York, NY 10017
(212) 687-8425

ENGLEWOOD CLIFFS
333 Sylvan Ave.
Englewood Cliffs, NJ 07632
(212) 867-9181 (201) 567-4450

CHICAGO
262 East Illinois St.
Chicago, IL 60611
(312) 321-0275

ATLANTA
6520 Powers Ferry Rd.
Atlanta, GA 30339
(404) 955-3040

DETROIT
3221 W. Big Beaver Rd.
Suite 106
Troy, MI 48084
(313) 647-7677

LOS ANGELES
3400 Wilshire Blvd.
P.O. Box 70024, Amb. Sta.
Los Angeles, CA 90070
(213) 380-8840

ST. LOUIS
Suite 200
677 N. New Ballas Rd.
St. Louis, MO 63141
(314) 872-9512

DALLAS
2225 E. Randol Mill Rd.
Suite 223
Arlington, TX 76011
(817) 461-9653

NEW ORLEANS
P.O. Box 8271
3033 N. Causeway
Metairie, LA 70010
(504) 834-8658

PORTLAND/SEATTLE
157 Yesler
Seattle, WA 98104
(206) 623-0096

PHILADELPHIA
Dublin Hall - Suite 324
1777 Walton Rd.
Blue Bell, PA 19422
(215) 542-0232

tisers can use preprinted inserts by providing either rolls of newsprint with their advertisement on one side or freestanding or loose inserts which may vary from a single sheet to a 32-page booklet. In both cases the insert has several advantages to the advertiser:

1. The advertiser can control the printing quality from newspaper to newspaper. This may be important when color is used.
2. A national advertising supplement may be localized with the name of the individual retailer.
3. The space and production costs of inserts printed in bulk can be significantly lower compared to the costs of purchasing the same space in individual newspapers.
4. Inserts can provide coupons and long copy which would be impractical or expensive if run as a regular advertisement.

Some newspapers offer zoning of insert distribution. This regionalization of circulation allows smaller retailers as well as national firms the opportunity to use inserts. Some newspapers are experimenting with the delivery of advertising material to households not subscribing to them. Since the newspapers already have distributors who pass each household, this allows the newspapers to increase their profits by operating as a delivery agent to all households, not just subscribing households. It also provides 100 percent household coverage for the advertiser, regardless of newspaper penetration. In the future newspapers will provide means of delivering supplemental material which will give them an even greater advantage over their local media competitors.

The shopper. In the 1960s the free delivery, all-advertising shopper was aggressively promoted in many markets. The early shoppers were either delivered to each household in a market or were available free through retail outlets, most of which were also advertisers. The initial reaction of newspapers was to ignore the shopper and hope it would go away. However, favorable public response as well as more sophisticated marketing by these publications has made them a viable competitor to newspapers in many markets.

In some instances newspapers have started their own shoppers or have bought out competitors' publications in order to serve advertisers in both type of outlets. Harte-Hanks Communications, Inc., a major communication corporation with newspapers and broadcast stations throughout the country, has found shoppers (or "pennysavers" as it calls them) to be among its most profitable enterprises.

Shoppers promise extensive coverage at a very low cost to advertisers. They are unaudited, and so there are no circulation guarantees comparable to those of other media. As a matter of policy many advertisers, particularly national firms, will not advertise in unaudited publications. Consequently, the shopper tends to be a local advertising vehicle whose success depends on the ability of the advertising sales force and the value of the local newspaper.

In recent years the trend has been for shoppers to accompany the advertising with a limited amount of editorial material. Usually the material is more filler than meaningful information. However, some shoppers have actually evolved into regular weekly newspapers with a full news staff. One of the more popular shopper formats is the local television schedule. This gives the consumer a reason to pick up the shopper in the first place and increases the average life of the publication.

Inflation. The typical daily newspaper is unlike many businesses in that it is both labor and capital intensive. That is, it needs many skilled workers and is also faced with the task of finding funds for the purchase and maintenance of equipment which is constantly being updated. Newspaper equipment changed more in the 20 years between 1960 and 1980 than in the 80 years between 1880 and 1960. The cash reserves required to maintain this increasing pace of change and adaptation continues to put pressure on newspapers, even those with a history of favorable cash flow.

American newspapers employ almost 400,000 people; this does not include the more than 1 million newspaper carriers, who are considered contract workers rather than regular employees. Only the U.S. steel and automotive industries employ more people. Over one quarter of newspaper employees are women, and 40 percent are production employees. With such a large number of employees, many of whom are highly skilled, it is natural that wage inflation is a serious problem for newspapers. Of even more concern is the inflation of newsprint and equipment costs. Whereas inflation during the last decade increased 80–100 percent for the American economy as a whole, the cost of newsprint increased more than 250 percent. Newspapers also began the transition to electronic editing and production during this period, necessitating massive amounts of new capital. All of these factors have contributed to higher subscription and single-copy prices to readers and rapid increases in advertising prices. Among the major media only television time costs have increased at a rate greater than the costs of newspaper advertising since 1970.

The youth market. One of the most discussed topics of the last several years has been how to get and keep the young adult reader. The ability to solve this problem successfully may determine the future of the newspaper as an effective advertising medium. Two crucial problems exist for newspapers in their quest for the youth market. First, the young adult of 18–34 is a prime target audience for many national advertisers. Second, the person who is not a regular newspaper reader by the age of 20 is probably not going to become one in later years. Newspapers have recently devoted considerable research to the problem of appealing to younger readers. The studies have indicated that in addition to hard news, features, how-to-do-it articles, and personality pieces appeal to these readers.

The electronic newspaper. Much has been written in recent years about the electronic nature of the modern newspaper. With the development of electronic editing much of the production process has been moved from the back shop to the newsroom. Some newspaper executives foresee a day when the newspaper will be delivered electronically to readers who use a video display terminal (VDT) and who order only those portions needed for future reference in the form of "hard copy."

Some people in the newspaper industry are also predicting the advent of one or more national newspapers with a basic national edition sent by satellite to many markets where local news and features can be added. *The Wall Street Journal* is already doing this with a limited number of local editions.

Such an electronic revolution has major implications for newspaper advertising. While the practical possibilities are many, let's look at one potential tie-in between advertising and the "electronic newspaper."

All of us are familiar with the coded symbols on most common consumer items. This Universal Product Code (UPC) was originally intended to facilitate inventory control and reduce labor costs at the retail level. However, the UPC may one day become the center of a marketing information system among retailers, distributors, manufacturers, advertising agencies, and the media. Figure 7–15 demonstrates a projected use of the UPC in such a network.

Here the UPC, in combination with other facilities, could go far beyond simple inventory control in coordination with various components of the marketing system. Data reflecting a retailer's current stock would constantly be coded into a central computer. Printouts would then be transmitted to the manufacturer by either satellite or ordinary telephone lines. The manufacturer in consultation with its advertising agency could then adjust inventories and promotion to the current local market situation. The advertising agency could prepare advertisements and transmit them by satellite to a newspaper or other local medium equipped with a receiving disk. Advertisements in tomorrow's newspapers could be based on today's sales activity.

Extensive utilization of the UPC for implementing marketing strategy is still some years away. However, in certain test cities marketing research is using the UPC as part of a realistic advertising measurement technique. One device, called Behaviorscan, provides a con-

Figure 7–15
Advertising and the electronic newspaper

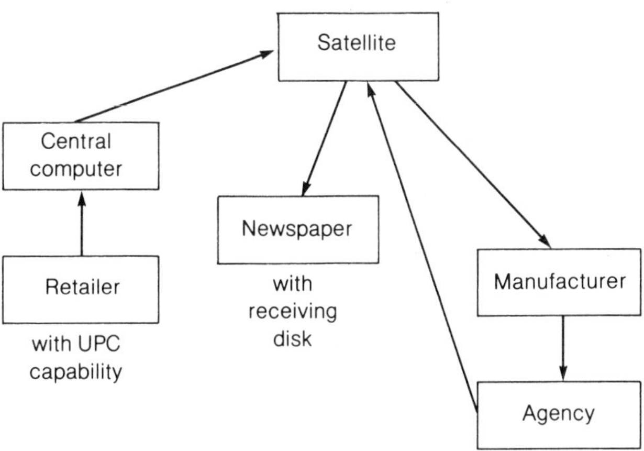

sumer panel with supermarket credit cards. The supermarkets are equipped with UPC scanner so that a continuing measurement of sales can be made. The system also allows matched subgroups of panelists to be reached with different television commercials through cut-ins and newspaper split runs.[6]

The variations of electronic technology uses for this and other purposes are limitless. However, both newspapers and advertisers must adjust to the era of electronic communication as the traditional boundaries between print and electronic media continue to disappear.

Despite the growing competition faced by newspapers and the many problems yet to be solved, the newspaper's future seems bright. It is evident that the newspaper will maintain its predominant position as an advertising medium for some time to come.

QUESTIONS

1. Briefly describe the advantage of newspapers as an advertising medium.

2. Discuss the major categories of newspaper advertising.

3. What is the Newspaper Advertising Bureau, and what are some of its services?

[6] *Media Science Newsletter,* October 15–31, pp. 4–5.

4. Discuss the role of cooperative advertising in newspapers.

5. How much would a 5-column, 14-inch ad cost at 10 cents per line?

6. Briefly define the following:
   a. Flat rate.
   b. Short rate.
   c. Minimil rate.
   d. ROP.
   e. ABC.
   f. ACB.

7. Discuss the national/local rate differentiation of newspapers.

8. What are the implications of the Universal Product Code for newspaper advertising research.

8 MAGAZINES

THE MAGAZINE medium is commonly divided into several distinct media, especially consumer, business, and farm publications. However, as we shall see, each of these categories can easily be divided into several subcategories.

Although many areas of similarity exist among the categories and subcategories of magazines, there are enough distinctions for the three categories to be treated separately in the present discussion. The first section will begin with the category most familiar to you, consumer magazines.

CONSUMER MAGAZINES

Consumer magazines are intended for the ultimate customers of most retail goods and services; these magazines have experienced recent prosperity after several years of adapting to changing forces in the marketplace. In 1979 magazines had advertising revenues of more than $2.5 billion, continuing the recent trend of 10–20 percent annual increases. Most observers see a bright future for magazines, especially among national advertisers that must contend with increasing costs and high demand for television time.

It is only a minor simplification to say that the modern consumer magazine's opportunities and problems center on two factors: (1) costs and (2) selectivity.

Costs

The optimism magazine publishers are currently experiencing is usually tempered by an awareness of escalating costs. The primary costs associated with magazine publishing are paper and distribution. In addition publishers have experienced higher labor and printing costs (either for in-house equipment or for contract printing by outside firms). However, paper and distribution (usually postage) are two costs over which publishers have little control.

While costs and supplies of paper run in cycles, most major publishers have enough coated paper stock to meet short-term requirements. In some cases magazines are substituting uncoated stock for certain portions of their publications. For some time *Redbook* has run its feature-length fiction supplement on a grade of uncoated paper similar to newsprint. While supply shortages are not the problem anticipated at the beginning of 1979, paper costs have risen to $600 per ton, and this is a major concern of publishers.

Most publishers see postage as a more serious long-term problem than paper. The creation of the quasi-independent U.S. Postal Service (USPS), with its mandate to operate at break-even prices, has produced dramatic increases in second-class postal costs. In managing these cost increases, publishers have three options:

1. *Lobby Congress for USPS rate relief.* The Magazine Publishers Association (MPA) has done this almost from the inception of the USPS. Any success publishers have had in keeping mailing costs down has been largely one of delaying rather than preventing programmed increases.

2. *Open additional outlets for newsstand sales.* Both the number of magazine outlets and the number of titles carried by retailers have increased markedly during the last several years. However, it is rare for a supermarket or convenience store to carry more than 50 of the almost 800 consumer magazines. Consequently, while a few large magazines benefit from the new distribution outlets, most magazines do not. In addition the retailer's commission (up to 35 percent) offsets much of the savings gained by not mailing.

3. *Use alternative delivery systems.* Approximately 1.2 million magazines are home-delivered monthly by private companies.[1] To date only major publishers have experimented with such a system, and then only in large markets. Generally the problems of not being able to distribute nationally with any single private carrier, of not being able to use mailboxes (due to government prohibition), and of inconsistent delivery quality from market to market have outweighed the advantages of this method. However, as postal costs continue to increase and more experience is gained in private delivery, it may become a viable alternative to the USPS.

Selectivity

What is "new" in the marketing of magazines is really the completion of a cycle that began in the 19th century. The magazines of the mid-1800s were characterized by high cost to readers, little or no advertising, and literary or political content intended for the educational and

[1] "Publishers Called to Private Delivery," *Advertising Age,* November 12, 1979, p. 1.

financial elite. The magazine of the 1980s, while anything but devoid of advertising, will be much more expensive to the reader and will generally be intended for a selective audience.

The magazine of 1850 was selective by necessity rather than design. The magazines of the day, such as *North American Review, Harper's Weekly, Century,* and the *Knickerbocker,* catered to an upscale portion of the population who were literate and interested in current affairs and the arts. It was not until the decade of the 1890s that the mass circulation magazine came into its own. Editors such as Frank Munsey (*Munsey's* magazine), S. S. McClure (*McClure's* magazine), and Edward Bok (*Ladies' Home Journal*) saw in the development of national distribution of goods an opportunity for magazine advertising. Utilizing the formula that newspapers had adopted a half century earlier, magazines cut their prices to readers, popularized their content, and aggressively promoted their advantages as an advertising medium.

By 1900 the *Ladies' Home Journal* had a circulation of over 1 million and the era of the mass circulation magazine had begun. The advent of radio, two world wars, and a great depression did little to alter the place of magazines as the major medium for national advertisers.

In 1947 television arrived on the scene, and magazines were totally unprepared to cope with this new competitor for the national advertising dollar. Magazines had largely ignored any sales criteria except circulation—the biggest magazine was automatically the best. Magazines panicked when faced with television, which could deliver more people at a cheaper cost per thousand. Instead of selling the unique qualities of their medium (color, long life, selective editorial content, and audience flexibility), they chose to meet television head-on and play the "numbers game."

Simply put, the numbers game meant that magazines sold readership (circulation multiplied by readers per copy) without regard to the quality of the audience. Unfortunately for magazines, even these inflated audience figures could not keep up with television audiences and their lower CPM figures. By 1965 the situation was desperate for magazines. Many national advertisers either ignored the mass circulation magazines or used them only as an occasional supplement to television. Some of the oldest and most prestigious publications (*Life, Look, Saturday Evening Post, Collier's,* and *Woman's Home Companion*) had either died or were in imminent danger of doing so. Clearly something had to be done.

The answer to the magazine crisis had already been found by a few specialized publications which had been founded in the 1950s and had prospered. *Sports Illustrated, Hot Rod,* and *Playboy* had all succeeded, while their more famous, well-established contemporaries had failed. Today the formula for magazine success is to deliver an acceptable editorial format to an audience segment which is important to some group of advertisers. With the exception of a few general circulation magazines (notably *Reader's Digest*), virtually every consumer magazine is now targeted to a limited audience.

Magazines are specialized in two ways. The most obvious way is represented by the relatively low circulation and specialized editorial matter of a publication such as *Gourmet.* A second approach to selectivity is to divide a magazine's circulation into regional and/or demographic editions. Magazines which already reach a specialized audience, such as *Business Week,* usually limit themselves to regional editions. The general circulation magazines, such as *Time* or *Newsweek,* offer advertisers both regional and demographic editions (see Figure 8–1). These regional and demographic editions account for approximately 15 percent of all magazine advertising revenues. The point is that most magazines have repositioned themselves as a segmented audience (or specific target) medium, not a mass medium in the television sense.

Recently, industry-wide promotions by organizations such as the MPA have attempted to show that there are certain people whom national advertisers will miss if magazines are not included in the media schedule. Since magazines (and television) have their own special audiences, both media must be used to reach the total audience. Hence the term *Media Imperatives* and the individual segments, called either "Television Imperatives" or "Magazine Imperatives" (see Figure 8–2).

It should be mentioned that there is some controversy, especially in television circles, as to the validity of the research technique involved. Without debating this issue here, the Media Imperatives concept is important in that it shows the radically different approach that magazines have adopted in their competition with television since the black days of the 1960s.

A final point should be made about magazine selectivity. While selectivity offers most magazines their best chance to compete effectively for national advertising, it does not guarantee the success or survival of any particular magazine. In the late 1970s *Viva, New Times, Muse,* and *Your Place* all failed despite being aimed at narrow markets.

Overall, however, the selective approach to magazine marketing has been successful. Magazines offer advertisers a narrowly targeted, usually upscale, audience; selective editorial material for good association between advertiser and reader interest; and a cost per *prospect* competitive with television.

Figure 8–1
Time demographic editions

TWO SURE ROADS TO THE TOP.

We're expanding two of our ultra-high demographic editions in response to advertisers' needs and the dramatic increase in affluent households. Your TIME representative has all the details for you.

TIME T: to cover the top of the business market

Circulation: 550,000 b&w page: $13,875 4-c page: $21,645

The good news about TIME T is that its circulation is increasing by 83%, and its cpm is *down* by 20%.

It means that TIME T's circulation is now within hailing distance of that of the three so-called business books and is exactly that of Newsweek E.

But where TIME T circulates makes all the difference. It's delivered exclusively to top management households, while none of the others delivers as much as half of its circulation among top management.

Besides its top management coverage,

	Circulation	% Top Management
TIME T	**550,000**	**100**
Business Week	820,000	45
Forbes	690,000	45
Fortune	670,000	43
Newsweek E	550,000	39
USN Blue Chip	425,000	37

TIME T will deliver a *bonus* circulation of 25,500 airline subscriptions, 19,000 comp copy subscriptions, and copies delivered to members of Congress and other government leaders.

If you've a need to talk to the top of business, and not all that many bucks to help you do the talking, why not take a close look at TIME T. It's a bigger and better buy than ever.

TIME A+: to cover the top of the consumer market

Circulation: 950,000 b&w page: $19,330 4-c page: $30,150

We've had the pleasure of watching TIME A+ grow like a snowball on a mountainside since its birth a little more than two years ago. Advertising has come from all kinds of categories, with imported cars, travel and resorts, cameras and watches leading the way. Since the top of the consumer market continues to burgeon, we're increasing the circulation of A+ by nearly 60% to keep pace.

This makes TIME A+ about twice the size of The New Yorker with comparable demographics. As a matter of fact, if there's another medium with as felicitous a combination of size and demos as A+, we'd like to hear about it.

As in the case of TIME T, this edition will provide hefty bonus circulation through airline, comp list and Congress- and other government-leader copies.

If you're on a tight budget and looking for room at the top of the consumer market, TIME A+ is hard to beat.

TIME A+ Subscriber Demographics	
Average Household Income	$65,000
Professional/Managerial	100%
Graduated College	75%
Attended College	90%
Own a Home	88%
Average Home Value	$128,000
Took Airline Trip in Past Year	76%

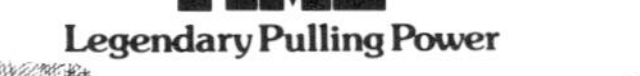

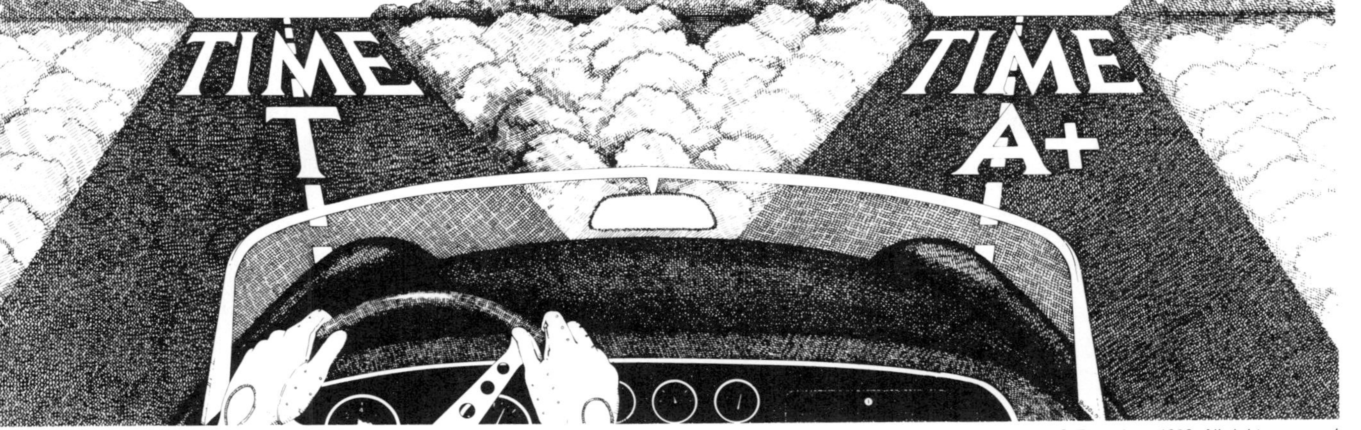

Figure 8–2
The media imperatives concept

The General Foods Media Imperatives.

TV or not TV isn't the question. And magazines and only magazines isn't the answer.

General Foods Corporation is one of the top 100 television advertisers.

But recently, General Foods has been turning more and more to magazines.

According to P.I.B./L.N.A. records, General Foods doubled its magazine advertising in 1976. And, in the first nine months of 1977, the increase was another 122 percent—from $12,192,640 to $27,069,343.

And General Foods is not alone. In the first half of 1977, 70 of the top 100 advertisers increased their magazine advertising investments.

The increases for 31 of these leading companies were at least 50 percent. The increases for 15 of them were 100 percent or more. And each of these top advertisers has its own reasons for increasing its use of magazines.

In the case of General Foods, magazines are second to none when it comes to zeroing in on women who are shopping for ideas and products—from Birds Eye® vegetables and Jell-O® desserts to Dream Whip® topping mix and Maxwell House® coffee.

And General Foods is using magazines for all they're worth—with pull-out recipe booklets that help promote other food products, with cents-off coupons that generate supermarket sales, and with corporate advertising that links the General Foods philosophy and products.

In short, magazines offer the kinds of readership and salesmanship that can help sell anything from a corporate idea to a consumer product. For General Foods. For anyone.

If your company and your agency wish to re-evaluate television and magazines, a new research concept can help you determine an effective media balance based on media and market potential.

The concept, called the Media Imperatives®, can help you draw [illegible] line between two kinds of prospects—the Television Imperatives who are big on television and not so big on magazines and the Magazine Imperatives who are big on magazines and not so big on television.

For information regarding a Telmar computer run based on your prospects and using either Simmons or T.G.I. data, simply write Magazine Publishers Association, Inc. 575 Lexington Avenue, New York, New York 10022.

MPA

Sources: P.I.B., L.N.A. and W. R. Simmons

The Television Imperatives represent 1.7 million heavy users of frozen vegetables.

The Magazine Imperatives represent 2.3 million heavy users of frozen vegetables.

Yet the fact remains that while industry averages have been booming, individual magazines continue to fail. Why do some magazines succeed, while others, similar in content, do not? Obviously, successful magazines must appeal to both readers and advertisers. It is also clear that magazines which appeal to a sizable number of readers can fail if advertising support is lacking.

WHY ADVERTISERS BUY MAGAZINES

As discussed earlier in this chapter, advertisers normally buy magazine space to reach a particular market segment. In addition advertisers choose magazines for several other reasons. Let's examine the major advantages and disadvantages which must be considered when making a magazine buy.

Strengths

1. *Audience selectivity.* Probably the major factor, as already discussed.

2. *Selective editorial content which complements the advertiser's message.* Advertisers must choose magazines on the basis of qualitative judgment as well as quantitative audience information. Some advertisers demand compatibility between their customers' attitudes and preferences and an advertising medium's editorial emphasis. Sometimes this is obvious such as when a golf club manufacturer advertises in *Golf Digest.* Other associations are subtler. For instance Kraft Foods will not advertise in fashion magazines because it feels that a woman thinking of fashion will not be in the proper frame of mind to read recipes.[2]

3. *Excellent color reproduction.* Although magazines no longer have color as a unique selling feature, it remains a major strength of the medium. Products which seek label identification and food products find magazines an excellent advertising medium.

4. *Long issue life.* Magazines are the only medium which regularly acquires repeat exposures. It is not uncommon for many types of magazines (home service, hobby and special interest, and business) to be kept for long periods and referred to often.

Weaknesses

1. *Lack the geographic flexibility offered by other media.* While a few large-circulation magazines offer metropolitan editions, most

---

[2] "The Courtice Recipe," *Marketing and Media Decisions,* November 1979, p. 136.

magazines offer only broad areas if less than national circulation is available.

2. *Are one-dimensional.* Magazines find that their major problem in competing with television is that they lack the sound and movement desired by so many national advertisers. Television proponents claim that television, with sight, sound, color, and movement, is at a disadvantage with magazines only in the area of message publishability.

3. *Lack audience reach.* If reach (or the accumulation of new audience) is an advertising objective, then magazines may not perform well. Magazines tend to reach the same audience over long periods of time. Consequently, in a selected magazine schedule, frequency levels will be acquired at the sacrifice of reach with a given budget.

BUYING BY THE NUMBERS

Despite all the discussion of audience selectivity and other strengths and weaknesses, magazines, like other media, are still bought "by the numbers." Advertisers divide magazine vehicles into acceptable and nonacceptable categories, but the final buy is usually made from those with the highest audience figures (and the lowest CPM).

What is an audience? This seems like a silly question, but magazines, by accident or design, have made it complex. There are really three ways to answer the question:

1. *Paid circulation.* The number of people who subscribe to or buy a magazine at the newsstand is normally called circulation or primary readership. Primary readers are generally considered more valuable than pass-along readers since primary readers are more interested in a magazine and, we assume, in the advertising it carries.

An example of CPM/prospects

We are considering placing magazine advertising in one of two travel magazines, *Diversion* and *National Motorist.* We have no interest in New England coverage. Given this assumption, let's work out a CPM/prospects comparison.

	Diversion	*National Motorist*
Total circulation	210,000	73,000
Cost/B&W page	$2,425	$838
CPM	$11.55	$11.48
New England circulation	12,918	1,985
Prospects (total circulation—New England)	197,082	71,015
CPM/prospects	12.30	11.80

2. Readership. Another method of defining magazine audiences is to compute the sum of the primary readers and the pass-along readers or the product of the total copies circulated and the readers per copy. This is usually called either readership or total audience.

3. Prospects. Consider only the prospects for your product in the total audience. This is probably the fairest method of comparing one magazine with another, and it usually combines both prospects and cost of advertising to figure the CPM/prospects. (see example, p. 206.)

When the two magazines are compared on the basis of their total circulation, they are almost identical. However, since *Diversion* has a much larger New England circulation than *National Motorist,* it fares much worse when only prospects are considered.

SOURCES OF MAGAZINE CIRCULATION

Regardless of the particular "audience" an advertiser is using, figures should be readily available. Several major sources are used by advertisers to obtain audience information.

1. Independent auditing companies. Most major magazine circulations are audited or checked by an independent company. Among the best known of these are the Audit Bureau of Circulations (ABC), the Business Publications Audit of Circulations, Inc. (BPA), and the Verified Audit Circulation Corporation (VAC). The reports of these organizations are normally carried in other rate and circulation directories such as those of the Standard Rate and Data Service (SRDS). The rate cards of individual magazines will also note that the circulation has been audited (see Figure 8–3).

2. Rate cards. Individual rate cards must be used if a magazine is not audited. Rate cards must often be used to obtain circulation of regional and/or demographic editions since only a limited number are carried in SRDS.

3. Syndicated research services. Audits and circulation figures tell only part of the story. Most of this information is confined to readers and their territorial distribution (see Figure 8–4). However, the figures give no information about the demographics of magazine audiences (occasionally magazines will provide limited information in promotional pieces) or about purchase behavior. Most advertisers use one of the major syndicated services to obtain such information.

THE SYNDICATED MAGAZINE SERVICES

In recent years the measuring of magazine readership has been one of the most controversial areas of media research. Currently the two major services are Magazine Research, Inc. (MRI), and Simmons Market Research Bureau (SMRB). While space does not permit a full

Figure 8–3
ABC magazine audit report

ABC Audit Report-Magazine

PROTOTYPE MAGAZINE
New York, New York

CLASS, INDUSTRY OR FIELD SERVED: Devoted to the interest of the outdoor sportsman and his family - hunting, fishing, boating, camping, conservation, dogs, travel, photography and the equipment and apparel necessary.

1. AVERAGE PAID CIRCULATION FOR 12 MONTHS ENDING DECEMBER 31, (Year).

Subscriptions:	1,525,893	
Single Copy Sales:	239,009	
AVERAGE TOTAL PAID CIRCULATION		1,764,902
Advertising Rate Base and/or Circulation Guarantee during Audit Period.	1,775,000	
Average Total Non-Paid Distribution	56,182	

2. PAID CIRCULATION BY ISSUES: (Total of subscriptions and single copy sales)

Issue (Year)		Issue (year)	
January	1,835,490	July	1,762,002
February	1,794,139	August	1,755,303
March	1,782,249	September	1,761,318
April	1,778,344	October	1,759,085
May	1,716,461	November	1,770,817
June	1,718,681	December	1,744,931

AVERAGE PAID CIRCULATION BY QUARTERS for the previous three years and period covered by this report.

Calendar Qtr. End.	(Year)	(Year)	(Year)	(Year)
March 31	1,873,945	1,912,603	1,765,665	1,803,959
June 30	1,807,370	1,842,569	1,771,572	1,737,829
September 30	1,850,890	1,871,683	1,769,596	1,759,541
December 31	1,906,794	1,915,877	1,819,311	1,758,278

AUDIT STATEMENT

The difference shown in average total paid circulation, in comparing this report with Publisher's Statements for the period audited, amounting to an average of 14,639 copies per issue, is accounted for by deductions made for: additional copies served on credit subscriptions cancelled for nonpayment, 10,146 copies; additional newsdealer returns Publisher having underestimated returns in compiling statements to the Bureau, 4,493 copies.

The records maintained by this publication pertaining to circulation data and other data as reported for the period covered have been examined in accordance with the Bureau's bylaws, rules and auditing standards. Test of the accounting records and other auditing procedures considered necessary were included. Based on ABC's examination, the data shown in this report present fairly the circulation data and other data as verified by Bureau auditors.

September, (Year).
(04-0000-0 - #120000 - RAB - RH)

AUDIT BUREAU OF CIRCULATIONS
123 North Wacker Drive, Chicago, Illinois 60606

M-2-

Figure 8–4
Rate card, Sports Illustrated

NATIONAL EDITION 2,250,000 (Average Net Paid Circulation)

The rates below apply to all general advertisers. Bleed premium 15%. Frequency discounts are generally earned by using 13 or more insertions in any edition or editions, either national, regional, metropolitan, other less-than-national editions, or any combination thereof. However, any Regional/State/Metro ad appearing in a single issue, regardless of the number of markets, counts as one insertion. No rate holders accepted. Maximum discount allowed is 25%.

Black & White	1X	13X	17X	26X	39X	52X
Full Page	$28,880	$27,725	$27,290	$26,570	$25,990	$25,415
2 Cols.	21,950	21,070	20,745	20,195	19,755	19,315
½ Page Hor.	17,325	16,630	16,370	15,940	15,595	15,245
1 Col.	11,260	10,810	10,640	10,360	10,135	9,910
½ Col. Vert.	5,775	5,545	5,455	5,315	5,200	5,080
Agate Line	83.90	80.55	79.30	77.20	75.50	73.85
Two-Color†						
Full Page	$36,390	$34,935	$34,390	$33,480	$32,750	$32,025
2 Cols.	27,660	26,555	26,140	25,445	24,895	24,340
½ Page Hor.	21,830	20,955	20,630	20,085	19,650	19,210
1 Col.	14,555	13,975	13,755	13,390	13,100	12,810
½ Col. Vert.	7,275	6,985	6,875	6,695	6,550	6,400
Agate Line	105.80	101.55	100.00	97.35	95.20	93.10
Four-Color						
Full Page	$45,050	$43,250	$42,570	$41,445	$40,545	$39,645
Back Cover	58,070	55,745	54,875	53,425	52,265	51,100
2 Cols.*	36,040	34,600	34,060	33,155	32,435	31,715
½ Page Hor.*	29,285	28,115	27,675	26,940	26,355	25,770
⅓ Page Sq.*	19,375	18,600	18,310	17,825	17,440	17,050

†Black and one color. *Units available on a limited basis.

REGIONAL EDITIONS

Eastern 685,000 (Average Net Paid Circulation)

See page 17 for available dates.

Bermuda, Connecticut, Delaware, District of Columbia, Jamaica, Maine, Maryland, Massachusetts, Nassau, New Hampshire, New Jersey, New York, Pennsylvania, Puerto Rico, Rhode Island, Vermont, Virginia, Virgin Islands, West Virginia.

Black & White	1X	13X	17X	26X	39X	52X
Full Page	$11,348	$10,894	$10,724	$10,440	$10,213	$ 9,986
2 Cols.	8,511	8,171	8,043	7,830	7,660	7,490
½ Page Hor.	6,809	6,537	6,435	6,264	6,128	5,992
1 Col.	4,539	4,357	4,289	4,176	4,085	3,994
½ Col. Vert.	2,837	2,724	2,681	2,610	2,553	2,497
Agate Line	40.50	38.88	38.27	37.26	36.45	35.64
Two-Color†						
Full Page	$14,298	$13,726	$13,512	$13,154	$12,868	$12,582
2 Cols.	10,724	10,295	10,134	9,866	9,652	9,437
½ Page Hor.	8,579	8,236	8,107	7,893	7,721	7,550
1 Col.	5,719	5,490	5,404	5,261	5,147	5,033
½ Col. Vert.	3,575	3,432	3,378	3,289	3,218	3,146
Agate Line	51.03	48.99	48.22	46.95	45.93	44.91
Four-Color						
Full Page	$17,710	$17,002	$16,736	$16,293	$15,939	$15,585

Advertisers wishing to buy more (or less) markets than those covered by this single region should consult the Regional/State/Metro section. Full-page advertisers combining regions and metros or states in a single issue must use the Regional/State/Metro pricing tables. The national discount structure applies to all regional rates. Circulation includes a limited number of air-lifted copies for U.S. military and foreign distribution.
†Black and one color.

Midwestern 635,000 (Average Net Paid Circulation)

See page 17 for available dates.

Illinois, Indiana, Iowa, Kansas, Kentucky, Michigan, Minnesota, Missouri, Nebraska, North Dakota, Ohio, South Dakota, Wisconsin.

Black & White	1X	13X	17X	26X	39X	52X
Full Page	$10,457	$10,039	$ 9,882	$ 9,620	$ 9,411	$ 9,202
2 Cols.	7,843	7,529	7,412	7,216	7,059	6,902
½ Page Hor.	6,274	6,023	5,929	5,772	5,647	5,521
1 Col.	4,183	4,016	3,953	3,848	3,765	3,681
½ Col. Vert.	2,614	2,509	2,470	2,405	2,353	2,300
Agate Line	37.32	35.83	35.27	34.33	33.59	32.84
Two-Color†						
Full Page	$13,176	$12,649	$12,451	$12,122	$11,858	$11,595
2 Cols.	9,882	9,487	9,338	9,091	8,894	8,696
½ Page Hor.	7,905	7,589	7,470	7,273	7,115	6,956
1 Col.	5,271	5,060	4,981	4,849	4,744	4,638
½ Col. Vert.	3,294	3,162	3,113	3,030	2,965	2,899
Agate Line	47.02	45.14	44.43	43.26	42.32	41.38
Four-Color						
Full Page	$16,321	$15,668	$15,423	$15,015	$14,689	$14,362

Advertisers wishing to buy more (or less) markets than those covered by this single region should consult the Regional/State/Metro section. Full-page advertisers combining regions and metros or states in a single issue must use the Regional/State/Metro pricing tables. The national discount structure applies to all regional rates.
†Black and one color.

East Central 510,000 (Average Net Paid Circulation)

See page 17 for available dates.

Illinois, Indiana, Kentucky, Michigan, Ohio, Wisconsin, Minneapolis/St. Paul, St. Louis.

Black & White	1X	13X	17X	26X	39X	52X
Full Page	$ 8,676	$ 8,329	$ 8,199	$ 7,982	$ 7,808	$ 7,635
2 Cols.	6,594	6,330	6,231	6,066	5,935	5,803
½ Page Hor.	5,206	4,998	4,920	4,790	4,685	4,581
1 Col.	3,470	3,331	3,279	3,192	3,123	3,054
½ Col. Vert.	2,169	2,082	2,050	1,995	1,952	1,909
Agate Line	30.96	29.72	29.26	28.48	27.86	27.25
Two-Color†						
Full Page	$10,932	$10,495	$10,331	$10,057	$ 9,839	$ 9,620
2 Cols.	8,308	7,976	7,851	7,643	7,477	7,311
½ Page Hor.	6,560	6,298	6,199	6,035	5,904	5,773
1 Col.	4,372	4,197	4,132	4,022	3,935	3,847
½ Col. Vert.	2,733	2,624	2,583	2,514	2,460	2,405
Agate Line	39.01	37.45	36.86	35.89	35.11	34.33
Four-Color						
Full Page	$13,541	$12,999	$12,796	$12,458	$12,187	$11,916

Advertisers wishing to buy more (or less) markets than those covered by this single region should consult the Regional/State/Metro section. Full-page advertisers combining regions and metros or states in a single issue must use the Regional/State/Metro pricing tables. The national discount structure applies to all regional rates.
†Black and one color.

Courtesy: *Sports Illustrated*

explanation of the various concerns of subscribers to these services, the major characteristics are highlighted below.

1. Methodologies. Although MRI and SMRB are similar in approach, their methods are dissimilar in some major ways. Briefly the two services operate as follows.

SMRB. The SMRB report uses a sample of 15,000 persons who are interviewed twice a year. The service uses a two-methodology approach: (1) For approximately 40 magazines with circulations of more than 5 million, it uses a "through the book" method of actually screening magazines with respondents and carefully going through five–ten magazines, asking the respondents whether they have seen certain things in the magazines to determine readership. (2) For another 100 magazines, it simply shows respondents magazine logos and asks them whether they have read the magazine during some period of time. This is called a "recent reading technique." SMRB then gathers demographic and marketing information.

MRI. MRI has a yearly sample of 30,000, with 15,000 respondents interviewed in the spring and another 15,000 interviewed in the fall. The MRI methodology is called the "modified recent reading technique." The object is to establish whether the respondent has read or looked into each title during its most recent publication interval. For example the last 7 days for a weekly, the last 30 days for a monthly, and so on. This is achieved by having the respondent sort a deck of logo cards in two steps. In the first step, all the cards (after shuffling) are sorted to show whether the magazines have been read during the last six months. This step takes about five minutes. Those cards sorted as "No—sure have not" (generally 90 percent or more of the total) are then put aside, and the remaining titles are separated into weeklies, monthlies, and so on. In step 2, these "screened-in" cards are resorted to show whether the magazines were read during the publication interval (different sorting boards being used for each frequency). Only those persons who are sure they have read or looked into the magazine during the appropriate period are counted as readers.[3]

The interview, including the time required to obtain magazine data, information about other media usage, and demographic information, takes about 45 minutes. At the conclusion of the fall interviews respondents are given a questionnaire covering product information and information on television shows viewed; this is to be returned by mail. MRI issues two magazine readership reports annually and a spring report detailing product usage.

2. Measurement of total readership only. The services measure only readership, not primary circulation. Some advertisers think it a mistake to give equal weight to paid circulation and pass-along readers. A pilot study of primary readers was recently completed by Starch INRA Hooper, but its high cost makes it problematic whether this service will gain wide acceptance.

3. Respondent fatigue. With the number of magazines to be

[3] Magazine Research, Inc., *Plan for Reports, 1979–80,* p. 6.

measured and the additional buying behavior collected by the services, there is a concern about wearing out the respondent. Some observers think a larger sample with shorter interviews is the answer, but this would significantly increase the cost of the studies.

4. Number of magazines surveyed. Fewer than 150 magazines are included in these reports. The lower circulation, specialized magazines so important to many advertisers are excluded. This not only leaves advertisers with virtually no consumer information regarding the excluded magazines, but can prevent these magazines from attracting additional advertising revenue. Some advertisers will buy space only in magazines that are included in a readership service.

5. Discrepancies between the two services. Perhaps the major concern of advertisers as well as the area of the harshest criticism is the differences between the audience figures of MRI and SMRB. In a recent report comparing the two services, MRI audience estimates ranged from 161 percent higher to 34 percent lower among the 104 magazines measured by both services.[4]

In 1980 the Advertising Research Foundation issued two reports concerning the controversy surrounding magazine research methodologies. The reports indicated that audience measurement differences exist among different types of magazines (notably monthlies and weeklies). Furthermore, the studies indicated that these differences result from the methodologies, not their execution.

Still to be determined is whether the different methodologies can be adjusted to make their results comparable. If not, then industry-wide agreement on a single audience research methodology might be necessary. In the meantime advertisers should not compare magazine audiences measured with different methodologies.

HOW ADVERTISERS BUY MAGAZINES

Buying space in a magazine involves several steps with many decisions to be made by the advertiser. Let us assume that we have decided on *Time* as the magazine we will use. Now we can follow the process from the time we decide to buy space in the magazine to the time the consumer sees our advertisement.

Where?

Perhaps the first question which the advertiser must answer is: Where will the advertisement run? *Time* (like many other major magazines) offers various possibilities. For *Time,* these include:

[4] "Does MRI Have the Answer?" *Marketing and Media Decisions,* November 1979, p. 66.

Full national circulation.

Eleven regional editions.

Twenty major spot markets.

Over 100 supplemental spot markets.

Twenty-two state editions bought individually or in combination with metro editions.

Eight major demographic editions.

In addition the advertiser can buy split-run editions which allow him to run several advertisements in the same issue. Split runs may be divided along regional or demographic lines. The advertiser may also buy half the circulation (called Half-Time). Many of these editions have special requirements. For instance supplemental spot markets are sold in full-page units only.

What format?

Having decided on the edition (in this example we will buy the full circulation), we must next decide on the format of our advertisement. The first question is one of size. Magazines normally sell space by the fractional page. However, many publications offer other alternatives such as inserts (either booklets or single cards), gatefolds, and cover positions. Normally only the second, third, and fourth covers of consumer magazines are available for advertising space.

Assume that we have decided on a full-page advertisement. Now we must decide on color or black and white. Costs for color vary widely from magazine to magazine, but an extra charge of 10–15 percent for two-color and 20–30 percent for four-color is usual. Magazines such as *Time* also offer bleed color (no margins) for a premium of about 15 percent over regular color.

How much?

Once the size and format of our advertisement have been decided, our next step is to determine how much we will spend. The one-page, four-color rate for *Time* costs more than $70,000; it is obvious why advertisers want to take steps to reduce their costs. The major way to cut per-unit costs is through discounts given larger advertisers. Magazine rates, like newspaper rates, are subject to rebate and short-rate adjustments. See Chapter 7 for a full discussion of these adjustments.

Common magazine discounts

1. Frequency discounts. These are offered for the number of pages (or page equivalents) run during a year or other contract period. Sometimes frequency discounts are figured on dollar volume rather than insertions. The dollar volume discount is often used when an advertiser is using regional buys.

2. *Multiple-page discounts.* Advertisers wishing to run several pages in the same issue are normally given special discounts.

3. *Multiple-edition discounts.* An advertiser buying more than one regional/demographic edition will be given a discount for each extra edition bought. For example the discounts on *Time* demographic editions are as follows:

Number of editions	*Percent of discount*
2	4%
3	6
4	8
5	10
6	12

4. *Standby (remnant) space.* In *Time,* an advertiser who gives the publisher complete flexibility in placing his ads will be charged 65 percent of the national cost per thousand.

Most magazines offer discounts similar to these. In taking advantage of these discounts, however, an advertiser must be certain that his advertising stragegy calls for frequency rather than reach. Multiple insertions which gain discounts rather than fulfilling advertising and marketing goals constitute a shortsighted savings for the advertiser.

An advertiser who plans to advertise in a publication throughout the coming year should consider signing a space contract with the publisher. Normally such a contract will give the advertiser some protection from rate increases. Signing a contract does not always mean that rates cannot be increased during the year, but it may mean that the magazine will agree to give four or six months' notice instead of five–eight weeks'. With the uncertainties of inflation publishers are less willing to lock themselves into long-term advertising rates than was the case several years ago. However, the advertiser should inquire about a contract even if it is not mentioned in rate information from the publisher.

THE MAGAZINE NETWORK

Another potential cost savings for the larger magazine advertiser is the magazine network. Networks allow an advertiser to purchase space in several magazines simultaneously at a significant savings over buying them individually. There are two types of network:

1. *The publisher network.* Here a publisher combines several re-

lated magazines (alone or in cooperation with other publishers), all of which an advertiser can buy at the same time. The Petersen Action Group, an example of such a network, offers the following:

Hot Rod	*Hunting*
Motor Trend	*Skin Diver*
Car Craft	*Motorcyclist*
Guns & Ammo	*Photographic*

Being a member of a magazine network normally does not prevent a magazine from selling advertising space individually.

2. *The independent network.* The independent network contracts with several publishers to sell advertising on a regional basis. The advertisements are usually bound as an insert, but conform to the style of the individual magazine.

SCHEDULING MAGAZINE ADVERTISING

The advertiser, after deciding on the vehicle, format, and price of the advertising must determine the schedule for the advertising. The scheduling decision will be made according to the advertising and marketing goals discussed earlier.

The mechanical problems of scheduling require careful planning by the advertiser. A checklist for scheduling, such as the following, might be helpful in planning magazine advertising.

1. *Closing dates.* The closing date is the date by which an advertisement must reach the publisher in order to be carried in a particular issue. Often a magazine will have different closing dates for color advertisements, regional editions, and special services such as split runs. Some magazines will accept a limited number of advertisements on short notice (five days as compared to five–seven weeks). However, there is a significant price increase for this service. It should also be pointed out that most magazines will not accept cancellations after the closing date.

2. *Mechanical requirements.* The advertiser must make certain that his advertisement conforms to a magazine's mechanical requirements. Most major magazines' requirements are listed in the SRDS Print Media Production Data. However, it is a good idea to get mechanical information directly from the publisher prior to making a mechanical layout.

3. *Addresses.* Many magazines have different addresses for their advertising sales offices and their printing operations. Don't assume that advertising material should be sent to the advertising sales office.

4. *Insertion orders.* Carefully check the insertion order to make

sure it includes the issue to carry the advertisement, the size of the ad, and the cost. If a prior contract has not been signed, an insertion order/contract may be combined in the order.

THE GUARANTEED CIRCULATION

Most magazines guarantee their paid circulation to advertisers. Normally a magazine makes this guarantee on its average six-month circulation. If a magazine fails to meet its guarantee, the advertiser is due a rebate of some portion of the advertising dollars he invested during the past six months. Guarantees are set conservatively and rebates are seldom given, but when they are, it is damaging to the reputation of a publisher.

A new wrinkle on the idea of the rebate was introduced in the fall of 1979 by *People* magazine. *People* computes ad charges on the basis of issue-by-issue circulation (the rate base is currently 2,300,000). When the per-issue circulation goes below the base, the advertiser receives credits. When the circulation goes above the base, the magazine gets credits. At the end of a six-month period, if the advertiser has credits he will be paid. On the other hand, if the magazine has credits, the advertiser will not be assessed further. In this system an advertiser accrues credits even when the magazine meets its base for the six-month period if the specific issues used fail to meet the average circulation.

Esquire magazine has developed another type of guarantee. Beginning in February 1980, *Esquire* introduced a "no clutter guarantee." Under this offer an advertiser need not pay if his full-page ad faces another full-page ad or if the editorial percentage of the issue in which his ad appears dips below 57 percent.[5]

THE FUTURE OF THE CONSUMER MAGAZINE

In the beginning of this chapter the bright future of magazines was discussed. However, no medium can be successful if it is allowed to become stagnant. The opportunities and accompanying problems for magazines in the 1980s are multiple and diverse. Some of the major areas are discussed here.

1. Special interest. Development of new, special-interest magazines will continue in the 1980s. As education and income continue to increase, the opportunities for leisure activities will become more plentiful. Magazines devoted to hobbies and special interests should

[5] "*Esquire* Lures Advertisers with No Clutter Guarantee," *Advertising Age*, November 12, 1979, p. 12.

prosper in this environment. Even the prospect of energy shortages may help these magazines as more people look to at-home outlets for their leisure time.

2. Inflation. There seems to be no end in sight to increases in the cost of paper, postage, and labor for magazine publishers. Publishers will be forced to manage scarce resources more efficiently and look for additional revenue in the future. Magazines may cut back on coated stocks for all or a portion of their pages. Further reduction in page size may be a possibility, especially for publications with non-standard page sizes. Alternative delivery systems may become more popular if second-class postage rates continue their anticipated rise.

3. Competition from cable television. The new broadcast technology (see Chapter 5) will bring the opportunity for broadcast audience segmentation. Audience fragmentation into small special-interest groups through electronic communications can be a major threat to the special-topic magazine. Some observers think broadcast segmentation will complement magazines by cresting superficial, preliminary interest in topics which can then be developed in depth by specialized publications. In any case the magazine of the future will have to find a way to compete with this new technology.

4. The city magazine. Perhaps the ultimate specialty magazine is the city publication. While not an innovation, city magazines have been demonstrating added vitality and respectability as an advertising medium. In a 1979 survey by the City and Regional Magazine Association, the city magazine was shown to be extremely strong among upscale audiences and to have very little duplication with national magazines. In the future it is expected that the city magazine will become a significant medium among advertisers seeking a high-income, well-educated, geographically concentrated audience.

BUSINESS MAGAZINES

In the previous section we discussed magazines directed to the ultimate consumer. In this section we will examine magazines intended for the industrial, middleman, and professional groups within the marketing channel. Figure 8–5 outlines the position of each of the categories of magazines discussed in this chapter (except farm publications, which are treated separately in the last section of the chapter).

The general category of business publications involves those industrial, merchandising, and professional publications which are intended for groups in the marketing channel short of the ultimate consumer.

The general business press comprises some 2,500 major publica-

Figure 8–5
Magazines and the marketing channel

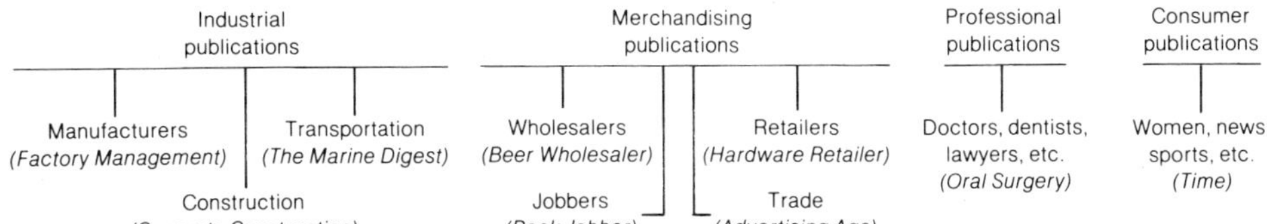

tions accounting for advertising revenues of more than $1.5 billion per year. As compared to consumer publications, business magazines are generally lower in circulation, higher in CPM, and more precisely targeted to a specific audience. Like consumer magazines, they sell advertisers on audience selectivity, long reading life, and close association between readers' advertising and editorial interests. However, it would be a mistake to characterize the business press as simply magazines directed to nonconsumers. Despite many similarities between business and consumer magazines, the business press has unique features which make it distinct from other print media.

Marketing strategy for business publications

The typical business publication advertisement is different from consumer advertisements in several significant ways. First, it is usually directed to a small, knowledgeable audience of experts. The types of product puffery and general media strategy used to reach a general consumer audience are inadequate in successful business advertising.

The purpose of most consumer advertising is to create long or short-term sales. Business advertising is more often designed to complement personal selling. With current estimates of a personal sales call running close to $100 (see Figure 8–6), it is imperative that the salesperson be "introduced" to the prospect prior to the call. Business advertising may accomplish this.

Competition from other media

The dollars allocated to any particular consumer medium often could have been placed in any number of competing advertising vehicles. Business publications tend to compete in a much narrower arena. The major competitor of business publications is direct mail. Direct mail offers many of the advantages of the business press. The higher

Figure 8–6
The average cost of a personal sales call

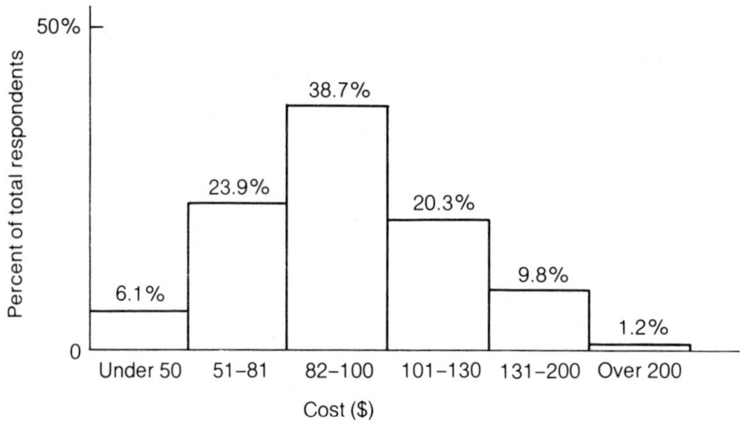

The average cost of a personal sales call in 1978 was $97.67.

Source: CARR Reports, Cahners Publishing Co.

cost of direct mail and, in the minds of some, its lower prestige work against direct mail in competing with business publications. However, while estimates are difficult to obtain, direct mail probably brings in more business advertising dollars than do business publications.

Circulation

Many business publications do not charge for subscriptions. Such magazines are said to have "controlled" circulations. The term is used since the publisher determines who is to receive the publication and thereby "controls" the circulation. Magazines may also offer a combination of paid and controlled circulation. For instance *Marketing and Media Decisions* is sent free to those who "plan, approve, and implement media buys." Others can subscribe for $25 a year. In the last several years many controlled circulation magazines have gone to a paid basis to offset increased costs.

Earlier in this chapter we mentioned that magazines are audited by three major organizations: VAC, BPA, and ABC. While all three audit controlled circulation, the ABC has special requirements which must be met before it will agree to audit a business publication. The publication to be audited by ABC must meet one of three conditions:

1. Have at least 70 percent of its total distribution as paid circulation.

2. Have at least 70 percent of its circulation as paid and choose also to report further nonpaid circulation to the field served.
3. Have at least 70 percent nonpaid direct request or a combination of at least 70 percent paid and nonpaid direct request.

In addition business publications with more than 50 percent paid circulation must report percentage of renewals of paid subscriptions.

Another feature of business publications is the use of the Standard Industrial Classification (SIC) in reporting circulation (see Figure 8–7). The SIC is a seven-digit code which classifies all industries and subcategories of industries. For most purposes only the first four levels are used. SIC was established by the U.S. Office of Management and Budget. The Business Publications SRDS lists the basic two-digit code for many industrial publications to allow advertisers to identify the circulation breakdowns of these publications.

Figure 8–7
An example of the Standard Industrial Code

20	Food
202	Dairy products
2021	Creamery butter

The Business Publications SRDS also requires that most magazines fill out a sworn statement. It breaks down circulation into census areas, paid and nonpaid circulation, and a business analysis which divides circulation into various groups. Magazines are required to provide a notarized statement twice a year.

Finally industrial publications are often characterized as either vertical or horizontal. A vertical publication covers all aspects of an industry. A horizontal publication covers one job which cuts across several industries (see Figure 8–8).

FARM MAGAZINES

The smallest category of magazines in number, circulation, and advertising revenues is the farm press. However, like its larger contemporaries, the farm press has experienced significant increases in advertising revenues during the last several years. In 1979 the revenues of farm magazines exceeded $130 million.

In many respects the farm press has followed the same pattern as consumer magazines during the last decade. During the 1960s several specialized farm journals were founded, which began to compete

Figure 8–8
Horizontal and vertical business publications

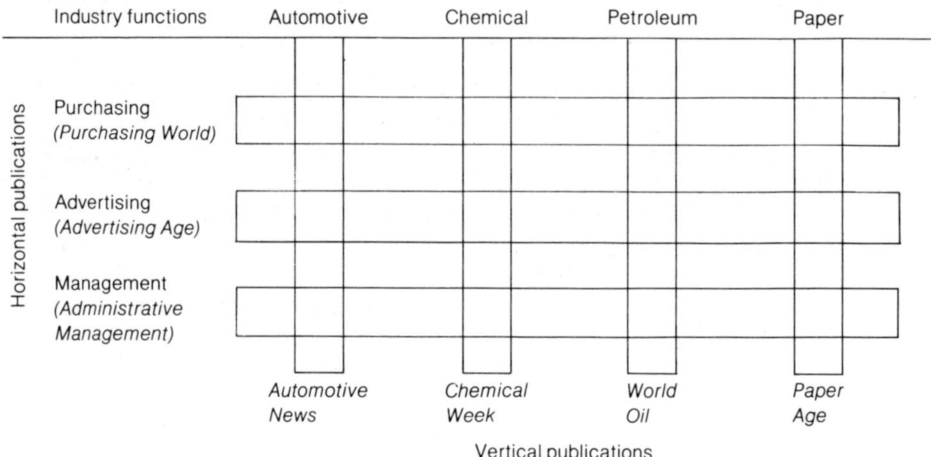

effectively with the more general farm journals. The large-circulation farm magazines were hurt by reductions in the number of farm families and by the growing sophistication and specialization of agribusiness. The "consolidated farm" made magazines which treated the farm family as a unique lifestyle increasingly unnecessary. The college-educated, higher income farm family was concerned with modern fashion, world events, and farm commodity prices. The farm family was reading *The Wall Street Journal, McCall's,* and *Agri Finance* rather than *Progressive Farmer.*

By the late 1960s the major farm publications had almost eliminated features about homemaking and had begun to emphasize the business aspects of farming. They also eliminated rural subscribers who were not farmers, thus cutting circulation but offering a more valuable audience to advertisers. They followed the lead of consumer magazines by aggressively selling regional and demographic editions to compete with the new regional publications. Some of the larger farm magazines have gone a step further and offered regionalized editorial material as well as advertising. For instance *Successful Farming* offered a regional insert for Southern cotton farmers in 1980.

Today the farm press offers advertisers market segmentation which is often more sophisticated than the market segmentations developed by either consumer or business publications. Target marketing of farm publications is necessary for two reasons. First, the farm audience is extremely diversified by climate, crops, and soil conditions. Second, agricultural businesses have shown a willingness to use a variety of media to reach their customers. In competing for the agribusiness advertising dollar, farm magazines must position themselves against radio, direct mail, outdoor, and in many major farm markets, television and newspapers.

To compete for this fragmented farm market, farm publications have developed extensive regional and demographic editions. A farm magazine may simultaneously offer regional editions, crop editions, and a general publication. Farm magazines may even increase their frequency of publication during peak growing seasons or put out special editions to certain reader segments. For instance, *Farm Journal* publishes 15 times a year—monthly except for two issues in February and March and a combined June–July issue.

Unlike the advertising in consumer magazines, in which national advertising is supplemented by regional/demographic advertising, most farm magazine advertising is placed on a regional basis. The only major category of farm advertisers which routinely uses national runs is farm equipment. Chemical companies, the largest category of farm advertisers, must adjust their advertising to various crop and geographic conditions. In fact, most farm advertisers would like even more specialized editions of major farm publications than are available at present.

Despite the demographic/regional breakouts offered by the major farm publications, specialized magazines have flourished in the agricultural sector. It could be said that most of the regional/demographic editions offered by the major farm publications have been a result of the growth of small, specialized farm magazines. Here the large-circulation farm publications have followed the same patterns as the major consumer publications. Farm publications differ from consumer publications in that they offer both advertising and editorial material on a regional basis. Regionalized editorial material is rarely offered in business publications and almost never offered in consumer magazines.

The number of specialized farm magazines has more than doubled in the last decade. The trend in these smaller circulation farm publications is toward both regional and vocational specialization. Magazines such as *Southern Hog Producer* are typical of the newer narrow-interest publication.

Structure of the farm press

The farm press is divided into four categories:

1. *General-circulation farm magazines.* The largest of the big three is *Farm Journal* (circulation 3 million). The other two are *Successful Farming* and *Progressive Farmer.*

2. *Regional farm magazines.* These publications aim specifically at farmers in different parts of the country. Examples of this class of farm publications are *Michigan Farmer* and *Buckeye Farm News.*
3. *Vocational farm magazines.* These publications are also called crop-specific/livestock-specific magazines. Often, a single magazine combines both regional and vocational elements, as is the case for the *New Mexico Stockman* and *Pecan South.*
4. *Agribusiness publications.* These magazines address the complexities of farming as a business. They include both business (*Agri Finance*) and technological (*Crops and Soils Magazine*) publications.

QUESTIONS

1. Discuss consumer, farm, and business publications from the perspective of the advertisers using each type.
2. Discuss the transition of magazines from a mass medium to a class medium.
3. Discuss the Media Imperatives concept as a device for selling magazine advertising.
4. How does the Audit Bureau of Circulations differ from the major syndicated magazine readership services?
5. Discuss flexibility as it relates to magazines.
6. What is a magazine network?
7. In what ways is the magazine rebate different from the newspaper rebate?
8. Why are magazines concerned with the growth of cable television?
9. Name three types of business magazines, and give an example of each.
10. In what ways have the farm magazines shown patterns of development similar to those of the consumer magazines during the last several years?

9

OUT-OF-HOME ADVERTISING

OUTDOOR is considered to be the oldest form of advertising and one of the most ancient forms of communication. The ancient Egyptians posted roadside commercial messages on stone tablets called stelae. Later the Romans and Greeks set aside space in public places for ads and announcements of sport contests.[1]

In the United States the growth of outdoor advertising coincided with the development of automobile travel. Early in this century, outdoor advertising moved away from the bill posting of the 1800s to become a standardized, self-regulated industry. By the 1930s it had a strong trade association, the Outdoor Advertising Association of America (OAAA), and an organization to provide outdoor circulation figures, the Traffic Audit Bureau (TAB).

OUTDOOR ADVERTISING TODAY

Today outdoor advertising is a major medium with revenues greater than those of network radio and farm publications and only slightly below those of women's magazines. Annual outdoor revenues are about $600 million, with 70 percent coming from national advertisers. From 1975 to 1980, outdoor advertising averaged an annual increase in revenues of about 10 percent.

A major concern of the outdoor advertising industry is criticism from special-interest groups and legislative bodies. Some of this criticism may be warranted. However, the organized outdoor industry thinks, with some justification, that the public often confuses outdoor with nonstandardized or on-premise signs. In recent years a large portion of industry-wide efforts has been marshaled to educate the public and lawmakers about the outdoor industry.

---

[1] *The First Medium,* Institute of Outdoor Advertising, 1975, p. 2.

OUTDOOR AS A REGULATED INDUSTRY

Self-regulation

Because of the criticism directed at outdoor advertising the industry has engaged in a self-regulation program which is stronger than that of any other medium. The initiative for this industry-wide effort is provided by the OAAA, although many local outdoor firms also engage in public education programs. These self-regulation efforts have been successful among OAAA *members.* In nearly all instances member organizations adhere to the OAAA regulations regarding outdoor advertising practices. Unfortunately for these OAAA members, the public does not always distinguish between members and nonmembers in its call for legal restrictions on outdoor advertising.

Legal regulation

The major federal legislation affecting outdoor advertising is the Highway Beautification Act, which was passed by Congress in 1965. It was known as the "Lady Bird Bill" because Mrs. Lyndon Johnson lobbied for the bill when it was being considered by Congress. The act was intended to regulate and control both outdoor advertising and junkyards.

The act requires a 660-foot buffer along interstate and major federal highways, with some exemptions in industrially zoned areas and near businesses being advertised. It provides penalties of up to 10 percent of federal highway funds for states found to be in noncompliance. It also provides that "just compensation" is to be paid for removed signs. The act is administered by the Federal Highway Administration.

The major obstacle to implementation of the act has been the failure of Congress to allocate funds to fully compensate sign owners. It would cost an estimated $400 million to remove the 200,000 signs which fall under the provisions of the act. In the last ten years Congress has budgeted a little over $100 million, but this money has been earmarked for junkyard screening as well as outdoor poster removal. In recent years Congress has been reluctant to allocate funds, and in his 1980 budget President Carter did not seek any new money for the program.

The lack of decisive action by Congress has left the outdoor industry in a difficult position. Owners of outdoor advertising companies do not know which of the following Congress will decide to do:

1. Fund additional poster removal.
2. Put the program in a holding pattern by leaving present signs alone.
3. Drop the program altogether by repealing the act.

In the meantime the outdoor industry must deal with local and state legislation which is contradictory to the federal regulations.

In the future such legislation may present a bigger problem than any federal legislation. The outdoor industry generally takes the position that it can operate successfully under a fair federal control program. However, since the outdoor industry depends on standardized, national advertising, local rules which specify varying sizes of outdoor posters would be impossible to deal with. For this reason some in the outdoor industry favor federal legislation which would take precedence over any local laws.

TYPES OF OUTDOOR ADVERTISING

The outdoor industry has three categories: posters (or paper), painted bulletins, and one-of-a-kind spectaculars.

Posters

The basic poster sizes are the 24- and 30-sheet posters and the bleed posters. The standard poster panel is built to accommodate all three sizes. In major markets an advertiser should be able to use one of these sizes. However, the 30-sheet poster is the most widely used size and has replaced the 24-sheet as the standard unit. There is no difference in advertising costs for the three sizes, although production costs are greater for the larger types.

In some markets two smaller posters are available. These are the junior panel or eight-sheet poster, which has a copy area 5 feet by 11 feet, and the three-sheet poster, which measures 46 inches high by 30 inches wide. These posters are generally used for pedestrian traffic and are often placed in shopping center parking lots or on the sides of buildings. Because of their smaller size and their unavailability in some markets, these posters have greater usage among local advertisers.

Painted bulletins

The painted bulletin is an individually designed and painted sign. Because bulletins are painted one at a time, they offer greater opportunities for creativity and individuality than do posters. Painted bulletins may use extensions to highlight certain aspects of the poster, and in some cases a high-gloss paper may be used in connection with these signs.

Figure 9–1 shows the mechanical specifications for the various sizes of outdoor posters. Advertisers often buy rotary plans which

Figure 9–1
Mechanical specifications for outdoor posters

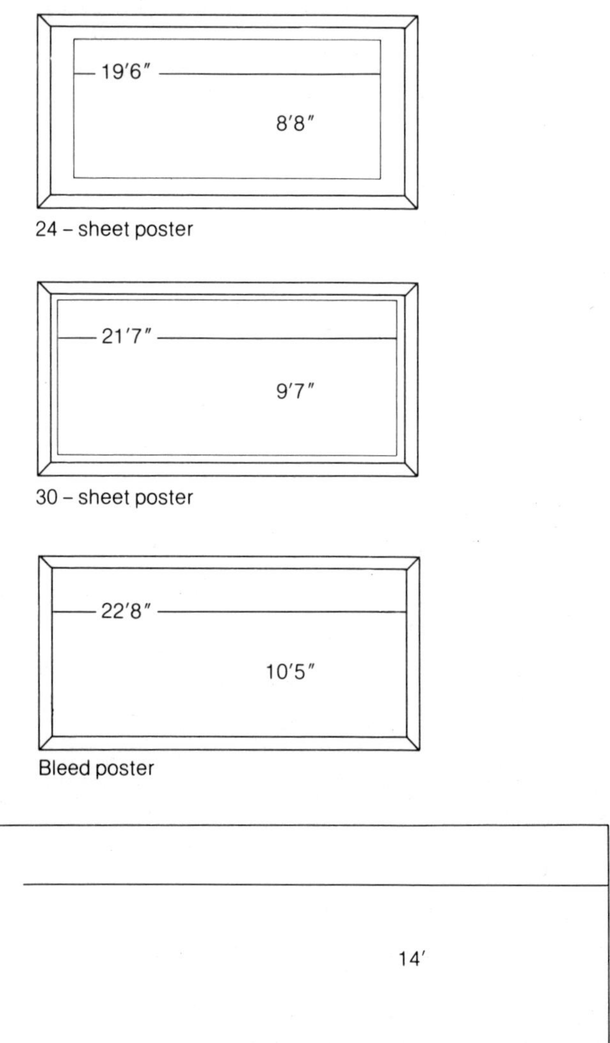

move the message from one location to another to increase audience reach. Figure 9–2 is an example of a typical rotary bulletin plan.

Spectaculars

The final category of outdoor advertising comprises the spectaculars. These custom-built displays are usually large, with extensive use of lighting, movement, and intricate designs. Because of the high cost of construction and maintenance, only the largest advertisers customarily contract for spectaculars, and then only in the most heavily traveled locations. Spectaculars are bought for specific locations, and their cost is determined by production costs and, to a lesser extent, traffic flow.

In recent years outdoor signs have been developed which offer greater durability, lower maintenance costs and higher visibility than do traditional paper posters. These new outdoor signs combine certain elements of paper posters, painted bulletins, and spectaculars. One example is 3M's Panagraphics, which places a series of lamps behind a vinyl-type material called Penaflex. Like paper the sign is relatively easy to change; it has the durability of paint; and it distributes light more evenly for better night visibility than do the usual spotlight-illuminated posters.

PLANTS

Outdoor advertising is purchased through individual operators or plants. Approximately 600 plant operators in the United States offer outdoor advertising in more than 900 markets. A plant usually leases space for its poster panels and then sells this space to advertisers. Many of the larger plants offer some creative services, but this is not generally a plant function. National outdoor campaigns are purchased through one or more national outdoor buying organizations. Using one of these services allows the advertiser to buy several markets and pay only a single bill and deal with one company instead of several plants.

OUTDOOR AS AN ADVERTISING MEDIUM

Strengths

1. *Broad reach and high frequency levels.* Outdoor is a high-intensity medium. It generates high levels of coverage as well as multiexposures. It is also excellent for reaching all segments of the population. Only the very young and very old are not prime prospects

Figure 9–2
A typical rotary bulletin plan

Atlanta Metro Rotary Bulletin Plan

MAGNA—FACE BULLETIN
COPY AREA: 14' X 48'

RATE SCHEDULE:

THREE YEAR CONTRACT	$1,161.00 Per Mo.
TWO YEAR CONTRACT	$1,225.50 Per Mo.
ONE YEAR CONTRACT	$1,290.00 Per Mo.

The rates indicated above reflect a 5% continuity discount for two year and 10% for three year noncancellable contracts, respectively. Rate protection is provided throughout the term of noncancellable contracts.

Three year contracts cancellable at the end of the first and second year shall not have rate protection beyond the anniversary dates and the monthly rate shall be as follows: First year $1,290.00; second year $1,225.50; third year $1,161.00.

Advertising agency commissions will be allowed on the net rate after applicable discounts.

THE BASE MONTHLY RATE INCLUDES:

- Three copy changes per year*
- All night illumination
- Sixty day rotation
- Cost of fabrication, painting, and rotation of up to 100 sq. ft. of cut-out extension is included in the initial copy design*

*Repaints and cut-out allowances may not be accumulated, nor will credits be issued for unused repaints or cut-out square footage.

SHORT TERM CONTRACTS:

Rates furnished upon request, based on availability.

PRINTED BULLETINS:

Advertisers furnishing 14' x 48' printed posters to be displayed on a 60 day basis for a minimum of 12 consecutive months will receive a $50.00 monthly allowance.

CUT—OUT EXTENSIONS:

The fabrication, painting and rotation of up to 100 square feet of flat surface cut-out extension for the initial copy is included in the contract cost, provided the contract term is a minimum of 12 months. The cost for additional square footage during the contract term will be $9.00 Gross (subject to agency commission) or $7.50 Net (not subject to agency commision) per square foot.

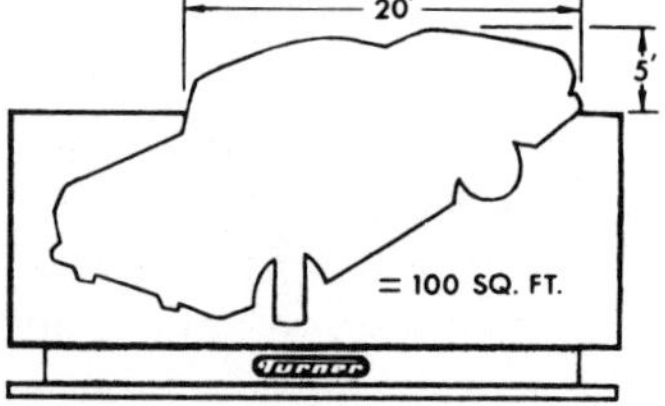

CUT—OUT LIMITATIONS: Side 2' 6" Bottom 2' 0" Top 5' 0"

ILLUMINATED AND CUT—OUT LETTERS, TRIVISION, AND OTHER SPECIAL TREATMENT:

Prices will be quoted upon request.

Courtesy: *Turner Advertising Company*

for outdoor advertising. Note in Figure 9–3 that outdoor advertising is efficient in reaching virtually all market segments.

2. Flexibility. Since outdoor advertising can be purchased in virtually every community, the media planner has flexibility in choosing the geographic pattern. The medium can be used selectively to accommodate specific market problems or in a general national campaign.

3. Low cost per thousand. Outdoor advertising is the least expensive major medium by a wide margin. Generally posters achieve a CPM of 30–40 cents, while the cost of the more expensive painted bulletins averages about $1/1,000.

4. Impact. One of the greatest strengths of outdoor advertising is its size. Combining visual dominance and color, it offers advertisers excellent opportunities for brand and package identification.

Figure 9–3
Outdoor reach and frequency by selected demographic characteristics (30 days)

	25 showing		*50 showing*		*100 showing*	
	R	*F*	*R*	*F*	*R*	*F*
Adults	72.6%	7	81.2%	13	86.7%	24
Men	73.1	8	80.8	15	85.8	29
Women	72.2	6	81.7	11	87.5	20
Female homemakers	71.9	6	81.3	11	87.2	20
Managers/ professionals	80.7	9	86.7	16	90.7	29
Heads of households	72.1	8	80.6	14	85.7	27
Age						
Age 18–24						
Adults	80.1%	8	86.2%	15	91.2%	28
Men	79.3	9	85.1	17	89.6	32
Women	80.8	7	87.2	13	92.7	24
Age 25–34						
Adults	78.6	9	87.6	16	91.3	30
Men	78.9	10	87.5	19	91.1	36
Women	78.3	7	87.7	13	91.5	25
Age 35–44						
Adults	73.6	7	81.4	13	86.3	24
Men	74.2	8	80.2	15	84.8	28
Women	73.1	6	82.7	11	87.7	20
Age 45–54						
Adults	70.6	7	80.2	12	86.2	22
Men	71.6	8	80.7	14	85.3	26
Women	69.7	6	79.8	10	87.0	18
Age 55 +						
Adults	63.4	6	73.3	10	80.5	17
Men	67.7	6	71.9	11	79.0	20
Women	63.3	5	74.3	8	81.6	15

Figure 9–3 (*continued*)

	25 showing		50 showing		100 showing	
	R	*F*	*R*	*F*	*R*	*F*
Individual employment income						
$25,000 +						
Adults	79.2%	9	85.0%	17	90.2%	31
Men	79.4	9	85.1	17	90.0	31
Women	71.6	8	81.3	18	96.3	27
$20,000 +						
Adults	80.0	10	86.1	18	90.5	34
Men	79.9	9	86.0	18	90.4	34
Women	81.5	9	87.0	19	92.0	36
$15,000 +						
Adults	80.0	9	85.8	17	90.3	32
Men	79.9	9	85.7	17	90.0	32
Women	81.8	8	87.9	15	93.4	28
$10,000 +						
Adults	79.0	9	85.7	16	89.7	31
Men	78.5	9	85.0	17	89.0	32
Women	81.3	8	89.2	14	92.8	27
Household income						
$25,000 +						
Adults	78.0%	8	84.9%	15	90.1%	27
Men	78.2	9	84.3	17	89.2	31
Women	77.8	7	85.5	12	91.0	23
$20,000 +						
Adults	78.7	8	85.5	15	90.5	27
Men	79.1	9	84.7	17	89.8	31
Women	78.4	7	86.3	12	91.3	23
$15,000 +						
Adults	76.8	8	84.0	14	89.4	26
Men	77.6	9	83.7	16	88.7	31
Women	76.0	7	84.4	12	90.1	22
$10,000 +						
Adults	75.3	8	83.0	14	88.4	25
Men	75.9	9	82.6	16	87.5	30
Women	74.6	6	83.4	11	89.3	21

Courtesy Institute of Outdoor Advertising

5. *Out-of-home audience.* Outdoor advertising reaches an audience which is already in the marketplace. It is an excellent medium to complement other advertising as a last reminder before purchase.

Weaknesses

1. *Nonselectivity.* Outdoor advertising is a *mass* medium in every respect. Used correctly, the medium can accomplish many marketing

objectives with its wide coverage. However, the medium is difficult to use to reach a particular market segment or target audience. Occasionally painted bulletins may provide such coverage in a particular geographic area of a market, but under normal circumstances outdoor advertising cannot be used to provide selective demographic coverage.

2. *High absolute cost.* Despite the low CPMs achieved by outdoor advertising, it is not an inexpensive medium for a multimarket

Figure 9–4
Estimated outdoor poster costs for top 300 Metro areas*

		Cost per month	
Metro market	*Population (000)*	*50 showing*	*100 showing*
Rank 1– 10	47,989.5	$ 328,586	$ 597,519
Rank 1– 20	66,382.1	470,526	878,939
Rank 1– 30	80,913.8	569,776	1,077,548
Rank 1– 40	91,136.6	651,704	1,222,042
Rank 1– 50	98,399.8	704,351	1,325,159
Rank 1– 60	104,637.8	760,965	1,431,808
Rank 1– 70	110,636.9	803,687	1,511,085
Rank 1– 80	115,177.5	834,830	1,573,141
Rank 1– 90	119,891.4	866,649	1,635,374
Rank 1–100	123,777.5	891,162	1,679,213
Rank 1–125	131,531.0	956,668	1,799,133
Rank 1–150	137,589.3	1,011,915	1,898,139
Rank 1–175	142,482.7	1,058,618	1,984,175
Rank 1–200	146,826.2	1,093,337	2,048,323
Rank 1–225	150,006.8	1,123,468	2,100,082
Rank 1–250	152,627.2	1,149,262	2,144,060
Rank 1–275	155,058.3	1,181,164	2,199,631
Rank 1–300	156,632.8	1,198,094	2,228,729

* Hawaii and Alaska excluded.

Source: Institute of Outdoor Advertising, *Buyers Guide to Outdoor Advertising,* January 1979.

campaign. This is especially true for advertisers who need extensive coverage of the top 10 or top 50 markets. Figure 9–4 shows some comparative cost data.

3. *Short exposure time.* Outdoor advertising derives benefit by being attractive to a mobile, out-of-home audience. However, this characteristic is also a detriment to communication. Outdoor advertising functions best when it is asked to deliver a visual image—a package, a brand name, or a short slogan. It is not designed to com-

municate lengthy advertising copy. An outdoor message which must be "read" is not as effective as one which may be "seen."

4. Audience measurement. A major problem which some advertisers think prevents outdoor advertising from achieving equal status with other media is a lack of verified audience measurement. The Traffic Audit Bureau (TAB) is the circulation-auditing organization for the outdoor industry. The auditing procedure is merely a traffic count in areas adjacent to poster locations.

It is obvious that a simple count of traffic is not adequate in determining the overall value of an outdoor poster. To estimate the overall value of a location the TAB assigns a Space Position Value Rating (SPV) to a poster. The SPV reflects the visibility of the poster, its angle to traffic flow, the number of panels in a location, and the speed of the traffic. The combination of visibility and circulation determines the value of any single poster (see Figure 9–5).

To ensure that the poster positions sold meet minimum requirements for visibility the TAB has developed the following guidelines to serve as standards for comparisons within a market or against other

Figure 9–5
Space Position Valuation Table

Form D

SPACE POSITION VALUATION TABLE
Code and Scale of Values for Poster Panels TAB

APPROACH			TYPES OF PANELS									
			Angled Single (AS) Angled nearest the Line of Travel (AE)		All Other Angled (A): In a Two Panel Facing		All Other Angled (A): In a Facing With More Than Two Panels		Parallel Single (PS) Parallel End of a Group (PE)		All Other Parallel (P)	
PEDESTRIAN	VEHICULAR: Fast Travel	VEHICULAR: Slow Travel	CODE	VALUE	CODE	VALUE	CODE	VALUE	CODE	VALUE	CODE	VALUE
Over 125 ft.	Long Approach Over 350 ft.	Over 250 ft.	1AS 1AE	10	1A	10	1A	9	1PS 1PE	8	1P	7
75 to 125 ft.	Medium Approach 200 to 350 ft.	150 to 250 ft.	2AS 2AE	8	2A	7	2A	7	2PS 2PE	6	2P	5
40 to 75 ft.	Short Approach 100 to 200 ft.	75 to 150 ft.	3AS 3AE	6	3A	5	3A	5	3PS 3PE	4	3P	3
Under 40 ft.	Flash Approach Under 100 ft.	Under 75 ft.	AF	4 3 2 1 0	AF	3 2 1 0	AF	3 2 1 0	PF	2 1 0	PF	1 0

Courtesy Traffic Audit Bureau

Space position values in shaded areas are below AAAA standards.

markets. These guidelines, utilized with the Space Position Valuation Table, ensure that the advertiser buys only positions meeting the standards of the American Association of Advertising Agencies.

GUIDELINES FOR SPACE POSITION VALUATION

Rule 1: All standard poster panels must be rated and assigned a code in accordance with the standards acceptable to TAB members —both buyers and sellers. Visibility standards reflect four variables: the length of approach, the speed of travel, the angle of the advertising structure to the street, and the position of the advertising structure to adjacent advertising structures.

Rule 2: Advertising structures not up to AAAA standards, if sold, must be clearly marked non-AAAA standard. National buyers have agreed to accept reporting of panels with high standards: e.g., 1AS 10, 1AE 10, 1A 10, 2AS 8, 2A 7. When panels that do not come up to these standards are sold, an explanation must be given of why they have been included for sale.

Rule 3: The approach distance applicable to an advertising structure is the distance measured along the line of travel from the point at which the panel becomes fully visible to the point at which the traffic stream passes by the center of the panel. If the panel is obstructed, or is at a reverse angle to the street, or is set back from the street, use only the approach distance to the point where the copy ceases to be readable.

Rule 4: The maximum visibility limit of a poster panel is set at 500 feet. If obstructions occur within the permitted 500 feet, either horizontally or vertically, only the visible distance may be used. Signs in front of advertising structures will be disregarded at the point where the advertising can be read.

Rule 5: Slow traffic is defined as all arterials where posted speeds are not over 35 mph. Fast traffic is defined as all arterials where posted speeds are over 35 mph.

Rule 6: Setback reductions must be applied to panels. SPV should be reduced by the following points:

	Reduce value of poster panel by:		
Setback distance (feet)	*Long approach*	*Medium approach*	*Short approach*
150–200	1	2	3
200–250	3	4	No rating allowed
250–300	5	No rating allowed	No rating allowed

Rule 7: The primary SPV is established by the street which has the highest circulation when a panel may be seen from two or more streets.

Rule 8: SPV ratings should reflect the average lane used by traffic. Example: With three lanes of traffic approaching a panel, rate the panel from the middle of the center lane.

Rule 9: Minimum secondary SPVs that may be assigned: No values lower than grade of 5 may be used.

Rule 10: Where a panel has more than a short approach from two directions and is not a parallel panel, use the total street circulation.

Rule 11: Angled panels are advertising structures built so that maximum visibility will be given to vehicles approaching the structure. Advertising structures are classified as angled when one end is more than six feet back from the other end. Six feet is a minimum, and TAB recommends greater angles of construction for more efficient viewing.

Rule 12: A panel is classified as single if it is 25 feet away from another panel along the line of traffic or 50 feet away from a bulletin.

Rule 13: The poster nearest to the street is classified as an "AE" (in a multiple-panel facing), or if a single panel, as an "AS." Panels adjacent to an "AE" are classified "A" if angled. A parallel panel is classified as a "PS" if it is a single structure. Parallel panels of multiple facing will be classified as "P."

Rule 14: Panels vertically built (decked) will be coded so that the lower is "AE" and the upper is "A," with the distance coded according to length of approach.

Rule 15: Approach distance for parallel panels should be applied as defined in this rule. (*a*) *For a two-way street:* Add approach from both directions. This cannot exceed twice the distance from the center of the panel to the center of the street at the panel. (*b*) For a one-way street: The approach distance cannot exceed twice the distance from the panel to the center of the street. (In both cases, obstructions must be adjusted for.)

Rule 16: The circulation that can be applied for parallel panels can only be one half the total circulation on the street.

Rule 17: Situations not covered in these rules must be referred to TAB for ruling. TAB has established a rating system to encourage the construction of panels with excellent standards of visibility. Buyers frequently make field trips to make their own personal judgment about the visibility and potential effectiveness of panels. TAB is not involved with these personal evaluations but strongly recommends the following guidelines: *"Look at a panel and ask yourself: If you were spending money for it, would you buy it? If you have any doubts, take it down."*

BUYING OUTDOOR ADVERTISING

The Gross Rating Point

The terminology for purchasing outdoor advertising has changed during the last several years. Formerly outdoor's basic unit of purchase was the "100 showing." A 100 showing was defined as the number of outdoor posters which would be seen by 100 percent of the mobile population (approximately 96 percent of the total population) in a 30-day period. This definition was unsatisfactory since it was fundamentally an attempt to measure reach (or unduplicated audience) when, in fact, the audience measurement techniques used in outdoor advertising had no practical means of distinguishing new from repeat exposures.

To overcome this problem, the outdoor industry redefined the term *100 showing.* It used the term *100* to define a level of *daily* coverage equal to the population of the market. Therefore, in a market of 100,000 persons, a level of intensity that provided 100,000 exposures was said to be a 100 showing.

This change in terminology provided a definition of what had been measured all along—duplicated audience. In 1972 the outdoor industry adopted its current definition of audience coverage, the Gross Rating Point. By using GRP, the medium could sell more easily to national advertisers who were comfortable with this television terminology. As used by outdoor advertising, "a rating point is 1 percent of the population one time." GRPs are based on the daily duplicated audience as a percentage of a market. If three posters in a community of 100,000 population achieve a daily exposure to 75,000 persons, the result is 75 Gross Rating Points. The formula can be stated as follows:

$$\text{GRP} = \frac{\text{Average Daily Effective Circulation (ADEC)}}{\text{Population of the market}}$$

ADEC is defined as follows:

Daily is 12 hours for nonlighted signs and 18 hours for illuminated signs.

Effective is a measure of audience proximity to a sign rather than communication.

Circulation is a measure of the total number of duplicated people passing a sign rather than the total number of different people.

GRPs are sold in units of 25, with 100 and 50 being the two most often purchased levels. Intensities of more than 100 may be purchased, but this is rare. Some plants still use the term *showing,* al-

Figure 9–6
Outdoor rates and markets

INDIANA 13

OUTDOOR RATES AND MARKETS

PLANT NO.	MARKET NO.	MARKET NAME	COUNTY NAME	POP.	EFF. DATE	GRP/SHOW	COVERAGE POSTERS NON ILL.	ILL.	COST PER MONTH	DIS.
1065.0	00050	ADVANCE IND	BOONE	.6	07/01/0	•100	1		110.00	11
4505.0	00150	ALBANY MKT IND SEE MARKET NO. 13-15550**	DELAWARE	2.3	07/01/0	•100	1		120.00	32
1052.0	00200	ALBION FOW	NOBLE	1.5	07/01/0	100	1		125.00	11
1060.0	00250	ALEXANDRIA IND SEE MARKET NO. 13-00400**	MADISON	5.6	07/01/0	•100 • 50	2 1		220.00 110.00	11 11
1060.0	00300	AMBOY IND	MIAMI	.5	07/01/0	•100	1		110.00	11
1060.0	00400	ANDERSON MKT IND --SUB MKTS. (ALSO SOLD SEPARATELY) ALEXANDRIA ELWOOD HUNTSVILLE LAPEL-FISHERSBURG MIDDLETOWN PENDLETON	MADISON	138.0	07/01/0	100 50 25	7 4 3	13 7 3	2800.00 1540.00 840.00	11 11 11
1052.0	00450	ANGOLA FOW	STEUBEN	5.1	07/01/0	100 50	2 1		260.00 130.00	11 11
1065.0	00700	ATTICA IND	FOUNTAIN	4.3	07/01/0	•100 • 50	2 1		220.00 110.00	11 11
1050.0	00750	ATWOOD SBN	KOSCIUSKO	.2	07/01/0	100	1		125.00	11
1052.0	00800	AUBURN FOW SEE MARKET NO. 13-07470**	DE KALB	7.3	07/01/0	100 50	2 1		260.00 130.00	11 11
3825.0	00850	AURORA-LAWRENCEBURG-GREENDALE CIN	DEARBORN	12.7	01/01/0	•100 • 50	6 3		612.00 306.00	23 23
3295.0	00900	AUSTIN LSV	SCOTT	4.9	07/01/8	•100 • 50	2 1		190.00 95.00	
8190.0	00980	BAINBRIDGE IND	PUTNAM	.7	09/01/0	•100	1		115.00	34
3825.0	01100	BATESVILLE-OLDENBURG CIN	FRANKLIN	4.6	01/01/0	•100 • 50	4 2		384.00 192.00	23 23
3825.0	01130	BEDFORD MKT LSV --SUB MKTS. (ALSO SOLD SEPARATELY) MITCHELL	LAWRENCE	38.0	01/01/0	•100 • 50	6 4	2 1	816.00 510.00	23 23
8190.0	01230	BELLMORE TER	PARKE	.1	09/01/0	•100	1		115.00	34
4505.0	01250	BERNE FOW SEE MARKET NO. 13-18250**	ADAMS	3.0	07/01/0	•100	1		120.00	32
4057.0	01300	BEVERLY SHORES CHI SEE MARKET NO. 13-14100**	PORTER	.9	06/01/0	•100	1		120.00	49
3825.0	01350	BICKNELL TER	KNOX	3.7	01/01/0	•100 • 50	3 2		288.00 192.00	23 23
3825.0	01400	BLOOMFIELD TER	GREENE	2.6	01/01/0	•100 • 50	2 1		192.00 96.00	23 23
3825.0	01450	BLOOMINGTON MKT IND	MONROE	84.4	01/01/0	100 75 50	5 4 3	5 4 3	1140.00 912.00 684.00	23 23 23
6300.0	01500	BLOUNTSVILLE IND	HENRY	.2	01/01/0	•100	1		96.00	25
1052.0	01550	BLUFFTON FOW	WELLS	8.3	07/01/0	100 50	2 1		240.00 120.00	11 11
6300.0	01650	BOSTON DAY	WAYNE	.2	01/01/0	•100	1		96.00	25
1065.0	01700	BOSWELL LAE	BENTON	1.0	07/01/0	•100	1		110.00	11
3825.0	01850	BRAZIL MKT TER	CLAY	9.8	01/01/0	•100 • 50	4 2		384.00 192.00	23 23
1050.0	01900	BREMEN SBN SEE MARKET NO. 13-20800**	MARSHALL	3.8	07/01/0	100 50	2 1		250.00 125.00	11 11
1052.0	01950	BRIMFIELD FOW	NOBLE	.3	07/01/0	100	1		125.00	11
1065.0	02000	BROOKSTON IND	WHITE	1.2	07/01/0	•100	1		110.00	11
3825.0	02050	BROOKVILLE CIN	FRANKLIN	2.9	01/01/0	•100 • 50	3 2		288.00 192.00	23 23
3825.0	02130	BROWNSTOWN IND	JACKSON	2.4	01/01/0	•100	1		102.00	23
3825.0	02200	BRUCEVILLE TER	KNOX	.6	01/01/0	•100	1		96.00	23
4505.0	02300	BRYANT FOW SEE MARKET NO. 13-18250**	JAY	.3	07/01/0	•100	1		120.00	32
1060.0	02350	BUNKER HILL IND	MIAMI	1.0	07/01/0	•100	1		110.00	11

ADI CODE SEE NOTE TO BUYER
**FIRST 2 DIGITS INDICATE STATE
9000.0+·OAAA NON-MEMBER

GRP GROSS RATING POINTS, EXCEPT **SHOWING

SEPTEMBER 1980

though in most cases they will also use GRPs. In recent years the term *showing* has come to mean that an outdoor campaign of some level of intensity was used (e.g., a showing of 50 GRPs). See Figure 9–3 for an example of this usage.

Rate information

Outdoor advertising is one of the few media for which no Standard Rate and Data volume is available. Advertising rates are published in the *Buyers Guide to Outdoor Advertising,* published twice a year by the Institute of Outdoor Advertising. Figure 9–6 shows an example of the information contained in the guide. Note that the guide gives GRP costs, market population discounts, and the number of posters in a GRP allotment and also cross-references overlapping markets.

Individual plants have their own rate cards (see Figure 9–7). The format of these cards is usually similar to that of the standard buying guide. However, the local rate cards often give more local market information as well as CPMs for the various GRP levels. When CPM is computed, remember that we are dealing with daily circulation so some conversion must be made in the CPM formula to obtain the equivalent of the monthly CPM costs used for other media.

CPM conversion for outdoor:

$$\text{Outdoor } CPM = \frac{\frac{\text{Monthly cost}}{30} \times 1{,}000}{\text{Daily circulation}}$$

Or using the 100-GRP level in Figure 9-7:

$$\text{Outdoor } CPM = \frac{\frac{\$25{,}420}{30} \times 1{,}000}{1{,}690{,}800} = \frac{\$847 \times 1{,}000}{1{,}690{,}800} = 50 \text{ cents}$$

Advertisers must consider outdoor production costs as well as space costs. In most other media, production costs are a small percentage of total advertising costs. This is not true in outdoor advertising. Production costs for painted bulletins and spectaculars comprise significant portions of total outdoor costs.

Buying procedures

As mentioned earlier, the "medium" for outdoor advertising is the plant. The agency or advertiser works in much the same way with the

Figure 9–7
A local rate card for outdoor advertising

Turner Advertising Company
Atlanta, Georgia

POSTER DISPLAY RATE CARD #26
Effective **December 15, 1979**

12 MONTH POSTING CONTRACTS EARN 20% RATE DISCOUNT

Standard Eight County Metro Coverage Plan

COUNTIES INCLUDED	POPULATION	GRP INTENSITY	ACTUAL GRPs DELIVERED	ALLOTMENTS				MONTHLY RATE	AVERAGE DAILY EFFECTIVE CIRCULATION (ADEC) †	AVERAGE COST PER PANEL	CPM
				NON ILL	ILL	TOTAL	% ILL				
Clayton Cobb	142,000 261,600	100	99.9	34	90	124	73%	$25,420	1,690,800	$205.00	50¢
DeKalb Douglas	463,000 49,100	75	75.6	26	68	94	72%	$20,300	1,279,800	$215.96	53¢
Fulton Gwinnett	577,900 134,900	50	50.5	16	46	62	74%	$13,850	853,600	$223.39	54¢
Newton Rockdale	32,700 30,800	25	25.2	8	23	31	74%	$ 7,700	426,800	$248.39	60¢
Total 8 County Population	1,692,000										

† Based on August 1978 T.A.B. Audit

MAXIMUM FLEXIBILITY/MINIMAL COST INCREASES
Turner Advertising Company's 1980 Rates and Allotments have been calculated to offer maximum flexibility with minimal cost increases to the advertiser. In the spirit of compliance with the President's Voluntary Wage-Price Guidelines, rate increases range from 6.8% to 7.3% per panel. Also, Turner will continue to offer a 20% continuity discount to twelve-month advertisers (see reverse).

STANDARD EIGHT COUNTY METRO COVERAGE PLAN
This plan offers a general distribution of panels throughout Turner's eight county marketing area. The allotments for all intensities have been increased slightly over 1979 allotments to reflect a 1.4% population growth during the past twelve month period (source: Sales & Marketing Management's annual "Survey of Buying Power"). The T.A.B. plant averages of 15,900 per illuminated panel and 7,640 per non-illuminated panel were utilized in establishing the appropriate allotment, GRP, and ADEC levels.

Turner's Eight County Metro Coverage Area encompasses 90.2% of the population and 90.6% of the households in the 15 county Atlanta SMSA.

CONTINUED DRAMATIC GROWTH IN POSTER CAPACITY AND DISTRIBUTION ANTICIPATED
Turner has erected over 300 new panels since late 1978 with special emphasis on locating these new structures in the fast growing suburban areas of the market. Plans call for further expansion of Turner's poster plant by approximately 200 panels in 1980 to supplement existing coverage and to add new coverage in areas which merit it.

Peter A. Dames — *General Manager*
Richard W. McGinnis — *General Sales Manager*
B. F. "Bud" Whitham — *Sales Manager*

Turner Advertising Company
732 Ashby St., N.W., Atlanta, Georgia, 30318
(404) 875-0822

ALL-NIGHT ILLUMINATION
Atlanta's highly mobile consumer population is constantly in motion . . . day and night . . . traveling to work, to shop, to play. For this reason, Turner offers dusk until dawn illumination on the great majority of its poster displays.

TRANSPORTATION HUB
Transportation remains the key to Atlanta's economy. Served by the world's second busiest airport and six Interstate highways, it is the region's most important distribution, wholesaling and corporate office center. In mid-1980, Atlanta will begin to open its new $400-million terminal complex that is slated to board 52 million passengers annually; by 1981, Atlanta's airport is expected to be the world's busiest.

Atlanta Metro Market (15 County SMSA)		NATIONAL RANKING
Population	1,874,900	19th
Households	639,300	20th
Total Retail Sales	$7,825,140,000	16th
Eating & Drinking Place Sales	$ 871,500,000	12th
Gen. Merchandise Store Sales	$1,310,018,000	15th
Automotive Dealer Sales	$1,747,536,000	12th
Registered Passenger Cars ..	1,009,820	19th

Items 1 thru 6 from SM/Item 7 from SRDS

Courtesy: *Turner Advertising Company*

plant as with other media. Agency and client first decide whether outdoor advertising can meet marketing and advertising objectives. Then a decision is made concerning the markets and exposure level to be used. Finally, the contracts and insertion orders are completed.

National advertisers and their agencies normally work with a national organization rather than with separate plant operators. Currently the largest such organization is the Out of Home Media Service (OHMS). OHMS serves as the media-buying department for its clients. An advertiser contracts with OHMS to purchase outdoor advertising in specified markets. OHMS also supervises transit advertising media buys. OHMS not only handles the buying of out-of-home media but also conducts field inspections to verify that buys were made properly and to investigate complaints.

The cost of the OHMS services varies with the types of media and with the number of services requested. The agency is billed 3.5 percent of gross billings for total service, which includes both administrative and field services. Administrative services alone cost the agency 2.5 percent of gross billings, and transit is serviced for 2 percent of gross billings. The organization is particularly advantageous to advertising agencies since it frees them from the overhead of a large in-house out-of-home buying staff.

After the purchase is made, the advertiser should require some proof of performance by the plant. Usually an affidavit, often with accompanying pictures of poster locations, is provided. In addition regional and national buying services provide on-site inspection of the posters they purchase.

The agency commission

The outdoor advertising industry is unique in that it offers a commission of 16.67 percent to advertising agencies. The "bonus" of 1.67 percent over the commission offered by all other media has traditionally been used to encourage agencies to consider the outdoor medium in making media recommendations to their clients.

OTHER FORMS OF OUT-OF-HOME ADVERTISING

Out-of-home advertising usually means posters and painted bulletins. However, there are other opportunities to advertise to this population. Many advertisers have promoted their products by placing messages on trash containers, bus stop shelters, and freestanding displays in shopping malls as well as by employing more unusual methods such as skywriting. See Figure 9–8 for other examples of out-of-home advertising.

Figure 9–8
Shopping list of out-of-home options

Arrival departure boards	Panagraphic displays
Balloons	Port-a-panels
Banner towing by planes	Roach coaches (mobile display canteens)
Beetleboards (privately owned Volkswagens)	Sailboats
Book covers	Shopping bags
Bus advertising	Shopping carts
Bus benches	Shopping center specials
Bus shelters	Spectacolor (Times Square)
Cablecar advertising in San Francisco, at resorts	Sports arenas
Delivery trucks	Sports events sponsorships
Egg cartons	Stadium signs
Greyhound, Trailways, other bus lines	Subway advertising
Holographic displays	Sugar packets
Individual spectaculars	T-shirts
Junior panels	Taxicabs
Kiosks and other public receptacles	Timetable programs
Lavatory advertising	Trash baskets
Lifeguard chairs at beaches	Trucks
Metroforms	Three-sheets
Clocks in off-track-betting parlors	Umbrellas
	Urban panels

Source: *Media Decisions,* July 1977, p. 71.

The problem with these outdoor media is that their impact is largely unmeasurable. The advertiser who uses these methods must rely on intuition to decide what types of displays to use and how much to spend. In addition there is the public relations problem of environmental pollution associated with such promotions. The potential customer backlash as well as the clutter associated with massive introduction of outdoor devices should cause advertisers to carefully weigh costs and benefits from out-of-home advertising.

THE OUTLOOK FOR OUTDOOR ADVERTISING

Outdoor advertising continues to grow at a rate slightly greater than secular inflation. In many markets the demand for outdoor posters and bulletins is greater than the available space and will continue to be in the foreseeable future. Currently the outdoor industry is a major beneficiary of television's high cost and its exclusion of some product categories. It is estimated that as much as 30 percent of all outdoor advertising is devoted to liquor and cigarette advertising. These products, with large advertising budgets and limited media in which to place their advertising, form the financial base of the outdoor industry. For other products, advertisers use the outdoor medium as an alternative to costly television advertising.

It is likely that television advertising costs will continue to increase, and it is unlikely that either cigarette or liquor ads will be permitted in broadcasting. Therefore, the elements for continued success for outdoor advertising will continue into the 1980s. The major barrier to continued growth in ad revenues is that of finding more space to accommodate the existing demand for posters and bulletins.

Despite the strong demand for outdoor advertising, potential problems for the industry exist during the next decade (see Figure 9–9). Public criticism and legislative action can be expected to continue in the coming years. It seems, however, that the intensity of active criticism directed toward the outdoor industry in the 1960s and early 70s has abated. The failure of the Highway Beautification Act to achieve its full objectives and recent reluctance by Congress to fund the act indicate a lack of public enthusiasm for new limits on outdoor advertising.

The outdoor industry is still faced with various state and local sign ordinances which restrict outdoor advertising. In some cities more stringent zoning laws have cost outdoor plants thousands of dollars. One of the most restrictive outdoor advertising markets in the country is Washington, D.C., where only 35 posters are allowed in the entire city.[2]

A final hazard for the outdoor industry is the effects of energy shortages. Outdoor advertising depends on automobile traffic for exposure. The visibility of outdoor signs from mass transportation vehicles is usually inferior to that from an automobile. During the Arab oil embargo of 1973 some communities outlawed illuminated posters. This restriction cut the effective viewing period by 20 percent during winter months. Energy shortages which produce a move to public transportation could have an impact on the outdoor industry.

TRANSIT ADVERTISING

Most people give only passing thought to transit advertising and have little understanding of the industry. However, it is prospering, and most industry indicators predict that its prosperity will continue in the 1980s. Annual gross revenues for transit advertising currently exceed $70 million.

Transit advertising is purchased from firms called operators, which have leased space from municipal authorities. The largest operator is Metro Transit Advertising (MTA), which operates in several of the top

[2] "Out-of-Home Explosion!" *Media Decisions*, July 1977, p. 70.

Figure 9–9
An editorial advocating billboard control

The Atlanta Journal

Covers Dixie Like the Dew

Since 1883

James M. Cox Chairman 1939 1957 --James M. Cox Jr. Chairman 1957 1974

Tom Wood, President

Durwood McAlister, Editor Jim Minter, Managing Editor

4-A ★★★★★ JANUARY 3, 1980

Billboard Control

ARGUMENTS can be advanced in behalf of billboards along Georgia highways, most notably that they provide information of convenience for the motorist.

But there are billboards and there are billboards. Some are a credit to the product or service that is advertised. And some are an utter disgrace to the state. Some are tasteful and some are atrocious. Some are located in such a way as to blend in with the scenic view and some are blatantly hideous.

Thus there must be rules and regulations regarding billboards. There must be a measure of control, and that control must be effectively enforced by the state.

Because of that we endorse the move by the Georgia Department of Transportation for legislation which would close existing loopholes in billboard control.

The DOT notes that there are some 31,000 billboards along Georgia's primary and interstate highways. Of that number a mere 3,300 are legal, complying with 1971 state law. Classified as illegal are 5,600 billboards. And the remaining 22,000 billboards are rated as non-conforming—which means they were erected before the 1971 law and do not comply with it. The state must purchase non-conforming billboards in order to remove them.

Legislation to be considered by the forthcoming General Assembly would authorize DOT to issue permits for non-conforming signs until those signs could be purchased. Thus only illegal signs would not have a permit and could be identified more readily, thus making them easier to remove.

Proposed legislation would also authorize DOT personnel to go on private property and remove an illegal sign without being personally liable.

We believe in highway billboards that are a credit to the state. But as DOT statistics point out, those in compliance with the 1971 law are definitely a minority.

For that reason we support DOT Commissioner Tom Moreland's efforts to improve billboard control, and we urge local governments to enact zoning ordinances which would further strengthen that control.

20 markets. In some respects the operator functions much like the outdoor plant. It receives printed material from agencies (through specialty printing houses) and maintains space inside and outside vehicles and in transit stations.

The operator pays a 15 percent agency commission (not the 16.67 percent paid by outdoor). In addition transit rates are available through the transit advertising edition of SRDS. There is some movement toward an industry-supported rate guide which would be the major source of transit rates in the same way that the IOA's *Buyers Guide* is the major source of outdoor rates.

The transit medium is divided into three major categories:

1. Car cards. Car cards are displayed inside mass transportation vehicles, primarily buses and subway trains. The recent move to mass transportation systems has improved the appeal of car cards to advertisers. The most obvious change has been the increased ridership of mass transportation systems caused by the high cost of driving. A less obvious but no less important change has been the improvement in the demographics of public transportation, which in all but a few markets has been at the lower end of the socioeconomic scale. Today, with the introduction of such systems as the Bay Area Rapid Transit (BART) system in San Francisco and new or renovated transportation systems in Washington, D.C., and other markets, advertisers can reach a more upscale audience through car cards.

Despite the development of a broader audience, car cards and transit advertising must be considered a mass medium. There are few practical opportunities to reach a specific market. In this respect the strategy for transit advertising is usually similar to that used in outdoor advertising. Because of this similarity the term *out-of-home* is being used increasingly to designate the broad concept of nontraditional media.

Car cards are 11 inches by 28 inches in most markets and are sold on the basis of a "full run." A full run means that every vehicle (or car in the case of subways) in the system has one card. An advertiser may also purchase half run (every other car) or double runs (two cards in every car). Minimum contracts for car cards are generally 30 days, with discounts based on 3-, 6-, and 12-month contracts.

Costs are based on six-month average ridership of a system. Circulation figures are compiled by the Transit Advertising Association (TAA) and are simply a matter of counting passengers. As with outdoor advertising, the circulation figures supplied by TAA are estimates of the potential audience, since there is no way of telling from these figures what segment of the audience saw any particular car card.

2. Outside space (traveling displays). Outside space is pur-

Figure 9–10
Basic sizes of outside signs

Traveling displays	21 inches × 44 inches (basic unit)
	21 inches × 36 inches
	21 inches × 17 inches
Queen size	21 inches × 88 inches
King size	30 inches × 144 inches
Rear end	21 inches × 72 inches
Front end	11 inches × 42 inches

Source: *Transit Advertising SRDS.*

chased on the back, front, and sides of mass transportation vehicles. Exposure to exterior signs is not confined to riders of mass transit vehicles but extends to a wider audience of pedestrians and other riders. In most respects, outside transit posters are comparable to outdoor advertising. They are seen by the broadest possible audience; their viewing time is short, necessitating a concise message. Audience measures, when they exist, report potential rather than real impact.

There are several sizes of outside signs. At one time the only standard-size exterior sign was the 21-inch by 44-inch traveling display. Some operators still refer to all exterior signs, regardless of their size, as traveling displays. In recent years operators have offered two additional widths of traveling displays: the so-called king- and queen-size outside posters. Figure 9–10 outlines the sizes available for exterior signs. Seldom are all sizes available in any single market, and most multicity advertisers use either the king size or the 21-inch by 44-inch traveling display.

Outdoor signs are sold by the unit and also on the basis of showings. However, since circulation figures are only estimated, the advertiser is buying largely on the basis of judgment. Figure 9–11 shows the cost of both a car card and an exterior transit campaign in the top 50 markets.

3. Station posters. Most station posters are found in the very largest markets. There are a wide variety of standardized and custom displays in the various markets. The standard station poster comes in four basic sizes:

	Height (inches)		*Width (inches)*
One-sheet poster	46	×	30*
Two-sheet poster	46	×	60
Three-sheet poster	84	×	42
Six-sheet poster	60	×	144

* White space copy area.

Figure 9–11
Transit advertising

	100 showing: Exterior bus space, 30-inch × 144-inch posters		*Full run: Interior bus space, 11-inch × 28-inch cards*	
Basic markets	*Posters*	*Monthly cost*	*Cards*	*Monthly cost*
1–10	3,670	$234,000	30,300*	$ 66,700*
11–20	1,520	77,100	6,280	19,900
21–30	660	41,000	2,920	9,400
31–40	465	26,500	1,430	4,360
41–50	440	23,900	1,410	3,080
1–50	6,755	$402,500	42,340	$103,440

50 showing and half-run rates and allotments are approximately 65 percent of 100 showing. Exterior and/or interior space may not be available in all markets.

* Includes subway cards in New York City.

Source: For permission to use this material the authors are indebted to McCann-Erickson Worldwide and Campbell-Ewald Worldwide, members of the Interpublic Group of Companies. From *1979/1980 Media Planning and Buying Guide* (New York: McCann-Erickson Worldwide, 1979) and *1979/1980 Media Information Guide* (Warren, Mich.: Campbell-Ewald Worldwide, 1979).

The most common types of station posters are the one- and two-sheet sizes. Costs range from approximately $1,000 per one-sheet poster in New York City to $60 in San Francisco. The station poster is sold on a per-unit basis or by showings.

4. The basic bus. In recent years a few advertisers and operators have developed the idea of having a single advertiser take over an entire vehicle for its advertising messages. This concept, called the "basic bus," works best when a firm has several messages to communicate (such as a storyboard layout or before-after advertising) or when it wants to advertise several of its brands.

CHARACTERISTICS OF TRANSIT

Strengths

1. Mass appeal. Transit advertising not only reaches large numbers of people, but it brings advertising messages to them while they are in the marketplace. It is an excellent method of supplementing other media as well as providing package identification on a reminder basis.

2. Low cost. Transit advertising is among the least expensive media. Costs vary by market size, but the average traveling display costs about $60 a month in the top ten markets, and a car card costs less than $3 per vehicle in the same markets. CPMs range from 15 to 25 cents for all forms of transit advertising. In computing CPMs, the

Figure 9–12
Use of the Free-Form Spectacular to announce the King Tutankhamen exhibit in Los Angeles

Courtesy 3M Company; graphic by Norm Gollin Design

advertiser must remember that there is no evidence concerning advertising exposure; even so, the low absolute costs and CPMs are impressive.

3. *Flexibility.* Transit advertising offers the advertiser geographic, format, and intensity flexibility in larger markets. The advertiser can choose among a variety of inside and outside signs which are available in excellent production processes. In most markets the advertiser can choose coverages as broad as a 200 showing (in station posters) to a specific bus route for a car card.

Recently more flexible formats have been tested successfully. For instance Metro Transit Advertising and the 3M Company have developed a plastic material which adheres directly to the outside of the vehicle. Called Metroform Spectacular, it eliminates frames, cuts down on maintenance costs, and permits large, unstandardized signs.[3] (See Figure 9–12.)

Weaknesses

1. *Lack of audience research.* Transit advertising suffers from a lack of in-depth audience research. While overall audience estimates are available, there is almost no information on demographics, impact, or reach/frequency levels. From time to time, audience research

[3] William T. Hadley, "Out-of-Home," *Media Decisions,* November 1977, p. 96.

studies have been conducted by A. C. Nielsen and other research organizations, but these have tended to be narrow in scope and to apply only to a single market.

2. Lack of prestige. Transit suffers from much the same problem of recognition that is encountered by outdoor, direct mail, and sales promotion. Often these media are not eliminated from a media plan; they are simply not considered in the first place. While educational efforts by the TAA and other industry groups have helped upgrade the image of transit advertising, it remains a poor relation to the major media.

THE OUTLOOK FOR TRANSIT ADVERTISING

The future of transit advertising appears positive. Current annual revenues are estimated at $60 million, and this figure should increase dramatically during the next ten years. Like outdoor advertising, transit benefits from the exclusion of cigarettes and liquor by the broadcast media. These two product categories account for more than 15 percent of total revenues. With space becoming an increasing problem in outdoor advertising, it is reasonable to assume that more advertising dollars will be diverted to transit.

Transit advertising will obviously benefit from continuing energy problems. In both numbers and upscale demographics, transit advertising is a more attractive medium now than it was prior to the oil crisis of 1974. In the next several years transit advertising may have the same problems in keeping up with demand that are now faced by outdoor advertising. Future expansion of transit advertising should not meet the type of public resistance which has been the bane of outdoor advertising. As more and better mass transportation systems are developed throughout the country, transit advertising can anticipate more lucrative situations.

QUESTIONS

1. Describe the three categories of outdoor advertising.

2. Discuss the use of Gross Rating Points as a measure of outdoor audiences.

3. What is the purpose of the Space Position Valuation?

4. What is the role of the plant in outdoor advertising?

5. Discuss the services provided by the Out of Home Media Service (OHMS) and the commission it receives for these services.

6. How is the success of transit advertising related to future energy conservation?

7. Discuss the major types of transit advertising.

8. What is the role of the operator in transit advertising?

10

DIRECT ADVERTISING AND SALES PROMOTION

DIRECT MARKETING

Direct marketing looks to the 1980s as a period of problems and opportunities unlike those faced by any of the other major media. On the positive side, direct marketers see the need for greater conservation leading to more in-home buying. The number of working women in the marketplace will also require timesaving methods of purchase such as direct marketing. In addition the application of computer technology makes direct marketing feasible in a number of areas which have been, to now, largely experimental.[1] When two-way communications systems such as QUBE (see Chapter 5) become widespread, direct marketing may become a major method of distribution, promotion, and selling. Approximately 5 percent of goods and services are now sold and/or delivered by direct marketing.

On the negative side, direct marketers see problems which may be exacerbated in the future. Despite the large expenditures in direct marketing (about $6 billion in direct mail alone in 1979), the public and many advertisers regard direct marketing with suspicion. The unfavorable attitude, the "junk mail" stereotype, hurts the credibility of most areas of direct marketing. In addition price inflation in printing, postage, and labor have hit direct marketing in the last few years. Finally, advertisers misunderstand the terminology used in direct marketing.

Terminology of direct marketing

"Direct marketing" is a term for marketing including distribution and/or advertising, which occurs directly between the seller and the consumer. Direct marketing requires no retailer or supplementary middleman to reach the consumer. It can be promoted through direct

[1] "Need for Direct Mail Expected to Grow," *Advertising Age*, October 29, 1979, p. 12.

channels or in traditional advertising media. This sometimes creates a misunderstanding. Direct mail is often confused with other related advertising terms. Therefore, it is necessary to make a clear distinction between what direct mail is and is not.

1. Mail-order advertising. Mail-order advertising refers to goods which are distributed directly from the seller to the buyer through the mails. The solicitation for such goods can be through any one advertising medium or any combination of advertising media, including direct mail. Many magazines carry classified sections for such mail-order advertising.

2. Direct advertising. Direct advertising is any form of promotion which passes directly from the seller to the buyer without first being placed in a medium. Political candidates, small retail stores, and car dealers often place their selling messages on car windshields as a form of direct advertising.

3. Direct mail advertising. Direct mail is the largest category of direct advertising. Some advertising practitioners prefer the term *direct-by-mail.*

Advantages of direct advertising and direct mail

The major appeal of direct marketing for most advertisers is selectivity, which can take many forms. For some advertisers the appeal of direct advertising is its flexibility of format; other advertisers use direct advertising because they cannot reach a widely scattered market segment efficiently through the traditional media; still other advertisers need the timing flexibility of direct advertising. The Direct Mail/Marketing Association has outlined ten major differences between direct advertising and other media:

1. Direct advertising can be used to reach specific individuals or markets with greater control than is obtainable by any other medium. An appeal can be directed to 100 handpicked millionaires just as readily as to a very select professional group of 100,000 book buyers. In many cases lists can be obtained with postage guaranteed up to 98 percent accuracy. How else, or how better, could a promotion be limited, yet assure absolute coverage, than through a direct approach by mail to present customers, or past customers, or recommended customers?

2. Direct advertising can be made personal to the point of being absolutely confidential. Whether a letter, order blank, confidential price list, or product information—regardless of the appeal or the number of people to be reached—a first-class mailing can do it. Not all direct mail is of a confidential nature; but when a confidential approach is needed, only this medium can provide the means.

3. Direct advertising is a single advertiser's individual message and is not in competition with other advertising and/or editorial matter. At the moment of reception, or when a piece of direct advertising reaches the reader, it has his complete attention. It will stand or fall on its appeal, just as will any other advertisement—but at least it will have a better chance because there is less competition for the reader's attention.

4. Direct advertising does not have the limitations on space and format of other advertising media. Almost no limit exists as to the size, shape, style, number of colors, and all of the other elements that enter into the makeup of direct mail and printed promotion. Direct advertising formats range from the small poster stamp and miniatures to booklets, brochures, and broadsides as big as the top of a desk, to accommodate any length of message or size of illustration. The piece can be made to fit the story, and the possibilities are as boundless as the ingenuity of the designer.

5. Direct advertising permits greater flexibility in materials and processes of production than any other medium of advertising. Production of direct advertising includes every phase of reproduction known to the graphic arts—printing, lithography, photo-offset, rotogravure, steel engraving, silk screen, Multigraph, mimeograph, Multilith, and so on. Added to these are the processes of die cutting, scoring, punching, tabbing, swatching, varnishing, laminating, mounting, and all kinds of binding and folding. Because of these facilities, and because each piece is individually produced, greater latitude exists in the use of materials—all kinds of papers, inks, plastics, and so on. These are the reasons why direct advertising can be custom made, can fit any pattern, can outdo any other form of advertising in physical presentation.

6. Direct advertising provides a means for introducing novelty and realism into the interpretation of the advertiser's story. Cutouts, pop-ups, and odd shapes and patterns are employed to good advantage by users of direct mail advertising. If a folder or booklet is wanted in the shape of a bottle, box, or barrel, the effect is easy to obtain. Even invisible colors and perfumed inks are used in some printed pieces for novelty and as powerful attention-getters.

7. Direct advertising can be produced according to the needs of the advertiser's own immediate schedule. For a quick promotion or an emergency mailing to take advantage of a situation, the production of direct mail can be geared to meet the need without waiting for a publication date or for some other medium of advertising to do the job.

8. Direct advertising can be controlled for specific jobs of research, reaching small groups, and testing ideas, appeals, and reac-

tions. Before the big campaigns in which other media may be employed, confidential questionnaires can be used for research and ideas, appeals, and reactions can be tested. Next to personal contact, direct mail affords the best medium for research and individual contact.

9. Direct advertising can be dispatched for accurate and in some cases exact timing, both as to departure of the pieces and as to their receipt. Material can be mailed according to set plan. Even departure schedules are available at the post office to help achieve good timing. Dealer material can be scheduled to reach dealer counters according to plan. Sales, holiday promotions, and stockholders' meetings as well as distributor, jobber, dealer, and consumer promotions can be timed for maximum results.

10. Direct advertising provides more thorough means for the reader to act or buy through action devices that cannot be used by other media. The business reply card and envelope make it easier for the recipient of direct advertising to take action. Complete order blanks and other action enclosures can also be used.[2]

Disadvantages of direct advertising and direct mail

These ten items give ample evidence of the versatility and selectivity of the medium. However, direct mail advertising is not suitable for many advertising purposes. Several potential disadvantages should be considered before a commitment to direct mail is made.

1. *Cost per thousand.* While most media sell time and space at a CPM of \$5–\$25, direct mail can easily run \$1,000/1,000. For example a first-class mailing will cost \$180/1,000 just for postage. Naturally the advertiser must consider factors other than cost:

Are prospects widely scattered?
Would personalized copy benefit the product?
Is long copy required to tell the story?
Is product sampling feasible through direct mail?
Is the market for the product relatively small?

Any one of these factors may mean that direct mail would be an appropriate medium.

2. *Updating mailing lists.* The per-exposure cost of direct mail mandates even greater efficiency than other media. Maintaining a current mailing list is expensive and time consuming due to the mo-

[2] Reprinted with permission from the Direct Mail/Marketing Association, Inc., from its publication *The Direct Mail/Marketing Manual.* Release No. 1201, May 1975.

bility of the U.S. population. An out-of-date list is not only inefficient in reaching prospects; it often destroys the personal contact which your message is attempting to convey. It is difficult to convince a prospect that you can solve his immediate problems when the envelope which carried your message has been forwarded from a previous address.

3. Improper timing. It is surprising how many users of direct mail do not take advantage of the control they have over the timing of their message. Commonsense rules, such as not mailing on the first of the month when bills are most likely to occupy the recipient, are often ignored to the detriment of the advertiser.

4. Improper format. Some advertisers fail to utilize the medium fully by sending an inappropriate message. There is no set of rules which will fit every direct mailing piece. However, some rules of thumb may be helpful:

First-class postage generally gets better response than bulk mail.

Stamped envelopes get better response than metered mail.

Messages on envelopes work for mass mailing, such as sweepstakes, but are generally inappropriate for selling most consumer goods.

Mimeographed or machine-copied messages are usually ineffective.

Consumers equate your product with the quality of the message which announces it.

Messages to businesses usually get opened (often by a secretary); those to home addresses are less likely to be seen.

Format

The most common direct mail format is the letter. For the majority of advertising messages the letter remains the most appropriate environment to carry a message. However, a format should be chosen only after full consideration has been given to the alternatives available to the direct mailer. Some of the major formats and their advantages are discussed in Figure 10–1.

The computer letter

One of the major innovations of the 1970s in direct marketing was the computer letter, where printers are connected directly to a computer. This direct connection is said to bring the printing unit "on line" with

Figure 10–1
Some major direct mail formats

Broadsides

Broadsides are large folders, used advantageously *when* the average folder is not adequate to convey the story and a booklet is not the form needed or wanted; *when* a smash effect is sought, particularly at the beginning of a campaign, or for a special announcement, or for a special emphasis of certain appeals; *when* a large surface is required for pictorial and bold copy expression; *when* the psychology of bigness is desired.

In designing broadsides, capture interest right at the beginning, and make sure that the interest is continued throughout, without confusion. Alhough large, a broadside should be designed for easy handling by the reader, with a physical makeup and layout that will lead the reader through in definite sequence quickly and impressively. Avoid smashing effects that confuse. They don't sell the reader. Broadsides are sometimes envelope-enclosed, but more often are self-mailers.

Booklets

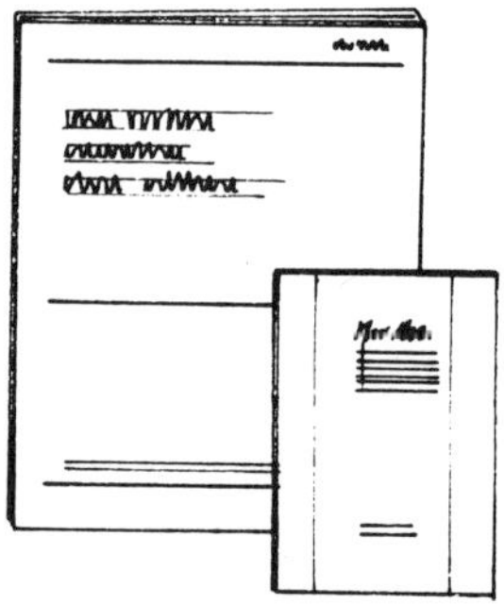

From the brief explanations covering the use of folders and broadsides, it is quite evident that booklets should be used when these two other formats are not adequate to convey the longer story, or lack sufficient prestige value or appropriateness for certain printed promotion jobs.

The use of booklets is almost as great and flexible as are the functions of their smaller brother, the folder. Usually designed for thorough reading and study rather than "flash" sales presentations, booklets must be attractive, interesting, and easy to read.

Booklets have a multiplicity of purposes. Booklets are to be used *when* the story is lengthy; *when* it cannot be accomplished by a folder or other lesser presentation; *when* dignity of approach is desired; *when* desired elaborateness does not reach the "brochure" classification.

Figure 10–1 (*continued*)

Catalogs, house organs, sales booklets, instruction books, directories, price lists, etc., are some of the functional purposes of booklets (and books).

Brochures

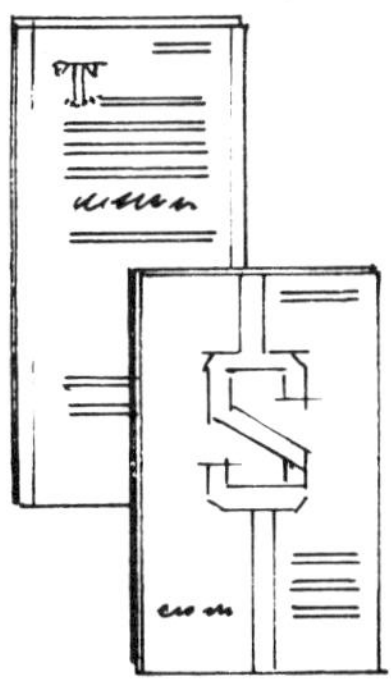

Brochures are for the glamorous phases of direct advertising and should be used *when* an elaborate presentation of company, product, or service is called for; *when* there is a need or desire to go beyond the ordinary booklet and broadside format for richness, power, and impressiveness in size, illustration, color, materials, bindings, etc.; *when* the presentation of a story must match the bigness of the selling job, must reflect the stature and dignity of the company responsible for its production.

Circulars

The circular, or flier, is the usually inexpensive form to adopt when you want to get across a strong message in a flash. Circulars are generally flat pieces up to a size that stops at the broadside category. The circular provides an opportunity for big, smash headlines, black and white, or full color. It can tell its story quickly, "loudly," and inexpensively.

Letters

Letters are perhaps the most widely used of all direct advertising forms. Letters perform almost every function in direct advertising. They are actually used for more different purposes than any other advertising form. They can be used alone or in conjunction with practically every other form of direct advertising. Letters lend the personality quotient to direct mail. They are the most adaptable, the most personal, and the most flexible of all forms of direct advertising. For the mailer with a small list, in many cases the cost of printed matter which involves typesetting and printing press work is prohibitive. Letters are

Figure 10–1 (*concluded*)

economical in small quantities as well as in large ones. There are various processes of producing letters: by multigraphing, mimeographing, printing, offset, or automatic typewriting. Letters may be personalized; or produced with an impersonalized salutation such as "Dear Friend," "Dear Reader," "Dear Customer"; or have a running head which functions as the salutation and headline. Illustrated letters afford the combination of the personal letter and the descriptive folder. All of these types of letters fit into a particular place in the direct advertising scheme.

Folders

Folders are the most commonly used of all printed advertising forms, because they are comparatively inexpensive and most flexible. Size, shape, and style are unlimited. In format, *folders* bridge the gap between *personal letters* and the *booklet.* That is the best rule to remember when considering the use of folders. Use them to precede and follow the more elaborate forms, books, and presentations. Use them for the short, direct, printed messages that hammer home selling points in a quick, concise manner. Use them for single shots or for a series. Use them when the sales message should have a compact form that the reader can grasp quickly. Inject them with novelty and color, but never at the expense or interruption of the natural flow of the advertiser's story to the prospect. Folders can be used alone, or in conjunction with letters and other forms, to inform, instruct, persuade, remind, or bring home the order.

Mailing cards

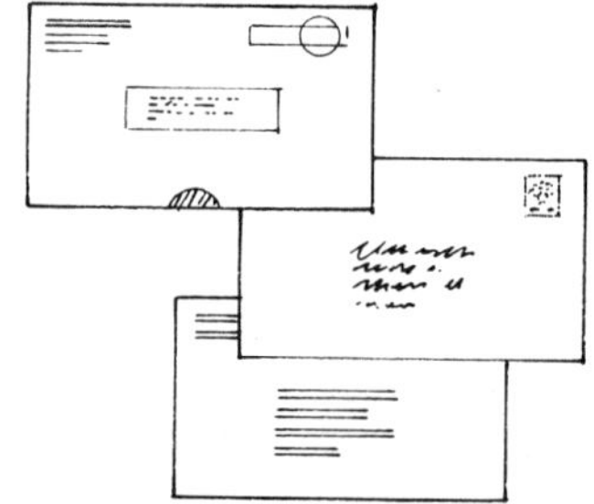

Mailing cards provide an inexpensive physical form of direct advertising, yet have great utility value. You can logically use mailing cards *when* brief announcements (not confidential) are desired; *when* budgets do not allow for more expensive format; *when* a teaser idea is used to introduce a campaign; *when* single messages or thoughts are

Figure 10–1 (*concluded*)

needed to influence prospects or obtain leads; *when* quick reminders are effective; *when* the element of time is most important; *when* notices, announcements, instructions, invitations, and other short direct messages lend themselves to this inexpensive, open, quick-reading format.

It is wise to check with your local post office for rulings on limitations of size, style, forms, folding, sealing, and postal regulations and requirements.

Unusual forms

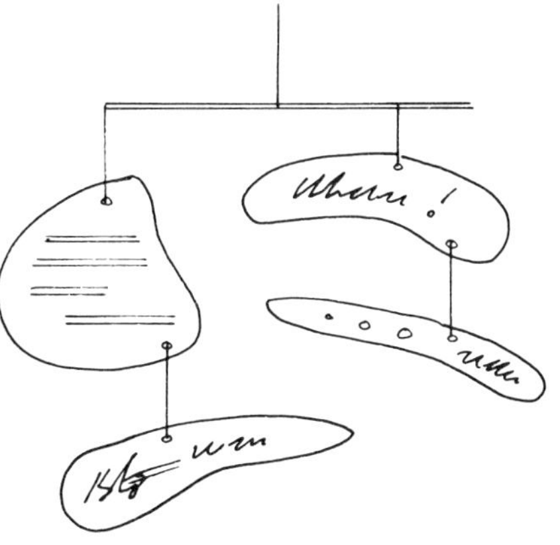

Cutouts, pop-ups, novelties, gadgets, and sample pieces can be used *when* realism is wanted; *when* it is important to make a fast, single impression on the mind of the prospect to gain immediate interest; *when* you want to show things that cannot be shown by other forms of advertising; *when* original, individual, and effective presentations of products and services, or their features, can be achieved through forms that are different, unusual, but extremely appropriate and forceful. In printed promotion, these effects are accomplished through die cutting, angle cutting, trick folding, unusual binding operations, gadgets, and so on.

Blotters

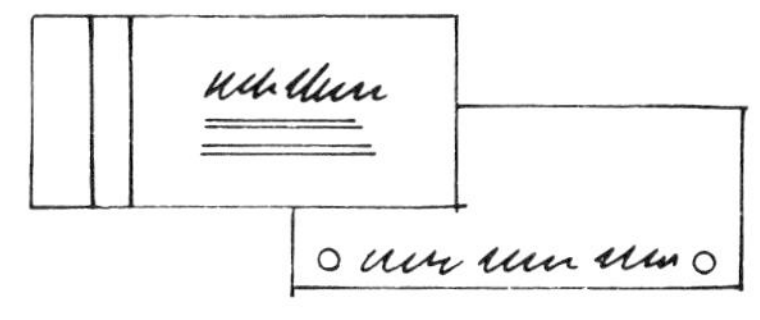

The blotter is an inexpensive type of direct mail used to carry short, strong sales messages, with or without illustrations; product or service information; directions for use; and so on. Blotters are also used at times as miniature house organs. Blotters and calendars are leading forms of "reminder" direct mail.

Source: Reprinted with permission from the Direct Mail/Marketing Association, Inc., from its publication *The Direct Mail/Marketing Manual*. Release No. 3001, November 1976.

the computer. Modern computers can print up to 775 lines per minute. The advantage of this system is that each letter can be personalized with references to the name of the addressee or other specific information about the locale.

Unfortunately the use of the computer letter demands prior planning and commonsense steps to avoid some glaring errors. A computer letter should read like a personal letter you would write. A letter with a mechanistic "tone" is no better than a printed message, and can be worse if it contains silly errors. One of the major errors made by computer letters is to pick up the addressee's name and insert it incorrectly in the body of the letter. Let's look at an actual example of how this can destroy a direct message.

Addressee: Mr. John Jones, Instructor Radio

Computer letter: Dear Mr. Radio:
In a few days the Radio family will be receiving a . . .

Needless to say, the "Radio" family received the accompanying product sample with something less than enthusiasm. Since a computer letter costs approximately three times as much as a printed letter, the damage caused by such mistakes is magnified.

The mailing list

The success of direct mail requires that three major elements work together: the format and message of the mailing piece, the product offered, and the mailing list. It would be a mistake to rank any of these elements as more important than the others. However, common sense indicates that a product offered to nonprospects will have no chance of success, however creative the message. The biggest mistake made by the inexperienced direct mail advertisers is to use an out-of-date, inappropriate, or duplicate-address list.

It is crucial to remember that lists have a high wear-out factor. For some lists this may mean that as many as 25 percent of addresses must be changed annually. It does no good to obtain a list, usually at considerable expense, unless provisions are made to keep it current.

Sources of mailing lists

In-house list. If it is feasible, an advertiser can save money by building his own list either from standard sources (city directories, chamber of commerce membership, etc.) or from customer account lists in the case of retailers. National manufacturers can rarely obtain a list of the consumers who buy their products. Techniques such as warranty cards enclosed in products are helpful for research, but rarely allow a complete list to be compiled.

Many retailers have done away with in-store credit in favor of bank credit cards. While shifting the credit function normally saves the retailers money, it causes them to lose contact with their customers. In cases where no in-house list is available, the advertiser should turn to a direct mail professional.

The list broker. The most common source of mailing lists is the list broker. List brokers function in the same way as other brokers in bringing buyers and sellers together. Most major list brokers are members of the Mailing List Brokers Professional Association. The list broker has knowledge of the thousands of lists available and can direct the advertiser to those most appropriate to his product or promotion.

A list broker does not sell lists, but rather rents them for a specified number of mailings. The actual list is not given to the advertiser. The mailing piece and the mailing list are delivered to a firm which specializes in folding, addressing, and mailing large commercial promotions. These mailing firms are called *letter shops.* Some printing firms have their own letter shops. In any case the printer and the letter shop must work closely together. The list broker is normally paid a 20 percent commission by the *list owner.* The costs of lists vary greatly, but $40–75 CPM would be an average range. The only names on a brokered list known to the advertiser are the names of those who respond.

The list broker should be regarded as more than someone who deals only with the mechanics of a mailing. A list broker can offer professional advice about the total direct mail program. The direct mail advertiser should use the expertise of the list broker in much the same ways as advertising agencies use the expertise of the media reps.

The list compiler. The list compiler is another source of lists. Unlike the list broker, who rents lists, the compiler sells them. Normally an advertiser that buys a list is a regular direct mailer. A firm may want to expand a present customer list, or a purchased list may be the first step in building an in-house list for a new firm. In either case the advertiser should make sure that the list under consideration is current and is made up of the right market segment. Lists are usually sold on the basis of so much/1,000. In the case of smaller lists the entire list must usually be purchased. Figure 10–2 shows an example of a list compiler catalog.

Standard Rate and Data. The most available source of list brokers and compilers is the *Standard Rate and Data Service Direct Mail List Rates and Data.* Under the volume's separate listings for list

Figure 10–2
List compiler catalog

—A—

Quantity	List	Price
677	AA Headquarters	$35/L
1,900	Abattoirs & Slaughterhouses	*35/M
4,700	Abstract & Title Cos.	**27/M
5,600	Executives	30/M
2,900	Leading Firms	30/M
127,000	ACCOUNTANTS - All	25/M
30,000	Corporate	25/M
115,000	CPA's	25/M
15,000	Public	30/M
14,000	ACCOUNTING FIRMS	25/M
56,000	Firms & Ind. Practitioners	25/M
34,000	Partners	25/M
20,300	Tax Preparation Firms	25/M
9,500	Bookkeeping Services	**27/M
85,000	CPA's - Private Practice	25/M
2,000	Acoustical Contractors	*32/M
3,800	Actuaries	27/M
9,700	Adding & Calculating Mach. Dlrs.	**25/M
5,300	Addressing and Lettershops	**25/M
5,300	Adjusters, Insurance	*32/M
	Administrators-see specific category	
15,000	ADVERTISING AGENCIES - All	25/M
3,640	Major Agencies	25/M
22,000	Major Agencies - Executives	25/M
7,000	Account Executives	25/M
3,150	Art Directors	25/M
3,500	Creative Directors	25/M
1,500	Agencies w/$1 million + billing	35/M
250	Agencies w/$10 million + billing	35/L
3,200	Direct Mail Assn. Members	30/M
5,300	Direct Mail Services	**25/M
5,300	Lettershops	**25/M
15,000	Managers-Largest Advertisers	28/M
1,900	Outdoor	*32/M
5,000	Specialty Jobbers	**28/M
1,800,000	ADVERTISERS - Classified Pages	***30/M
15,000	Leading - National	25/M
43,000	Leading - National - Execs.	25/M
	Affluent-see Wealthy, Who's Prominent	
	Agencies & Agents-see specific category	
4,900	Agribusiness - Top Companies	*30/M
15,000	Executives	**30/M

Quantity	List	Price
6,400	Agricultural - Agents (County)	$28/M
500	Associations	35/L
7,400	Farm Co-ops	25/M
22,500	Equipment - see Farms	**27/M
240	Publications	25/L
110	Schools	25/L
25,500	Air Conditioning Contractors	**25/M
18,100	Air Cond. & Refrig. Dlrs. & Svc.	**28/M
	AIRCRAFT	
230	Airlines	25/L
7,800	Executives	27/M
6,700	Airports - All	27/M
2,900	Larger	30/M
1,200	Airport Limousine	*40/M
6,000	Aviation & Aerospace Execs	30/M
3,800	Charter & Rental	*32/M
24,800	Control Tower Operators	27/M
27,400	Flight Instructors	27/M
3,500	Flying Clubs	40/M
177,000	Owners	25/M
745,000	Pilots - All	25/M
50,100	Airline	27/M
184,000	Commercial	25/M
303,000	Private	25/M
2,900	Parts & Supplies Mfrs.	35/M
2,600	Repair Stations & Schools	**32/M
5,400	Alaska Businesses	30/M
25,000	Residents	Inquire
4,800	Alcoholism & Drug Addiction Ctrs.	*35/M
1,000,000	Alumni - College	***25/M
2,000	Ambassadors, Consuls & Vice Consuls-Foreign in U.S.	*35/M
6,100	Ambulance Companies	**28/M
6,300	American Legion Posts	28/M
1,700	Amusement Arcades & Parks	30/M
1,700	Animal Hospitals	*32/M
5,600	Kennels	**27/M
5,000	Answering Services - Telephone	**28/M
24,400	Antique Dealers	25/M
13,400	Repairing	**27/M
23,600	Apparel Mfrs - All	**28/M
3,200	Top Companies	*30/M
17,400	Top Companies - Executives	**30/M
8,000	Children's/Infants'	**27/M
4,000	Men's	**28/M
10,500	Women's/Girls'	**28/M

Quantity	List	Price
28,500	Apparel Retailers - Men's/Boys'	$**25/M
55,000	Women's/Girls'	**25/M
5,200	Women's Specialty Shops	**30/M
62,600	Appliance Dealers	**25/M
2,200	Mfrs - Electric	*30/M
54,400	Radio & TV Dealers	**25/M
9,000	Appraisers - Real Estate	**28/M
250	Aquariums & Zoos	35/L
23,400	Architects - Assoc. Members	25/M
16,000	Contractors - Landscape	**28/M
9,000	Firms	25/M
22,000	Firms & Private Practice	25/M
2,515	Armored Car/Guard/Protect. Svcs.	**32/M
1,700	Army & Navy Stores	30/M
8,700	ART - Galleries & Picture Dlrs.	28/M
510	Museums	35/L
1,350	Schools	30/M
5,700	Supplies Dealers	25/M
8,000	Who's Prominent	27/M
7,700	Artists - Commercial	27/M
4,200	Arts & Crafts Supplies	*32/M
11,000	ASSOCIATIONS - National	35/M
	(inquire for specific categories)	
2,000	1,000 to 10,000 members	40/M
1,200	10,000 or more members	50/M
2,600	Business & Trade	30/M
745	Technical & Scientific	35/L
148,000	Athletic Coaches - by sport	30/M
240,000	ATTORNEYS - Private Practice	**25/M
130,000	Bar Assn. Members	**30/M
1,500	County & State	35/M
28,000	Firms - All	**27/M
9,500	Anti Trust	30/M
30,000	Corporation	27/M
6,500	Criminal	28/M
1,200	District & Prosecuting	35/M
4,300	Family Law	28/M
30,000	In Industry	27/M
10,500	Insurance	28/M
5,000	Labor	28/M
1,800	Maritime	30/M
8,200	Patent	30/M
2,200	Public Utility	30/M
12,000	Real Estate	30/M
17,660	Tax	27/M

Minimums: *2,000 **3,000 ***5,000 /L = total list /M per thousand Call: 212-969-8800 3

Source: *Catalog of Mailing Lists*, Customized Mailing Lists, Inc., 158–23 Grand Central Parkway, Jamaica Estates, New York 11432, 212-969-8800

brokers and compilers, hundreds of lists and their prices are enumerated.

Direct Mail/Marketing Association

One of the most aggressive media trade associations is the Direct Mail/Marketing Association (DMMA). The association has recently inaugurated a three-year $1,500,000 campaign of consumer education and lobbying to tell the direct marketing story. The two major problems which this campaign is attempting to overcome are (1) the idea that unsolicited direct mail is an invasion of privacy and (2) the ill will that has been engendered by the minority of fraudulent mail-order schemes.

Regulation of direct mail

Legislators at both the state and national level continue to advocate various forms of direct mail regulation, including the restriction of certain types of mailing lists. This trend toward more legislation assumes that the use of a person's name without permission is an invasion of privacy and that unwanted mail slows down the postal distribution system.[3] The DMMA has sought to counteract this adverse trend by research and public relations. According to one study, only 5 percent of respondents did not like any direct mail; 33 percent enjoyed all direct mail; and 85 percent had no general dislike for direct mail. The same study showed that 83 percent of respondents received less than ten pieces of direct mail per week.[4]

The major DMMA public relations program has been the Mail Preference Service, which was initiated in 1971. The service provides a "name removal form" which is made available to major direct marketers, who then remove the person's name from their lists. The service also provides an "add-on" form for requests to be placed on specific types of lists. Advertising promoting the Mail Preference Service has appeared in most major magazines during the last several years (see Figure 10–3).

The outlook for direct mail

The future of direct mail marketing appears to be positive, though there are a few warning signals on the horizon. The growing trend

[3] Louis A. Fanelli, "DMMA Rallies Support against Mailing Controls," *Advertising Age*, October 29, 1979, p. 12.

[4] *Study of Consumer Attitudes toward Direct Mail—A Summary*, Direct Mail Advertising Association, 1962, pp. 3 and 8.

Figure 10–3
DMMA Mail Preference Service advertisement

Want to get LESS advertising in the mail? MORE? The DMMA gives you a choice!

Who's the DMMA? We're the 1,800 member companies comprising the Direct Mail/Marketing Association. Many of the manufacturers, retailers, publishers and service companies you've come to trust most over the years are among our members.

☐ And we think you deserve a choice, as to how much—and what kind—of advertising you receive in the mail. If you'd like to get less, mail in the coupon on the left. We can't stop all your mail, but you'll see a reduction in the amount of mail you receive soon.

☐ If you'd like to receive more mail in your areas of interest—catalogs, free trial offers, merchandise and services not available anywhere else—mail the coupon on the right. Soon, you'll start to see more information and opportunities in the areas most important to you. Let's hear from you today!

LESS mail

I want to receive less advertising mail.

Mail to: DMMA Mail Preference Service
6 East 43rd Street
N.Y., NY 10017

Name (print)

Address

City State Zip

Please include me in the Name Removal File. I understand that you will make this file available to direct mail advertisers for the sole purpose of removing from their mailing lists the names and addresses contained therein.

Others at my address who also want less mail—or variations of my own name by which I receive mail—include:

MAIL PREFERENCE SERVICE OF DIRECT MAIL MARKETING ASSOC.
dm ma

MORE mail

I want to receive more advertising mail.

Mail to: DMMA Mail Preference Service
6 East 43rd Street
N.Y., NY 10017

Name (print)

Address

City State Zip

I would like to receive more information in the mail, especially on the subjects below (circle letter):

A All subjects
B Autos, Parts & Accessories
C Books & Magazines
D Charities
E Civic Organizations
F Clothing
G Foods & Cooking
H Gifts
I Grocery Bargains
J Health Foods & Vitamins
K HiFi & Electronics
L Home Furnishings
M Insurance
N Plants, Flowers & Garden Supplies
O Photography
P Real Estate
Q Records & Tapes
R Sewing, Needlework, Arts & Crafts
S Sports & Camping
T Stamps & Coins
U Stocks & Bonds
V Tools & Equipment
W Travel
X Office Furniture & Supplies

Courtesy Direct Mail/Marketing Association, Inc.

toward local marketing strategy can only help direct markets. The continually rising costs of traditional media make direct mail a more practical alternative than it has been. The use of the computer will help in the identification, production, and distribution of direct mail pieces.

The computer is being utilized in all phases of advertising and marketing to find profitable consumer groups and segment them from the general population. As the delineation of these groups becomes more specific, direct mailers can increasingly make a case for CPM/*prospect* efficiencies in comparison to other media. It is only a matter of time before the problems of the computer letter, discussed earlier, are solved. Already computers are being placed on line with formats other than the letter. Simple folders can be printed by computer printing systems, and soon more elaborate formats will utilize these systems.

Direct mail and direct marketing in general should benefit from concerns about conservation. The future should find the percentage of in-home shoppers on the rise. Conservation combined with the female work force expands the advantages of direct mail to a larger portion of the population.

On the negative side, direct mail must continue to upgrade its image and work to keep down costs. The efforts of the DMMA, outlined earlier, seem to be a step in the right direction. Whether these efforts will be enough to forestall anti–direct marketing attitudes by the public and legislatures remains to be seen. Despite the use of sophisticated computer techniques direct mail is an expensive means of reaching large groups of consumers. However, under certain circumstances direct mail can be a useful supplement, or even a substitute, for traditional media.

SALES PROMOTION

Strictly speaking, sales promotion is not advertising. The major difference between sales promotion and advertising is that sales promotion is direct promotion between the advertiser and the customer, whereas advertising operates through an impersonal, intervening medium of communication. Sales promotion consists of a wide range of techniques designed to help sell a product and to complement traditional media advertising. Sales promotion ideas are as endless as the companies which employ them. The major trade show, the "Can you draw me?" matchbook, and the handsomely designed point-of-purchase display are all forms of sales promotion.

Sales promotion, especially premiums and specialty promotions, is clearly related to advertising and is often included in a firm's advertising budget. Furthermore, the sales promotion program, like the advertising program, should be planned and coordinated with the overall marketing and advertising goals of the firm.

This section will discuss the three major forms of sales promotion closest to advertising: specialty advertising, premiums, and point-of-purchase.

SPECIALTY ADVERTISING

At the 1980 meeting of the Specialty Advertising Association International (SAAI) more than 15,000 different specialty items were on display. Advertising specialties range from beer mugs to fruitcakes and are limited only by the creativity and budget of the giver. The industry's sales volume was estimated at more than $3 billion in 1980, approximately the same as that of radio and magazines. A survey conducted by the A. C. Nielsen Company indicated a positive acceptance of specialty items by both the public and businesses.[5] Yet, for all its success, the specialty advertising business is not fully understood by either the public or advertisers.

[5] Henry R. Bernstein, "Specialty Ad Industry Forecasts Large Growth," *Advertising Age*, February 19, 1979, p. 72.

What is specialty advertising?

Specialty advertising has several characteristics which distinguish it from other forms of advertising and sales promotion. It consists of a wide array of items, usually imprinted with the name of the advertiser. These items are free gifts given with no obligation to selective target markets. In this regard the specialty item is different from the advertising premium, which usually is received only after a product has been purchased.

Specialty advertising is a complement to traditional promotion and is rarely the central focus of an advertising campaign. Specialties have the advantage of long life and should continually remind the customer of the advertiser's product. Since everyone enjoys a gift, specialties are an excellent method of building consumer goodwill.

The major disadvantage of the specialty item is its cost. Specialty items are not for mass distribution. Even the smallest gift is expensive on a CPM basis and should be used carefully to achieve a specific goal. However, the long life of many specialty items reduces their cost significantly since it eliminates the need for frequent repetition that exists in mass media advertising. It is important to exercise control over the distribution of specialty items to guarantee that legitimate prospects are receiving them.

Specialty advertising is generally divided into four major categories:

1. Novelties or advertising specialties, which account for about half of the industry's sales.
2. Advertising calendars, with 15 percent of sales.
3. Writing instruments, with 20 percent of sales.
4. Executive gifts, with 15 percent of sales.[6]

Novelties. The novelty category is by far the most extensive in number of items. Almost any item can be used as an advertising specialty, but advertising specialties generally have these two characteristics: (1) they are relatively inexpensive; and (2) they are imprinted with the name of the advertiser. (See Figure 10–4).

Calendars. Calendars meet the qualifications of the novelty category. However, they are treated as a separate category since they represent the largest source of revenue for the specialty industry. It is hard to estimate the number of calendars distributed for advertising purposes, but it is in the millions each year. Calendars have the advantage of daily communication with the recipient and represent

[6] Dan S. Bagley, *Specialty Advertising: A New Look* (Specialty Advertising Association International), p. 1.

Figure 10–4
A specialty advertising case study

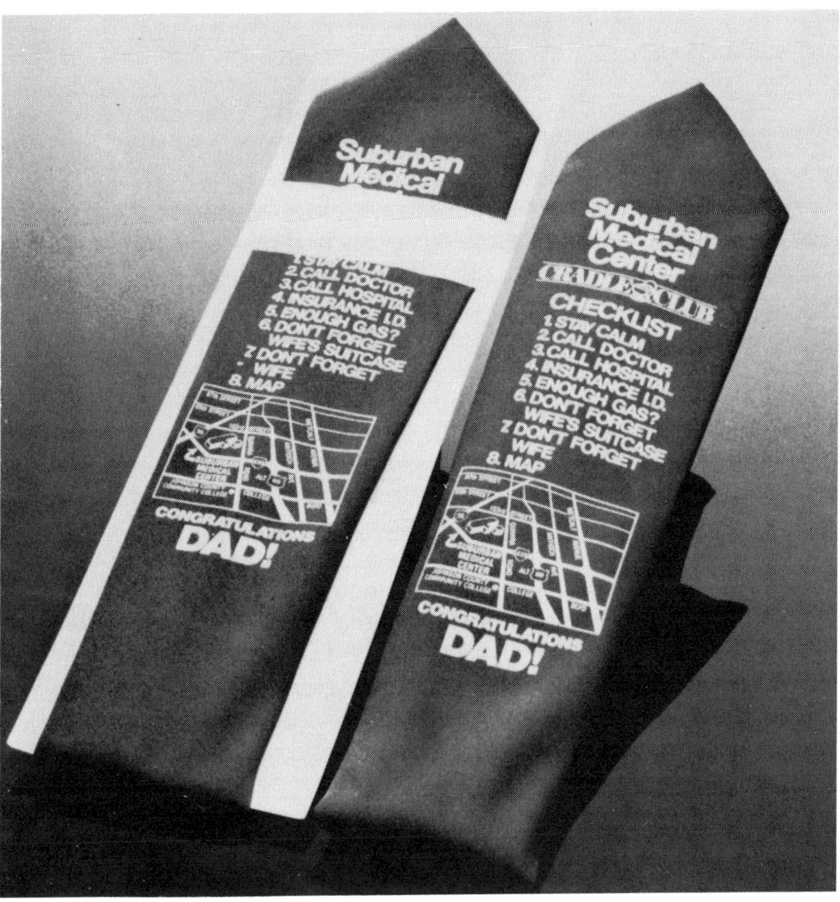

Advertiser: Suburban Medical Center

Type of specialty: Necktie

Marketing objectives:

1. To acquaint prospective fathers with the hospital's maternity clinic and facilities.
2. To provide information for the hospital's Cradle Club and give a checklist of dos and don'ts before the hurried delivery run to the maternity center.
3. To build goodwill among pediatricians who would be distributing the ties and recommending the hospital.

The maternity ward was booked solid, a fact attributed somewhat to the promotion and somewhat to the hard winter of 1977–78.

Courtesy: Specialty Advertising Association International

Figure 10–5
A specialty advertising case study

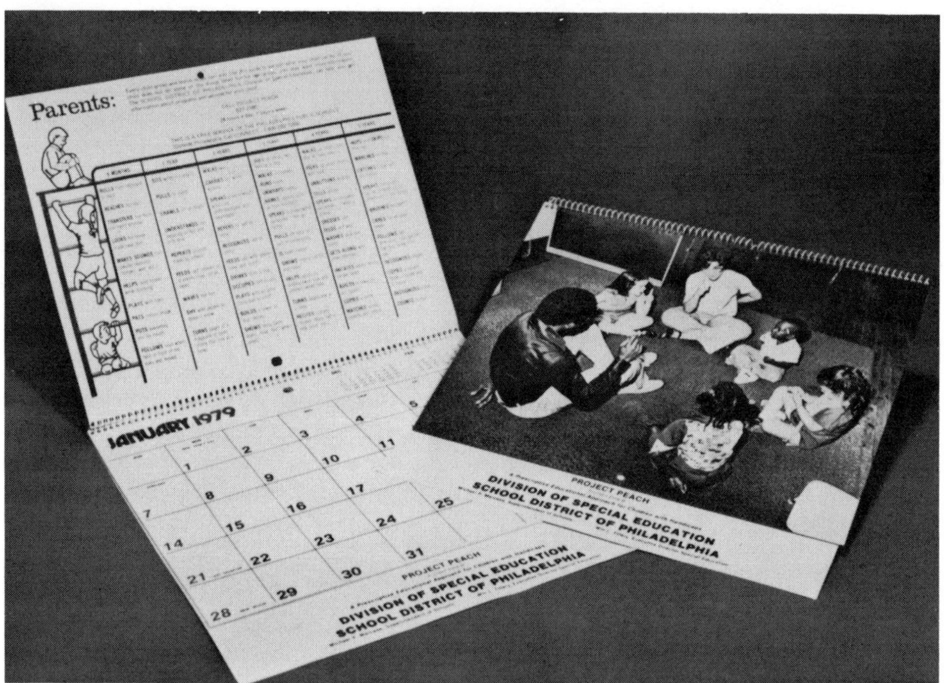

Advertiser: School District of Philadelphia

Type of specialty: Calendar

Marketing objectives:

1. To promote PROJECT PEACH (Prescriptive Educational Approach for Children with Handicaps) with special 12-sheet calendars issued to parents at PEACH workshops or to those believed to have high-risk children.
2. To tie in with television public service announcements and brochures to alert parents to expected task performance of children from six months to five years old.

The calendars, distributed at Christmas, produced 62 referrals in December and 111 in January, the latter a 95 percent increase over the same month the previous year.

Courtesy: Specialty Advertising Association International

one of the most practical gifts in the specialty category. Calendars are available in three basic formats: wall, desk, and pocket. The wall calendar is usually sent to the home, while desk and pocket calendars are more appropriate for business distribution.

Calendars have become so popular that a clutter problem has developed. Each year more and more calendars are being used as sales promotion. Normally only a few of these calendars are used, with the others discarded at a major expense to the advertiser. Unless an advertiser invests in a quality calendar which can compete with others received by the customer, another form of sales promotion should be considered. (See Figure 10–5.)

Executive gifts. Executive gifts differ from other forms of specialty items in that they are more expensive and do not carry the name of the advertiser. Gifts in this category are usually given by manufacturers or wholesalers to their retail customers rather than to the general public. Christmas is the customary time to give these gifts. Executive gifts can be as ordinary as a pen and pencil set or as unusual as a smoked ham. Often a company will give the same type of gift year after year, such as items of glassware, and thus become identified with a specific kind of gift.

Structure of the specialty advertising industry

The specialty industry is divided into three types of organizations: suppliers, jobbers and direct-selling houses.

Suppliers. The supplier is the source of the many specialty items available. Some suppliers specialize in a particular type of specialty, but most offer a wide array of merchandise. Suppliers may manufacture items, but more often they simply buy merchandise which they then imprint. These items are sold through jobbers for distribution to the advertising client.

Jobbers. Jobbers (or distributors) are independent salespeople who contact business for the sale of specialty items. The typical jobber has contacts with a wide range of suppliers, and most jobbers offer virtually any type of merchandise an advertiser might want to use as a specialty. A good jobber is not only a salesperson, but one who can work with a client to develop the most appropriate idea for a company's promotional program.

Direct-selling houses. The direct-selling house is a firm which combines the function of the supplier and the jobber. It manufactures specialty items and sells them through its own sales force. Occasionally a direct-selling house will sell to independent jobbers to cover areas or customers missed by its own sales force. For the client there is really no difference between dealing with a direct-selling house and dealing with a jobber. The distinction is of importance, however, within the industry.

Selection of the specialty item

The major failure of specialty advertising is choosing an item without proper planning. The advertiser should develop the specialty advertising program in the same way as he develops other aspects of the advertising program. When he contemplates a specialty sales promotion, he should ask, "Will it contribute to the overall marketing plan?" Only when the answer to this question is yes should the advertiser go forward.

Actual selection of the specialty item should meet several criteria:

It should be related to the product or to the company's promotional program.

It should have utility to the receiver, preferably in a way related to a job activity (for instance copy-fitting guides for printers, miles per gallon charts for traveling salespersons).

It should be of good quality; shoddy merchandise not only disappoints the receiver, but may reflect poorly on the product of the advertiser.

It should be practical to distribute and easy to imprint.

PREMIUM ADVERTISING

The advertising premium differs from the specialty item in that it is not a free gift. It is given as a reward for some action by the consumer. Usually the requirement for receiving a premium is to purchase the product. However, premiums are also given as traffic builders, such as a T-shirt for test-driving a car or a small appliance for viewing some property. In either case the premium should remind the customer of the product and should appeal to the same audience as the product.

Like all advertising programs, premium advertising programs should be conducted with the marketing objectives in mind. Among these objectives are:

Overcoming price competition by lower priced brands.

Encouraging purchases, or traffic, during slack seasons.

Introducing a new product.

Giving an edge to parity products.

Advertising premiums are designed to increase sales either by promoting products to consumers or by providing incentives at the wholesale or retail level. Premiums are normally used to deal with a specific problem during a relatively short period. In other cases premiums are a long-term complement to the product. In rare cases, such as baseball trading cards, the premium becomes as important as the product and is promoted as a separate product. Premiums normally supplement general media advertising by providing an added buying incentive. Consequently, one of the primary considerations in selecting a premium is that it should lend itself to advertising and merchandising.

Types of advertising premiums

As with advertising specialties, there is a wide selection of premiums from which an advertiser can choose. In this chapter we will discuss some of the major categories. We should note that a premium may fall into several of these categories since they are not mutually exclusive.

Factory pack premiums. The factory pack is the oldest and still the most popular type of premium. Since it is included with the product, it has the advantage of intimate association with the product and immediate reward for the buyer. In some cases factory packs are in the package—towels and dishes in boxes of detergent. In other cases they are attached to the package such as toothbrushes packaged with toothpaste. Sometimes the premium is the package. Glass jelly jars or decorated liquor bottles are examples.

Self-liquidating premiums. In recent years advertisers have turned to premiums which pay for themselves or can actually provide a profit. Self-liquidators are normally offered for proof-of-purchase and cash. The cost to the consumer covers the expense of handling and mailing as well as the cost of the premium itself. Self-liquidating premiums can be as inexpensive as a T-shirt or a toy, but may include expensive watches, bicycles, or clothing items. In recent years both Marlboro and Budweiser have set up subsidiaries to sell advertising premiums.

Traffic-building premiums. It is unrealistic to expect a premium to play a major role in the purchase of high-priced goods. However, premiums may be helpful in getting customers to inspect such products. A wide variety of premiums can be used for this purpose, including self-liquidators such as the Texaco toy fire engines and the Firestone Christmas records.

Continuity premiums. Continuity premiums build in value as the customer purchases more of the product. Among the more familiar continuity premiums are grocery store trading stamps and merchandise coupons such as those offered by Raleigh cigarettes. Continuity premiums may also be used as factory packs, for example in cases where a set of towels or dishes may be obtained after frequent purchases of a product.

Sweepstakes and contests. Normally a sweepstakes promotion is one in which prizes are awarded as a result of chance. In a contest prizes are awarded on the basis of skill, although the terms *contest* and *sweepstakes* are often used interchangeably. Publisher's Clearing House and *Reader's Digest* conduct two of the best-known sweepstakes, while the Ford Motor Company has for several years sponsored its "Punt, Pass, and Kick" contest as a traffic builder.

The advertiser should consider some of the problems associated with sweepstakes and contests before sponsoring either. Care must be taken to assure that the contest or sweepstakes is conducted fairly and that no state or federal regulations are violated. In addition an advertiser must remember that contests and sweepstakes result in many more dissatisfied "losers" than winners.

Dealer premiums. While most premiums are designed for consumers, many are used to encourage trade support by wholesalers and retailers. Usually a variety of gifts or cash prizes are offered based on sales performance. Some companies issue catalogs and offer dealer incentives as continuity premiums. In some cases dealer premiums include foreign travel or automobiles.

POINT-OF-PURCHASE

Point-of-purchase advertising is the last opportunity for a company to promote its product before a customer makes a purchase. Ideally, point-of-purchase ads should supplement other media advertising and also promote impulse purchasing. Often point-of-purchase ads will duplicate the creative message from a firm's advertising and promote tie-ins with celebrity endorsers. Not all store signs and displays are point-of-purchase advertising. Generally only manufacturer-supplied displays are included in this category. (See Figure 10–6.)

Point-of-purchase ads are usually handled directly by a company's sales force. The success of a point-of-purchase display is dependent on the aggressiveness of a company's sales force in obtaining space from retailers and, of course, on the promotional value of the display. Since the sale of consumer goods grows more dependent on self-service by the buyer, point-of-purchase ads will grow in importance.

Because of the number of displays available to retailers, manufacturers must provide point-of-purchase ads whose value is commensurate with the space required. Many proprietary drug manufacturers ship their products within point-of-purchase displays which give a more integrated appearance to the products and conserve space for

Figure 10–6
A point-of-purchase marketing case study

Advertiser: Time-Life "How to Do It" books

Type of display: Manual rotation book display

Marketing objectives:

1. To carry out the overall promotional theme "Time-Life Books Show America 'How to Do It' " and to gain off-shelf space on a permanent basis for additional sales by centralizing the five book categories in the Time-Life Books "How To" series in one display.
2. To upgrade the display of the Time-Life "How To" series by stressing the image of quality related to the company and the product line itself.

In test markets retailers reported that centralization of titles and easy visual and manual access to books, along with the attractiveness of the display, promoted increased sales and in some cases multiple purchases of the books in the series.

Courtesy Point-of-Purchase Advertising Institute, Inc.

the retailer. Combining product and display also enhances the chances of the display being used by the retailer.

In most cases a point-of-purchase display is free to the retailer. However, where a display involves considerable expense, the manufacturer and the retailer sometimes share the cost. In either case the retailer must be convinced of the promotional benefits of any point-of-purchase display for it to be used.

In the last few years point-of-purchase techniques have been combined with certain aspects of out-of-home promotion to use the strengths of both media. In the spring of 1980 On-Line Media introduced video monitors to deliver an advertising message to customers in supermarket checkout lines. The network, called the OMI System,

Figure 10–7
Percent of coupons distributed by media

	1977	*1978*	*1979*
Daily newspaper	56.9%	55.6%	52.3%
Sunday newspaper	8.5	7.7	9.5
Freestanding insert	11.8	13.4	14.9
Total newspaper	77.3	76.7	76.7
Magazine	12.5	11.4	12.2
Direct mail	3.0	3.0	3.2
In/on pack	8.2	8.9	7.9
Coupons distributed (billions)	62.2	72.7	81.2

Source: *Marketing & Media Decisions,* April 1980, p. 30.

displays a six-minute look of three-, five-, and ten-second commercials. CPM levels are in the $1.00–1.50 range.[7] Similar systems have also been introduced in other locations such as shopping malls and hotel lobbies.

COUPONING

Couponing has been a major area of sales promotion for decades. It is difficult to find a company in the food, soft drink, or soap/detergent category which has not recently utilized couponing on a regular basis. An estimated 100 billion coupons were distributed in 1980. (See Figure 10–7.)

Couponing has several purposes: (1) to offer price incentives to customers without tampering with the actual product purchase price, (2) to gain new customers or retain present customers, and (3) to introduce a new brand or a product innovation. Couponing, however, is not inexpensive. The average handling charge paid to retailers is seven cents, up from three cents as recently as 1974.

In addition to legitimate costs a major problem for coupon users is the misredemption of coupons. While it is difficult to estimate the number of illegally redeemed coupons, the number must be in the millions annually. Some unethical retailers send in hundreds of coupons which were not used to purchase the product. This practice costs manufacturers hundreds of thousands of dollars annually. Before undertaking a coupon promotion, the prudent marketer should

[7] "National In-Store Video Advertising Network to Debut," Ad-Media, January 1980, p. 8.

consult one of the several coupon houses that specialize in coupon promotion and security.

The marketing strategy of the advertiser will largely determine the type of coupon distribution used. The most common method is newspaper advertising which includes a coupon (as opposed to freestanding inserts containing coupons). Newspaper coupons reach both present and potential users of a product. Often an advertiser wants to encourage repeat purchases or keep customers in the face of new or more aggressive competition. In such situations the in-pack coupon might well provide the ideal solution.

Sources of sales promotion information

Direct Mail Marketing Association
6 East 44 Street
New York, New York 10017

National Premium Sales Executives
1600 Route 22
Union, New Jersey 07083

Point-of-Purchase Advertising Institute
60 East 42 Street
New York, New York 10017

Promotion Marketing Association of America
420 Lexington Avenue
New York, New York 10017

Specialty Advertising Association International
1404 Walnut Hill Lane
Irving, Texas 75062

QUESTIONS

1. What are the prospects for growth in direct marketing?
2. What are the major advantages and disadvantages of direct mail?
3. What is the role of the list broker? How does this differ from the role of a list compiler?
4. Compare and contrast advertising and sales promotion.

5. What is the major difference between specialty and premium sales promotion?

6. Give an example of the following premiums:
   a. Factory pack.
   b. Self-liquidating.
   c. Traffic building.
   d. Continuity.
   e. Sweepstakes.
   f. Contests.

7. What is the major medium for couponing?

11

MEDIA SELECTION AND ALLOCATION METHODS

SINCE THE EARLY 1960s professional advertising literature has reflected a growing use of mathematical models for media selection. Prominent among the methods has been linear programming.[1]

GRAPHIC SOLUTIONS TO LINEAR PROGRAMMING

In the appendix to Chapter 2, the notion of linear programming was introduced. Simple examples for maximization and minimization problems were presented. These were solved by first graphing the objective function and constraints, then checking the coordinates of each cornerpoint of the feasibility space for the optimum solution.

You can readily imagine that the problem of selecting an assortment of media classes and vehicles for an actual advertising campaign is much more complicated than the problem (in Chapter 2) of selecting the correct number of ads for two magazines. And as the problem becomes more complex, the power and usefulness of graphic solutions are diminished.

SIMPLEX METHOD OF LINEAR PROGRAMMING

Fortunately a method of linear programming called the *simplex method* has been developed which efficiently solves linear programming problems, even when a very large number of variables and constraints are to be considered. The simplex calculations are often performed on computers when the problem is large.

---

[1] See, for example, P. Kotler, "On Methods: Toward an Explicit Model for Media Selection," *Journal of Advertising Research,* no. 4 (1964), pp. 31–41; B. Brown, "A Practical Procedure for Media Selection," *Journal of Marketing Research,* no. 4 (1967), pp. 262–69; B. Brown and M. Warshaw, "Media Selection by Linear Programming," *Journal of Marketing Research,* no. 2 (1965), pp. 83–88; and A. Charnes et al., "A Goal Programming Model for Media Planning," *Management Science,* vol. 14 (1968), pp. B–423–30.

It is important for persons who use computer routines in solving problems to understand the method being used. An application of the simplex method is presented as an appendix to this chapter. You should recognize that the simplex method does not alter the general linear programming situation. That is, optimal solutions are always found at a cornerpoint of a bounded feasibility space. You should also recognize that the simplex method is not necessarily "simple," but that thousands of students and professionals use the method every day. You are encouraged to read the chapter appendix before continuing your study of the chapter text.

Simplex solutions consider all the possible, feasible solutions, variable by variable, and are therefore systematic. They employ a system of calculation based on the coefficients in the objective function and the constraints. These coefficients are arranged in a table or "tableau" to reduce the complexity of the calculations. And while potential problems are associated with the method (and these will be discussed later in this chapter), simplex offers a clear way to identify the optimum solution.

The problem solved in the chapter appendix indicates that the simplex method produces results identical to those obtained earlier by graphing. The simplex solution to the rework cost minimization problem from Chapter 2 is also included at the end of this chapter as an exercise for students who wish to improve their skill with simplex.

In the real world of advertising, media selection problems are almost never as simple as the example in the appendix. In fact, real media selection problems are almost always so complex as to defy graphic solutions. There are simply too many cornerpoints.

Let's look at a more realistically complicated problem. Let's say that the media objective for a particular campaign is to earn a target of 3,800 Gross Rating Points during a particular month among women between the ages of 18 and 49 in a particular market. The media plan calls for the exclusive use of spot television. The budget in this market for one month is $300,000. Your problem is to achieve the target level of GRPs in this month by the careful selection of television stations and dayparts for your 30-second spots, but you are not authorized to exceed the monthly budget. Further, several restrictions have been imposed on the buy. First, you must achieve a minimum of 1,000 GRPs from ads to run during primetime, and a minimum of 500 GRPs from ads to be aired during late evening broadcasts. Finally, you must make the purchase so as to earn no more than 100 GRPs during the daytime broadcasts of any single station. These restrictions were imposed so that there would be adequate coverage of those persons in the target market who are away

Figure 11–1
Daypart cost per 30-second commercial and rating among women 18–49.

Television costs/ratings/availabilities

Station	*Affiliation*	*Daytime*	*Early evening*	*Primetime*	*Late evening*
A........	ABC	$340/7	$1,260/19	Not available	$ 400/4
B	CBS	$212/5	$1,400/21	Not available	$ 580/6
C	NBC	$300/6	$1,320/20	$2,140/15	$1,000/9
D	Independent	$145/3	$ 700/10	$1,400/13	$ 680/8

Television cost per Gross Rating Point: Women 18–49

Station	*Affiliation*	*Daytime*	*Early evening*	*Primetime*	*Late evening*
A........	ABC	$48.57	$66.32	—	$100.00
B	CBS	42.40	66.67	—	96.67
C	NBC	50.00	66.00	$142.67	111.11
D	Independent	48.33	70.00	107.69	85.00

from home during the day. Costs, availabilities, and ratings for the stations in this market are presented in Figure 11–1.

This table shows, for example, that the independent station in this market will sell a 30-second spot during daytime television for $145 and that this daypart has an average rating of 3. Similarly a late evening 30-second spot on the NBC station costs $1,000 and has an average rating of 9.

You decide to use the simplex method of linear programming to guide you in your selection of what is initially a bewildering array of costs, ratings, and restrictions. The first step is to let the combination of stations and dayparts be represented by the following variables:

Daytime	*Early evening*	*Primetime*	*Late evening*
$A = X_1$	$A = X_5$	A—not available	$A = X_{11}$
$B = X_2$	$B = X_6$	B—not available	$B = X_{12}$
$C = X_3$	$C = X_7$	$C = X_9$	$C = X_{13}$
$D = X_4$	$D = X_8$	$D = X_{10}$	$D = X_{14}$

It is then possible to write the objective function and the system of constraints as follows:

$$Z_{max} = 7X_1 + 5X_2 + 6X_3 + 3X_4 + 19X_5 + 21X_6 + 20X_7 + 10X_8 + 15X_9 + 13X_{10} + 4X_{11} + 6X_{12} + 9X_{13} + 8X_{14}$$

Figure 11–2
Initial tableau for television buy

C			7	5	6	3	19	21	20	10	15
	Sol	b	X_1	X_2	X_3	X_4	X_5	X_6	X_7	X_8	X_9
0	S_1	300,000	340	212	300	145	1,260	1,400	1,320	700	2,140
$-M$	A_1	1,000	0	0	0	0	0	0	0	0	15
$-M$	A_2	500	0	0	0	0	0	0	0	0	0
0	S_2	100	7	0	0	0	0	0	0	0	0
0	S_3	100	0	5	0	0	0	0	0	0	0
0	S_4	100	0	0	6	0	0	0	0	0	0
0	S_5	100	0	0	0	3	0	0	0	0	0

Subject to the following constraints:

a. $340X_1 + 212X_2 + 300X_3 + 145X_4 + 1{,}260X_5 + 1{,}400X_6 + 1{,}320X_7 + 700X_8 + 2{,}140X_9 + 1{,}400X_{10} + 400X_{11} + 580X_{12} + 1{,}000X_{13} + 680X_{14} \leq 300{,}000$

b. $15X_9 + 13X_{10} \geq 1{,}000$

c. $4X_{11} + 6X_{12} + 9X_{13} + 8X_{14} \geq 500$

d. $7X_1 \leq 100$

e. $5X_2 \leq 100$

f. $6X_3 \leq 100$

g. $3X_4 \leq 100$

You can see that in the objective function we use the rating for each variable as the coefficient. Then by summing the function for the number of spots of each type purchased, we calculate the total GRPs of the buy.

The budget constraint is constructed by using the dollar cost of each type of spot as the coefficient for that variable. The entire cost of all spots purchased must not exceed $300,000.

The remaining constrants about maxima and minima for the GRPs earned in each daypart and station again use the ratings as coefficients.

We add slack variables, as discussed in the appendix, to constraints *a, d, e, f,* and *g* to convert these to equalities, or:

13	4	6	9	8	0	0	0	0	0	0	0	−M	−M
X_{10}	X_{11}	X_{12}	X_{13}	X_{14}	S_1	S_2	S_3	S_4	S_5	S_6	S_7	A_1	A_2
1,400	400	580	1,000	680	1	0	0	0	0	0	0	0	0
13	0	0	0	0	0	0	0	0	0	−1	0	1	0
0	4	6	9	8	0	0	0	0	0	0	−1	0	1
0	0	0	0	0	0	1	0	0	0	0	0	0	0
0	0	0	0	0	0	0	1	0	0	0	0	0	0
0	0	0	0	0	0	0	0	1	0	0	0	0	0
0	0	0	0	0	0	0	0	0	1	0	0	0	0

a. $340X_1 + 212X_2 + 300X_3 + 145X_4 + 1{,}260X_5 + 1{,}400X_6 + 1{,}320X_7 + 700X_8 + 2{,}140X_9 + 1{,}400X_{10} + 400X_{11} + 580X_{12} + 1{,}000X_{13} + 680X_{14} + S_1 = 300{,}000$

d. $7X_1 + S_2 = 100$

e. $5X_2 + S_3 = 100$

f. $6X_3 + S_4 = 100$

g. $3X_3 + S_5 = 1{,}000$

As described in the appendix, add artificial variables (and the corresponding necessary slack variables) to constraints *b* and *c* to convert these to equalities:

b. $15X_9 + 13X_{10} - S_6 + A_1 = 1{,}000$

c. $4X_{11} + 6X_{12} + 9X_{13} + 8X_{14} - S_7 + A_2 = 500$

From these equations, it is possible to construct the initial simplex tableau (Figure 11–2).

You can easily imagine that graphic solutions to such a problem would not be practical. Also, even hand calculation of the simplex method would be cumbersome, though the student who takes pride in meticulous work may wish to try.

Since the mechanics of the simplex method are readily programmed for computers, this problem was solved by computer. The final tableau is shown in Figure 11–3.

Since many organizations involved in media buying use computer routines to solve linear programming problems via the simplex

Figure 11–3
Final (11th) tableau for television buy

C			7	5	6	3	19	21	20	10	15	13	4	6
	Sol	b	X_1	X_2	X_3	X_4	X_5	X_6	X_7	X_8	X_9	X_{10}	X_{11}	X_{12}
20	X_7	99.15	0	0	0	0	.955	1.061	1	.530	.397	0	.045	.053
13	X_{10}	76.92	0	0	0	0	0	0	0	0	1.154	1	0	0
8	X_{14}	62.50	0	0	0	0	0	0	0	0	0	0	.5	.75
7	X_1	14.29	1	0	0	0	0	0	0	0	0	0	0	0
5	X_2	20.00	0	1	0	0	0	0	0	0	0	0	0	0
6	X_3	16.67	0	0	1	0	0	0	0	0	0	0	0	0
3	X_4	33.33	0	0	0	1	0	0	0	0	0	0	0	0
	$Z =$	3,882.74	7	5	6	3	19.1	21.22	20	10.6	22.94	13	4.9	7.06
		$C - Z =$	0	0	0	0	−.1	−.22	0	−.6	−7.94	0	−.9	−1.06

method, it is important that you understand such solutions. Can you recognize what the solution means for the media purchase problem?

The solution indicated by simplex is as follows:

Variable	Station	Daypart	Rating	Number of 30-second spots	Cost (dollars)	GRP
X_7	C	Early evening	20	99.15	\$130,878.00	1,983
X_{10}	D	Primetime	13	76.92	107,688.00	1,000
X_{14}	D	Late evening	8	62.50	42,500.00	500
X_1	A	Daytime	7	14.29	4,858.60	100
X_2	B	Daytime	5	20.00	4,240.00	100
X_3	C	Daytime	6	16.67	5,001.00	100
X_4	D	Daytime	3	33.33	4,832.85	100
			Total	322.86	\$299,998.45	3,883

You can see that by the purchase of about 323 commercial spots on the plan described above, the target level of GRPs is achieved (actually, slightly exceeded) without violating any of the restrictions and without exceeding the budget. The solution indicates that portions of a commercial are to be purchased, which it is impossible to do, but the number of spots for each station and daypart can be rounded to the nearest whole number without doing great harm to the optimality

9	8	0	0	0	0	0	0	0	$-M$	$-M$
X_{13}	X_{14}	S_1	S_2	S_3	S_4	S_5	S_6	S_7	A_1	A_2
.178	0	.001	−.037	−.032	−.038	−.037	.082	.064	−.082	−.064
0	0	0	0	0	0	0	−.077	0	.077	0
1.125	1	0	0	0	0	0	0	−.125	0	.125
0	0	0	143	0	0	0	0	0	0	0
0	0	0	0	.2	0	0	0	0	0	0
0	0	0	0	0	167	0	0	0	0	0
0	0	0	0	0	0	.333	0	0	0	0
12.56	8	.02	.261	.36	.24	.26	.639	.28	−.638	−.28
−.3.56	0	−.02	−.261	−.36	−.24	−.26	−.639	−.28	−M +.638	−M +.28

of the solution. Thus we would actually purchase ninety-nine, not 99.15, 30-second spots during the early evening period on station *C*.

Something else is implied by the above solution. As part of answering the question of how many commercials to buy, on which stations, during which dayparts, we have almost accidentally solved the problem of how to distribute our advertising budget allocation efficiently among the possible media vehicles. And by the same process we used above, it is possible to include other media classes, other objectives, or other constraints to produce a combined media purchase.

SENSITIVITY ANALYSIS

It is clear that linear programming, especially when enhanced by computer processing for the simplex method, is a powerful tool in selecting a media mix. Perhaps not so clear, but equally important, is the fact that linear programming solutions are very much captive of the decision maker's input. For example, if the constraints are wrong, or foolish, the solutions are also likely to be wrong or foolish.

One additional aspect of linear programming, called sensitivity analysis, provides an additional reassurance to the media purchaser. He could ask questions such as the following:

"What would happen to the solution if the budget were increased to $400,000?"

"What would be the effect of a new set of station-by-daypart ratings?"

"What would the TV buy become if a limit of 1,000 GRPs were imposed on early evening broadcasts?"

The prudent media planner can imagine many other such questions relating the sensitivity of the solution to changing conditions, objectives, or judgments. And while sophisticated procedures exist for assessing sensitivity, the most straightforward approach to this part of linear programming is to substitute the new values, recalculate the new optimal solution, and compare the results. In the final analysis no "black box," computer program, or computational method can relieve the decision maker of responsibility for a decision.

MORE ADVANCED APPROACHES TO CHOOSING MEDIA

In using models for technical problems, we often simplify "reality" so that its various aspects can be better understood. In the technical problem of advertising media selection (and the corresponding budget distribution among vehicles), we often simplify to improve our managerial abilities. Linear programming does this in two dramatic ways. First, it requires objective functions and constraints to be *linear* functions. Second, it considers the bounds of the feasibility space to be *inviolate.* Since neither of these simplifications reflects the way the advertising would really work, it is important to recognize that decision methods exist for making the media selection–budget distribution problem more realistic. And as you may suspect, this added realism comes at a price. In both instances, linearity and boundary rigidity, extra realism means more complicated analysis. However, our discussion will be limited to conversational descriptions of such methods.

NONLINEAR PROGRAMMING

In advertising many objectives are accurately modeled by nonlinear functions. For example, if we chart the reach of an advertising campaign as a function of the number of ads, we (realistically) expect to find something like the pattern shown in Figure 11–4. This pattern happens because of audience duplication. As we place increased numbers of advertisements in media, we begin to have persons in the

Figure 11–4
Reach as a function of the number of ads

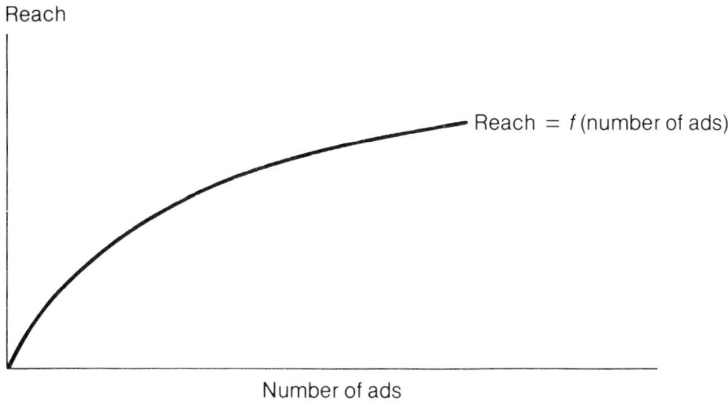

audience who have been exposed to our message more than once. The problem of audience duplication will be handled in greater detail later in this chapter. For the moment, though, imagine what this type of response does to the implied assumptions of linear programming!

Other real circumstances produce discontinuities in objective functions or constraints. For example an advertiser may have virtually saturated the newspapers in a market at an average CPM of $20. To include another class of media in the campaign, say metropolitan magazines, may produce a much different average CPM of $35. While each of the two portions of such a cost curve are linear, together they produce a function called a step function or a "piecewise" linear combination. In these examples, and in many other aspects of media planning, linear programming can produce grotesque oversimplifications. One way of producing added realism is to let the actual, nonlinear functions bound the feasibility space. Then, in principle, one must mathematically search the cornerpoints to find an optimal solution. You should not imagine that this is an easy calculation. However, you should be aware that computational methods and computer programs are available for nonlinear programming. Experience is the best guide for determining when the added complexity of these methods is warranted.

GOAL PROGRAMMING

In practice, objectives and constraints are not often stated with the rigidity implied by linear programming. For example a budget constraint might be set at $300,000 plus or minus 10 percent. This means that instead of a single straight-line constraint, we really have an "envelope" or family of budget constraints with a minimum value of $270,000 and a maximum value of $330,000. This improvement in realism makes traditional linear programming methods virtually impossible to work.

Goal programming, as developed by Charnes[2] and Lee,[3] provides a way of handling flexible aspects of media selection realistically. Lee,[4] for example, uses goal programming to select from among 47 media vehicles in seven media classes when some budget overexpenditure is permitted (5 percent) and when several measures of effectiveness and exposure are permitted to vary within specified limits. While Lee has developed both graphic and simplex approaches to goal programming, a full description of these approaches is beyond the scope of this text. However, you should recognize that goal programming is a way in which advertising problems can be formulated more realistically.

MEASURING AUDIENCE DUPLICATION FOR AN ASSORTMENT OF MEDIA

Anytime a media plan calls for more than one insertion in a single medium, audience duplication becomes an issue for the media planner. In Chapter 4, we discussed the notion of frequency and how *reach* differs from the duplicated audience for a media buy. Chapter 4 also suggested the problem of audience duplication for two media, television and magazines.

Audience duplication is a fact in virtually every advertising campaign. Some audience duplication is desirable, and this fact is expressed in frequency goals greater than one. In many actual campaigns, you will see examples where media planners call for monthly GRP levels of 250. As you know, this implies a monthly frequency of 2.5 if the reach is 100 percent of the market. If the reach is less than 100 percent, the implied monthly frequency is even greater. In other instances, multiple exposures above some target level for frequency can be wasteful. But whether audience duplication is "good" or "bad" in a particular media plan, the essential point here is that it must be considered in the media selection and scheduling process.

---

[2] Charnes, "Goal Programming Model for Media Planning," pp. B–423–30.

[3] S. M. Lee and L. J. Moore, *Introduction to Decision Science* (New York: Petrocelli/Charter, 1975), pp. 196–231.

[4] S. M. Lee, *Goal Programming for Decision Analysis* (Philadelphia: Auerbach, 1972), pp. 250–59.

The Agostini method

One of the first attempts to estimate audience duplication systematically appeared in the very first issue of the *Journal of Advertising Research.* The author, J. M. Agostini, proposed a method for estimating audience duplication for advertising carried in an assortment of magazines.[5] He suggested that C, the net (or unduplicated) coverage, was:

$$C = A \left[\frac{1}{1 + \frac{KD}{A}} \right]$$

Where:

A = duplicated audience for all vehicles used
D = Sum of the *duplicated* "readership" of all pairs
K = Agostini's constant, 1.125

You will notice that the value for A in a set of vehicles is simply the sum of each vehicle's readership. And subsequent research by Claycamp and McClelland[6] has shown that the value for K is not constant, but varies, dependent on the media consumption of the audiences for the particular set of vehicles chosen. Nevertheless, it is instructive to work through an example of the rather primitive Agostini model.

Assume that a set of five magazines have the readership indicated:

Magazine	*Readership*
A	20,000
B	30,000
C	40,000
D	30,000
E	20,000
Total	140,000

Next, the pairwise audience overlap is:

A–B, 5,000	B–C, 1,000	C–D, 1,000	D–E, 4,000
A–C, 2,000	B–D, 2,000	C–E, 5,000	
A–D, 3,000	B–E, 1,000		
A–E, 2,000			

[5] J. M. Agostini, "How to Estimate Unduplicated Audiences," *Journal of Advertising Research,* vol. 1, no. 1 (March 1961), pp. 11–14.

[6] H. J. Claycamp and C. W. McClelland, "Estimating Reach and the Value of *K*," *Journal of Advertising Research,* vol. 8, no. 2 (June 1968), pp. 44–51.

Here 5,000 readers of magazine A also read magazine B, etc. On reflection you will notice that this is the complete list of magazine pairs, since the A–B overlap is identical to the B–A overlap. The sum of these pairwise duplicated readership values, which is the term *D* in Agostini's formula, is 26,000. By inserting the various values, we can now solve for *C*, the net audience.

$$C = 140{,}000\left[\frac{1}{1+\dfrac{1.125(26{,}000)}{140{,}000}}\right] = 140{,}000\left[\frac{1}{1+.209}\right] = \frac{140{,}000}{1.209} = 115{,}798$$

Because of the importance of audience duplication estimates, and because of substantial dissatisfaction among media persons with the too simplistic Agostini method, more comprehensive methods for estimating audience duplication have been developed. Two prominent improvements, the Metheringham method and the beta-binomial method, will be discussed here.

The Metheringham method

In 1964, in an article published in the *Journal of Advertising Research,* R. A. Metheringham proposed the method of estimating net audience coverage which bears his name.[7] This method is implemented in two stages:

1. The probability is estimated that a single individual in the target audience is exposed to one, two, three, etc., vehicles in the vehicle assortment up to the probability that the individual is exposed to every vehicle used. The general relationship between number of vehicles, *M,* and probability of exposure to *N* of the *M* vehicles is graphed in Figure 11–5. Intuitively, the probability that some individual will be exposed to all 12 of the vehicles in an assortment containing 12 vehicles is much lower than the probability that the individual will be exposed to 1, 2, or 3 of the 12 vehicles.
2. The probabilities generated in the first stage are converted to information about the proportion of the total audience exposed to one, two, three, . . . *M* exposures.

Let's take the problem we used to illustrate the Agostini method and apply Metheringham's method to it. For purposes of this explanation, assume that a single advertisement/insertion was carried in each of the five magazines A through E.

---

[7] R. A. Metheringham, "Measuring the Net Cumulative Coverage of a Print Campaign," *Journal of Advertising Research,* vol. 4, no. 4 (December 1964), pp. 23–28.

Figure 11–5

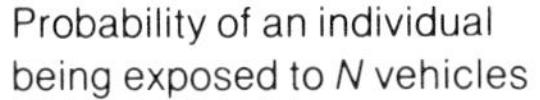

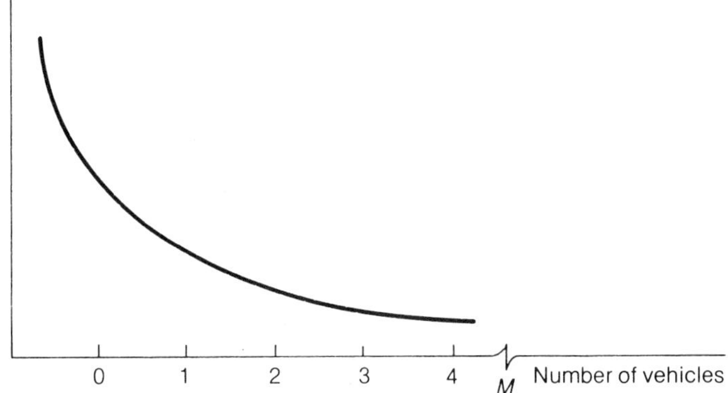

Now the probability that any audience member was "exposed" to the ad in at least one vehicle is 1.0. Notice that *exposure to the ad* is a different and more relaxed criterion than *readership of the ad.* You should recognize in this and subsequent steps that exposure to the ad is assumed to be synonymous with readership of the magazine issue.

The average probability of exposure to any two vehicles is given by the formula:

$$\text{Average } P_2 \text{ vehicles} = \frac{1}{10}\Big[p(A,B) + p(A,C) + p(A,D) + p(A,E) + p(B,C) + p(B,D) + p(B,E) + p(C,D) + p(C,E) + p(D,E)\Big]$$

The probability of any magazine pair is equal to the audience overlap divided by the combined audience for that pair. Therefore, the probabilities are:

Pair	*Overlap*	÷ *Combined readership*	= *Probability*
AB	5,000	(20,000 + 30,000)	.100
AC	2,000	(20,000 + 40,000)	.033
AD	3,000	(20,000 + 30,000)	.060
AE	2,000	(20,000 + 20,000)	.050
BC	1,000	(30,000 + 40,000)	.014
BD	2,000	(30,000 + 30,000)	.033
BE	1,000	(30,000 + 20,000)	.020
CD	1,000	(40,000 + 30,000)	.014
CE	5,000	(40,000 + 20,000)	.083
DE	4,000	(30,000 + 20,000)	.080

Therefore,

$$\text{Average probability of any two vehicles} = \frac{1}{10}(.100+.033+.060+.050+.014+.033+.020+.014+.083+.080)$$

$$= \frac{.487}{10} = .0487$$

In a similar way we would compute the average probability that an individual audience member would be exposed to any three vehicles, any four vehicles, and all five vehicles. To calculate these probabilities we would need the duplicated audience for all nonredundant combinations of three vehicles, the same figures for all nonredundant four-vehicle combinations, and finally the number of persons who read all five vehicles. Experience suggests that these probabilities would be very close to zero for this problem. And, obviously, the computational details for these probabilities are extensive, though not particularly difficult.

The beta-binomial method

On closer inspection, advertising scholars recognized that the means for generating probabilities of audience exposure in the first stage of Metheringham's method is called the *beta* distribution by statisticians. The second stage then uses what statisticians call a *binomial* distribution to calculate the proportion of the total audience exposed to one, two, three, . . . M exposures. Figure 11–6 presents these

Figure 11–6
The beta-binomial distribution and its components

Let:

m = Number of vehicles
r = Number of vehicles to which a reader is exposed
p = Probability of a given individual being exposed to a vehicle
$\acute{p}$ = Random variable which reflects the differences in p from person to person and is assumed to be independent over persons
$f_\beta(\acute{p}|a,b)$ = Density function for beta distribution with parameters a and b, both greater than -1
$f_b(r|m,p)$ = Density function for binomial distribution with parameters m and p

$$f_{\beta b}(r) = \int_0^1 f_b(r|m,\acute{p}) f_\beta(\acute{p}|a,b)\,d\acute{p}$$

This is the beta-binomial density function, which is obtained by compounding the beta and binomial distributions.

stages in statistical notation for those students who prefer this approach.

For students not familiar with complicated statistical notation, it is important to recognize that both the beta and binomial distributions and their properties can be used to answer the question of *net* audience coverage in campaigns with multiple insertions in a single vehicle and multiple vehicles. Further, R. S. Headen[8] and others have shown that the beta-binomial can be readily converted for broadcast media. They have also shown that this method does not require information about pairwise audience overlap.[9] This feature is of particular interest to those buying large amounts of spot TV, since the pairwise audience overlap values required by Metheringham's method are often unavailable.

A calculation of net audience coverage is provided in Figure 11–7. In this example the beta-binomial procedure is used directly, rather than in the somewhat roundabout way originally suggested by Metheringham. The direct beta-binomial procedures produce results virtually identical with those obtained by Metheringham's method.

A review of recent literature and actual practice suggests that while net audience coverage can be practically estimated via beta-binomial, other methods are also used. The binomial distribution derives its name from the fact that it relates to situations in which only two outcomes (hence "bi") are possible. In the advertising coverage examples, a person (or household) was either "exposed" or "not exposed." While exposure is important to advertising planning, other outcomes, such as "interest" or "intention to purchase," are also important. Here a *multinomial* distribution may be more useful than a binomial distribution in answering a real advertising management question.

As you can surmise, multinomial distributions are more complex than binomial distributions. And a detailed discussion of these is beyond the scope of this text. You should recognize, however, that procedures exist for estimating advertising coverage that permits more than two outcomes. When the situation seems to require them, these procedures can be employed with the help of qualified analysts to produce practical information.

BUILDING THE MEDIA SCHEDULE

In this chapter so far, we have discussed two of the important requirements for building a media schedule. Boiled down to simple terms,

[8] R. S. Headen, et al., "Predicting Audience Exposure to Spot TV Advertising Schedules," *Journal of Marketing Research,* no. 1 (1977), pp. 1–9.

[9] Ibid., p. 6.

Figure 11–7
Use of beta-binomial distribution to calculate net audience coverage

Problem: Estimate the complete exposure distribution (or number of households exposed at each level of exposure) and reach for the advertising schedule consisting of four insertions in vehicle A and three insertions in vehicle B.

Vehicle	*Audience*	*Two-insertion accumulation*	*Net audience*
A	.24	.41	.27
B	.10	.16	

Target audience = 20 million households.

Formulas:

$$\bar{R}_1 = \frac{\sum_{i=1}^{m} A_i n_i}{\sum_{i=1}^{m} n_i}$$

or reach of one insertion in the "composite" or average vehicle in the schedule

and
$$\bar{R}_2 = \left[\sum_{i=1}^{m} (n_{i2}) R_{2i}\right] + \left[\sum_{i=1}^{m} \sum_{j=i+1}^{m-1} n_i n_j R_{ij}\right]$$

or reach of two insertions in the composite vehicle

Where:

m = Number of vehicles
n_i = Number of insertions in vehicle i
N = Total number of insertions
R_{2i} = Accumulated audience for vehicle i
R_{ij} = Net audience of vehicles i and j
A_i = Audience of vehicle i
$\binom{n}{r}$ = Number of combinations of n things taken r at a time

$$\binom{n}{r} = \frac{n!}{r!\,(n-r)!}, \text{where } n! \ (n \text{ factorial}) = n(n-1)\ldots 1$$

$$a = \frac{\bar{R}_1 (\bar{R}_2 - \bar{R}_1)}{2(\bar{R}_1) - \bar{R}_2 - \bar{R}_1^2}$$

$$B = a\frac{(1-\bar{R}_1)}{R_1}$$

$$\text{Number of exposures} = \binom{N}{n_i} \frac{a(a+1)(a+2)\ldots(a+n_i-1)(B)(B+1)(B+2)\ldots(B+N-n_i)}{(a+B)\quad(a+B+1)\quad(a+B+2)\ldots(a+B+N-1)}$$

Figure 11–7 (*concluded*)

$$\bar{R}_1 = \frac{4(.24) + 3(.10)}{7} = .18$$

$$\bar{R}_2 = \frac{\left(\binom{4}{2}.41 + \binom{3}{2}.16 + (4)(3)(.27)\right)}{\binom{7}{2}} = .294$$

$$a = \frac{.18(.294 - .18)}{2(.18) - .294 - .18^2} = .611$$

$$B = \frac{.611(1 - .18)}{.18} = 2.783$$

$$N = 7$$

Then number of exposures:

$$0 = \binom{7}{0} \frac{(2.783)\ (3.783)\ (4.783)\ (5.783)\ (6.783)\ (7.783)\ (8.783)}{(3.394)\ (4.394)\ (5.394)\ (6.394)\ (7.394)\ (8.394)\ (9.394)} = .450$$

$$1 = \binom{7}{1} \frac{(.611)\ (2.783)\ (3.783)\ (4.783)\ (5.783)\ (6.783)\ (7.783)}{(3.394)\ (4.394)\ (5.394)\ (6.394)\ (7.394)\ (8.394)\ (9.394)} = .219$$

$$2 = \binom{7}{2} \frac{(.611)\ (1.611)\ (2.783)\ (3.783)\ (4.783)\ (5.783)\ (6.783)}{(3.394)\ (4.394)\ (5.394)\ (6.394)\ (7.394)\ (8.394)\ (9.394)} = .136$$

$3 = .087$
$4 = .055$
$5 = .032$
$6 = .016$
$7 = .005$

Thus, in this example .450, or 45 percent of the total audience, has zero exposures, 21.9 percent of the audience was exposed once; 13.6 percent was exposed twice; etc. And since reach is the entire target audience minus those households not exposed, reach equals 100 percent minus 45 percent, or 55 percent. Given a target audience of 20 million households, the reach is 11 million households.

Source: This example was developed by Professor John Leckenby, of the Department of Advertising, University of Illinois, and is used with his kind permission.

the foregoing material has been directed toward the answers to two questions:

"Which vehicles?"

"What effective audience?"

We should point out that these requirements exert a mutual influence. That is, the vehicle selection problem is to some extent influenced by audience overlap, while net audience coverage is certainly influenced by vehicle selection. In practice, an assortment of vehicles is often chosen on a trial basis; then net audience coverage is estimated, and, if necessary, the assortment is revised. This recursive process continues until both questions have satisfactory answers. The *timing* of the advertising insertions is the remaining decision area in this discussion.

MANAGERIAL OBJECTIVES

In reaching decisions about the timing of advertising, it is of paramount importance that the managerial objectives of the advertising campaign be incorporated into the decision process. First the intended reach and frequency for the campaign must be considered. Perhaps less obviously, other managerial objectives should also play an important role in the schedule.

Reach-dominant situations

For certain advertising projects, the principal objective is to maximize *reach* within a specified target audience. This situation is most likely to occur when the advertising is for a product class which is characterized by highly interested and well-informed prospective buyers. Often advertising for specialty goods has a reach-dominated objective. For example, DeBeer Consolidated Mines, Ltd., advertises diamond engagement rings to women 18–24 years of age. DeBeer assumes that this audience is highly sensitized to such products. The advertising objective is not so much to create large numbers of reminder-type advertisements as to reach the largest possible percentage of this audience with an appealing, impressive message. In situations like this, a relatively large number of vehicles are scheduled, at relatively low numbers of insertions per vehicle. Also, emphasis is placed on the long-lived media classes, such as magazines.

Frequency-dominant situations

In contrast, some advertising is focused on the creation of large numbers of impressions per audience member. A high-frequency objective may be appropriate when the product is likely to appeal to a broad group of prospects and when many reminder-type impressions are desirable. This kind of objective may be implied by advertising for the typical fast-food franchise. In such situations, the media schedule usually contains a relatively smaller number of vehicles and a larger number of insertions per vehicle. Also, greater use of the "perishable" media, particularly the electronic and outdoor media, is consistent with a high-frequency objective.

The general case—reach and frequency

In most advertising, both reach and frequency are important objectives. Even in the situations described in the foregoing discussion, the reach-dominant projects are likely to have target frequencies greater than one, while the frequency-dominant projects are likely to be concerned with obtaining adequate reach.

In the discussion of media selection and audience duplication, Gross Rating Points served as example objectives. GRPs are a measure which combines both reach and frequency. They are, therefore, an appropriate way to state the objective for advertising in some general-audience media. And GRP levels, when combined with constraints in the form of minimum frequency and minimum reach, can be adequate statements of the objectives of a campaign.

Audience and customer variables

When reach, frequency, and GRP level are used in combination as advertising objectives, the implied assumption is that audience members are homogeneous with respect to the advertised product. Yet common sense and research evidence suggest that this is not true. Some members of the audience are more inclined than others to respond to a campaign or to buy the advertised product. For instance young adult women may be one important group of prospects for diamond products. Perhaps another important group comprises married males in the 34–49-year age group who are likely to buy diamond products for their wives. Other good and poor groups could be specified for these products or for most other products.

One way in which to take account of this inequality among audience members is by *weighting.* We can use weighting to reflect differences in audience characteristics, such as demographic variations (recall here the Chapter 4 discussion of "demographic matching"). Other bases for differential weighting include differences in propensities to purchase the product class and differences in past purchase patterns.

Weighting influences not only the selection of vehicles but also the scheduling decision. Differences in the audience composition by daypart for broadcast media are an obvious example. Also, weighting can influence the scheduling of print advertising when periodic audience differences are detectable. For example, most daily newspapers have a "best food day," when grocery shoppers expect to find the most complete array of grocery advertising. Ads run on this day reach an audience group who are predisposed to look for "specials."

These ads may produce better results than ads run for grocery products on other days.

Product considerations

For many products, there is a distinct seasonal pattern in sales. Snow tires and tire chains sell briskly in the fall and early winter and shortly after major snowstorms. Sales of bathing suits, skis, vacations to warm climates, fashion apparel, fresh produce, and many other products follow seasonal trends. Marriages tend to occur more frequently in spring and summer, while warm, somewhat heavier foods are more popular during fall and winter.

The schedule of advertising for products with seasonal sales patterns tends to occur in one or more of three patterns. The most obvious scheduling pattern is to place a large proportion of the total advertising effort just before and in the early portions of the "season." Audiences are especially attentive to appeals at that time. And tie-in promotions linked to holidays such as Thanksgiving, Christmas, and the Fourth of July strive to reach audiences during the preparations for these festive occasions. A second scheduling pattern is to place advertising weight just after a major seasonal event has occurred. Thus ads for tire chains might be frequent just after the first major snowfall, and might be placed in the most time-flexible media, such as radio and newspapers. Similarly, ads for World Series or "Star Wars" paraphernalia might be run shortly after the series began or the movie was shown. Finally, a countercyclical or counterseasonal scheduling pattern may be used. Ads for vacations in warm places, emphasizing low off-season rates, may be run in summer.

Competitors' schedules

When the influence of competing advertising is being weighed, the scheduling decision usually requires the consideration of a basic trade-off. Ads placed at the "usual" time (such as the best food day) tend to reach more highly interested prospects, but at a time when competition for their attention is greater. Ads placed countercyclically tend to operate with fewer competing messages, but reach audiences which are less interested and are therefore harder to influence. As a rule, ads with frequency-dominated objectives tend to be scheduled along with competitors' ads, while ads with reach-dominated objectives can be scheduled with less regard to competitors' schedules.

Another managerial consideration

Capital budgeting was described in Chapter 3 as one method of developing the advertising allocation. In some instances the capital budgeting process can be influential in scheduling decisions. Recall that a basic element in the capital budgeting decision is the time shape of the cash flow. Thus both cash outflows in the form of media purchases and cash inflows in the form of sales returns are significant elements in the calculation. To the extent that advertising schedules are linked to sales, the scheduling decisions for advertising can be used to refine the capital budgeting process. And while such calculations are more commonly made in client organizations, media persons should be aware of these implications. The effect of incorporating the media schedule into the capital budgeting process is to delay media expenditures to their actual dates (rather than to assume that these expenditures occur at the beginning of the budget period). This refinement has the effect of increasing the rate of return on the advertising project.

APPENDIX

In the simplex approach to linear programming, several new concepts are required. These are presented as a glossary in Figure 11A–1. Each concept is also explained as its use is required by the simplex method.

To acquaint you with simplex, a listing of the steps required is presented in Figure 11A–2 and an example of the actual calculations is demonstrated, step by step. Finally, the process is reviewed and summarized.

Let's start learning the simplex method by using it to verify the optimum solution to the Sunset Farms problem of choosing the right mix of two magazines. You may wish to review this problem, which appears in the appendix to Chapter 2.

Step 1: Set down the objective function and the constraint functions. Since this is a maximization problem, it is not necessary to convert by multiplying the objective function terms by -1.

$$Z_{max} = 40(SL) + 37.5(SO) \qquad \text{Objective function}$$

Subject to:

$SL \geqslant 2$	Constraint 1
$SO \geqslant 2$	Constraint 2
$\$30{,}000(SL) + \$20{,}000(SO) \leqslant \$200{,}000$	Constraint 3

Figure 11A–1
Glossary of simplex method concepts

Artificial variable. A nonnegative variable, A_n, used to convert a "greater than or equal to" inequality to obtain a starting solution. Artificial variables are arbitrarily assigned a value of M, a very large number, in the objective function, which prohibits their presence in the solution.

Basic feasible solution. A solution in which, at most, a number of variables equal to the number of equations have positive values and all other variables have the value zero. For example, in a problem having two equations a basic feasible solution would have, at most, two variables with positive values, and the remaining variables would equal zero.

Basic solution. A solution in which there are an equal number of variables and constraints.

Basic variables. Variables in a basic feasible solution which have positive values.

Entering basic variable. A nonbasic variable used to "enter" or to replace a basic variable.

Leaving basic variable. A basic variable which has been replaced by an entering basic variable.

Nonbasic variables. Variables in a basic feasible solution which have the value zero.

Pivot column. The column of coefficients related to the nonbasic variable that has been identified as the entering basic variable.

Pivot number. The coefficient at the intersection of the pivot column and the pivot row. Also called pivot element.

Pivot row. The row of coefficients containing the current basic variable which has a coefficient of +1 and which is the leaving basic variable.

Slack variable. A nonnegative variable, S_n, used to indicate the presence of unused (or "slack") capacity of a constraint and to convert a "less than" or "equal to" inequality to an equality.

Starting solution. A system of equations, composed of the objective function and the constraint functions, in which all variables appear in all equations. Variables not originally contained in the equations are assigned a coefficient of zero.

Step 2: Add slack variables to convert each constraint of the "≤" type to an equality. Since constraint 3 is of this type, we must add a slack variable:

$$30{,}000(SL) + 20{,}000(SO) + S_1 = 200{,}000$$

In this revised constraint S_1 equals the budget dollars not spent, if any are not spent.

Step 3: Add artificial variables to each constraint of the "≥" or

Figure 11A–2
Steps required for simplex solution to linear programming problems

1. Set down the objective function and the constraint functions. If the objective function is to be minimized, convert it to a maximization problem by multiplying all terms by -1.
2. Add slack variables to convert each constraint of the "$\leq$" type to an equality.
3. Add artificial variables to constraints of the "$\geq$" or "$=$" type to produce a starting solution.
4. Create the tableau of coefficients for the starting solution.
5. Check solutions for optimality. Continue to step 6 if initial solution is not optimal.
6. Select the entering basic variable in order to improve the solution.
7. Select the leaving basic variable to be replaced.
8. Perform row operations to recalculate solution.
9. Return to step 5. Repeat steps 6 through 9 until optimum solution is obtained.

"=" type. Since constraints 1 and 2 are of this type, we must add an artificial variable to each. Also, you should recognize that each time an artificial variable is added, another slack variable must also be added. This is shown below:

$$SL = 2 + S_2 \qquad SO = 2 + S_3$$
$$SL - S_2 + A_1 = 2 \qquad SO - S_3 + A_2 = 2$$

Step 4: Create the tableau of coefficients for the starting solution. When doing this, keep in mind that each variable, *including slack and artificial variables,* must appear in every equation. This initial tableau is created by first creating a matrix of the coefficients in the form shown in Figure 11A–3.

In the topmost row of Figure 11A–4, labeled *C* for coefficients, are

Figure 11A–3
Starting the initial tableau—Sunset Farms

C			40	37.5	0	0	0	$-M$	$-M$
	Sol.	*b*	*SL*	*SO*	S_1	S_2	S_3	A_1	A_2
0	S_1	200,000	30,000	20,000	1	0	0	0	0
$-M$	A_1	2	1	0	0	-1	0	1	0
$-M$	A_2	2	0	1	0	0	-1	0	1

Figure 11A–4
Initial tableau—Sunset Farms

C			40	37.5	0	0	0	$-M$	$-M$	
	Sol.	*b*	*SL*	*SO*	S_1	S_2	S_3	A_1	A_2	$\phi = \frac{b}{\text{Pivot column element}}$
0	S_1	200,000	30,000	20,000	1	0	0	0	0	$\frac{200{,}000}{30{,}000}$
$-M$	A_1	2	(1)	0	0	-1	0	1	0	$\frac{2}{1}$ ←
$-M$	A_2	2	0	1	0	0	-1	0	1	$\frac{2}{0}$
	$Z =$	$-4M$	$-M$	$-M$	0	M	M	$-M$	$-M$	
		$C - Z =$	$40 + M$	$37.5 + M$	0	$-M$	$-M$	0	0	

Notes:

a. Pivot column is *SL*.
b. Pivot row is A_1.
c. Pivot element is 1.
d. Entering basic variable is *SL* (largest positive $C - Z$ value).
e. Leaving basic variable is A_1 (smallest positive ϕ value).

the original objective function coefficients. Since there were no slack variables in the objective function, these slack variables are assigned a coefficient equal to zero. We arbitrarily assign the artificial variables a coefficient of $-M$, which stands for a very large number. The purpose of this assignment is to prevent the artificial variables from appearing in the optimum solution since they would have no meaning there. If you wished, you could use some very large actual number, say -10^{10}; although this would be a more cumbersome procedure, it would produce the same results.

The second row merely provides column labels. The third row reflects the coefficients for each variable in the first constraint we altered by adding a slack variable. In addition we place the name of the variable added, which has a coefficient of $+1$ under the "solution" column, labeled *Sol.* Finally, we place that variable's coefficient from the objective function under the column labeled *C.* The remaining constraint function coefficients appear in the next two rows. The sixth row, labeled *Z,* is obtained by multiplying each coefficient in the *C* column by the corresponding coefficient in every column and summing down the column. Thus, for the *SL* column the value for *Z* row is $(0 \cdot 30{,}000) + (-M \cdot 1) + (-M \cdot 0) = 0+(-M) + 0 = -M$. Similarly, for the *SO* column the value for Z is $(0 \cdot 20{,}000) + (-M \cdot 0) + (-M \cdot 1) = 0 + 0 + (-M) = -M$. The final row, labeled $C=Z$, is calculated by subtracting the value of Z for that column from the objective function coefficient.

Step 5: The C − Z row furnishes our test for optimality. To be optimal, a solution must have all values in the $C-Z$ row either negative or equal to zero. Inspecting the initial tableau reveals that both the *SL* and *SO* columns have large positive values. We must therefore continue to another solution, and the next step.

Step 6: Select the entering basic variable. To do this, we identify the column with the largest positive $C-Z$ value, in this instance the *SL* column. This means that *SL* will be added to the variables originally appearing in the solution column (i.e., S_1, A_1, and A_2). It also means that *SL* will become the pivot column for this next trial.

Step 7: Select the leaving basic variable. This is the variable to be replaced by *SL* in this trial. To identify the leaving basic variable, we compute an index number, ϕ, for each row in the initial tableau. The value for ϕ is equal to the numerical value of that constraint, or b, divided by the associated element in the pivot column. For the S_1 row, $\phi = 200{,}000 \div 30{,}000$; for the A_1 row, $\phi = 2 \div 1$; for the A_2 row, $\phi = 2 \div 0$, which is a number so large as to be undefined. Therefore, A_1 is the leaving basic variable.

The leaving basic variable is always found in the row with the smallest positive value for ϕ. It is scheduled for replacement by the entering basic variable in this trial.

Step 8: Perform row operations which will produce the revised (second) tableau for this trial. This is done, step by step, below.

Row calculations for second tableau—Sunset Farms

1. Divide all elements in pivot row of initial tableau, element by element, by pivot element. This produces, for the entering basic variable, *SL:*

Pivot row, initial tableau	÷ *1*	*New* SL *= row*
2		2
1		1
0		0
0		0
−1		−1
0		0
1		1
0		0

2. Multiply old S_1 row by the element in the pivot column associated with this row. Subtract the result from the old S_1 row:

Old S_1 row	−	*(Old S_1 row, SL column element*	×	*New SL row)*	=	*Value of new S_1 row*
200,000		30,000		2		140,000
30,000		30,000		1		0
20,000		30,000		0		20,000
1		30,000		0		1
0		30,000		−1		30,000
0		30,000		0		0
0		30,000		1		−30,000
0		30,000		0		0

3. Multiply the old A_2 row by the element in the pivot column associated with this row. Subtract the result from the old A_2 row:

Old A_2 row	−	*(Old A_2 row, SL column element*	×	*New SL row)*	=	*Value of new A_2 row*
2		0		2		2
0		0		1		0
1		0		0		1
0		0		0		0
0		0		−1		0
−1		0		0		−1
0		0		1		0
1		0		0		1

This produces the second tableau (Figure 11A–5). Since this is not yet an optimum solution (all elements in the $C-Z$ row are not zero or negative), we return to step 6 and continue.

Row calculations for third tableau—Sunset Farms

1. Divide the elements in the pivot row of the second tableau, element by element, by the pivot element. This produces, for the basic entering variable, *SO:*

Pivot row, second tableau	÷ *1* =	*New SO row*
2		2
0		0
1		1
0		0
0		0
−1		−1
0		0
1		1

Figure 11A–5
Second tableau—Sunset Farms

C			*40*	*37.5*	*0*	*0*	*0*	*−M*	*−M*	
	Sol.	*b*	*SL*	*SO*	S_1	S_2	S_3	A_1	A_2	ϕ
0	S_1	140,000	0	20,000	1	30,000	0	−30,000	0	$\frac{140,000}{20,000}$
40	*SL*	2	1	0	0	−1	0	1	0	$\frac{2}{0}$
−*M*	A_2	2	0	1	0	0	−1	0	1	$\frac{2}{1}$
	Z =	80 − 2*M*	40	−*M*	0	−40	*M*	40	−*M*	
		C − *Z* =	0	37.5 + *M*	0	40	−*M*	−*M* − 40	0	

Notes:

a. Pivot column is *SO*.
b. Pivot row is A_2.
c. Pivot element is 1.
d. Entering basic variable is *SO* (largest positive $C - Z$ value).
e. Leaving basic variable is A_2 (smallest positive ϕ value).

Figure 11A–6
Third tableau—Sunset Farms

C			*40*	*37.5*	*0*	*0*	*0*	*−M*	*−M*	
	Sol.	*b*	*SL*	*SO*	S_1	S_2	S_3	A_1	A_2	ϕ
0	S_1	100,000	0	0	1	30,000	20,000	−30,000	−20,000	$\frac{100,000}{30,000}$
40	*SL*	2	1	0	0	−1	0	1	0	$\frac{2}{-1}$
37.5	*SO*	2	0	1	0	0	−1	0	1	$\frac{2}{0}$
	Z =	155	40	37.5	0	−40	−37.5	40	37.5	
		C − *Z* =	0	0	0	40	37.5	−*M* − 40	−*M* − 37.5	

Notes:

a. Pivot column is S_2.
b. Pivot row is S_1.
c. Pivot element is 30,000.
d. Entering basic variable is S_2 (largest positive $C - Z$ value).
e. Leaving basic variable is S_1 (smallest positive ϕ).

2. Multiply the old S_1 row by the element in the pivot column associated with this row. Subtract the result from the old S_1 row:

Old S_1 row	−	*(Old S_1 row, SO column element*	×	*New SO row)*	=	*Value of new SO row*
140,000		20,000		2		100,000
0		20,000		0		0
20,000		20,000		1		0
1		20,000		0		1
30,000		20,000		0		30,000
0		20,000		−1		20,000
−30,000		20,000		0		−30,000
0		20,000		1		−20,000

3. Multiply the old *SL* row by the element in the pivot column associated with this row. Subtract the result from the old *SL* row:

Old SL *row*	−	*(Old* SL *row, SO column element*	×	*New SO row)*	=	*Value of new* SL *row*
2		0		2		2
1		0		0		1
0		0		1		0
0		0		0		0
−1		0		0		−1
0		0		−1		0
1		0		0		1
0		0		1		0

This produces the third tableau. Since this is not yet an optimum solution (all elements in the $C-Z$ row are not zero or negative), we return to step 6 and continue.

Row calculations for fourth tableau—Sunset Farms

1. Divide all elements in the pivot row of the third tableau, element by element, by the pivot element. This produces for the entering basic variable, S_2:

Pivot row, third tableau	÷ *30,000* =	*New S_2 row*
100,000		$3\frac{1}{3}$
0		0
0		0
1		$\frac{1}{30,000}$
30,000		1
20,000		$\frac{2}{3}$
−30,000		−1
−20,000		$-\frac{2}{3}$

Figure 11A–7
Fourth tableau—Sunset Farms

C			40	37.5	0	0	0	−M	−M	
	Sol.	b	SL	SO	S_1	S_2	S_3	A_1	A_2	ϕ
0	S_2	3⅓	0	0	$\frac{1}{30{,}000}$	1	⅔	−1	−⅔	$\frac{3⅓}{⅔}$
40	SL	5⅓	1	0	$\frac{1}{30{,}000}$	0	⅔	0	−⅔	$\frac{5⅓}{⅔}$
37.5	SO	2	0	1	0	0	−1	0	1	$\frac{2}{-1}$
	Z =	288.33	40	37.5	$\frac{40}{30{,}000}$	0	−10⅚	0	10⅚	
		C − Z =	0	0	$-\frac{40}{30{,}000}$	0	10⅚	−M	−M − 10⅚	

Notes:

a. Pivot column is S_3.
b. Pivot row is S_2.
c. Pivot element is ⅔.
d. Entering basic variable is S_3 (largest positive $C - Z$ value).
e. Leaving basic variable is S_2 (smallest positive ϕ value).

2. Multiply old *SL* row by the element in the pivot column associated with this row. Subtract the result from the solution *SL* row:

Old SL row	−	*(Old SL row, S_2 column*	×	*New S_2 row)*	=	*Value of new SL row*
2		−1		3⅓		5⅓
1		−1		0		1
0		−1		0		0
0		−1		$\frac{1}{30{,}000}$		$\frac{1}{30{,}000}$
−1		−1		1		0
0		−1		⅔		⅔
1		−1		−1		0
0		−1		− ⅔		− ⅔

3. Multiply the old *SO* row by the element in the pivot column associated with this row. Subtract the result from the old *SO* row.

Old SO row	−	*(Old SO row, S_2 column*	×	*New S_2 row)*	=	*Value of new SO row*
2		0		$3\frac{1}{3}$		2
0		0		0		0
1		0		0		1
0		0		$\frac{1}{30,000}$		0
0		0		1		0
−1		0		$\frac{2}{3}$		−1
0		0		−1		0
1		0		$-\frac{2}{3}$		1

This produces the fourth tableau. Since this is not yet an optimum solution (all the elements in the $C-Z$ row are not zero or negative), we return to step 6 and continue.

Row calculations for fifth tableau—Sunset Farms

1. Divide all elements in the pivot row of the fourth tableau, element by element, by pivot element. This produces, for the entering basic variable, S_3:

Pivot row, fourth tableau	÷ $\frac{2}{3}$ =	*New S_3 row*
$3\frac{1}{3}$		5
0		0
0		0
$\frac{1}{30,000}$		$\frac{3}{60,000}$
1		$1\frac{1}{2}$
$\frac{2}{3}$		1
−1		$-1\frac{1}{2}$
$-\frac{2}{3}$		−1

2. Multiply old *SL* row by the element in the pivot column associated with this row. Subtract the result from the old *SL* row:

Old SL row	−	*(Old SL row, S_3 column*	×	*New S_3 row)*	=	*Value of new SL row*
$5\frac{1}{3}$		$\frac{2}{3}$		5		2
1		$\frac{2}{3}$		0		1
0		$\frac{2}{3}$		0		0
$\frac{1}{30,000}$		$\frac{2}{3}$		$\frac{3}{60,000}$		0
0		$\frac{2}{3}$		$1\frac{1}{2}$		−1
$\frac{2}{3}$		$\frac{2}{3}$		1		0
0		$\frac{2}{3}$		$-1\frac{1}{2}$		1
$-\frac{2}{3}$		$\frac{2}{3}$		−1		0

Figure 11A–8
Fifth tableau—Sunset Farms

C			*40*	*37.5*	*0*	*0*	*0*	$-M$	$-M$	
	Sol.	*b*	*SL*	*SO*	S_1	S_2	S_3	A_1	A_2	ϕ
0	S_3	5	0	0	$\frac{3}{60,000}$	1½	1	−1½	−1	
40	*SL*	2	1	0	0	−1	0	1	0	
37.5	*SO*	7	0	1	$\frac{3}{60,000}$	1½	0	−1½	0	
	$Z =$	342.5	40	37.5	$\frac{112.5}{60,000}$	16¼	0	−16¼	0	
		$C - Z =$	0	0	$-\frac{112.5}{60,000}$	−16¼	0	$-M + 16¼$	$-M$	

Notes:
a. All values in the $C - Z$ column are either zero or negative; therefore, this is the optimal solution.
b. The coefficient for *SL* in the optimal solution is 2.
c. The coefficient for *SO* in the optimal solution is 7.
d. The value for the objective function Z_{max} is 342.5.

3. Multiply the old *SO* row by the element in the pivot column associated with this row. Subtract the result from the old SO row:

Old SO *row*	−	*(Old* SO *row,* S_3 *column*	×	*New* S_3 *row)*	=	*Value of new* SO *row*
2		−1		5		7
0		−1		0		0
1		−1		0		1
0		−1		$\frac{3}{60,000}$		$\frac{3}{60,000}$
0		−1		1½		1½
−1		−1		1		0
0		−1		−1½		−1½
1		−1		−1		0

This produces the fifth tableau. Since all elements in the $C - Z$ row are zero or negative, this is the optimum solution.

Interpretation of Melissa and Hillary tableaux—Figures 11A–9 through 11A–12

In the fourth and final tableau (Figure 11A–12), cost is minimized at a value of $16,148. Recall that we changed signs (from + to −) when

Figure 11A–9
Initial tableau—Melissa and Hillary

C			-75	-35	0	0	0	0	0	$-M$	$-M$	$-M$	
	Sol.	b	X_1	X_2	S_1	S_2	S_3	S_4	S_5	A_1	A_2	A_3	ϕ
$-M$	A_1	30	0	1	0	0	-1	0	0	1	0	0	$\frac{30}{1}$
$-M$	A_2	300	1	1	0	0	0	-1	0	0	1	0	$\frac{300}{1}$
0	S_1	235	1	0	1	0	0	0	0	0	0	0	$\frac{235}{1}$
0	S_2	215	0	1	0	1	0	0	0	0	0	0	$\frac{215}{1}$
$-M$	A_3	141.2	1	0	0	0	0	0	-1	0	0	1	$\frac{141.2}{0}$
	$Z =$	$-2M$	$-2M$	$-2M$	0	0	$+M$	$+M$	$+M$	$-M$	$-M$	$-M$	
		$C - Z =$	$-75+2M$	$-35+2M$	0	0	$-M$	$-M$	$-M$	0	0	0	

Notes: X_1 is the variable for Melissa's work units assigned, and X_2 is the variable for Hillary's work units assigned. The artificial variables A_1, A_2, and A_3 are assigned a coefficient of $-M$, a very large negative number.

Figure 11A–10
Second tableau—Melissa and Hillary

C			-75	-35	0	0	0	0	0	$-M$	$-M$	$-M$	
	Sol.	b	X_1	X_2	S_1	S_2	S_3	S_4	S_5	A_1	A_2	A_3	ϕ
-35	X_2	30	0	1	0	0	-1	0	0	1	0	0	$\frac{30}{0}$
$-M$	A_2	270	1	0	0	0	1	-1	0	-1	1	0	$\frac{270}{0}$
0	S_1	235	1	0	1	0	0	0	0	0	0	0	$\frac{235}{1}$
0	S_2	185	0	0	0	1	1	0	0	-1	0	0	$\frac{185}{0}$
$-M$	A_3	141.2	1	0	0	0	0	0	-1	0	0	1	$\frac{141.2}{1}$
	$Z =$	$-1{,}050$ $-411.2M$	$-2M$	-35	0	0	$35 - M$	M	M	$-35 + M$	$-M$	$-M$	
		$C - Z =$	$-75 + 2M$	0	0	0	$M - 35$	$-M$	$-M$	$-2M + 35$	0	0	

Notes: X_1 is the variable for Melissa's work units assigned, and X_2 is the variable for Hillary's work units assigned. The artificial variables A_1, A_2, and A_3 are assigned a coefficient of $-M$, a very large negative number.

Figure 11A–11
Third tableau—Melissa and Hillary

C			−75	−35	0	0	0	0	0	−M	−M	−M	
	Sol.	b	X_1	X_2	S_1	S_2	S_3	S_4	S_5	A_1	A_2	A_3	ϕ
−35	X_2	30	0	1	0	0	−1	0	0	1	0	0	$\frac{30}{-1}$
−M	A_2	128.8	0	0	0	0	1	−1	1	−1	1	−1	$\frac{128.8}{1}$
0	S_1	93.8	0	0	1	0	0	0	1	0	0	−1	$\frac{93.8}{0}$
0	S_2	185	0	0	0	1	1	0	0	−1	0	0	$\frac{185}{1}$
−75	X_1	141.2	1	0	0	0	0	0	−1	0	0	1	$\frac{141.2}{0}$
	Z =	−11,640 − 128.8*M*	−75	−35	0	0	35 − M	M	−M + 75	−35 + M	−M	+M − 75	
		C − Z =	0	0	0	0	M − 35	−M	M − 75	−2M + 35	0	−2M + 75	

Notes: X_1 is the variable for Melissa's work units assigned, and X_2 is the variable for Hillary's work units assigned. The artificial variables A_1, A_2, and A_3 are assigned a coefficient of $-M$, a very large negative number.

Figure 11A–12
Fourth tableau—Melissa and Hillary

C			−75	−35	0	0	0	0	0	−M	−M	−M	
	Sol.	b	X_1	X_2	S_1	S_2	S_3	S_4	S_5	A_1	A_2	A_3	ϕ
−35	X_2	158.8	0	1	0	0	0	−1	1	0	1	−1	
0	S_3	128.8	0	0	0	0	1	−1	1	−1	1	−1	
0	S_1	93.8	0	0	1	0	0	0	1	0	0	−1	
0	S_2	56.2	0	0	0	1	0	1	−1	0	−1	1	
−75	X_1	141.2	1	0	0	0	0	0	−1	0	0	1	
	Z =	−161.48	−75	−35	0	0	0	35	40	0	−35	−40	
		C − Z =	0	0	0	0	0	−35	−40	−*M*	−*M* + 35	−*M* + 40	

All elements zero or negative. Therefore, this is the optimal solution.

Notes: X_1 is the variable for Melissa's work units assigned, and X_2 is the variable for Hillary's work units assigned. The artificial variables A_1, A_2, and A_3 are assigned a coefficient of $-M$, a very large negative number.

we converted the cost minimization to a problem in the form of a maximization; therefore the negative Z value.

In the optimum solution, we assign X_1 (Melissa) 141.2 work units and X_2 (Hillary) 158.8 units. Compare this to the solution in Chapter 2; the work assignments are identical to those obtained by graphing.

S_1 represents the slack in Melissa's production maximum constraint. It represents slack or surplus in this constraint. Its value, 93.8, when added to Melissa's actual assignment of 141.2 equals 235, the value for this constraint.

S_2 represents the slack in Hillary's production maximum constraint. It represents slack in this constraint. Its value, 56.2, when added to Hillary's actual assignment of 158.8 equals 215, the value for this constraint.

S_3 represents the slack variable required by the addition of artificial variable A_1 and has no real-world meaning.

QUESTIONS

1. What is a major limitation on the use of graphic solutions to solve real-world media selection problems?

2. In the simplex example for buying television time, a budget constraint of $300,000 was imposed. What general steps would you follow to assess the sensitivity of the solution to this constraint?

3. Linear programming simplifies the problem of media selection in two major ways. What are these?

4. What are some advantages and disadvantages of using the Agostini method to measure audience duplication?

5. What are the basic differences between the Agostini and Metheringham methods?

6. Discuss an advertising media situation in which product considerations are dominant.

7. Discuss the two types of variables which are required in the simplex method to obtain an initial tableau, and the types of inequalities which make each type necessary.

12 THE MEDIA PLAN

THE MEDIA PLAN is a concise description of the objectives, planning, and proposed implementation of the media strategy. The media plan serves two major purposes:

1. It gives a written summary of the media to be bought and the rationale for scheduling them. At this stage the media plan allows all parties (client, creative, account management) to react to the media department's strategy.

2. After its approval the media plan becomes a guide to the media department in implementing the media program. In this respect the media plan should be specific enough to allow media buyers to make their commitments to space and time purchases with no confusion.

COMPONENTS OF THE MEDIA PLAN

Media plans follow a number of formats adapted to the individual marketing and media needs of the advertisers. However, most media plans have certain elements in common.

General statement of product background

The media plan may include a short summary of the product and the major competition as well as some historical sales trend. The product development portion of this section is normally very short. When the media plan is part of a larger discussion of campaign strategy, the product development information would be included in a longer separate section.

Marketing considerations

The media strategy must be formulated as part of the client's larger marketing and advertising objectives. The media plan does not examine the client's overall marketing program. It does, however, highlight those aspects of the marketing program which must be accomplished through advertising and, more specifically, through the media plan. In this section the media plan may offer the justification and rationale for the thrust of the media program—for instance, why certain media vehicles were chosen to reach a particular target segment.

Creative considerations

The media plan next considers how the creative and media strategies complement each other. Again, there is no lengthy discussion of the creative rationale, but it shuld be noted that creative requirements are considered in development of the media plan.

The media platform

After the preliminary statements on the purposes of the media strategy and its coordination with other aspects of the advertising program, the media portion of the campaign is outlined. In the context of an advertising campaign report, the media portion sometimes starts with the media platform. However, it is worthwhile to restate the marketing and advertising objectives so that the media platform can be presented within this larger environment.

While postscheduling research is usually not presented as part of the media plan, it may be mentioned at the conclusion of the plan. A media schedule can rarely be measured without also considering the effectiveness of the advertising messages. Consequently, the results of the total advertising effort, including both creative and media considerations, are normally measured both during and after a campaign. Astute advertisers will consider methods of postadvertising research as they plan their advertising and will make provisions for such research.

Note that the media plan is designed to work from the general objectives to specific tactical decisions. The most frequent mistake of the novice media planner is to move directly to the media schedule without the necessary preplanning. Ideally the media schedule should flow directly from the marketing/advertising objectives and strategy and should be the easiest section of the media platform to accomplish.

The remainder of this chapter will discuss the general components of the media platform and an actual media plan for *Grease relief,* a Texize product. Note how this media plan flows from overall objectives to specific tactics. Also observe the research foundation for each step of the plan.

THE MEDIA PLATFORM

Media plans must take into account specific conditions which will be encountered in advertising a particular product or service. Therefore, each media plan is unique for a product and for the time during which the plan will be implemented. There are, however, certain general formats which media plans normally follow. The media planner should use the outline presented here as a guide around which a specific media plan can be developed.

Section I. Overall objectives

The media plan should introduce the broad media-planning concepts and demonstrate how they complement both the overall marketing objectives and the general creative plan. In essence this section provides a review of corporate advertising/marketing objectives and forces the media planner to focus the media function on overall corporate planning.

A. Statement of media philosophy. The media plan follows the introductory section with a statement of overall media objectives. This statement outlines what the media schedule should accomplish in concert with other marketing and promotional areas.

Section II. Media strategy

The planning of media strategy is crucial to the success of the overall media program. Here the media planner begins the process of identifying the appropriate target market(s) and developing the media strategy most suited to reaching them.

A. Prospect identification. The media planner begins the process of prospect segmentation. At this point the various consumer groups are identified in terms of demographics, product usage characteristics, and/or lifestyle criteria. Prospects are also identified geographically, both in broad regions (Southeast) and in smaller socioeconomic units (suburbs). Regardless of the manner in which prospects are identified, the categories should be compatible with similar categories used by the media in identifying their readers and viewers.

B. Timing considerations. The timing of media buys is a crucial factor in overall media planning and advertising budgeting. In this regard, factors such as flighting and seasonal sales trends must be considered.

C. Creative considerations. The media/creative team must arrive at necessary compromises between the media which are most appropriate to carry the message and these media which reach the target audience most efficiently.

At this stage the media planner begins specific planning for future media scheduling. Even at this stage the media plan should be based on the information available concerning the marketing and competitive situation. However, there is also some "thinking out loud" as the media planner experiments with alternative approaches to the media schedule. Most media departments provide their planners with flowcharts for use in the initial planning stages (see Figure 12–1). These flowcharts are largely for internal agency use and are not sent to either clients or the media as part of the media-buying process. They are most often used in buying television.

Section III. Media tactics

In the media tactics section the media planner begins to outline the specific principles of the media function which are designed to implement both overall corporate objectives and the overall media strategy.

A. Advertising impact

1. Gross Rating Point levels. The first step in media tactics is to decide what level of advertising weight is to be applied against various market segments and in various geographic locales. GRPs have become the standard measure for general levels of advertising, but

Figure 12–1
Agency flowchart for use in initial planning of media schedule

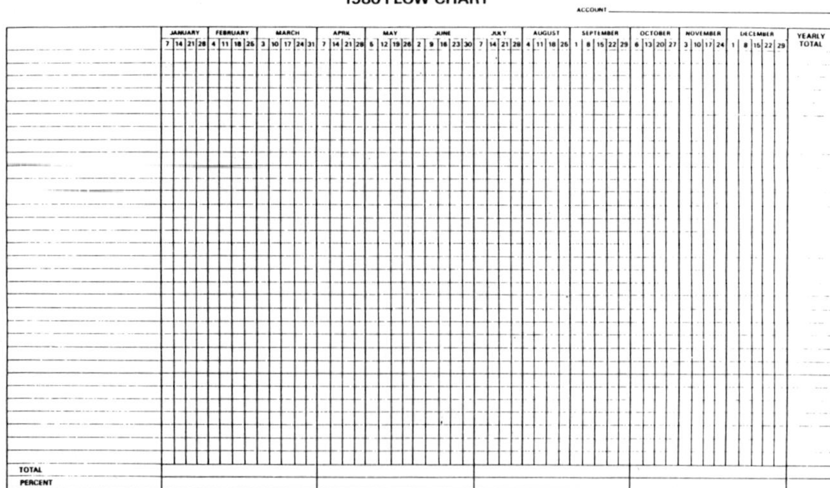

other measures may be more appropriate in specific cases (e.g., total exposures in magazines).

2. Reach versus frequency. Once the general weight of advertising has been decided, the next step is to analyze the pattern of exposure of the various target markets. These reach/frequency levels may be in terms of target segments, media, or both.

3. Competitive impact. Many advertising plans state goals in terms of some competitive strategy (taking away share points from a major competitor). The media planner should show how the campaign will meet such competitive goals.

B. Principles of media selection and justification

After general guidelines have been developed (Section IIIA), the media planner considers the more specific media factors which ultimately lead to the media schedule.

1. Selection of general media types and their justification. The media planner can present this section in a number of ways, but the example given in Figures 12–2 and 12–3 is typical.

Figure 12–2
General media plan and its justification

Medium	*Budget (percent)*		*Media vehicle types*	*Justification*
Television	$2,000,000	(50%)	Daytime soaps, barter syndication (Donahue, Douglas)	TV provides brand name awareness and excellent package identification; it reaches both women 25–49 (primary market) and women 50+ (secondary market)
Magazines	1,600,000	(40%)	Women's service books (*Family Circle*); specialized, upscale women's books (*Self*)	Magazines will be used to reach upscale and working women missed by a major portion of television advertising
Newspapers	400,000	(10%)	Dailies and major suburban papers	Newspapers will be used to complement other advertising with follow-up couponing in major markets

Figure 12–3
Budget allocation chart

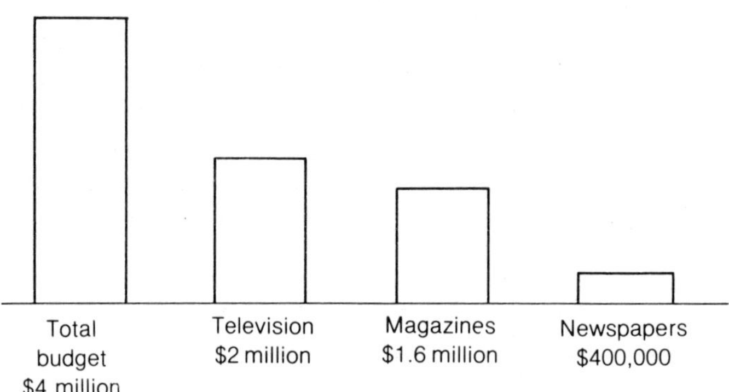

2. *Scheduling strategy.* After discussing the media to be used (Section IIIB), the media planner must delineate the scheduling strategy which will be used in each medium. This discussion should be regarded as an introduction to the media schedule. It should briefly highlight the major factors of the media strategy to be employed.

3. *Budget summary.* The way in which the budget is discussed in Section IIIB1 may make a separate budget summary subsection unnecessary. Even in such cases, however, the media planner may use the budget summary subsection to examine the budget constraints affecting the media plan. Usually budget problems of a major nature will be resolved before media planning is begun. On the other hand, if adequate advertising dollars are not available to carry out the overall advertising objectives, this should be noted by the media planner.

Section IV. The media schedule

The media schedule is a "calendar" of media buys. Depending on the diversity of the media types, the number of vehicles within these media, and the length and size of advertisements, the schedule may be simple or complex. At a minimum the following information is normally included in the media schedule:

1. Identification of each media vehicle to be used—*Time,* "The Jeffersons."
2. Time or space to be bought in each media and any special criteria for the buys—full position, four-color, ROP.
3. Dates advertisements and commercials are to run (and often insertion dates to media).
4. Cost—total for medium and per insertion with the exception of package buys in broadcast.

This information is sometimes included in media schedules:

1. Circulation, total audience, or prospects reached by each vehicle.
2. Cost per thousand, Gross Rating Points, cost per rating point, or weighted CPM by vehicle, medium, or entire schedule.
3. Coverage areas (broadcast).

From the media schedule actual media buys are made. In larger agencies the process begins with the account team (or account executive) notifying the media planner that media buys previously agreed upon should be made. The media planner prepares a media request form which starts the buying mechanism (see Figures 12–4

Figure 12–4
Print media request

OGILVY & MATHER INC. **MAGAZINE** PRINT MEDIA REQUEST

DATE

ESTIMATING ______ CLIENT ______

TRAFFIC ______ 1 – NATIONAL PRODUCT ______

FOWARDING ______ 2 – REGIONAL ESTIMATE ______

BUYER ______ 3 – TEST REVISION ______

OTHER ______ CANCELLATION ______

☐ MAGAZINE ☐ SUPPLEMENT ☐ TRADE

PUBLICATION	CIRC. 000	SPACE	ISSUE DATE	SPACE CLOSING DATE	GROSS COST

POSITION – SPECIAL INSTRUCTIONS

Courtesy Ogilvy & Mather, Inc.

Figure 12–5
Network buying request

OGILVY & MATHER INC.
Advertising

2 EAST 48 STREET, NEW YORK 10017
(212) MURRAY HILL 8-6100

NETWORK BUYING REQUEST

FROM: ______

Date: ______

TO: BROADCAST (N.Y.) ______
BROADCAST (.LA.) ______
ASSISTANT MEDIA DIRECTOR ______
ACCOUNT EXECUTIVE ______

CLIENT ______
PRODUCT ______ DAYPART ______ BUDGET $ ______ [ ] GROSS [ ] NET

INSTRUCTION: [ ] BUY [ ] CHANGE [ ] PREPARE BUY FOR REVIEW [ ] ORIGINAL or REVISION # ______

[ ] SPEND TO BUDGET
[ ] SPEND TO GRP'S
[ ] NOTIFY PLANNING GROUP OF OPPORTUNITIES

REACH OBJECTIVE
[ ] HIGH
[ ] MEDIUM
[ ] LOW

WEIGHT DISTRIBUTION TARGET

AGE	TOTAL	18-34	35-49	50+	25-49	18-49		TEENS		CHILDREN
MEN	[ ]	[ ]	[ ]	[ ]	[ ]	[ ]	M	[ ]	2-5	[ ]
WOMEN	[ ]	[ ]	[ ]	[ ]	[ ]	[ ]	F	[ ]	6-11	[ ]
	-$5M	$5-10M	$10-15M	$15M+			1-2	3-4		5+
INCOME	[ ]	[ ]	[ ]	[ ]	FAMILY SIZE		[ ]	[ ]		[ ]
	A	B	C	D						
COUNTY SIZE	[ ]	[ ]	[ ]	[ ]						

PRE-EMPTION POLICY: [ ] ACCEPT MAKE GOOD [ ] DURING FLIGHT [ ] OTHER TIMES [ ] ACCEPT CREDIT [ ] NOTIFY PLANNER

INCLUSIVE DATES ______ TOTAL # WKS ______

GROSS RATING POINT BASIS [ ] HOUSEHOLD [ ] WOMEN [ ] MEN [ ] CHILDREN OTHER ______

COST PER RATING POINT $ ______ $ ______ $ ______ $ ______ $ ______

DATES		GRP'S		WEEKLY BUDGET	NO. OF	SPECIAL INSTRUCTIONS
START	END	:30's	:60's	(GROSS)	WEEKS	
			TOTAL			

REMARKS

ASSISTANT MEDIA DIRECTOR SIGNATURE ______

ATTACH LATEST FLOW CHART

Courtesy Ogilvy & Mather, Inc.

and 12–5). Copies of the media request form are sent to traffic and creative as well as media, so that all aspects of the buy can be cordinated. From the media request forms insertion orders are submitted based on previously executed contracts with the media.

Contracts and insertion orders. The purchase of media involves two steps: contracting for time and space and submitting the advertisement or commercial insertion instructions to the given medium. The contract sets the price which the medium will charge over a set period. In some cases the contract also specifies or fixes the amount of time or space to be bought. In other cases, especially with newspapers, the final rate is computed after all the media buys have been made. In these cases the contract indicates the final discounts available and the price to be paid at each billing period.

The insertion order accompanies the advertisement or commercial (see Figure 12–6). It gives the date the advertisement is to run, reaffirms the cost, outlines any special requirements already agreed upon by the medium and the advertiser, and sometimes gives the advertising run to that time for discount purposes.

Section V. Summary

The summary is designed to show how the proposed media schedule accomplishes the advertising objectives. It should address the manner in which the media plan aids the client in meeting competitive challenges. Often the specific marketing goals (e.g., shift in a certain percentage market share) are reiterated here, and the methods by which the media strategy will aid in accomplishing these goals are discussed.

The media plan summary is an overview of anticipated accomplishments, reasonable chances of success, and potential pitfalls in the media portion of the advertising program. As mentioned at the beginning of this chapter, the media plan should both sell a client on the media program and guide the media department in implementing the plan.

THE MEDIA PLAN: AN EXAMPLE

Grease relief—a product of Texize, Inc.

Agency: Liller Neal Weltin, Inc.

1. Media objectives

a. Assist in increasing new-users trial to 20 percent during the fiscal year by reaching a mass female audience, with emphasis on the primary target

Figure 12–6
Insertion order

PLEASE SEND INVOICES TO
OGILVY & MATHER INC.
P.O. BOX 3708, GRAND CENTRAL STATION
NEW YORK, N.Y. 10017

Ogilvy & Mather Inc.
Advertising
2 EAST 48 STREET NEW YORK 10017 (212) 688-6100

INSERTION ORDER

TO PUBLISHER OF:

ORDER NO. B 112978
DATE
RATE
AGENCY COMM. %
CASH DISC. %

PLEASE INSERT THE ADVERTISING OF

DATE OF ISSUE	SPACE	P.O.	AD. NO.	CAPTION

Please advise at once if instructions are not clear.
Please check reproduction material against proof
to make sure it corresponds in every respect.
Please acknowledge receipt by return mail.
Schedule and instructions given above are subject
to the same conditions as in our contract.

A copy of each issue of your publication containing each advertisement should be sent promptly to the advertiser as well as to our office.

Ogilvy & Mather Inc.

Per ____________________

Member of
AMERICAN ASSOCIATION OF ADVERTISING AGENCIES

8-8E REV. 5-76
PRINTED IN U.S.A.

Courtesy Ogilvy & Mather, Inc.

of homemakers 18–49 years of age with household incomes of $10,000 and over.

b. Maximize coverage of the above target audience at a frequency of at least four impacts per month or one per week on the theory that it is prudent to reach her (our target) at least as often as she shops.

c. Optimize total advertising impressions nationally.
d. Vary the overall impact of *Grease relief* advertising to reflect the seasonal aspects of sales.
e. Test a high-level spending plan in two low brand development markets to ascertain whether sales can be increased commensurately.
f. Maintain a degree of flexibility of media funds to allow for possible changes in the media plan in response to differing competitive activities and/or consumer research.

2. Media strategies

a. Employ media that will deliver a mass audience of homemakers skewed toward our primary target to assist in increasing the rate of trial.
b. Select media vehicles to maximize coverage of our target audience at a frequency of four per month.
c. Utilize national media vehicles only (except for the high-level spending test described in point *e*) to deliver the greatest number of impressions for the brand.
d. Schedule media with varying intensity to match seasonality of sales and/or change commercial rotation to reflect differing seasonal usage patterns.
e. Add 50 percent more media spending in two test markets.
f. Commit funds only on a quarterly basis to permit a high degree of flexibility.

3. Media rationale

To fulfill the media objectives and strategies enumerated earlier, the basic media tactic for fiscal year 1976–77 will be to use a media mix comprising magazines and television. The recommendation calls for a 50–50 split of the budget (approximately $1 million in each medium) on the premise that we can do an effective job for *Grease relief* at this level in each medium.

The utilization of this media mix permits the presentation of *Grease relief's* attributes and selling proposition to consumers from different vantage points, as opposed to total concentration in one medium. This is important because the registration of the same basic copy points among viewers of TV and readers of magazines can be markedly different. A study on Chef Boy-Ar-Dee advertising done some years ago by Audits & Surveys dramatized this point:

	Major elements recalled	
	Quick and easy to prepare	*Taste and quality*
Magazines	5%	15%
TV	16	8

Another important reason for recommending a media mix of magazines and TV is the realization that TV, as it matures, is not the advertising panacea it once was or was thought to be. It is no longer generally true that entire families sit eyes glued to the tube for hours at a time. Today, not only have most viewing groups become smaller (parts of families or only one member), but these smaller units effectively screen out up to 80 percent of all commercials aired, which has the effect of reducing commercial recall, as seen below:

	Recall decline
Daniel Starch, 1956–68	52%
Grey Advertising, 1961–70	48

Concern about loss of message impact or recall when reverting to a media mix rather than using all TV is ill founded, as studies done by Audits & Surveys, W. R. Simmons, Hooper, and Grudin/Appel/Haley all indicate at least a parity of magazines with TV.

All media have usage patterns similar to the concentration seen for TV, where the top 40 percent of viewing homes account for about two-thirds of all viewing on a total-day basis and for over 80 percent on a daytime-only basis. These Nielsen quintile data for TV and magazines are tabulated as follows:

NTI			*NMS*	
Viewing Quintiles	*24-hour*	*Day*	*Reading quintiles*	
Top 20%	39%	56%	Top 20%	45%
Next 20	26	27	Next 20	28
Next 20	20	13	Next 20	18
Next 20	14	4	Next 20	9
Last 20	1	—	Last 20	—

Although these data are about ten years old, the principle of concentration still applies today and has been verified by W. R. Simmons (1973). And, significantly, the homes that comprise these quintiles tend to be different homes; hence, they complement each other to even out impact levels. A Brand Rating Index Study revealed that exposure to magazines tends to be heavier among homes with upper incomes and adults under 49 years of age, while the reverse is true for TV. Homes with three or more members do both more reading and viewing than with one or two members.

The two recommended media and their vehicles and usage patterns are discussed in the following sections.

Magazines are recommended because of their ability to provide above-average coverage of and frequency against our target audiences and home-makers in the fourth and fifth TV quintiles, who do little TV viewing. This matter of frequency in print advertising has not been thoroughly researched and documented recently, as the only element of frequency that appears in any of the syndicated services' printouts is that created by duplication of readership between magazines. Completely ignored by the researchers is the matter of multiple referrals by the same homemaker. It is our belief that print frequency could conservatively be double the levels reported. As evidence, please note the number of read-days per book recorded by the Simmons study of 1973:

	Reading days per reader
Reader's Digest	4.5
Good Housekeeping	3.3
Better Homes & Gardens	3.0
Family Circle	3.5
Woman's Day	3.8
McCall's	3.5

Further, except for one general-interest magazine, the selected magazines are edited for women and will afford us the privilege of speaking to her in her language, while borrowing interest from a compatible editorial environment. This editorial furnishes our prospects with ideas, information, and help, which provoke reader involvement, action, and response.

Insertions will be scheduled during all months of the year to provide the continuity believed necessary to remind our prospects to buy and try *Grease relief.* Four-color bleed half-page spreads are recommended in six national and one regional magazine. These facing units are envisioned as an effective way to sell more than one usage of *Grease relief.* The recommended magazines are discussed below.

Good Housekeeping, Better Homes & Gardens, Family Circle, and *Woman's Day* are truly the service magazines in the women's grouping and are the magazines to which homemakers refer frequently when performing household duties. Following is the proportion of service editorial in major women's magazines as reported by Lloyd Hall in 1975:

	*Service editorial**
Good Housekeeping	53%
Better Homes & Gardens	58
Family Circle	66
Woman's Day	74
McCall's	51
Ladies' Home Journal	48
Redbook	36

* Beauty, children, food, health, home, and apparel.

Reader's Digest is the basic coverage magazine of all magazines with its mass circulation of 18 million and its audience of 15 million among women of 18–49 years. This magazine alone reaches 34 percent of all women with each issue.

These audience levels exceed those of most primetime TV shows. Again, it should be noted that despite its great audiences, the *Digest* does skew in the direction of our target audience, with almost 40 percent coverage of women in households with incomes of $15,000 and more, or 60 percent greater than its level among women in homes with less than $5,000 income. And, as with the reading patterns of the women's magazines, readers refer back to the *Digest* several times during the life of each issue.

In addition to the above usage of *Reader's Digest,* we are recommending two coupon carriers as follows:

a. Carolyn Davis Shopping Values Unit in May 1977 as an overlay to the off-label promotion on 32 oz.
b. Four-color, one-half page bleed with Pop-Up Coupon "Co-op with Glass*Plus" in August 1976.

McCall's was selected over the other remaining women's magazines because of its editorial thrust toward the "new suburban homemaker" and the fact that it is currently the most vital in the sense of ad page gains from a year ago. Interestingly too, it is becoming more service oriented, with a 14 percent gain in editorial pages during the first half of 1975.

Southern Living is a must for inclusion despite its relatively high CPM (all regionals are quite high) because there is a 16 percent deficiency in the combined circulations of the national magazines in the South. *Southern Living* is *the* magazine of the South and has shown a steady growth since its inception, in terms of both circulation and advertising pages.

On the other hand, certain other magazines were considered but not recommended for this fiscal year at our budget level for the following reasons:

Ladies' Home Journal because it is not considered as vital as *McCall's.*

Redbook and *Cosmopolitan* because they have the smallest circulations and audiences within our target groups, add the least unduplicated reach to our combination, and are generally less efficient.

Sunset was not included as there is no evidence of a deficiency in either gross circulation or time spent reading per page of the recommended national magazines among women on the West Coast. This is not to say that *Sunset* should never be used for *Grease relief,* because there are readership pluses for *Sunset* with respect to all other print vehicles. However, at the current budget level it is not affordable.

Television is again recommended as the other primary medium for *Grease relief* because it is an effective way of demonstrating product attributes to consumers.

Within the medium of television, we are recommending the use of daytime only by reason of its being the basic daypart for reaching full-time homemakers frequently and efficiently. Full-time homemakers are thought to be the best prospects for *Grease relief,* and it is common knowledge that heavy buyers of most household commodities buy four–five times as much as other buyers, so it is important to concentrate on these better prospects.

A Nielsen study of the past on the subject of maximizing reach at a specified frequency clearly displayed that at a frequency of four or more commercials per home per month, daytime only was superior to either a combination of half day and half prime or half day and half fringe. The same spending level was used in all three alternatives, and the division within daypart combinations was on the basis of equal dollars. These data are tabulated below:

	NTI—four weeks		*Reach @ four or more*	*Larger families (three or more)*	*Housewives under 50 years*
All homes	*Reach*	*Frequency*			
All daytime	53.7%	5.9	28.0%	28.6%	28.6
Half day–half prime	58.3	3.8	21.7	21.8	21.3
Half day–half fringe	55.9	4.4	25.6	27.3	28.9

Further, the reach of daytime only was greater in each of the top three quintiles of daytime viewers, where most of the full-time homemakers are found:

	NTI—quintile analysis		
	Day	*Half day and half prime*	*Half day and half fringe*
Top 20%	85%	81%	78%
Next 20	81	77	73
Next 20	74	68	66
Next 20	36	48	44
Last 20	*	28	27

* Less than 1 percent.

The above level of TV usage is higher than that which we contemplate, but the expenditure is probably close to our planned expenditure due to the substantial increases in media costs over the past several years. Also, the lower the level of activity, the better daytime only looks comparatively.

The recommendation calls for 48 weeks of television during the year—24 weeks of 50 GRPs of daytime 30s and 24 weeks of 45–50 points of daytime 10s (product mentions on daytime game shows for name registration), modified by the seasonality of category sales (two-thirds light duty and one-third soil/stain). The 30s will be scheduled during the first six weeks of each quarter year, followed directly by six weeks of 10s.

Except for *Southern Living* and 50 percent additional spending in the test markets, we are not contemplating the use of any other local/regional media because national media are far more efficient and the $2 million media budget does not permit the luxury of regional heavy-ups.

As in the past, we have not recommended special efforts in either Alaska or Hawaii because their TV rating levels are quite similar to those in the rest of the United States, and all of the magazines have fair representations in both states.

Working women, although not our primary target audience, were not neglected in our considerations. In terms of our daytime TV efforts, the impact levels will be about 70–75 percent as great against all women, while our magazines are 7 percent above average against working women.

Other media plans were reviewed but not recommended. The two most promising alternatives were either all TV or all magazines, but neither was as desirable as the half-and-half plan, because the all-print plan lacked provable frequency (duplicate referrals by the same woman), while the all-TV plan was lower in reach:

	Estimated per cycle	
	Reach	*Frequency*
Recommended plan (half TV, half magazines)	85%	5–6
All TV (half day, half fringe)	70–75	7–8
All magazines	80	3–4

4. Media plan: 1976–1977 fiscal year

Network television	$ 991,125
Day 30s—1,230 GRPs—$915,900	
Day 10s—1,110 GRPs—$75,225	
Magazines	$1,064,722
a. Half-page, four-color bleed spread units	
Better Homes & Gardens—$51,061 (1 ×), $45,794 (2 ×)	$ 142,649
Family Circle—$44,572 (2 ×), $37,886 (1 ×),$40,115 (1 ×)	167,145
Good Housekeeping—$32,803 (4 ×)	131,212
McCall's—$34,299 (3 ×)	102,897
Woman's Day—$42,981 (2 ×), $35,780 (1 ×)	121,742
Reader's Digest—$64,995 (3 ×)	194,985
Southern Living—$16,148 (4 ×)	64,592
	$ 925,222
b. Other units—*Reader's Digest*	
Carolyn Davis Shopping Values unit	$ 58,750
Four-color, half-page bleed with pop-up coupon	80,750
	$ 139,500
Total media	$2,055,847

Expenditures by quarter

	Magazines	*Television*	*Total*
1976			
First quarter, July–September	$ 355,951	$299,028	$ 654,979
Second quarter, October–December	235,798	225,480	461,278
1977			
Third quarter, January–March	240,607	179,745	420,352
Fourth quarter April–June	232,366	286,872	519,238
Total	$1,064,722	$991,125	$2,055,847

Figure 12–7
Flowchart of *Grease relief* television advertising schedule, 1976–1977 fiscal year

texize ADVERTISING SCHEDULE

BRAND GREASE RELIEF - TELEVISION

Mondays: July 30, 7, 14, 21; August 28, 4, 11, 18; September 25, 1, 8, 15, 22; October 29, 6, 13, 20; November 27, 3, 10, 17, 24; December 1, 8, 15, 22; January 29, 5, 12, 19; February 26, 2, 9, 16; March 23, 2, 9, 16, 23; April 30, 6, 13, 20; May 27, 4, 11, 18, 25; June 1, 8, 15, 22

	FIRST QUARTER (July–August)	FIRST QUARTER (August–September)	SECOND QUARTER (October–November)	SECOND QUARTER (November–December)	THIRD QUARTER (January–February)	THIRD QUARTER (February–March)	FOURTH QUARTER (April–May)	FOURTH QUARTER (May–June)	$
DAYTIME 30's									915.9
GRP's/WEEK	65/wk		45/wk		40/wk		55/wk		
GRP's/FLIGHT	390		270		240		330		
TOTAL = 1,230 GRP's									
DAYTIME 10's									75.2
GRP's/WEEK		60/wk		40/wk		35/wk		50/wk	
GRP's/FLIGHT		360		240		210		300	
TOTAL = 1,110 GRP's									
TOTAL TV DOLLARS									991.1
4 Week									
All Homes									
Reach	50–55%	50%	45–50%	40–45%	40–45%	35–40%	50%	50%	
Frequency	5	4–5	3–4	3–4	3–4	3–4	4–5	4	
Target Group									
Reach	55%	50%	50%	45%	45%	40–45%	50%	50%	
Frequency	5–6	5	4	3–4	3–4	3–4	5	5	
Flight									
All Homes									
Reach	60%	60%	50–55%	50%	50%	45–50%	55%	55%	
Frequency	6–7	6	5	5	4–5	5	6	5–6	
Target Group									
Reach	60–65%	60%	55%	50–55%	50%+	50%	60%	55–60%	
Frequency	6–7	6–7	5–6	5	5	5	6–7	6	

Figure 12–8
Flowchart of *Grease relief* magazine advertising schedule, 1976–1977 fiscal year

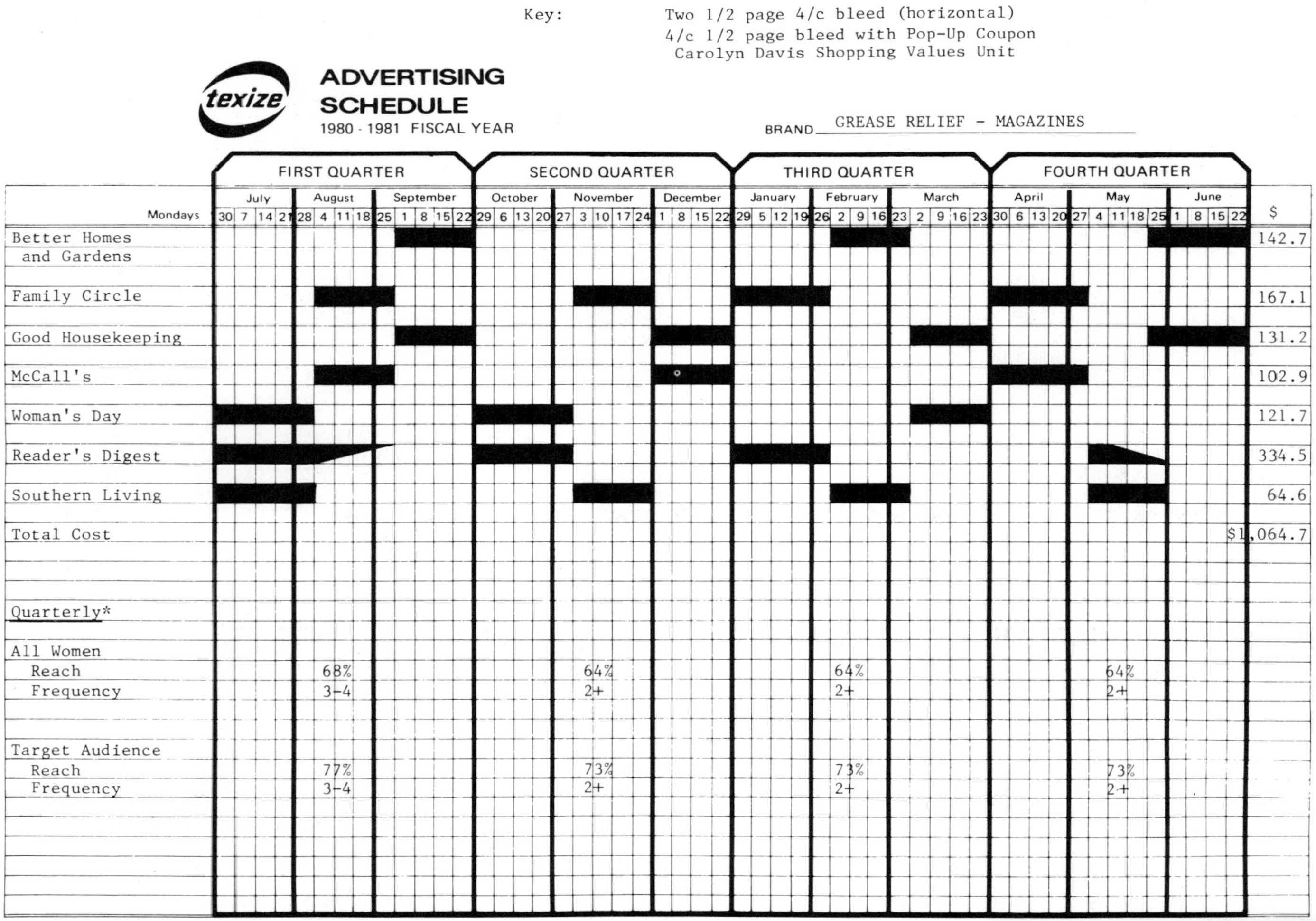

Key:
Two 1/2 page 4/c bleed (horizontal)
4/c 1/2 page bleed with Pop-Up Coupon
Carolyn Davis Shopping Values Unit
texize
ADVERTISING SCHEDULE
1980 - 1981 FISCAL YEAR
BRAND GREASE RELIEF - MAGAZINES
FIRST QUARTER
SECOND QUARTER
THIRD QUARTER
FOURTH QUARTER
July
August
September
October
November
December
January
February
March
April
May
June
Mondays
30 7 14 21 28 4 11 18 25 1 8 15 22 29 6 13 20 27 3 10 17 24 1 8 15 22 29 5 12 19 26 2 9 16 23 2 9 16 23 30 6 13 20 27 4 11 18 25 1 8 15 22
$
Better Homes and Gardens 142.7
Family Circle 167.1
Good Housekeeping 131.2
McCall's 102.9
Woman's Day 121.7
Reader's Digest 334.5
Southern Living 64.6
Total Cost $1,064.7
Quarterly*
All Women
Reach 68% 64% 64% 64%
Frequency 3-4 2+ 2+ 2+
Target Audience
Reach 77% 73% 73% 73%
Frequency 3-4 2+ 2+ 2+

* Based on Simmons run—*Southern Living*'s reach and frequency estimated.

Expenditures by month

	Magazines	Television	Total
1976			
July	$ 116,923	$229,190	$ 346,113
August	155,164	57,838	213,002
September	83,864	12,000	95,864
October	107,976	174,150	282,126
November	60,720	43,080	103,800
December	67,102	8,250	75,352
Six-month totals	$ 591,749	$524,508	$1,116,257
1977			
January	$ 102,881	$137,600	$ 240,481
February	61,942	34,833	96,775
March	75,784	7,312	83,096
April	78,871	222,310	301,181
May	74,898	54,512	129,410
June	78,597	10,050	88,647
Six-month totals	$ 472,973	$466,617	$ 939,590
Twelve-month totals	$1,064,722	$991,125	$2,055,847

Estimated *Grease relief* quarterly audiences, TV and magazines combined

	All homes	Target group
First quarter		
Reach	90–95%	90–95%
Frequency	10–11	11–12
Second quarter		
Reach	90%	90%
Frequency	7–8	8–9
Third quarter		
Reach	85–90%	90%
Frequency	6–7	7–8
Fourth quarter		
Reach	90–95%	90–95%
Frequency	8–9	9–10

Grease relief magazines, division of reading*

	Quarterly	
	Reach	*Frequency*†
Among reading quintiles		
All women	67%	2.2
Top 20%	90	3.7
Next 20	85	2.4
Next 20	75	1.8
Nex 20	5	1.2
Last 20	25	1.0
Among day-viewing quintiles		
All women	67%	2.2
Top 20%	61	2.1
Next 20	67	2.2
Next 20	70	2.3
Next 20	70	2.3
Last 20	67	2.2

* Estimated from Nielsen quintile data.
† Does not include frequency created by duplicate referrals.

Grease relief television,* division of viewing:†
Day-viewing quintiles

	Quarterly	
	Reach	*Frequency*
All women	65%	6–7
Top 20%	95	11.7
Next 20	90	6.0
Next 20	80	3.3
Nex 20	45	1.8
Last 20	20	1.0

Grease relief magazines and television, division of reading and viewing: Day-viewing quintiles

	Quarterly	
	Reach	*Frequency*
All women	90%	8–9
Top 20%	98	12.7
Next 20	96	7.1
Next 20	94	4.4
Next 20	85	2.8
Last 20	70	2.1

* Day 10s included at one third the weight of day 30s.
† Estimated from Nielsen quintile data.

1975–1976 revised plan versus 1976–1977 recommended plan

Network television

	1975–76		1976–77	
	Total GRPs	*Number of weeks*	*Total GRPs*	*Number of weeks*
Prime 30s	556	4	—	—
News 30s	640	8	—	—
Day 30s	2,048	23	1,230	24
Day 10s	2,120	40	1,110	24

	1975–76	*1976–77*
Network television	\$2,729,434 (86%)	\$ 991,125 (48%)
Magazines	\$ 455,594 (14%)	\$1,064,722 (52%)
Total budget	\$3,185,028 (100%)	\$2,055,847 (100%)

QUESTIONS

1. What are the two major purposes of the media plan?

2. How does the media plan fit into the total marketing program of a firm?

3. What is the purpose of a media flowchart?

4. How does the media schedule differ from the media strategy section of the media platform?

5. Discuss the purpose of each of the following:
   a. Media request form.
   b. Space or time contract.
   c. Insertion order.

13

POSTSCHEDULING MANAGEMENT TECHNIQUES

ONCE THE MEDIA schedule has been prepared, four tasks remain in the advertising process. First, the media must actually be purchased. Second, the schedule must be monitored so that ads appear at the planned time and place. Third, adjustments to the schedule must be made when circumstances require them. Finally, the efficiency of the media plan as well as the success of the advertising campaign should be measured.

SUPERVISING THE ACTUAL MEDIA PURCHASE

In the purchase of broadcast media time, negotiation is the primary basis for transactions. In Chapter 5, an example chronology for buying network television time (Figure 5–6) is presented, as are the procedures for purchasing spot and local television time. Similarly the general negotiation process for radio time purchase is detailed in Chapter 6.

Any business negotiation has the objective of producing an agreement, between buyer and seller, on the terms and conditions of a sale. In order to produce this agreement, each party advances proposals, has them evaluated by the other party, who then offers counterproposals. In theory this process continues until either a mutually agreeable contract is arrived at or until no further discussion is necessary since agreement seems beyond reach.

GUIDELINES FOR SUCCESSFUL NEGOTIATION

In other areas of business, where negotiations are often public and bitter, and where agreement is often not reached, several guides to successful negotiation have emerged. Some of these are listed below:

1. Learn to prepare for the negotiation. Buyers should know the details of the available money and the budget tolerances (overages-shortages), if any, the nominal or published rate and discount structure, and the performance of the medium (e.g., show or daypart ratings) insofar as possible. Obviously, the purchase of time in future shows deals with situations for which there is no available rating.

2. Learn about the persons with whom you will deal. Especially during the first meeting, try to establish a relaxed, friendly, cooperative atmosphere.

3. Learn the value of a change in subject. If it seems that agreement on a particular issue (say, the price of an ad in a particular show or daypart) is not near, table this issue and go on to others. Often resolution of the tabled problem will emerge as part of other discussions.

4. Learn to be a good listener. It is good psychology to let a person finish a statement. If the term or condition or price is different from what you will accept, there will be time to discuss the difference *after* the other party finishes presenting the proposal.

5. Learn that haste makes waste. Generally, attempts by one party to "hurry" the negotiation are resented by the other, and this resentment can poison the bargaining. A pause in the bargaining, in the form of a coffee or lunch break, or a late afternoon suggestion to pick up talks again in the morning can provide a creative opportunity for both parties to evaluate the progress made so far.

6. Learn how to be a good questioner. Try to question the "facts" and the statistical evidence offered by the other party in a way that will let you learn what these data really mean.

7. Learn to identify which processes and techniques work best. No one benefits from anger, emotion, and irritation.

8. Learn to avoid public statements or positions until the agreement is reached. Public positions are much harder to adjust by compromise than nonpublic positions.

9. Learn to emphasize areas of common agreement. These can be the negotiating bridge to areas of remaining differences.

10. Learn that it never pays to take advantage of the other party. It is sometimes tempting to seize an unfair short-term advantage. However, over the interval of many seasons, many campaigns, and many media negotiations, taking unfair advantage (setting aside whatever ethical demerits this may produce) is almost certain to result in present bitterness and future retribution.

As you can see from these suggestions, negotiation is more art than science, and more demanding of interpersonal skills than are other areas of media management. And the problems of television time supplies and radio "network" variations have already been covered.

INTERMEDIA EQUIVALENCIES

For either broadcast or print media schedules, the media plan begins with a statement of objectives. Then the media mix is selected with an eye toward meeting these objectives. An important aspect of this mix is the development of comparable units among media.

Chapter 4, you will recall, listed and described ten standards for media evaluation. These were reach, composition, cost per thousand, frequency, audience turnover, ratings, audience share, Gross Rating Points, audience overlap, and cost per rating point. Some of these measures, especially Gross Rating Points and audience overlap, have been discussed in the intervening chapters. We refer to these to emphasize the role some "standards" play in developing intermedia comparisons.

The practitioner relies most heavily on GRPs to make intermedia comparisons. If one keeps in mind the substantive, fundamental differences between the broadcast media and other media, this method of comparison can work reasonably well. For instance, consider the recent acceptance of the GRP standard by the outdoor advertising industry, although you will easily recall that an "outdoor" GRP is different from, say, a "TV" GRP.

In print advertising, the use of cost per thousand seems to emerge as the method of comparing media or media classes. Newspapers thus become more comparable with magazines in spite of the fact that newspapers compete more directly with other media for audiences.

What has largely eluded media planners is general agreement about the print versus broadcast equivalencies. While cost per thousand (of target market members) can be and sometimes is applied to broadcast advertising, the application of ratings to print advertising has never been enthusiastically attempted. In practice, advertising objectives for a single campaign are often set in the form of GRPs for broadcast media and CPM for print media. Further, both reach and frequency objectives are often stated.

In a recent study of intermedia equivalencies, Sissors[1] reviewed

[1] Jack Z. Sissors, "Problems of Finding an Adequate Response Function for Media Planning," in *Making Advertising Relevant, Proceedings of the 1975 American Academy of Advertising,* ed. L. W. Sanfranco, pp. 152–54.

nine practical bases for intermedia comparisons. He concluded that the fundamental problem is the absence of an adequate response function and that the major contributing factor is a lack of agreement over what should be measured, especially the "dependent" variables.

MONITORING THE ADVERTISING CAMPAIGN

The second major managerial responsibility for a media schedule is the monitoring activity by which the scheduled times and places are verified. Not only must the advertising appear as planned (and the verification here can be more complicated than you would expect), but the adjacent communications must also be scrutinized.

Verification of broadcast advertising

For radio and television, verification should take the form of an affidavit signed by a broadcast station official that a particular ad was run at a specified time and entered in that station's program log. This affidavit has been cooperatively expanded by the Radio Advertising Bureau (RAB), the Television Bureau of Advertising (TvB), and the Association of National Advertisers to include not only the air time information but also the price of the commercial and a copy of the script. This combined form is particularly useful in preventing abuses in cooperative retail advertising, discussed more fully later. An example is presented in Figure 13–1.

Verification of print advertising

For print advertising verification, the usual procedure is for the medium (e.g., the newspaper) to "tear" out the entire page on which the advertisement appears and to furnish this to the advertiser or the agency. In addition a duplicate of the invoice showing effective prices is sometimes furnished. In certain cases, especially legal notices, an affidavit is also furnished.

Makegoods, rebates, and rip-offs

The verification procedures described so far are incomplete in some respects. They do not, of themselves, monitor the immediate environment in which an ad is broadcast, nor do they completely preclude opportunities for chicanery.

To handle the problem of the messages which surround a particular broadcast ad, broadcasters furnish advertisers with certain guarantees. These are often stated on rate cards or in the SRDS rate

Figure 13–1
Broadcast verification form

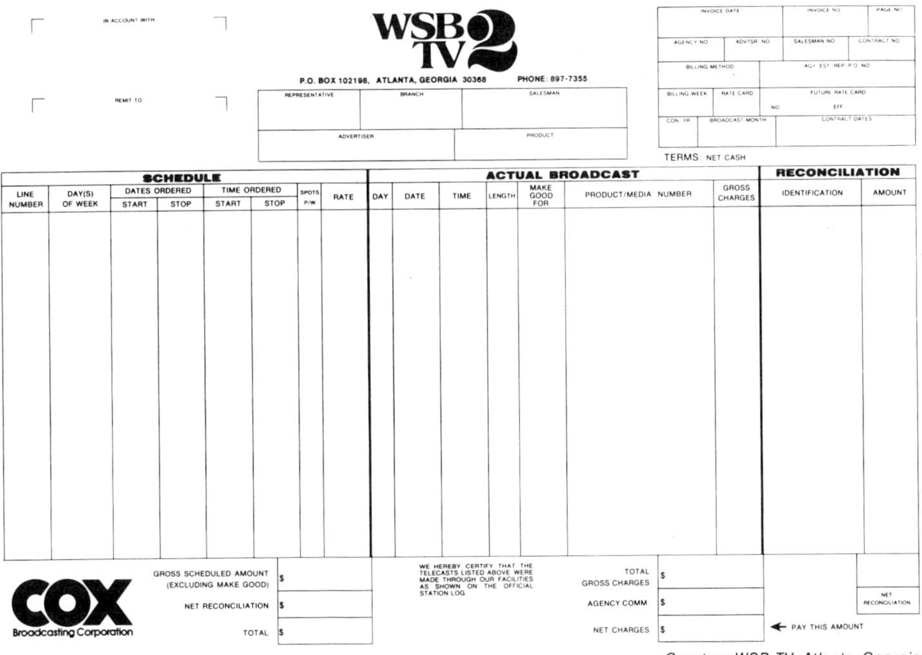

IN ACCOUNT WITH

REMIT TO

WSB TV 2

P.O. BOX 102198, ATLANTA, GEORGIA 30368 PHONE: 897-7355

REPRESENTATIVE	BRANCH	SALESMAN
ADVERTISER		PRODUCT

INVOICE DATE		INVOICE NO		PAGE NO
AGENCY NO	ADVTSR NO	SALESMAN NO	CONTRACT NO	
BILLING METHOD		AGY EST REP P.O. NO		
BILLING WEEK	RATE CARD	FUTURE RATE CARD NO EFF		
CON YR	BROADCAST MONTH	CONTRACT DATES		

TERMS: NET CASH

SCHEDULE								ACTUAL BROADCAST							RECONCILIATION	
LINE NUMBER	DAY(S) OF WEEK	DATES ORDERED		TIME ORDERED		SPOTS P/W	RATE	DAY	DATE	TIME	LENGTH	MAKE GOOD FOR	PRODUCT/MEDIA NUMBER	GROSS CHARGES	IDENTIFICATION	AMOUNT
		START	STOP	START	STOP											

COX Broadcasting Corporation

GROSS SCHEDULED AMOUNT (EXCLUDING MAKE GOOD) $

NET RECONCILIATION $

TOTAL $

WE HEREBY CERTIFY THAT THE TELECASTS LISTED ABOVE WERE MADE THROUGH OUR FACILITIES AS SHOWN ON THE OFFICIAL STATION LOG.

TOTAL GROSS CHARGES $

AGENCY COMM $

NET CHARGES $ ← PAY THIS AMOUNT

NET RECONCILIATION

Courtesy WSB-TV, Atlanta, Georgia

books. They can be negotiated as part of the advertising time purchase. Examples of such guarantees by broadcasters, often called "product protection" promises, are:

> "Station will endeavor, but cannot guarantee, to provide product protection of at least ten minutes."
>
> "Station will use reasonable care at all times to avoid scheduling of advertising in an obviously competitive atmosphere."
>
> "Station will endeavor to provide a minimum of 15 minutes' separation between directly competitive products when both commercials are originated by the station."
>
> "Station guarantees against running competitive products back to back only."

Most broadcasters offer advertising credits, or "makegoods," only when ads for directly competing products are aired back to back and when the station (as opposed to the network and station) originates the advertising message. Management of the media schedule usually involves spot checks of the client's advertising (or the station logs) to ensure that product protection contract clauses have been observed by the broadcaster. If such promises are not kept, the broadcaster usually provides either a "free" ad in an "equivalent" time or else credits the advertiser with the cost of that particular ad.

In the short run, similar "conflicts" may exist between ads and the surrounding editorial or program material. Examples of such conflicts can be found in a political ad which is aired during a movie portraying politicians as venal or in an ad for a particular product which is placed within a story disparaging that product. Virtually no media enterprise offers product protection guarantees against this eventuality, though its regular occurrence would have unfavorable consequences for the broadcaster's or publisher's advertising revenues. This problem is most often handled in the negotiations for space or time, especially by advertisers who use the medium regularly.

Verification procedures also require the prevention (or, more realistically, the minimization) of "double billing" and "double stapling." These abuses occur most often in cooperative retail advertising, in the print and broadcast media, respectively. While the details of such scams are varied, they are basically the substitution of an "unauthorized" message or an "inflated" rate for advertising purchased cooperatively by the manufacturer and the retailer. Verification procedures have been tightened by the industry to prevent double billing. However, since this rip-off requires conspiracy between media officials and retailers, such measures as affidavits are only a partial answer. Complete verification procedures should include reasonable measures to detect double billing, especially for advertising campaigns which employ significant amounts of co-op advertising.

ADJUSTING THE SCHEDULE DURING THE CAMPAIGN

In the discussion of media-buying processes presented in Chapter 4, we suggested that it would be foolhardy to construct a media plan in ignorance of what advertisers of similar products are doing. It would be equally foolish to disregard changes in the competitive environment during the life of the campaign.

Changes in the competitive environment

As you recall from Chapter 4, the size and the timing of competitive pressure were incorporated into the media plan in one of three ways: wave theory, media dominance, or media concentration. All three methods of dealing with competition reflect the fact that most advertising budgets are not large enough to overwhelm all competition in all media at all times. In fact, there are good managerial reasons for not even attempting to outspend all competitors on all fronts. But depending on the strategy used in building the media plan, changes in the competitive environment during the campaign can produce a situation which requires adjustments to the media plan.

In *wave theory,* a large "wave" (or burst or flight) of advertising is followed by a hiatus (or pause). It is hoped that the wave's impact will be sufficient to produce audience impressions which will carry through the hiatus.

Recall also the problem identified in Figure 4–4, where a planned wave theory campaign is simply overwhelmed by competitive expenditures. In this situation, continuing with the planned schedule is likely to produce disappointing results. Among the adjustments which might be considered are:

Increasing the budget to "competitive" levels.

Increasing the expenditure during the wave period, and increasing the length of the hiatus, so that fewer, larger bursts of advertising match the competition without increasing the total budget.

Switching to an alternative strategy.

The second strategy, *media dominance,* permits the advertiser to "beat" the competition in a single medium for a specified time period, then switch to the dominance of a second medium, and so on. Of course this strategy is likely to have maximum success only if the medium used is, in fact, "dominated."

If, during a campaign planned around media dominance, competitive expenditures are much larger than expected, the planned dominance may not be achieved. In this instance, some of the possible adjustments are:

Increasing the budget to "competitive" levels.

Rearranging the sequence in which media are to be used. For example the sequence newspaper—metro magazine—outdoor might become newspaper—outdoor—metro magazine. Such a rephasing of the schedule, even without additional expenditure, may permit the reestablishment of dominance.

Incorporating wave theory into the plan. In the dominated medium, the advertiser might use a burst-pause sequence which creates the impression of "dominance" among the audience.

Switching to an alternative strategy.

The third strategy, *media concentration,* can also encounter unexpected competitive pressure. Since this strategy requires the selection of a single "best" medium, an unexpected competitive development can turn "best" into "not so good" or worse. Here the alternatives for adjustment include:

Increasing the budget to "competitive" levels.
Selecting another "best" medium.
Incorporating wave theory within the single medium used.

Changes in the editorial environment

The development of a media plan must, of course, take account of the editorial environment in which the advertising is to appear. Media planners are required to look beyond the numbers (such as GRP or CPM) to select editorial formats which will be harmonious with the advertising messages.

This editorial ambience can be pictured as the intellectual and emotional river which carries the advertiser's canoe. And as is the case with wilderness explorers, when the direction of the river deviates from the planned route, it may become necessary to leave the river and use another route.

Editorial environments are almost never static. However, changes in these environments can occur at either of two rates: evolutionary and revolutionary. Examples of evolutionary change include the expansion or contraction of a particular section in a newspaper or magazine, minor reformatting of a television news show, and the addition or deletion of a syndicated feature by a local radio station. Revolutionary changes can be produced by major changes in editorial policy (such as the recent decision of two television networks not to accept an advertisement of a major energy corporation) or by external events. Strikes which force the suspension of publication or major criticism of a television show by an influential group are examples of such externalities.

Changes in the client organization

In a fundamental sense, media planning is a staff function undertaken in support of the client organization's marketing objectives. When these objectives change, the supporting media plans must be reexamined and often recalculated to be consistent with the new objectives. Among the events which can produce revised marketing objectives for the advertiser are a new corporate philosophy, a new chief executive, technological breakthroughs which result in new or modified products, new competitive products, governmental action in the form of product recalls, the granting of patents, and new licensing for production and sale. These and many other events can produce changes in marketing objectives which must, in turn, be reflected in altered media plans.

Regardless of their source, adjustments to a carefully prepared media plan are not without risk. Adjustments which take the form of spending more money for advertising increase the capital investment. In the language of capital budgeting, such decisions increase the cash outflow and thereby increase the overall risk of the capital project. Adjustments which alter the placement, timing, or media mix of the original plan are accompanied with the very real prospect of canceling out bulk or continuity media discounts which had been an important part of the plan. And, of course, some media, especially television, have at least short-term limitations on the available inventory of space or time available for sale. Finally, the process of adjustment and replanning is itself a cost-incurring activity.

Prudence requires that adjustment costs be considered before adjustments to the media plan are implemented. But prudence also requires that a media plan which has been seriously invalidated by changes in the competition, the editorial environment, or the advertiser's marketing objectives be reconsidered. Adjustments which can be accomplished at reasonable cost and materially improve the prospects for advertising success are an important part of postscheduling management of the media plan. The calculation of "reasonable" costs can be developed by use of a decision tree of the type discussed in Chapter 2. The measurement of advertising success is the subject of the next section of this chapter.

EVALUATING THE EFFICIENCY OF THE MEDIA PLAN

It may seem evident that for advertising to be successful it must be efficient. And we can intuitively relate to the axiom that advertising, which is a cost-incurring activity, must produce returns above its costs to be economically justified. But to develop a more systematic understanding of advertising success, it is helpful to understand the concept of efficiency.

What is efficiency?

The most useful notion of efficiency is an amalgam of economic theory and simple arithmetic. In this notion efficiency is defined as the simple ratio of output to input when both are measured in constant units, say dollars. Thus, if some process costs $10 to perform and produces $15 of returns, its efficiency is $15 ÷ $10, or 1.5.

In the physical and mechanical world in which we live, many processes are notoriously inefficient. If we measure the energy value of gasoline and the energy value produced by gasoline engines in autos, we find that the efficiency ratios fall in the range of .15 to .30. That is, less than a third of the energy value of the gasoline we put in a car is converted to energy used to move the car. The balance is wasted, mostly in the form of heat. And one of the most efficient areas of agriculture, fish farming, requires about 1.15 pounds of feed to produce a pound of fish. This is equivalent to an efficiency of $1 \div 1.15$, or about 87 percent.

In regard to advertising efficiency in general, and media efficiency in particular, it is relatively easy to measure the input side of the ratio. Net advertising expenditures (after allowances, discounts, and rebates) are combined with the cost of the human resources employed (i.e., wages and salaries) and the administrative or overhead costs required to produce the campaign. The sophisticated practitioner (and student) will then use these dollar inputs to calculate the net present value of the advertising project. This produces a relatively unambiguous measure of the input required for a particular advertising effort.

Unlike the horsepower of auto engines and the weight of catfish, which are outputs amenable to relatively unambiguous measurement, the output of an advertising campaign is often the subject of lively debate and disagreement among the interested parties. This controversy about advertising output can be divided into two problems: What is the proper set of goals or objectives for the ad campaign, and what are the proper methods of measuring the level at which those goals or objectives were realized.

As was suggested in Chapter 1, advertising objectives can be stated on one, two, or three levels: communications output, sales output, or profitability output. Of these three levels, the first two are the most frequently used measures of advertising success. These two are most often measured by syndicated research services or by other "custom job"–type research firms. You may wish to review, from Figure 2–7, the identities and sizes of the major advertising research firms in the United States.

Communicative efficiency of the media plan

In circumstances where the communications level has been chosen to express advertising objectives, the measurement of advertising output or results ideally produces answers to three questions:

1. How many persons were exposed to the ad(s)?
2. Who were these persons?
3. To what extent were the exposed persons involved in the ad(s), and what was the nature of this involvement?

A moment's reflection will suggest that the most familiar media statistics, such as reach, frequency, and Gross Rating Points, are largely methods of answering the first question, the extent of exposure. For the broadcast media, the *rating* and subsequent calculations derived from it are based on the exposure level of the program in which the ad was embedded—not necessarily on the exposure level of the ad per se. In print advertising, analogous measures of exposure as well as problems in calculating actual exposure to the ad (versus exposure to the medium) are found in circulation figures. Traffic counts for outdoor locations measure a similar exposure potential rather than a true exposure figure.

Answers to the second question, about audience identity, most often take the form of demographic profiles of the exposed audience or of subgroups within this audience. From the advertiser's viewpoint, this method is usually more useful than research which reveals the identity (name, address, etc.) of individual audience members, though direct mail can furnish the answer to this question in both forms.

Answers to the third question, about the extent and nature of audience involvement with the ad message, are the most varied and are subject to the highest level of controversy. Here mechanical, physiological, psychological, and many other measures have been employed.

You are already familiar with the most prominent measures of exposure and audience identity, those furnished by Nielsen and Arbitron for broadcast advertising. You are also cognizant of services such as Starch, which provide indications of audience involvement in print advertising. To provide a better overview of how advertising practitioners calculate communicative success, as well as the role which research firms play in furnishing these answers, Figure 13–2 has been prepared. While this is not an exhaustive list of such research companies, the firms listed have given permission to be included in this text. Their services are representative of the available measurements of advertising success.

Sales efficiency of the media plan

The second level of advertising objectives, sales results, has the benefit of being measured in the same units as advertising inputs, namely dollars. Thus, the expressions of advertising and media efficiency are more directly formed than the expressions of communication objectives. Sales objectives can also be expressed in terms such as brand share, market share, repurchase rate, and other measures which convert to dollar values.

The crucial problem in using sales as a measure of efficiency is the

Figure 13–2
Examples of firms which provide advertising research

Research firm	*How much exposure?*	*Who were exposed?*	*Nature/extent of involvement?*	*Dependent or criterion variable(s) measured*	*Most common regular reports/comments*
A. C. Nielsen Company (Media Research Services Group)	Yes	Yes	No	Ratings, audience demographics	See Figure 5–10 for listing of major Nielsen TV reports
ADTEL (Burke subsidiary)	Yes*	Yes	Yes	Copy, media schedule, budgets, promotion, products distribution * Via Nielsen ratings	Custom reports primarily designed to show sales effectiveness of TV ads. Incorporates cable-broadcast ads.
Arbitron Company	Yes	Yes	No	Ratings, audience demographics	Network Program Analysis Syndicated Program Analysis Arbitron Television USA Supersweep Television Markets and Rankings TAPP Reports Also basic research reports on methodology, reliability, control of research contamination
Burke Marketing Research Company	No	Yes	Yes	Audience profiles, recognition, recall	Burke D.A.R. (for television) and Burke Standard Print test for magazines.
Cahners Publishing Company	Yes	Yes	Yes	Recognition, recall, audience profiles, market position studies, buyer behavior studies	*CARR* reports, others
CASS Student Advertising, Inc.	No	Yes	Yes	Attitudes, audience profiles, and buyer behavior of college students	CASS *Profile of Students as Consumers, National Rate Book* (for college publications)
Leferman Associates, Inc.	No	Yes	Yes	Attitudes, advertising, trading, corporate identity, many other marketing variables	Custom reports

Market Statistics	No	No	See →	Extensive series of integrated market statistics from public and private sources	*Survey of Buying Power*
McCollum-Spielman	No	No	Yes	Brand awareness, message comprehension, intentions to purchase, sales response	AC-T reports for television; similar reports for other major media
National Family Opinion, Inc.	*	*	*	*	* Providers of mail and telephone research which can be applied to advertising measurements
Plog Research, Inc.	No	No	Yes	Motivations, attitudes, and buyer behavior	Emphasizes custom designs and reports
Rabin Research Co.	No	No	Yes	Perceptions, attitudes, and intentions toward advertised brands	*SEARCH* reports, ohers
Research Systems Corporation	No	Yes	Yes	Brand preference, delayed recall buyer behavior	Uses labratory simulation
Sherman Group, Inc.	No	No	Yes	Recall, comprehension, emtional responses, intentions to purchase	BUY © TEST reports plus custom-designed features
Starch INRA Hooper, Inc.	No	No	Yes	Ad readership levels	Starch Message Report Service
Telcom Research, Inc.	No	No	Yes	Recall plus eye movement and looking intensity measures	Reports available for "visual" media—TV, print, outdoor—and for radio
Winona	No	Yes	Yes	Concept evaluation studies, forced-exposure copy testing, campaign tracking	Custom reports only

accurate linking of sales to the advertising which produced them. In earlier chapters some methods have been suggested for evaluating sales response and decay (e.g., via Vidale-Wolfe or other methods) and for discounting nonadvertising influences (e.g., via experimentation). Here it is important to recognize that not only the client, ad agency, and media enterprise can combine to produce the data required for such a sales-efficiency test of advertising. Some of the research firms which offer such measurement services and examples are identified in Figure 13–2.

TWO METHODOLOGICAL NOTES

The advertising research process was discussed in outline form in Chapter 2. Subsequent chapters, especially Chapters 3, 4, 11, and 12, have provided more detail on how research processes are applied to specific media problems such as budgeting, selecting, buying, and evaluating advertising media. Thus you have already used most of the important concepts first presented in Chapter 2. However, two concepts, *metricity* and the *cost of information,* deserve a final comment in the context of this discussion of advertising research firms.

Regarding metricity, you should be aware that a large volume of basic research suggests that data for variables such as attitudes, opinions, and intentions are nonmetric. While it is true that some scholars and practitioners argue that this feature of such behavioral variables is unimportant—and that metric analysis can be used—you should be aware that substantial decisional risks can be created by using an inappropriate tool. Many of the research firms listed above have the capacity to furnish nometric analysis of nonmetric data. You should consider this in purchasing research which uses these variables.

Regarding the cost of research information, some research reports, such as the CARR Report prepared by Cahners Publishing (and some of the media trade associations), are furnished at no cost. The costs of standard reports, such as those of Arbitron or Nielsen, begin at under $100 per copy. The costs of custom research begins at about $3,000–4,000 for studies using very small samples. The cost for a well-designed custom research project to measure recognition and recall, using a sample of around 300 subjects, is likely to cost $10,000–20,000.

BEYOND SALES RESPONSE

To restate the problems of measuring advertising (and therefore media) efficiency, some dependent variables are less than satisfactory. It is also true that more preferred outcomes are difficult to measure. Virtually all parties agree that exposure measures, such as GRPs, represent only a partial measure of advertising success. On the other hand, attitudes, intentions, and other behavioral measures of inclination to purchase are difficult to measure precisely, and even then are not perfect correlates of sales. Net sales, the most theoretically pleasing dependent variable, is often contaminated by factors other than the current advertising campaign. Such contamination reduces the power of net sales as an output measure for efficiency calculations.

One alternative is to use "owner wealth" measures as the output part of the efficiency calculation. This is easy to do for publicly held firms, since the financial press provides daily figures for the value of common stocks. In this way, the collective wisdom of an information-efficient stock market, after looking at a company's overall success, places a value (price) on its common stock. Thus not only advertising success, but success in the other areas of the firm, is reflected in the price of its stock.

This approach to efficiency is still in its infancy, and not even its enthusiasts claim that it is problem free. It too suffers from some of the measurement contaminants associated with the net sales criterion. And while the possibility is unlikely, this approach could obscure the facts in the firm where poor-to-ordinary advertising is combined with superior performance in other management areas. And in the not-for-profit organization the approach is not possible.

Perhaps the strongest claim for the owner wealth approach is that it brings the question of advertising efficiency into conformity with the "acid test" used by the business community for business success. The units of measurement (dollars) are the same for both sides of the efficiency ratio. And if work progresses in this area, profitability measures of advertising success have great potential as a tool for the overall management of the media function.

QUESTIONS

1. What is the primary basis for the transactions required to purchase advertising media? What are some of the ways in which these transactions are facilitated?

2. How would you summarize the progress made to date in developing effective measures of intermedia equivalency?

3. Construct a sound argument for the abolition of makegoods.

4. List the probable reasons why employees of media enterprises might participate in a double-billing scheme. Make a second list of the reasons why national advertisers continue to tolerate a situation in which double-billing can occur.

5. How can a hiatus be used, under a strategy of media concentration, to make adjustments to changes in the competitive environment?

6. Construct a defensible definition of advertising efficiency.

7. Of the three standards for the communicative efficiency of the media plan, which would be most useful to the advertising client? Why?

14

FUTURE TRENDS IN ADVERTISING MEDIA: EMPLOYMENT AND OPPORTUNITIES

AT THE CONCLUSION of each of the chapters dealing with the various mass media (Chapters 5–10), a particular medium's future outlook was discussed. It is obvious that each of the media faces problems and opportunities which are both unique to itself and dependent on outside forces or related to intermedia developments. The media planner of tomorrow must be both a specialist and a generalist to deal with these problems and opportunities. Naturally the media planner will continue to be a highly trained specialist in media strategy. However, the media planner, and for that matter the business executive with advertising responsibility, will also have to understand the interrelations between advertising media and the firm's basic marketing objectives. This final chapter will concentrate on the media management function. In addition the final section of the chapter will discuss academic training and employment opportunities in advertising media planning.

THE MARKETING REVOLUTION

The past–World War II period was marked by the development of the so-called marketing concept, which supported the idea that the consumer should be the focus of a firm's planning and development. This awareness of the consumer based on a research orientation and an integration of a firm's activities for marketing has significant application for advertising media.

In recent years advertising has come to be viewed as a segment of marketing. Few would question the fact that advertising objectives must flow from the marketing plan and that advertising which operates in ignorance of the firm's general marketing goals is probably going to fail. The problem with this concept of advertising as complementary to marketing is that it is too often neglected in the day-to-day operations of marketing and advertising agencies. The marketing/advertising marriage is often a shaky one, with advertisers sometimes wanting to do "their own thing" in the absence of a thorough knowledge of the marketing plan. Unfortunately the usual result of this attitude is clever, even award-winning, advertising which entertains but rarely sells potential customers. The media planner must resist the temptation to be anything but a marketing professional. While virtually any aspect of advertising planning must have its foundation in marketing, this is especially true for the media function.

Marketing and the financial risks associated with it have made audience segmentation a vital area of study. The job of the media planner centers on the notion of audience segmentation as it logically proceeds from the consumer orientation of the marketing concept. The media planner must first determine the best prospects and then match them with the advertising media most likely to reach these prospects economically.

The media planner must consider two major aspects of advertising media: those which are external to the advertising function and those which are part of the advertising function but not directly under the control of the media department. The media function is a subcategory of two larger functions, advertising and marketing. Within both marketing and advertising strategy certain constraints guide the media planner. Generally it is easier for the media planner to reach compromises among the various parts of the advertising function than to reach compromises between the advertising strategy and the marketing strategy. The marketing plan, on the other hand, generally dictates advertising activities, including media planning.

External marketing constraints on the media planner

1. Budget. Normally the media planner is *given* a budget. Despite the fact that advertising media purchases may account for up to 80 percent of a typical advertising budget, the input of media departments at the initial stages of corporate budgeting remains woefully inadequate.

2. Target audience and competition. The media planner does not determine who is to be reached. Normally the client knows who his best prospects are and the degree of competition which will be encountered in attempting to gain them as customers. As the number of prospects or the aggressiveness of competitors increases, the media buyer must become more efficient with the budget allocated.

3. Price and distribution. The choice of distribution channels and the pricing policy of a product often dictate the choice of advertising media. Decisions in these areas often determine the demographic profile of the potential audience. As discussed in Chapter 4, demographic matching is most often utilized in purchasing media time and space.

4. *Specific product restrictions.* Legal and regulatory restrictions are playing a larger role in advertising than ever before. In addition to the obvious broadcast restrictions applying to advertising for such products as liquor and cigarettes, the media buyer must be aware of a number of other restrictions, including those developed by individual media vehicles. For instance many broadcasters will not accept certain feminine hygiene products and almost 15 percent of weekly newspapers refuse to carry liquor advertising.

Internal marketing constraints on the media function

1. *Creative considerations.* Obviously the adoption of some creative strategies eliminates certain media buys. Product demonstrations are difficult in the print media and impossible in radio. A strategy of coupon promotions must be confined to print vehicles.

2. *Qualitative factors.* Media people are often criticized, and probably with some justification, for an overdependence on numbers. The media buyer must recognize that regardless of what research tells him about reach, frequency, and cost efficiency, the image of the product must be matched with the tone of the various media alternatives.

3. *Message complexity.* In addition to considering the creative approach and the tone of the advertising message, the media planner must consider its length and complexity. For example television and outdoor advertising are unsuitable vehicles for long messages, since only a small amount of information can be conveyed in a 30-second television commercial or an outdoor poster.

Factors largely controlled by the media planner

1. *Choice of media vehicles.* The media planner largely determines which media vehicles will be purchased. These decisions are based on primary and secondary research and may be made in consultation with other members of the advertising and marketing departments. However, the final decision and responsibility for it usually lie with the media planner.

2. *Media scheduling.* A primary responsibility of the media planner is the scheduling of advertising among the media vehicles selected. The skill with which the number and frequency of insertions

are determined separates the professional media planner from the novice. The media planner who makes excessive commitments in certain media vehicles will expend the budget before effectively reaching all prospects. The media planner who buys too many vehicles may spread the advertising impact so thin that effective communication does not take place.

3. Allocating the total budget to the various media components. It is the media planner who initially decides what proportions of the advertising media budget will be allocated to the various components of the media mix. This decision will, of course, be made in consultation with other members of the advertising staff or, in an agency, with the account team.

In summary it should be clear that the media planner, like all advertising personnel, should be marketing oriented. This appreciation of the total marketing program by advertisers is not a one-way street. The wise marketing executive, even where an outside advertising agency is employed, should develop a knowledge of and appreciation for the overall advertising program.

THE MANAGEMENT REVOLUTION

Media planning and the management function

In a simplistic fashion the typical corporation can be characterized as consisting of production, marketing, and finance functions. Corporate management seeks to maximize profitability by operating each of these areas in the most efficient manner possible. While this approach seems commonsensical, it is easier to approve in the abstract than to accomplish in reality.

The management of the advertising function is twofold. First, corporate leadership must be aware of the expense and the accompanying risks of advertising media expenditures. Second, the media function must be creatively managed by those with primary advertising responsibility.

The media function as managed by executives outside the advertising department

The type of control exercised by corporate management over advertising will vary, but typically the media function is carried out by advertising agencies or other outside organizations. However, the responsibility for the control and approval of media selection, or any other advertising task, is the job of the executive overseeing the advertising program. The person in charge of advertising will often be the vice president for marketing or someone in a similar position. Basically the job of this executive is to:

1. Inform the advertising agency of corporate marketing objectives and develop research from which the advertising plan is developed in consultation with the agency.
2. Review and approve the overall advertising strategy developed by the agency.
3. Coordinate the marketing and promotional activities of the firm with advertising. These include, but are not limited to, public relations, sales promotion, sales management, and distribution. The communication function also includes such tasks as representing the advertising department to top corporate management.

The interest of corporate management in advertising has grown in proportion to the greater investment required and the resulting sales success, especially in television advertising, among national advertisers. With annual corporate advertising expenditures often exceeding $50 million and sometimes representing 10 percent or more of total sales, advertising may be a firm's single largest expenditure.

The media responsibility of corporate management is not confined to ensuring the efficient use of advertising expenditures. Top management must also be aware of the public's reaction to the media in which the firm's advertising appears. Despite disclaimers to the contrary, much of the public regards the purchase of time or space as an endorsement of media editorial or entertainment content. Sears Roebuck made a corporate decision to pull its television commercials from such shows as *Charlie's Angels* in response to public criticism of the program's sexual overtones. General Motors has never run an advertisement in *Playboy* despite the fact that the demographics of *Playboy*'s audience match well with the buyers of some GM cars.

The media function and the corporate advertising department

Too often we assume that when a company employs an advertising agency, there is little to be done by the corporate advertising department. Actually several major functions must be performed by the advertising department even when an outside agency is being used:

1. Client-agency liaison. The corporate advertising department has major responsibility for developing a smooth liaison between the agency and the company. This liaison includes checking to make sure that the agency's work meets the client's requirements and that the media budget is being spent efficiently. The degree of input concerning media expenditures varies widely. A few firms leave the media buying solely to the discretion of the agency, while a firm such as Colgate-Palmolive has its own media director to work in concert with its several agencies.

2. *Developing the marketing plan.* Ideally the advertising department should be consulted in the firm's preparation of its overall marketing plan and its advertising budget. Enlightened firms give major input to the advertising department while developing marketing strategy. However, too many firms still complete their marketing strategies without consulting the advertising department and then simply direct the advertising department or the outside agency to draw up a complementary advertising plan.

3. *Choosing an advertising agency.* Normally the advertising department is given a major share of the responsibility for choosing an advertising agency. Often the advertising department is asked to prepare a profile of several agencies and a recommendation. The final selection is then based on this recommendation.

4. *Preparing creative material.* Often the advertising department is given the task of preparing creative materials which are noncommissionable for an agency. Direct mail pieces, point-of-purchase displays, and various types of specialty items are examples.

The in-house agency

In the previous discussion we have assumed that the company has hired an outside full-service advertising agency. However, many companies use an in-house agency which can be one of two major types: (1) an in-house agency which prepares the total advertising program for the firm and, more commonly, (2) an in-house agency which performs some advertising functions and contracts outside for other services such as media placement. In either case the size of the internal advertising staff and its breadth of responsibility are much greater than they would be in the more usual client/full-service agency relationship.

TECHNOLOGY AND MANAGING THE MEDIA FUNCTION

Much has been written about the dramatic changes in media technology during the last decade. The media planner and those responsible for the advertising program must be aware of two basic types of technological changes related to advertising media:

1. Those changes affecting the opportunities for using the media more effectively for advertising.

2. Those changes affecting the ways in which the media function itself is carried out.

Advertising and the changing media environment

To some extent every change in media technology has an effect on advertising. However, some recent innovations offer, or will offer, dramatic opportunities and problems for media planners. The following discussion gives an idea of these changes and their potential ramifications for advertising.

Cable and satellite communication. The advent of home cable and satellite distribution of programming brought quality reception to homes in fringe areas and has begun to deliver programming from great distances. The dramatic predictions of the potential consequences of cable include the demise of local stations in favor of a few supernetworks communicating directly to home receivers.

Today, however, cable is largely ignored by major advertisers. Many advertisers think that 30 percent is the minimum household penetration needed to make cable buys attractive media alternatives. Cable is currently presenting some problems for media planners because of the audience fragmentation which can occur even though cable programming itself is largely ignored. Previously the media planner's decisions were confined to a three-network choice during primetime. Now the audience is being segmented increasingly among 12 or more channels, including pay television services which exclude advertising but siphon off viewers. What makes the problem more acute is that the fragmentation is generally occurring among an upscale audience. A recent survey by Video Probe Index showed that 37.2 percent of the respondent households subscribing to pay cable had incomes of more than $25,000.[1]

If the home video recorder and the videodisc gain in acceptance, the media planner will find audience fragmentation more difficult to deal with. Magnavox marketed the first videodisc player (with tapes of movies such as *Animal House* selling for $65). RCA, Sony, and other manufacturers are experimenting with similar systems. How advertising will fit into pay television systems remains a question. Some see a willingness on the part of a large segment of the population to pay to exclude advertising altogether. Others think that the audience willing and able to pay the full cost of programming is very small and that some type of advertising will eventually enter most of these pay systems. Predictions include videodiscs with and without advertising messages, with those including advertising priced lower,

[1] "Update on Cable TV," *Media Decisions*, January 1979, p. 62.

and the inclusion of a limited amount of advertising between programming on regular pay television.

In December 1977 Warner Communication began an era of two-way mass communication with the introduction of QUBE to Columbus, Ohio, cable subscribers. A small cable control mechanism allows viewers to answer quiz show questions, place orders for merchandise, and participate in straw votes on local political topics. Some restaurant advertisers have taken reservations from QUBE, and travel brochures can be ordered during commercials. While a complete evaluation of two-way cable is still some years away, it is evident that television advertisers will be making dramatic adjustments to current advertising practices.

Cable also offers opportunities for realistic research in a home environment. With the coming of two-way cable, researchers can inexpensively document the cable audience and gather information about specific commercials. A. C. Nielsen and the Young & Rubicam advertising agency recently announced a joint research effort to study the cable audience. Perhaps this pilot effort will mark the beginning of a new era of cable research and more sophisticated television research generally.

Other companies plan to escalate the timetable for in-home satellite reception. Sears and Comsat (Communications Satellite Corporation) have announced a joint venture to bring satellite transmission directly to households. Comsat will provide the programming, and Sears will market a small receiving disk capable of picking up the Comsat signal. If this plan is successful, it will no doubt be only a matter of time until other programmers, including the networks, begin to utilize such direct broadcasting. The Sears/Comsat proposal has obvious implications for the structure of the television industry and in particular that of local network-affiliated stations.

Print media selectivity. Magazines and, more recently, newspapers have been faced with the problem of competing with the broadcast media for advertising dollars. The print media have long recognized that immediacy and timeliness are attributes which must be conceded to broadcasting. Magazines were the first, followed more recently by some newspapers, to respond to the challenge of the broadcast media by building their audiences on in-depth specialization of content that the broadcast media are at present unable to provide.

Selective content is an advantage to a medium only if it can be directed to a selective audience which can then be delivered to advertisers. In the future, as broadcast covers the mass audience, print will succeed through appeals to audience subgroups. Advertisers will expect both magazines and newspapers to offer audience breakouts by geography, demographics, and ultimately perhaps by product preference. Only recently *Newsweek* magazine has begun to offer ADI Metro Editions which match *Newsweek* circulation with television coverage of major markets (see Figure 14–1). (For a discussion of ADI, see Chapter 5.)

Technology and the media planning environment

In addition to the many aspects of media that are currently being changed by new technological developments, technology is changing the methods used by the media planner. It is bringing greater sophistication to the media-buying process. Basically the media planner is adapting to computer research and the buying opportunities which it makes possible. Media planning has improved dramatically in three major areas in the last few years.

1. Methodological improvements. The selection of the research sample to a great extent determines the value of the information provided by a study. During the last decade organizations such as the Advertising Research Foundation, faced with industry criticism of media research methodology, have given increasing attention to the problem. Some of these industry-wide efforts have met with limited success. For instance the Radio Advertising Bureau's Task Force on Radio Ratings was criticized for not limiting its examination to the top 25 or 50 markets.[2]

Despite the problems of ascertaining the validity of media research, one must be encouraged by the interest in the topic. Some concrete changes in methodology can be cited. An example is the so-called Extended Sample Frame (ESF) used by Arbitron in placing radio diaries. The technique electronically selects telephone numbers at random. This overcomes the problem of unlisted telephone numbers and includes a more representative sample of the listening population than is obtained when the sample is confined to households with listed telephone numbers.

2. Improvements in timeliness of media research information. Advertisers often complain about the excessive amount of data available. Nielsen and Arbitron together publish more than 300 reports annually at costs which can exceed $100,000 for a large agency. A major problem with media research is that we can produce more information than can be analyzed properly. Much of it is duplicated by other sources. Unfortunately a great deal of this information leaves much to be desired. The current controversies over magazine audience accumulation, out-of-home radio audience, and discrepan-

[2] *Media Decisions,* January 1977, p. 57.

Figure 14–1
***Newsweek* ad for its ADI metro editions**

NOBODY PUTS YOU IN THE RIGHT PLACES

If you want your products to be seen selectively in the nation's top markets, you should know about Newsweek's 20 ADI Metro Group I editions. They offer very special advantages that planners should take note of.

ADI Metros enable you to make inter-media comparisons with leading metropolitan newspapers or spot TV. They offer a special opportunity to test a new campaign or product in more concentrated areas. Or to cope effectively with seasonal product usage. They also give you the added efficiency—and profitability—of spending media money where it will count the most for your product.

And if you want the 10 largest ADIs in one super-efficient package, Newsweek's Top Ten ADI edition is just that. And it qualifies for combined regional and national frequency discounts.

For those who wish to target *additional* major U.S. markets, there are Newsweek's Metro Group II editions as well. Each covers one of the next 20 largest American metropolitan areas and conforms closely to standard ADIs.

In all, 40 ideal opportunities to reach the nation's key metro areas, plus one well-assembled edition to reach the 10 biggest. Make them the marketplace for your products.

To find out more, contact your Newsweek representative or Bill Allbaugh, Advertising Director, Newsweek, 444 Madison Avenue, New York, N.Y. 10022 (212) 350-2900.

LIKE NEWSWEEK

cies in Nielsen and Arbitron data indicate that improvements in media research are needed. With the continuing growth of syndicated research services a major job of the media planner is to decide which service to invest in.

3. Sophistication of data analysis. The computer has created a type of mini-industry devoted to analyzing, restructuring, and modeling the information provided by syndicated research companies. Most major agencies and advertisers subscribe to at least one of these services. Companies such as Telmar, Interactive Market Systems (IMS), and Marketronics are becoming as important to media planners as the syndicated services themselves.

EDUCATIONAL TRAINING FOR MEDIA PLANNING

Before we discuss the academic background needed for a successful career in media planning, we should first examine the type of skills and personality needed for a career in media. The media-planning function demands both analytical skills and a people orientation, a combination that is not often found in the same individual. The media buyer and planner must be thorough and careful, but must also be able to negotiate effectively in making media purchases and to communicate the media plan to other advertising executives. While no one can give a formula for success in any field, there are four areas which the student should consider in planning a career in advertising media.

1. Strong marketing foundation. If there is one absolute necessity for a successful career in advertising, it is a strong foundation in basic marketing principles. No one can fully understand advertising without a knowledge of the larger marketing area of which it is a part. Virtually any marketing course would be of some value to the advertising student. However, the basic marketing course, market research, and consumer behavior should constitute the core of any marketing program designed to complement advertising.

2. Research emphasis. All areas of advertising, but especially media, are becoming increasingly analytical. To interpret and analyze the abundance of data necessary for media planning the student should have a facility for analytical skills. An introductory course in statistics is essential, and an additional statistics course and a research methodology course would be extremely helpful. The student should keep in mind that the major purpose of research training is to allow decision making and forecasting based on valid and reliable data. Obviously, unless a person has the background to make such judgments, serious error can result.

3. Practical experience and internships. Advertising is an extremely competitive field, and any practical experience a student brings to the job market is an advantage. Perhaps the best type of experience is summer internships coordinated between employers and colleges, often with academic credit. The college placement office will usually have a list of summer jobs and internships, but students should also write employers directly about employment.

Students should not limit themselves to advertising agency internships when looking for a part-time job. Media reps, media advertising and circulation departments, and corporate advertising departments all may provide part-time employment. In addition many campuses have commercial media run by students and requiring student advertising salespersons. Finally, directories such as *The Student Guide to Mass Media Internships* are often available at college placement offices and list both advertising and circulation openings.

Employers place major importance on outside activities of students as well as grade-point averages. Students should participate in college advertising clubs and volunteer for communication jobs in other organizations. Advertisers are looking for energetic, intelligent self-starters. This is the image you should project.

EDUCATION FOR A CAREER IN ADVERTISING

Advertising professionals have varying opinions about the best preparation for a career in advertising, but two consistent themes are heard. A broad liberal arts education is beneficial, and some marketing background is helpful. In specialized areas such as account management the Master of Business Administration degree is often preferred, while those students interested in art may be encouraged to attend an art institute or a department of commercial art.

EMPLOYMENT OPPORTUNITIES

Advertising agencies. Entry-level jobs in the media area, like all advertising jobs, are competitive. Over the last several years agency employment has represented a stable market at best. In 1965, 75,000 people were employed in advertising agencies, but this number dropped to 74,000 in 1975. However, the job market is better in media departments than in many other advertising agency departments. A survey conducted by the American Association of Advertising Agencies (4 A's) showed that of 529 entry-level positions, 214 (40.4 percent) were in the media department of member agencies, with the majority going to persons holding only the baccalaureate degree.[3]

[3] Edward J. Rogers, "A Practitioner's Thoughts on Advertising Education," in *Sharing for Understanding, Proceedings*, 1977, p. 194.

Media jobs, both entry-level and more senior positions, tend to pay less than creative or account management jobs. The salary differential between an agency creative director and his counterpart in media often amounts to $10,000–20,000. However, media departments offer an excellent opportunity for advancement within agencies, especially into account management.

Figure 14–2 outlines the starting salaries in job markets throughout the country.

Typically the entry-level media position in a larger agency is that of the media estimator. The media estimator, sometimes called an assistant media buyer, gathers cost and scheduling information to support the actual media buys done by more experienced personnel. The next level is that of the media buyer. This person negotiates for broadcast buys and supervises the contracting and scheduling of space and time. The coordinator of media strategy is the media planner, who, in consultation with the account team and the client, develops the broad direction of the media strategy for one or several accounts. Depending on the size of the agency, there may be one media planner or several working under an overall media director who is usually an agency vice president. In a small agency these functions are carried out by fewer people, and in some cases a very small agency may elect to have the account executive handle the media-buying function.

Nonagency media jobs. To the surprise of many students the majority of entry-level advertising media positions are not in advertising agencies. These jobs may lead to agency employment or may themselves provide satisfying lifetime jobs.

Media time and space salespersons. Even the smallest newspaper, magazine, or broadcast station employs media salespersons. At smaller media these positions not only offer excellent experience, but the salary plus commission for an aggressive space and time seller are usually far above the income obtainable from comparable news and editorial entry-level jobs. Because the turnover is relatively high among smaller media, jobs are available if a person is willing to move to a small town.

Sales among media in the top 20 markets, as well as broadcast networks and national magazines, can be lucrative. A top salesperson for a large medium will often earn more than top agency media directors, although the competition to get and hold these jobs is fierce.

Media representatives. As discussed earlier (see Chapter 4), the media representative, commonly known as a rep, is the middleman between advertising media buyers and sellers. Usually the rep deals directly with advertising agencies, although it is not uncommon for reps to go directly to the client.

The advertising rep holds a specialized job. An individual salesperson normally deals with only one medium such as newspapers or

Figure 14–2
Media job market at a glance (salaries in $000)

Job title	*New York and Chicago*			*Second job market area (Atlanta, Dallas, Detroit, Pittsburgh, Philadelphia, Cleveland, Houston, Minneapolis, Kansas City, St. Louis, Los Angeles, San Francisco)*		*Third job market area (Baltimore, Boston, Cincinnati, Richmond, Birmingham, Denver, Memphis, Des Moines, Miami, Oklahoma City, Phoenix, San Antonio, Nashville, Little Rock, New Orleans)*
	Large ($50 million +)	*Medium ($10–50 million)*	*Small ($5–10 million)*	*Large (over $10 million)*	*Medium (under $10 million)*	
Media director	$45–65	$35–50	$25–35	$30–40	$15–25	$18–25
Associate media director or media supervisor	30–45	25–30	—	20–25	—	—
Broadcast media director	30–45	25–35	—	—	—	—
Senior media planner	18–25	16–22	16–22	14–17	—	—
Media planners	10–18	10–16	10–20	10–16	10–14	10–14
Media buyers (all categories)	10–25	10–23	10–20	10–18	8–15	8–15

Source: Jerry Fields estimates; ncte that figures represent high and low ranges. Adopted from "Where the Money and the Jobs Are," *Media Decisions*, June 1977, p. 178.

television. Media planners often depend on reps for detailed media information, so the rep's job is not for an amateur. However, large rep organizations do employ media estimators who perform a function similar to that performed by media estimators in agencies.

Independent media-buying services. Independent media-buying services are employed primarily by companies which do not use full-service agencies and by very small agencies which use them as a media department. Since the independent media buyer survives through skillful negotiation usually in broadcast time, entry-level positions normally are not available.

The future. Media buying and selling offer an exciting and lucrative career for men and women. With the current competition for advertising jobs and the specialized skills needed for media, the student must analyze his talents objectively before pursuing a media career. The relatively rare combination of a faculty for numbers and a people orientation is a prerequisite for success in media. Only those who are willing to work hard and who find fulfillment in analyzing marketing and media information should consider media planning as an occupation.

QUESTIONS

1. How does the media function relate to the marketing concept and marketing segmentation?

2. Briefly discuss three external and three internal marketing constraints on the media function.

3. What are some of the major media responsibilities of a corporate advertising department in a firm employing an outside advertising agency?

4. Discuss how the "electronic revolution" will affect (*a*) television, (*b*) print, and (*c*) direct response advertising.

5. Discuss the basic function of the following:
   a. The advertising agency media department.
   b. Media reps.
   c. The individual medium's salespersons.

GLOSSARY

"A" counties. Counties located in the 26 largest metropolitan areas.

Adjacency. The time between programs. Commercials during this period are usually sold by local stations.

Advertising allocation. The total funds planned for advertising for a time interval or for an entire campaign.

Advertising Checking Bureau. Organization which provides advertisers with tear sheets of their advertisements. Often used to verify cooperative advertising.

Advertising decay. The diminishing but still present effect of past advertising on present demand.

Advertising elasticity of demand. The proportional change in demand, given a unit change in advertising expenditures.

Advertising exposure. One person or home exposed to a single medium. Advertising exposures are often accumulated for all media in an advertiser's schedule.

Advertising response. The effect on sales (or some other measure) produced by advertising.

Affiliate. A radio or television station which contracts with a network to carry some portion of the network's programming.

Agate line (or simply **line**). A measurement of newspaper space, one column wide and 1/14 of an inch deep.

Amplitude modulation (AM). Oldest and most popular form of transmitting radio signals.

Annual discount. Advertising discount based on number of advertisements placed during a 52-week period.

Appropriations budget. A budget containing a fixed level of expenditure and/or revenue.

Arbitron. With A. C. Nielsen, one of the two major broadcast rating services. Also the name of the electronic data-gathering device used to monitor television set usage.

Area of Dominant Influence. A geographic area consisting of all counties in which the home market stations receive a preponderance of total viewing hours.

Artificial variable. A nonnegative variable, A_n, used to convert a "greater than or equal to" inequality in order to obtain a starting solution. Artificial variables are arbitrarily assigned a value of *M,* a very large number, in the objective function, which prohibits their presence in the solution.

Audience composition. The percentage of some market segment within the total audience of a medium.

Audience turnover. The rate at which a medium accumulates audience over time. It is determined by dividing the reach by the average audience.

Audilog. The listener diary used by A. C. Nielsen.

Audimeter. The electronic recorder used by A. C. Nielsen to measure set usage.

Availabilities (avails). In broadcasting, the time available for sale by the station.

"B" counties. Couties with populations over 150,000 that are not "A" counties as well as counties that are a part of the metropolitan area of cities in these counties.

Barter. In media, usually refers to trading space or time by a medium in return for merchandise. In broacasting, an advertiser may provide a program free of charge to a station in exchange for having the station run the program. The program will normally carry commercials for the advertiser who provides it as well as open time that can be sold by the station.

Basic feasible solution. A solution in which, at most, a number of variables equal to the number of equations have positive values and all other variables have the value zero. For example, in a problem having two equations, a basic feasible solution would have, at most, two variables with positive values, and the remaining variables would equal zero.

Basic solution. A solution in which there are an equal number of variables and constraints.

Basic variables. Variables in a basic feasible solution which have positive values.

Billable services. Services not covered by agency commission and therefore billed to clients.

Billing. In media billing, refers to the total amount of money purchases for a client by an advertising agency.

Brand demand. Demand for a particular, branded product.

Budget. A financial plan.

Bulk discount. Discount offered to advertisers who contract for a certain quantity of insertions on a monthly or yearly basis.

"C" counties. Counties with populations of over 50,000 which are neither "A" nor "B" counties. Also counties which are part of the metropolitan areas of cities in "C" counties.

Capital budget. A financial plan for projects lasting longer than one year which takes into account the time value of money.

Car card. An advertising message which appears within a public vehicle.

Card rate. The time or space cost appearing on a medium's published rate card.

Cash budget. A short-term plan, usually for no longer than a year, for the use of cash.

Cash discount. A 2 percent discount given by media to advertisers for prompt payment. It is calculated after deducting the 15 percent agency commission.

Census. The collecting of information *from every member* of some statistical population.

City zone. The center city of a market. One of the ways in which newspapers report their circulation.

Clearance. Refers to the time which affiliates make available for network programming.

Closing date. The date by which all advertising materials must be at the medium if the advertising is to appear on a certain date.

Coincidental telephone. A data-gathering technique in which interviews are conducted simultaneously with the activity being measured.

Combination rate. A lower rate given to the advertiser for buying two or more media. In the case of one-owner morning and evening newspaper combinations, this is often mandatory.

Continuity. The period of time over which an advertising schedule will run.

Continuity of impression. Term associated with flighting. The period during which advertising is reduced but audience still retains the advertising previously communicated.

Contract. In media, a space or time contract sets the price that an advertiser will pay for time or space during some specified period.

Controlled circulation. That portion of a publication's circulation which is delivered free.

Convenience sample. A sample in which the sampling units are chosen on a nonprobability basis.

Cost per rating point (**CPP** or **CRP**). Means of comparing broadcast costs based on delivering one rating point. CPP is often used to compare the costs of reaching 1 percent of a market segment. In this case it may be referred to as the cost per demographic point.

Cost per thousand. The cost of reaching 1,000 circulation. Circulation may be expressed as households, individuals, or some market segment.

Cover positions. Premium positions sold in magazines. First cover—front cover; second cover—inside front cover; third cover—inside back cover; fourth cover—back cover. Only business publications routinely sell their first covers to advertisers.

Coverage. In broadcast, refers to geographic area over which station gets a certain level of listeners or viewers. In print media, it can refer to the geographic area in which the publication has some acceptable level of penetration.

Cooperative advertising. Advertising placed by retailers but wholly or partly financed by national manufacturer or wholesalers.

Cumulative audience (cume). The number of different people or households reached by a medium or media over some period of time.

Cut-in. A commercial which replaces a network announcement. Often national advertisers will make such substitutions for purposes of local testing.

"D" counties. All counties which are not "A," "B," or "C" counties.

Demarketing. Activities designed to destimulate demand.

Demographic edition. A portion of a magazine's total circulation which can be bought by an advertiser and distributed to some market segment.

Display advertising. Print advertising which includes both copy and pictures. In newspapers the term is used to distinguish it from classified advertising.

Double billing. An abuse most frequent in cooperative retail advertising, in which the participating retailer, with the connivance of the media enterprise, substitutes an unauthorized message or submits an inflated media bill, or both.

Double stapling. A double-billing scam in broadcast advertising in which the cooperating retailer airs an unauthorized advertisement.

Drive time. Periods during morning and evening weekdays when automobile radio usage is considered to be at its highest.

Duplicated audience. The number of people reached two or more times in a media schedule.

Earned rate. The amount an advertiser pays for space and time and figuring all discounts.

Efficiency. The ratio of outputs to inputs.

Entering basic variable. A nonbasic variable used to "enter" or to replace a basic variable in the simplex method.

Estimators. Usually entry-level media buyers who figure costs of schedules prior to making actual buys. Also can refer to the many reference books used by media buyers to estimate media costs.

EVPI. Expected value of perfect information.

Exposure. The media making contact with an individual or a household.

Facing. In outdoor advertising, refers to the direction and the number of boards in a location. A double south facing has two boards visible to northbound traffic.

Fifteen and two. Common agency discounts given by media. The traditional agency discount is 15 percent, and 2 percent is given by some media for prompt payment. Often expressed as 15/2.

Flat rate. An advertising rate for which no discounts are available.

Flexible budget. A budget which permits specified variations in revenues and/or expenditures.

Flighting. A concentration of advertising over a short period of time followed by a reduction in advertising and then another burst of advertising.

Frequency. The average number of times an individual or household is exposed to a medium over some period of time.

Frequency discount. Advertising discounts based on the number of insertions during either a month or a year.

Frequency modulation (FM). Fastest growing sector of commercial radio. Offers better sound reproduction than AM radio.

Fringe time. In broadcast, the periods before and after primetime.

Generic demand. Demand for an entire product class.

Gross Rating Points. The total rating achieved by several advertisements or commercials. A duplicated audience measure for the equivalent reach achieved with a particular advertising schedule.

Horizonal publication. An industrial publication directed to a particular job category in several industries. For instance, *Purchasing.*

Households Using Television (HUTs). The number of households tuned in at a specific time.

Hypothesis. Statement of a problem in research form.

Independent station. A broadcast station which is not affiliated with one of the major networks.

Insert. An advertisement, usually prepared by the advertiser, which is provided to a newspaper or magazine. Inserts may be either freestanding or bound into the publication.

Insertion order. Instructions sent by the advertiser or agency to the media outlining how and when an advertisement or commercial is to be run.

Junior panels. Eight-sheet posters available to outdoor advertisers in many large markets.

Koyck function. An expression for the carry-over effect of past performance on present performance.

Leaving basic variable. A basic variable which has been replaced by an entering basic variable.

Local rate. A medium's rate to local advertisers which is lower than the rate which the medium charges national advertisers. Most common in newspapers.

Macroeconomics. The economics of a nation or a society.

Makegood. An adjustment in which an advertising credit is provided to an advertiser when the ad is aired in violation of the broadcaster's product protection policy.

Management. The process of achieving organizational objectives by planning, organizing, staffing, directing, and controlling.

Market share. The percentage of the total generic market held by an individual brand.

Maximil rate. The maximum cost per line per million newspaper readers. See *Milline rate.*

Media schedule. The "calendar" which details the future advertising for a client. Gives the exact date, time, and cost of advertising placements.

Metricity. The ability of a measurement device to produce data which are of interval or ratio quality.

Microeconomics. The economics of an individual firm.

Milline rate. A method of comparing newspapers of different circulation. The milline rate is figured by the following formula:

$$\frac{\text{Cost/line} \times 1 \text{ million}}{\text{Circulation}}$$

Minimil rate. Same as the milline rate except that it uses the lowest rate available in computing the cost. See *Milline rate.*

Network, broadcast. Two or more stations simultaneously broadcasting the same program originating from a single source.

Network, print. Several print media vehicles which can be bought simultaneously whether or not they are commonly owned.

Nonbasic variables. Variables in a basic feasible solution which have the value zero in the simplex method.

Nonbillable services. Services normally covered by agency commission.

Null Hypothesis. Hypothesis which posits that no actual relationship exists between two (or more) phenomena.

Off-the-card rates. Rates offered to advertisers which do not appear on the rate card. In print media the use of such rates is a very controversial practice and is considered unethical in many quarters.

Owned and operated stations (O&O). Stations which are not only affiliated with a network but are actually owned by the network.

Package plan. A plan under which an advertiser is offered a lower rate for buying a group of broadcast commercials. Individual stations and networks offer many types of package plans.

Painted bulletin. Outdoor sign whose message is painted rather than papered. Generally used in high-traffic areas and bought for longer periods than are paper posters.

Parameter. Numerical value of some state of nature.

Pass-along readers. See *Secondary readers.*

Penetration. The coverage of a market, an audience, or a segment of the market by a particular medium.

Pivot column. The column of coefficients related to the nonbasic variable that has been identified as the entering basic variable in the simplex method.

Pivot number. The coefficient at the intersection of the pivot column and the pivot row. Also called the pivot element in the simplex method.

Pivot row. The row of coefficients containing the current basic variable which has a coefficient of + 1 and which is the leaving basic variable in the simplex method.

Plant. The medium for outdoor advertising. The plant operator is responsible for installing and maintaining outdoor signs on property he owns or leases.

Posters. Highway billboards. Standard units of posters are 24 sheet, 30 sheet, and bleed.

Preemptible spot. A broadcast commercial that can be replaced on short notice by an advertiser who is willing to pay a higher rate.

Primary data. Facts collected by the decision-making organization.

Probability sample. A sample in which the sampling units are chosen on a probability basis.

Rate differential. The practice among most newspapers of charging national advertisers a higher rate than is charged local advertisers.

Regional edition. That portion of a magazine's total circulation which can be bought by an advertiser and distributed in a single area.

Reliability. The property or ability of a measurement device to produce "repeatable" results.

Representative (Rep). An independent company which acts as the salesperson for a number of media, taking a commission on what it sells.

Retail trading zone. An area outside the city zone, reached by newspaper circulation, whose residents trade in the city.

Run of paper (ROP). An advertisement placed at the discretion of the publisher. In broadcast this is known as run of schedule (ROS).

Sampling. The collecting of information from a portion of some statistical population.

Scatter plan. A package buy which emphasizes a number of vehicles or programs, with little weight given to any one of them.

Scientific method. The problem-solving method, used in both the physical and social sciences, in which the problem is defined, pertinent information is collected and analyzed, and a solution is developed and implemented.

Secondary data. Facts collected by others for the decision-making organization.

Secondary readers. Readers who do not buy or subscribe to the medium but receive it on a pass-along basis.

Sets in use. See *Households Using Television.*

Share of audience. The percentage of people with sets in use who are tuned to a particular show.

Shopper. An advertising sheet with little or no editorial material, usually a weekly and distributed free in most cases.

Short rate. Charge made by medium to an advertiser who fails to earn a discount which was granted at the beginning of a contract period.

Showing. In outdoor, formerly a measurement of purchase. Now normally refers to a number of posters in a market which are bought on the basis of Gross Rating Points.

Slack variable. A nonnegative variable, S_n, used to indicate the presence of unused (or "slack") capacity of a constraint and to convert a "less than or equal to" inequality to an equality in the simplex method.

Split run. When an advertiser runs two different advertisements in the same issue of a publication. Such advertisements can be placed on an every-other-issue basis or on a regional basis.

Spot advertising. When national advertisers buy commercials on a station-by-station basis rather than on a network basis.

Standard Metropolitan Statistical Area. Major U.S. cities and the counties surrounding them.

Starting solution. A system of equations, composed of the objective function and constraint functions, in which all variables appear in all equations. Variables not originally contained in the equations are assigned a coefficient of zero.

Syndication. Broadcast programming that is sold to stations on a market-by-market basis.

Tear sheet. A verification procedure in print advertising in which the publisher furnishes the advertiser (or agency) a copy of the entire page on which the ad appeared.

Ultra high frequency (UHF). In television, channels 14–83. UHF stations are often nonaffiliated in major markets, and most UHF stations have weaker signals than VHF stations.

Unduplicated audience. See *Reach.*

Validity. The ability of a measurement device to measure what it claims to measure.

Vertical publication. A business publication that editorially covers an entire industry. For instance, *Automotive News.*

Wild code. Impossible or highly implausible values for a variable.

Zero-based budgeting. The development and justification of budget allocations "from scratch," without regard to historical budget allocations.

INDEX

I–J–K

L

M

N

O

P–Q

R

S

This book is set VIP in 10 and 9 point Helvetica, leaded 2 points. Chapter numbers are Weiss Roman, and chapter titles are 20 point Helvetica. The size of the type page is 30 x 47 picas.